Slow Boat Through England

Come into a fascinating new world!

Behind those old warehouses, beyond the railway line, over the fields you can see from the jammed, noisy main road, is a hidden world, only just recently being recognised for its own fascination and for what it can offer to holidaymakers and weekenders. The canals and navigable rivers of England thread their way behind, under, and around the overcrowded holiday areas, and they are waiting to be explored.

Frederic Doerflinger has been exploring them for fifteen years. His book is a tempting guide to the first-timer, an easy introduction for the novice, a reminder of holiday delights for the experienced boater. By the time you reach the last page, your ideas for next year's family holiday may have changed radically.

Slow Boat Through England

Frederic Doerflinger

Foreword by Roger Pilkington

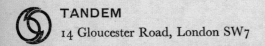

TANDEM
14 Gloucester Road, London SW7

First published in Great Britain by
Allan Wingate (Publishers) Ltd, 1970

Published by Universal-Tandem Publishing Co. Ltd, 1970

To the First Mate
who neither jibs nor jibes

Made and printed in Great Britain by
The Garden City Press Ltd, Letchworth, Herts

CONTENTS

ILLUSTRATIONS

Between pages 128 and 129

FOREWORD

IN A WAY I was responsible for this book. Not that I suggested it, for it was the publishers who did that, and they chose the man who could best write it. No, my responsibility goes back fifteen years, to a June day when Fred Doerflinger and his wife Lisa chugged down the Upper Thames on my boat from above St John's Lock to the Rose Revived. As a result of that one day on the water Fred Doerflinger began to develop a strange malaise.

The symptoms of his growing addiction followed the usual pattern. If he was driving and came to a humped bridge he had a compulsive urge to stop and get out of the car to see if there were any boats in sight. At home, his study floor began to be covered with canal maps and his desk littered with pieces of paper on which were sums in peculiar units which he would explain to be 'lock miles'. A year or two later you might find him sitting on a bollard in darkest Camden Town or furthest Fenland, pensive as the ancient mariner about to hook a wedding guest and tell him about his latest voyage.

Fred Doerflinger's addiction to water sometimes showed itself under the most surprising circumstances. Once a very very important person from behind the Iron Curtain came to London and held a press conference at which he outlined his scheme for uniting Europe, or dismembering it— I forget precisely which. At the end of his prepared statement the very very important person indicated that if any of the world's press wished to ask a very very important question he might answer it. There was an awed silence, then Fred spoke up. What was the depth of water in the canal that led from Berlin across Poland to Moscow?

That Fred Doerflinger is a canal fanatic nobody could deny. But he does not want to keep the waterways for himself. The canals and rivers, he writes 'are in fact a key to a way of life almost unchanged since the eighteenth century, and they are all yours to explore and enjoy'. As I read that, I remembered how on an April evening Fred had rowed us dreamily along part of the Regent's Canal. Overhead the buds were breaking on the elms, the rooks were cheerfully sorting themselves into pairs. My wife and I sat in the stern of the dinghy, she trailing her fingers in the water and I myself looking up dreamily at the silhouette of the trees against the evening sky, amazed that such peace and beauty could exist right there in London. Only 30 ft above us the traffic was jammed motionless on Blow-up Bridge, but it seemed to belong to another world, incredibly remote. And so it did.

On the bend towards Maida Vale Fred eased off to lean out and pick up a used motor-tyre. It was a fine one, white-walled and expensive. No doubt it had once belonged to just such a smart executive saloon as those which were edging irritably along the road beyond the trees. Fred thought it would serve us as a fender, as it did through eight countries in the following years. Every time I hung it against a quayside it brought back to me a whiff of those canals which we had cruised with him, the Llangollen or the Oxford, the Grand Union and the River Weaver, and the nostalgic dereliction of Ellesmere Port. And often I wished Fred Doerflinger would write about those voyages so that others could explore for themselves the same world and the same way of life.

This he has now done, and what particularly delights me is not just his encounter with the mole-catcher, the story of Ben who spent a lifetime legging in Braunston Tunnel, or the rescue of Worcester the ginger cat, but that he has set out to provide all the information a newcomer to the waterways can possibly need. And he has done so in exactly the right way. So many of those who have written about the waterways have adopted an intolerance quite foreign to such a pleasant way of exploring the Britain which still survives, as genuine and unspoiled as ever, between the strands of a web of hurrying motorways. In this book, where his purpose is partly to tell people *how* to voyage into adventure, he is the gentlest of advisers, never hinting that if you don't think as he does about some aspect of boating or waterways you must be deranged.

Fred Doerflinger loves the canals and rivers, and he has travelled them more widely than anyone else I have met. There are not many English locks which he has not wound, and as lock-wheelers his family have padded scores of miles of towpath. I hope that many others will cruise the same canals and rivers, and find as he does that whatever water-ways they may happen to have chosen they will have entered a new world.

ROGER PILKINGTON

CHAPTER I

OUR INLAND WATERWAYS

IT WAS all due to our golden Labrador, Brandonwood Bracken of Denewood, more affectionately known as 'Wiggers' because of the continual happy movement of his tail, that we became a family of inland waterway addicts. We enjoy holidaying as a family and our three children were adamant about including the dog in any travel plans. This, of course, ruled out holidays abroad and set us searching for holiday venues in Britain that would genuinely welcome children and dogs and cater for everyone's idea of fun and relaxation.

Such criteria are difficult enough to agree, let alone satisfy, but Britain's inland waterways proved to be the ideal passport to pleasure for every single member of the family, 'Wiggers' included, and although we have already cruised literally thousands of miles up and down the rivers and canals of this country they continue to offer new, different and more exciting adventures each year. I must warn you at the outset, until you have experienced boating on inland waterways you cannot imagine or appreciate how the habit surreptitiously creeps up and envelops you. Your first cruise will almost certainly be the forerunner of many more and if you are not careful you will quickly become an enthusiast.

The water roads of Britain, for that is what the inland waterways essentially are, constitute another world. The peace and quiet they offer are in striking contrast to our congested, noisy, smelly and dangerous roads and to our pounding and often unsightly railways where speed is undisputed king. Who goes for a drive for pleasure or relaxation these days? Who travels by train to see the countryside? Roads and railways are no more today than methods of transport, a means of getting from A to B and usually in the fastest possible time.

But the shallow, narrow ribbons of canal waters, defying the barriers of the watersheds with their tunnels, locks and aqueducts to form links with deeper and wider rivers and then the sea, almost magically convey us like explorers into a way of life touched only on the periphery by the so-called advances of the last two centuries. On a boat on the inland waterways the pressure is off and you are as free as the open air. The waterways greet you as a friend and companion and act as a catalyst to initiative.

Today, thanks to the vigorous campaign led for over two decades by an almost fanatically devoted Inland Waterways Association, and the recent belated but welcome recognition by the British Government of the tremendous amenities for recreation and leisure provided by the nation's inland waterways, more and more people are beginning to discover the countless attractions and peace of the 3,000-mile network of navigable rivers and canals that the vast majority of an increasingly tension-ridden public have strangely failed to notice for generations.

Once you cruise the inland waterways you will begin to delve deeply into many aspects of their fascinating story. For each of your holidays afloat will introduce you to many strange, unusual and unexpected phenomena, sights and people, as the accounts of some of my own boating holidays in later chapters reveal in some detail. A lot of places we come across look magical at first glance, but the waterways go on being constantly surprising.

Their courses silently penetrate a very different Britain

from that we are accustomed to in the course of our busy and hectic lives. Unspoiled and uncrowded even if pleasure-craft traffic were suddenly to double or treble overnight (and it has already done so on the River Thames and the Norfolk Broads) the inland waterways of Britain are uniquely remote yet easily accessible to anyone with the slightest tinge of inquisitiveness in their make-up.

For the most part our rivers and canals today are lost trade routes with little prospect of ever again contributing an important chapter to the economic and social history of the country. But in this crowded island where there are so few opportunities to escape from the burdensome effects of modern civilisation, the inland waterways are a unique heritage which, if you care to claim it, can add a new dimension to your leisure. Our canals and rivers remain part of another age when the pattern of trade and transport was quite different. This pattern has been long forgotten or ignored by modern business and indeed by the masses of the public. So the canals and rivers are in fact a key to a way of life almost unchanged since the eighteenth century, and they are all yours to explore and enjoy.

Although the inland waterways still flow through or near a number of cities and towns and villages across the land they do not enmesh you and your craft in the snarls of traffic on flyovers, roundabouts and shopping centres, nor grind you to a halt in noisy, teeming railway termini after a tour of back-door slum districts. You will be agreeably surprised at the way waterways tend to avoid congested conurbations, ribbon developments, power plants, industrial estates and other conglomerations of this technological age. Well over nine-tenths of the canals and rivers wander peacefully through a remote countryside on winding courses bordered by meadows and fields, pretty flowers and bird-laden rushes, isolated cottages and picturesque inns.

You will, as my family and I have, become smitten with certain waterways and even particular spots on particular waterways, but there isn't any waterway anywhere that doesn't possess a host of attractions and cater for a myriad interests. I find that each river and canal has a distinctive charm and character of its own and conjures up different memories from varied personal experiences. One thing, you will never be bored, for even though a holiday cruise sometimes brings you back over the same or much of the same outward route you will discover that they really do look entirely different when travelling in the reverse direction.

A glance at the map of the inland waterways will show you that the threads of water are rather like a massive spider's web, somewhat tattered admittedly, but nevertheless sprawling over much of the country, with odd bits of cobweb seemingly blown by the winds from the centre to some outlying areas. Boating holidays open up vast areas of the countryside which you might otherwise never really see or explore.

Whatever waterways you choose for most of your holiday you will be away from it all—free to potter or press on; free to bypass this town or that village unless you want to shop or sightsee; free to visit that stately home or country church or pleasure ground; free to picnic in that pleasant glade; free to dine in that handy waterside inn; free to take the children to that bird sanctuary or zoo or craftsman's cottage; free to swim or paddle or fish; free to saunter along that towpath with your dog, and like him, thoroughly enjoy nature's sights and sounds and smells.

You will pass over rivers and streams from time to time on aqueducts, some rather small and quaint and others breathtakingly noble and massive. You will slip under countless road bridges, most of them sited in the middle of nowhere and devoid of traffic except for a mooing cow or a farmer with a load of hay. There will be railway bridges too, most of them deserted and many 'Beeching'd', but should you by chance spot a train rumbling across, a hoot on your boat horn will often spark the response of a whistle or a wave of the driver's arm.

Suddenly, you will begin to appreciate the functional and aesthetic beauty of the different kinds of locks, from the ordinary to the staircase and guillotine types; the different designs of bridges dating back even to medieval times and including those delightful swing and split bridges; the period lock cottages, many with colourful gardens; the old wharves and warehouses; the stables now perhaps converted to a pub storeroom; and scores of other relics of yesterday when architecture and craftsmanship were based on ingenuity, good taste and durability.

You will also notice little things like worn bollards and battered balance-beam caps, cast-iron name plates, bridge numbers and curious signs that from another era warn you that this or that bridge 'is insufficient to carry a traction engine or any other extraordinary weight'. The youngsters may collect lock names or pub names or spot mileposts as you cruise along. It isn't just that your leisurely pace gives you time to take things in properly, but that from a boat you have a different perspective. It's only when you get on the water that you begin to take notice of so many things that are usually taken for granted.

While the inland waterways map in one sense only hints at the lost world we can so easily recapture it does usefully chart the many routes to pleasure across so much of this island. Whether in the North, South, East, West or Midlands there are waterways that will carry you into a fresh and refreshing appreciation of your own country.

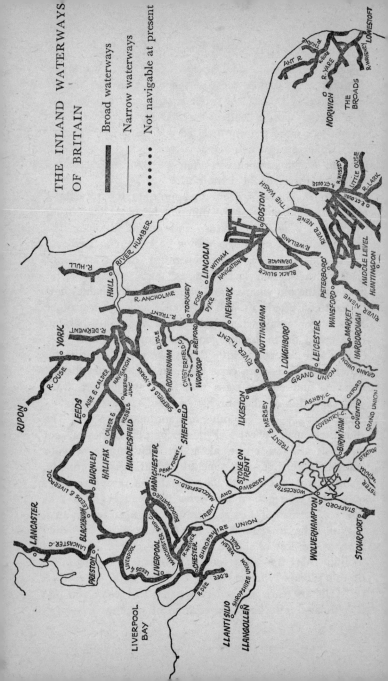

THE INLAND WATERWAYS
OF BRITAIN

Broad waterways
Narrow waterways
Not navigable at present

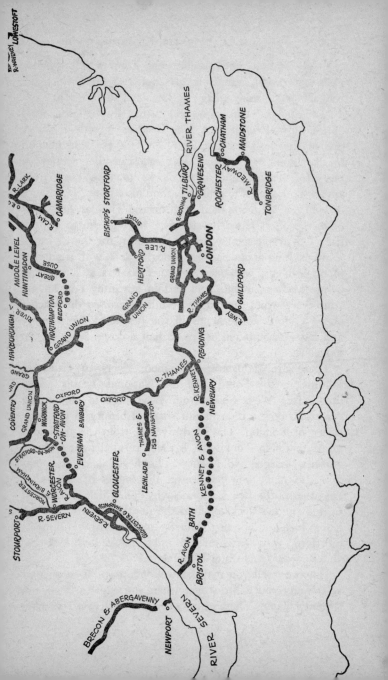

In the South, London's river, the Thames, is the major river navigation, navigable for over 200 miles from the tiny Gloucestershire village of Lechlade to the tidal locks at Teddington in London, and thence through the heart of the capital to the sea. The Thames is without doubt one of the most popular waterways for pleasure boating in the country, boasting an almost endless series of beautiful reaches and broad locks to take craft from kayaks and canoes to really substantial cruisers. Thousands of boat owners moor their craft on the Thames, and fleets of hire cruisers based on the river have grown to quite a size. This won't spoil your fun, however, for there's something exciting about passing through a lock with a number of other boats, with meeting other boaters at a mooring beside a cheerful pub, and certain advantages in having your every whim catered for. We have cruised the reaches above Oxford at weekends in the height of the summer and have encountered as few as half a dozen boats on the move.

There are smaller more remote rivers to cruise in solitude in the South, like the National Trust's pretty little River Wey, which from Weybridge to Godalming contributes more than its fair share of beauty to the periphery of London. The Medway too, from the tidal lock at Allington to Tonbridge, is sheer rural delight with its ancient bridges, wild garlic, hopfields and the odd 'folly' to make you ponder on the foibles of humanity. And there's the Lee & Stort Navigation which carries you from London's dockland into the depths of Hertfordshire along pleasant winding courses to Hertford or Bishop's Stortford, with views of old mills, stocks and lock-ups, water gardens and water-lilies galore.

However well you may know London you'll be amazed at the city you will discover when you explore it via the Regent's Canal. There's much more to it than a few miles

of waterway with a baker's dozen of locks. It takes you
into dockland, the East End and the curious hinterland
running from the City of London to Camden Town and
beyond. There are a couple of short tunnels, Regent's
Park with 'Blow-up Bridge' and the zoo, attractive Little
Venice, and more. From it you can enter the Lee
Navigation, the tidal Thames or cruise along the Paddington Arm into the Grand Union Canal proper.

The Grand Union—our youngsters on their first trip
along it dubbed it the 'Grand Onion'—is the major water
link between the South and the Midlands. With its broad
locks, the longest tunnel still open to boats in Britain, a
smattering of commercial narrow-boat traffic, the fascinating Waterways Museum at Stoke Bruerne, charming canal
villages and the changing panoramas of its pounds, this
canal, whether you follow it from the Thames to Birmingham or to the Trent, will give you a little bit of everything
that canal holidays have to offer.

Another route to the Midlands from the Thames is the
Oxford Canal, without doubt one of the most beautiful
canals in England, winding along the contours of the hills
through unspoiled countryside with only rare contact with
towns or villages. This is a shallow canal with narrow
locks and delightful lifting bridges and with an intimate
association with nature.

The canals of the Midlands are centred on Birmingham
whose network of local navigations reflects the industrial
England of a century or so ago. It's a rather sorry page
of history to explore but with its own fascination, and
many surprisingly pleasant and interesting stretches. From
Birmingham the canals probe outwards in all directions
with a choice of many different routes for years of holiday
pleasure. To the south lies the recently restored Stratford-
on-Avon Canal, several dozen miles of heavily locked
waters, including a flight of nineteen locks in $1\frac{1}{2}$ miles,

plunging through lovely Shakespeare country. Then there's the thirty-odd miles of the Worcester & Birmingham Canal running through hilly country to the River Severn. Although all the fifty-eight locks on this canal are concentrated in sixteen miles they are easy to work, and the famous Tardebigge Flight, the longest in the country and consisting of thirty locks with a total fall of over 200 ft, is an experience you'll always remember. Progress here will be slow but the magnificent scenery is in any case worth dawdling over.

The River Severn is also connected to the Midlands and indeed the River Trent by the Staffordshire & Worcestershire Canal, which averages less than a lock per mile in its forty-six-odd miles through really beautiful country, the haunt of many wild birds. On this canal you'll find such things as a 'canal lake', locks with picturesque names like 'Bumble Hole' and 'Stewponey', unusual split bridges which allowed the towline on horse-drawn craft to be passed through without unhooking, in addition to scenic splendour, good inns and attractive castles and manor houses.

The River Severn has few locks and few places to moor but it is a rather grand concourse connecting, via Tewkesbury, with the River Avon, which we find so idyllic and enjoyable that we return to it again and again. The word 'lovely' is too weak to describe the Avon along its twenty-eight miles between Tewkesbury and Evesham. The wooded countryside, the charming old mills, the pretty towns and villages, the unusual locks, the ideal moorings, the enchanting walks—and the local 'scrumpy' —are among the attractions that bring us back to the Avon so often.

From the Birmingham area the Shropshire Union Canal will take you over sixty-six miles through recurring deep cuttings with rocky and heavily wooded slopes, under towering bridges and over ingenious aqueducts to Chester, and beyond to Ellesmere Port and the Manchester Ship Canal. It is one of the most exciting and thoroughly pleasant canals we have ever cruised, every mile offering new prospects for admiration. The forty-six additional miles of the Welsh Section or the Llangollen Canal, from Hurleston Junction on the main line to Llantisilio in Wales, is, in the view of my family, the most beautiful canal in the country. It has simply everything from fine scenery including the Vale of Langollen and the 'Little Lake District' through narrow locks and lift bridges and tunnels and even an inland port to the thrilling Chirk and Pontcysyllte aqueducts, the latter over 1,000 ft long and carrying the canal breathtakingly over 120 ft above the rushing River Dee.

Not so spectacular but interesting in their own ways are the canals to the east of Birmingham, the Birmingham & Fazeley, the pretty Northern Arm of the Oxford Canal, the decaying Coventry Canal, all of which, while perhaps not selected as holiday venues in themselves, make possible circular tours which enable the exploration of a number of waterways on a single holiday. All have particular attractions worth seeking out as you get to know the waterways a little better.

Also part of the Midlands waterways is the Leicester Line of the Grand Union Canal incorporating the delightful River Soar Navigation, stretching over seventy-five miles from Norton Junction on the Grand Union main line to Birmingham to the Trent & Mersey Canal and the River Trent. It is a canal of great contrasts, varying from narrow to broad gauge locks, from canal to river navigation, from wild untidy country to pastoral landscape. It runs through fascinating villages and interesting towns and cities, features haunted tunnels, intriguing staircase locks and is one of the highest canals in the country, the summit level being 412 ft above sea level, with glorious views.

The River Trent and the Trent & Mersey Canal, you will note from the waterways map, form a vast semi-circle connecting the Mersey in the north-west to the Humber and ports of the north-east. The Trent & Mersey Canal is nearly a hundred miles long from Preston Brook on the Bridgewater Canal to Derwent Mouth on the River Trent, and from it you can also explore such scenic gems as the Macclesfield and Peak Forest Canals. The Trent & Mersey is another of those canals that combine broad and narrow locks, and a narrow-beamed craft with under 6 ft headroom is in any case essential because of the safe but sagging Harecastle Tunnel, which has a height gauge at each end which your boat must clear to be admitted. This 2,919-yard tunnel is only one of the exciting adventures on the Trent & Mersey as it wends its way through the Potteries and some of the most enchanting reaches anywhere in the country. Where the Trent & Mersey joins the broad sweep of the River Weaver in Cheshire you'll find the only boat lift in Britain. The Anderton Lift raises boats in massive caissons from the level of the Weaver some 50 ft to the canal level above, and passing up or down in your own boat is an exhilarating experience, to say the least.

The River Trent is tidal for fifty-two miles from the Humber to Cromwell Lock some five miles below Newark and, frankly glorious as these tidal reaches are, you must accumulate some boating experience before venturing along them as we have done into the Humber & Yorkshire Ouse and beyond to the city of York. A little experience will contribute to a greater enjoyment of the many canals of the North including the Sheffield & Yorkshire, Stainforth & Keadby, Calder & Hebble and the bustling Aire & Calder, famous for its trains of coal-

carrying 'Tom Pudding' compartment boats which can still
be seen daily. The finest cruising canal in the North, well
suited to amateurs and rated the most pleasing in the
country by many enthusiasts, is the 127-mile-long Leeds
& Liverpool which takes you through the rugged moor-
lands of Yorkshire and Lancashire, and the farm lands
of the Pennines. A broad canal with ninety-one locks and
two tunnels, it mingles rustic scenery with grand navigation works like the unique sets of locks, grouped in sets
of two, three and five, and the Burnley embankment which
carries the canal literally over the centre of the town. The
summit level of the Leeds & Liverpool canal is some
497 ft above sea level, and although the canal does run
through some industrial areas many of the buildings are
mellowed with age and quite interesting, while the open
countryside is nothing less than magnificent.

The northernmost navigable canal in England is the
Lancaster, separated from the main canal system and more
like a river than a canal in appearance. There are no
locks except on the short Glasson Arm leading to the sea,
and the canal is beautiful with splendid sea views over
Morecambe Bay.

And then there are the waterways of East Anglia. The
ancient Fossdyke and Witham Navigations, a heritage
from the Romans, penetrate rural Lincolnshire in almost
the same straight line as a Roman road and are in a
class of their own. They are mainly of academic interest
to the enthusiast rather than of much interest to holidaymakers. We cruised them solely as a contrasting side-trip
from a voyage on the Trent, but bird-watchers and anglers
will find the Witham Navigable Drains at the Boston end
most interesting.

It is the Fenland waterways of East Anglia that are
unique, totally different in character from the other waterways of the country. They have qualities which can only

be described as partly primitive, partly medieval. What we call the 'Nowhither Nene' is connected to the canal system by the heavily-locked and narrow Northampton Arm, and a cruise along this lovely winding river is not only scenically enchanting but a kind of historic pilgrimage. Our first love, however, is that conglomerate of rivers composed of the Ouse and its tributaries, the Cam, the Lark, the Wissey and the Little Ouse. Here there are hundreds of miles of the most unsophisticated cruising grounds in the country where you will move from one delight to another. These are perfect waters for the beginner and are guaranteed to convert amateur into enthusiast.

Of course, East Anglia also contains the Norfolk and Suffolk Broads, the most popular holiday centre in the country for boaters. The Broads have changed out of all recognition from what they were even a few decades ago. Today they are a commercialised holiday centre where three major rivers and their tributaries, broadening from time to time into inland seas, have been intensively developed to cater for those who want every facility and other holidaymakers about them. The Broads offer yet another kind of boating holiday which appeals particularly to young families who in pretty surroundings enjoy making new friends.

You'll find, once you board a boat for a holiday cruise, that whatever waterway you happen to have chosen, you have entered a new world where you are completely absorbed and there is never a dull moment. Each waterway, even after decades of boating holidays, offers new adventures and opens up new interests. Messing about in boats on our inland waterways becomes an engrossing hobby that opens the door to the wonders of nature and the achievements of humanity through the ages. On them you will find the closest thing to perfect peace in the world.

CHAPTER 2

HOW TO CHOOSE A
SUITABLE HOLIDAY CRAFT

A BOAT is the most important element in a boating holiday, but before broaching to family and friends the idea of getting on to the water for a holiday you will want an assurance that novices can easily cope with boats and boating. As you will all literally be living aboard a boat for a week or more, everyone will want to know if boats are safe and comfortable, if they can be handled easily by the inexperienced, what kind of boat should be selected for your particular holiday and how to go about obtaining a holiday craft.

When you set off on your first boating holiday on our inland waterways you won't exactly be ranked in history with Brendan the Navigator, Leif Ericsson, Christopher Columbus, Ferdinand Magellan or even Sir Alec Rose or Robin Knox-Johnston. Quite a few people living on or near the water have long been messing about in boats and they all began as amateurs. Although annual boating holidays by non boat-owners are a relatively recent development they are becoming increasingly popular.

At the start of this century it would have been fair to say that the inland waterways network was almost virgin territory. It wasn't until L. T. C. Rolt produced his classic *Narrow Boat* in 1944, triggering off the founding of the Inland Waterways Association, that public interest in our inland waterways network as a venue for holidays began to be aroused. Before the Second World War our

waterways network carried very few people indeed on
pleasure cruises. When the I.W.A. was formed in 1946,
apart from the Broads and the Thames, only two firms
offering hire craft were in existence.

With a small but growing band of enthusiasts creating
a demand for more and more hire craft and spreading
the word about the fun of exploring the waterways, a
whole new industry catering to boating holidays gradually
developed and spread to virtually every navigable waterway.

Types of hire craft

Today there are scores upon scores of hire craft operators
based strategically over the length and breadth of the
waterways system. They make it possible for the novice
to enjoy a convenient and economical holiday on any
particular stretches of navigable water that may take his
fancy. Many types of craft are available for hire on our
inland waterways. For those who want to see what a boating holiday is like without the responsibility of commanding a boat, cabins are available on hotel boats which
cruise on a number of the waterways. These are usually
pairs of converted traditional narrow boats, one with a
motor and the other on tow. There are also bigger hotel-
barges which operate on broad rivers. Both types have a
professional crew who will let passengers steer or work
locks if they wish, but the elderly or inactive passenger
need not lift a finger if he doesn't want to.

Even cheaper holidays are available on hostel-boats,
converted canal boats pulled by a horse. Accommodation
on these is of dormitory type and passengers are expected
to assist the professional crew.

Traditional camping skiffs and punts may be hired on
some rivers like the Thames. These are flat-bottomed
craft, usually paddled or poled, sleeping two to four. They

are fitted with awnings which stretch over metal frames
to form a tent, and cooking utensils and equipment can
also be hired. The camping pontoon or barge, housing
four to six, and motor-powered, has recently become
available on a number of waterways. These inexpensive
camping-cum-boating type holidays appeal particularly to
groups of youngsters.

Sailing craft for hire on inland waterways are available on the Norfolk and Suffolk Broads and on rivers like
the Warwickshire Avon. Most are equipped with an
auxiliary engine and sleep from two to six people. Some
skill is required to handle sailing yachts, however, and
operators' brochures will spell out what degree of skill is
necessary.

By far the most popular type of craft for inland waterway holidays are motor cruisers. Various types of modern
craft are available with from two to ten berths and fully
fitted with all modern conveniences and equipped with
everything needed for a family holiday on the water.
There is a choice of diesel or petrol engine and some of
the smaller craft are powered by outboard motor. On
rivers these craft are usually broader beamed and fitted
with wheel steering, while on the canals the cruisers are
mostly narrow-beamed, of shallower draught, and many
are equipped with tiller steering. On some canals too it
is possible to hire converted traditional narrow boats 70 ft
long and 6 ft 10 ins in beam, and while they are somewhat more difficult to manoeuvre than the shorter cruisers
the novice need have no fears about handling them.

I can readily recommend the self-drive river or canal
cruisers as being ideal for family holidays. They give you
the independence you want without having to rough it.
They are safe and comfortable, easy to handle and are
available right across our vast network of inland waterways so that your choice of holiday venue is unlimited.

Advantages of hiring

Hiring a river or canal cruiser for a holiday is the simple way to enjoy the pleasures of boating. For when you hire there is someone else to do the worrying and to cope with the countless details that are part and parcel of owning and running your own craft, from licensing and insurance to maintenance and servicing. For the first-timer, in fact, it would be folly to invest in a motor cruiser. Without any experience of boats and waterways you will not, quite apart from the financial investment required, know precisely what you want from your boat and what you want to do with it. Bringing a boat into a family should never be undertaken until you have spent some time on the waterways in boats owned by others and are not only enthusiastically fired by the idea of owning a boat but have an 'ideal' craft in mind.

Hiring gives you the opportunity to skipper different types of craft, including bigger and more lavishly equipped boats than you can probably afford to buy. Hiring not only provides you with a means of learning about boats but of acquiring sufficient waterways know-how to enable you to invest intelligently in the right type of boat for family use for years to come.

Early booking essential

Despite the rapid growth in the number of hire firms and the size of hire fleets the demand for hire cruisers is greater than the supply. To find a craft to suit your family on a particular waterway at a particular time it is essential to get your holiday dates settled and select the waterway on which you wish to cruise well in advance. Most hire firms get the bulk of their bookings for the season, which usually extends from late March to late October, very early in the New Year. This does not mean, however, that those who cannot, because of circumstances, make a firm hire cruiser booking before March will have to abandon hope of a holiday on the water. You may be lucky or fall heir to a cancellation and there are always other waterways—all of which are fun. But the earlier you book and the more flexible your holiday dates, the wider is your choice of both boats and waterways. Hire cruiser charges, which are scaled according to the number of berths per craft, are also .caled according to season, and are cheaper in spring and autumn than in the peak months of July and August.

Hire firm lists

Once you know when you can get away on holiday and have selected your holiday venue—the bulk of this book is devoted to detailed first-hand reports on the many waterways open to you, to help you and your family make an appropriate choice—you will need a list of hire firms. There is an extensive list of hire firms in the Appendix but no book can keep pace with the mushroom growth of this industry. Annually updated lists of hire firms can be obtained from a number of sources.

The Inland Waterways Association at 114 Regent's Park Road, London, N.W.1, publishers for 2s post free, an annual *Waterways Holiday Guide* containing a list of hire firms offering all types of craft on all waterways. The British Waterways Board, Melbury House, Melbury Terrace, London, N.W.1, will provide information on the craft they have for hire at various bases on the nationalised waterways. The Association of Pleasure Craft Operators, The Wharf, Norbury Junction, Stafford, will, on receipt of a stamped self-addressed envelope, send you a copy of the Association's brochure listing names and addresses of their fifty-odd member firms describing the holidays they offer on the canals and some rivers. The Thames Hire

Cruiser Association, W. Bates & Son, Bridge Wharf,
Chertsey, Surrey, will provide a list of member firms who
between them offer over 200 hire craft on the River
Thames. The Great Ouse Boatbuilders and Operators
Association, Riverside Boatyard, Ely, Cambridgeshire, has
a list available of member firms with hire craft at seven
bases on East Anglia's Fenland Waterways. On the Norfolk
and Suffolk Broads there are over a hundred hire firms
offering well over 2,000 craft, most of them motor cruisers,
and most of them can be reached through three associations that have been formed, each with central booking
facilities. Craft belonging to the Norfolk and Suffolk
Broads Yacht Owners Association can be booked through
Blakes (Norfolk Broads Holidays), Wroxham, Norwich,
NOR 41Z, who will provide a free colour booklet. The
Broadland Owners Association publish a big colour
catalogue obtainable from Hoseasons, 60 Oulton Broad,
Lowestoft, Suffolk, and the Red Whale Boat Owners
Association also produce a free colour brochure available
from Bradbeer Ltd, Lowestoft, Suffolk.

Making enquiries

You need only enquire about craft in the first instance
from those hire firms or trade associations which are based
on the waterways or combination of waterways of your
choice. If you state the number in your party and the dates
or probable dates of your holiday it helps the hire firms
to advise you about availability of suitable craft. And you
should, before booking, always advise the hire firm of
where you propose to take your hire cruiser, to ensure that
the craft you book is suitable to your route. Of course, hire
cruisers will always be suited to the waterways on which
they are based and many firms offer hire craft that can
range far afield, on broad and narrow canals and rivers
as well. But problems can arise. For example, some hire

craft on the River Thames may have superstructures too tall to pass under the low bridges of the upper Thames waterway between Oxford and Lechlade. If you intend to combine cruising on the Thames with a jaunt along the Oxford Canal you will require a narrow (6 ft 10 ins in beam) cruiser which can pass through the 7 ft wide locks of the narrow Oxford Canal. Should you plan to move from the broad Grand Union Canal to the broad River Nene a narrow canal cruiser is essential because the Northampton Arm, which links the two waterways, has locks only 7 ft wide. Another reason to advise the hire firm of your planned itinerary is that often canal cruisers are licensed for the nationalised waterways and not the Thames or Nene, and conversely Thames craft may not be licensed for the canals, and so on.

Preliminary spadework

It isn't necessary to plan your boating holiday in detail before you hire a cruiser, but if you have a particular itinerary in mind some preliminary spadework is advisable. It is relatively simple to figure out roughly just where and how far you can cruise in a given period with the aid of Stanford's Inland Cruising Map obtainable from Stanford's Ltd, 12 Long Acre, London, W.C.2, or the Inland Waterways Association, price 10s including postage. This useful map gives mileages, shows which waterways are broad and which are narrow, and gives the number and location of locks. We happen to enjoy locks, and have been known to average over a hundred a week on a three-week boating holiday, but the first-timer will not be so keen and will probably prefer a waterway or a route with relatively few locks.

There is usually a speed limit of four miles an hour on canals and six to eight miles per hour on rivers, depending upon whether you are cruising upstream or downstream. Speed limits should be strictly adhered to, to avoid damage to banks and harm to moored craft from excessive wash and indeed trouble with your own cruiser. It is rarely possible, in any case, to go much faster than the speed limit on canals because they are almost invariably shallow. Without going into technicalities attempts at excessive speed on canals will only result in your own wash overtaking you and slowing you down and can even cause your own cruiser to go aground.

Your speed is, of course, affected by locks. While experts can pass through locks in a few minutes when the gates are open and the lock ready and beginners will take only a few minutes more, the time taken to pass through locks is extremely variable. Timing can depend not only upon the proficiency of your crew but whether paddles or guillotine gates are stiff or easy to operate, upon the size of the lock and how long it takes to empty or fill, upon whether a lock is with you or against you, upon whether you have to wait for other craft using the lock or waiting to pass through, upon whether a lock-keeper holds you up until other boats in sight can join you in passing through, and upon whether locks are far apàrt or in flights where crew members can move ahead and get locks ready in advance, a process called 'lock-wheeling'.

The 'Lock Mile'

I have kept an accurate and detailed log of all my holiday cruises and experience shows that cruising time can be surprisingly accurately estimated by equating a mile of waterway with a lock. By adding locks to miles on any cruising route you get a total figure which can be quoted in 'lock miles'. Thus 60 miles of waterway and 60 locks would equal 120 lock miles, as would 90 miles of waterway and 30 locks. While it actually takes less time on average to pass through a lock than to navigate a mile

. .

of waterway, allowing equal time in your calculations will cover the variables in passing through locks mentioned earlier as well as others, including infrequent but nevertheless possible instances of rubble or rubbish obstructions preventing the complete closure of a lock gate. At times too you may pick up weeds on your propeller shaft, or a plastic bag or inner tube round your propeller, which will take time to clear.

My experience over the years shows without exception that it is safe to estimate that you can travel 4 lock miles per hour on canals and 6 lock miles per hour on rivers. River locks are generally bigger, deeper and take longer to empty and fill so that time gained on the open waterways is lost at the locks.

This calculation takes into consideration time lost on canal pounds or river reaches by the odd going aground, by slowing down for moored craft and fishermen, by easing off for blind corners and oddly angled bridge holes and the like. A combination cruise of rivers and canals can be estimated in the same way, i.e. a cruise involving roughly equal lock mileage on river and on canal will result in an average speed of 5 lock miles per hour.

Knowing in advance your cruising speed is helpful in planning an itinerary for your boating holiday, but there remains the question of how many lock miles you can comfortably cover in a day with ample time for seeing the local sights, shopping, visiting the local pub, chatting with interesting acquaintances, fishing, swimming, picnicing, bird-watching, sunbathing or just idling about.

A day's cruising is different for different people and different craft. Professional boaters with a pair of narrow boats will travel at a steady 60 to 70 lock miles a day. Experienced enthusiasts can manage up to 100 lock miles in a day in a canal cruiser, but these lock mileages are chalked up by being on the move for 12 hours or more, eating meals while under way, shopping only while in locks, consistent lock-wheeling at every opportunity, and what's more keeping on the move even in torrential rain. This is not for the holiday maker, whether a first-timer or a veteran of the waterways.

The beginner in a river or canal cruiser should not plan on covering more than two dozen lock miles per day on average. On canals this means 6 hours cruising, on rivers 4 hours, and on a combination of rivers and canals just under 5 hours cruising per day on average. As you gain experience this can be stepped up to 30 lock miles per day, which is what we have averaged over the years, but no more. This may seem a very short distance but I am talking about averages. Each day's cruising will be different. Some canal pounds and river reaches offer more in the way of sightseeing and other amenities than others. By planning on a 24 lock-mile-per-day average you will have ample time to 'sleep in', see the most interesting sights, complete your shopping, swim or fish or just laze about. And should it pour with rain all morning you can still do your 24 lock miles in the afternoon. An itinerary based on 24 lock miles a day will not exhaust you, however many locks are involved in the total cruise, and provides leeway not only for bad weather but for the odd battery failure or breakdown which can happen. It allows for lingering from time to time in particularly appealing places and ensures against straining the strength and patience of your crew.

So a week's boating holiday will mean 7 days at 24 lock miles a day, or 168 lock miles. For two weeks the total is simply doubled to 336 lock miles and for three weeks trebled to 504 lock miles. If you, as a beginner, plan your cruising itinerary on this maximum lock mileage basis, you will not be over-reaching yourself or be asking too much of your family or crew of friends. Your cruise will be halved, of course, if you return to the same starting point on a similar outward and return route. But in many areas of the country you can plan round trips on a combination of waterways so as not to retrace any of your outward journey or only a part of it. Then, too, quite a number of boat hirers operate from a number of bases and will make arrangements for your cruiser to be left at some other place, thus facilitating a holiday in which every day can be spent exploring new country.

I have provided these calculations as a guide only, a maximum which the beginner will not find it difficult in any way to achieve. It enables you to plan an itinerary with confidence and approach boat hire firms with sufficient information to enable them in turn to advise you that the craft you have in mind is suitable, or to advise you on what craft they have available for your planned cruise. If your planned itinerary is impracticable or will involve additional charges for licence fees on waterways for which the hirer's craft are not automatically licensed you will know the score in advance. The hirer is in a position too to suggest an alteration in your itinerary if necessary.

Writing for brochures

So with your holiday dates established and a feasible itinerary calculated you are ready to write for brochures to hire firms based along your chosen waterways route. One word of warning here. It is unwise to borrow a cruiser from a friend who may own one. Like borrowing money from a friend, it can lead to a broken friendship and on more practical grounds can lead to a spoiled holiday, for your friend's craft may not be properly serviced and you can hardly call him out should you break down with his boat. Nor should you hire a boat from the little man who can let you have it cheap, for it is unlikely to be in tip-top condition, and perhaps not even licensed for the waterways or insured. And the little man is rarely on tap to effect repairs in the event of a breakdown.

The professional hire firms belong to associations which require certain standards regarding the condition of craft let for hire, telephone repair services and fair conditions of hire.

Hire firm brochures vary enormously. Some are quite small and basic, while others are massive and packed with cruising hints and other helpful data. Do not be put off, therefore, if some boat hirers make a small charge for their brochure. Generally you will find it worth the token charge made to cover printing costs. All brochures will contain a bit of information on local waterways and usually a map of the waterways on which the firm's boats are permitted to cruise. There will be either a map or directions for reaching the boatyard by road and/or rail. There will be photographs, layouts, specifications and descriptions of the firm's hire craft, specimen inventories of equipment on board according to size of craft, hire terms (scale of charges for each craft according to season), notes regarding cancellation and baggage insurance, a booking form, conditions of hire and general information, often including advice on clothing to take, recommended holiday routes and even a list of booklets or guides you may wish to purchase. Some firms will send an up-to-date availability list of craft, while others will ask you to make alternative choices of craft in the event of your first choice being already hired.

It is a wise precaution to read carefully the all-important conditions of hire so that you know exactly where you stand before you book, what deposit is required, what extras may be involved and what responsibilities you have to assume.

Criterion for hire craft

Is it possible to make a wise choice of craft from brochures? What should one look for in a hire craft? The vast majority of brochures are accurate and truthful and you have the protection of the Trade Descriptions Act. Our first hiring was such a success with the craft more than living up to its photograph and description that we booked from another firm on another waterway for the following year on the strength of the firm's brochure. When we arrived at the boatyard to start our cruise we found, to our dismay, that the firm's hire craft were very old and that maintenance was not all that it should have been. Our craft, while big and comfortable, not only leaked badly when it rained but the bilge needed pumping completely twice a day. Even though the firm slipped the craft to repair the leaks in the hull, losing us half a day, the repairs were not adequate. On the last day but one of our holiday, on a run of six hours after empty-ing the bilge, we moored at the boatyard with water lap-ping our floorboards. We found that other hirers had had similar experiences, one family abandoning their hire craft in mid-holiday and demanding their money back. That particular firm went out of business a few years later, which didn't surprise us in the least. As a result of that unhappy experience we have ever since visited the boatyard to check our hire craft before actually booking it. It has in every case proved unnecessary but we have come to enjoy these outings and hire firms have always welcomed our personal visit.

The first criterion in choosing a hire craft is its suit-ability for your planned itinerary. This will not arise, of course, if you decide just to potter along on the waterway on which the craft is based, or if you are booking a craft for a cruise on isolated waterways, such as the Broads, the

South Level of the Fenland Waterways, the Medway, the Lancaster Canal, etc. But if you are planning a cruise covering both broad and narrow waterways or a combination of river and canal, you will have to ensure that your craft will go where you want it to.

As a simple guide you can cruise virtually anywhere on the navigable waterways—except through the Harecastle Tunnel on the Trent & Mersey Canal where headroom is restricted to 5 ft 9 ins—with a craft with maximum dimensions of 45 ft in length, 6 ft 10 ins in beam, headroom 6 ft 6 ins and a draught of up to 2 ft or a bit more. Many canals and rivers will take craft up to 70 ft or more in length but you may not be able to enter some connecting waterways because the locks will not be big enough to cope with a boat this size. If the beam of the craft is over 6 ft 10 ins you will automatically be excluded from the narrow canals and limited to rivers and broad canals. All broad waterways will accommodate craft up to 10 ft 6 ins in beam and some will take boats up to 12 ft 6 ins or 13 ft wide. But once the beam reaches 14 ft most canals will be out of your reach and you will only have the larger rivers left as cruising grounds. If the draught is over 2 ft 6 ins canal cruising also becomes rather limited.

As long as you inform a hire firm where you want to go on your holiday you will have no worries. They will advise you of craft suitability including the aspect of size and whether the craft is licensed for the waterways on your itinerary or involves you in supplementary fees for travelling on non-nationalised waterways. There is one other important point. Many canal and river cruisers are equipped with flush toilets but there are waterways, like the Thames for example, which insist on chemical closets and do not even permit washing-up water to be drained into the river. Therefore, if your itinerary includes the Thames and you are hiring a craft from a boatyard on the Grand Union or Oxford or other canals within reach of the Thames, you will have to acquire one with a chemical closet and ensure you have a washing-up bowl aboard.

As important as the suitability of the craft for waterways is its suitability for your family or group of friends. Although the larger the boat the bigger the hire charge, it is unwise to hire a craft with insufficient room for a holiday cruise in comfort. The difference in handling boats of different size is minimal but you will certainly not enjoy being cramped for space. Most of our own boating holidays have been a combination of canal and river cruises and we usually hire a narrow cruiser. But on those occasions when we cruised exclusively on rivers or broad waterways we have invariably hired a broader-beamed motor cruiser.

Study the specifications and layouts of the craft in the brochures. Note how they are described in terms of berths upon which charges are based. Some brochures will give the exact number of berths, while others will quote adaptability, i.e. 2-3 berth, 2-4 berth, 4-6 berth, 6-8 berth, and so on.

Layouts will show you whether upper bunks are involved or if some of the crew will have to sleep under a boat canopy. Layouts of hire craft can vary tremendously and some layouts are much more spacious and comfortable than others, with better access, standards of privacy, deck space and sanitary and showering facilities. We inevitably select a craft for hire which is just a bit bigger than necessary.

It is impossible to describe in words the ideal layout in a hire craft, but you will find on page 40 good examples of a well designed narrow cruiser and a really comfortable river cruiser, both accommodating our basic five with guests from time to time. You will note that while the

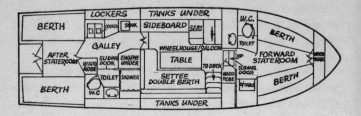

6 berth cabin cruiser

Length 34 ft. 6 in. Displacement 4.25 tons

Beam (maximum) 10 ft. 4 in. Draft 2 ft. 3 in.

Overall height 7 ft. 6 in. approx., normal waterline to top of windscreen

Headroom 6 ft. 0 in. minimum

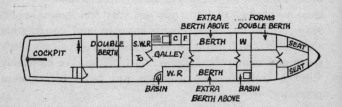

6/8 berth narrow cruiser (*Flying Mexican*)

Length 43 ft.

Beam 6 ft. 10 in. Draft 2 ft. 0 in.

Headroom 6 ft. 4 in.

river cruiser is broader beamed than the canal cruiser, the latter is usually longer than the former.

Many factors contribute to a comfortable layout. It is convenient if not essential to have a shower aboard. Even if you arrange baths for your crew in waterside hotels a shower provides extra storage room. Chapter 4 will cover what you should take with you on a boating holiday, but let me say at this stage that you will need at least one drawer per crew member and at least one hanging cupboard, apart from storage space for galley supplies.

A refrigerator or insulated cold box with renewable ice pack is a boon in hot weather and a worthwhile amenity at any time. We like ice in our drinks, the facility to have ice cream aboard, the convenience of frozen vegetables and meat at times, and butter that doesn't run.

Most craft, however large or small, have Calor gas stoves and even ovens, a sink and washbasins with running hot and cold water. While you will often dine ashore many meals will be prepared aboard and the scope of these as well as ease of preparation will depend upon the facilities. We find an oven a great advantage not only in providing more varied meals but in keeping food hot when delayed by locks or when running on a bit further to find a better mooring. Ovens can also be used for drying wet clothing and warming a craft on a cold or wet day.

You'll find that on boating holidays, you will be on your craft more of the time than inside her, so deck space should be available for every member of the crew, either in the steering well, in a bow well and/or on the superstructure. Crew members will want to see the sights as you cruise along or will want to sunbathe. I wouldn't hire a boat without a catwalk for ease in getting about the craft. It is a confounded nuisance to have to pass through a craft or climb over the top to get from stern to bow, particularly when dealing with warps or mooring lines.

Cruisers accommodating four crew or more should always have two points of access.

Water-flushed toilets are less trouble than chemical closets which have to be disposed of at least once a day, either at chemical disposal points or buried with the spade or shovel provided. But if you cruise on waterways which ban flush toilets you will have no choice in the matter and I would be prepared to bet that within the next decade more and more waterway authorities will insist on chemical closets, and introduce many more regulations against pollution.

Fuel and particularly water tank capacity on hire craft are important. Most craft carry enough fuel to take you through your entire holiday but many are fitted with inadequate water tanks. Watering points can at times be over a comfortable day's cruising apart. This can be inconvenient and I would say that every hire craft should carry at least fifteen to twenty gallons of water per person. You will be surprised how much water you will use on a boat and your crew will have to learn quickly not to let taps run.

Whether your engine is a diesel or petrol doesn't matter much although diesel engines are somewhat cheaper to run. On the other hand diesel engines are usually noisier than petrol engines. You will have to exercise special care with petrol engines because petrol is more inflammable than diesel fuel and although incidents are extremely rare, explosions and fires resulting from carelessness with Calor gas on petrol-driven craft are not unknown. I prefer a diesel engine every time and our entire crew has come to enjoy its distinctive throb.

Depending upon what waterways you choose for your holidays, you may have a choice of steering. River cruisers invariably have wheel steering, with the steering position either aft or in a centre cockpit. There is little to choose between them. Centre cockpit steering provides greater visibility as a rule but naturally affects deck space and general layout of the craft.

Canal cruisers usually have tiller steering, which is admittedly more direct, but which I personally find less comfortable. But many cruisers have wheel steering, some aft and some amidships, and I plump for wheel steering every time. This enables you to sit on a stool instead of standing. It is possible to sit while tiller steering but this can be awkward at times and controls can be inconveniently placed. I have found too that one gets much wetter at a tiller than at a wheel, for with wheel steering you have the benefit of bulkhead protection for most of your body. Many boating friends, however, prefer tiller steering. I don't honestly dislike it, indeed have found it fun, and would recommend beginners to compare it with wheel steering for themselves.

Both canal and river cruisers, particularly smaller craft, are sometimes designed to incorporate folding canopies. You will find that only on rare occasions can you cruise along with the canopy up, for there is usually a bridge hole too low on your course. Some hire firms insist that canopies can only be used when moored. My family and I enjoy an open cockpit even when it is raining, although not in torrential downpours. We have been on many cruises when we have never raised the canopy the entire time. On some craft, however, it is essential to erect a canopy when it rains, either because cockpit space under the canopy is required for sleeping space or because the combination of wind and rain makes it desirable. The important thing about folding canopies is to check that they are in good condition and all side curtains are aboard. Previous hirers may well have cruised with the canopy up and damaged it.

Take a good look at the layout of the craft you have in

mind from the standpoint of accommodation and privacy. Single bunks allow more space for each person than double bunks, for which reason my wife and I always sleep head to toe on the latter in sleeping bags. This makes the double bunk every bit as comfortable as the single. Age and sex of crew, whether family or friends, have to be taken into consideration when choosing a craft, so always work out which berths each member of the crew will occupy before a booking. If a friend or friends are joining the family a reallocation of berths may be necessary. Upper bunks are as comfortable as lower ones as a rule, and it is possible to tuck even a restless sleeper in one of these to obviate the danger of a fall. But those who sleep under an upper bunk will get less air, and this can matter to those people who like to sleep normally with bedroom windows wide open. You will want to be sure that cabins are separated by doors of one kind or another instead of being merely open gangways, for those times when privacy is desired. Doors should fasten back easily in an open position too because, particularly in hot weather, you will want them all open and a breeze flowing through the boat for sleeping comfort.

Cruiser equipment

Cruiser inventories listed in brochures do provide practically everything you will need afloat in the way of domestic equipment as claimed, and you will find it all supplied clean and ready for use. These inventories will vary somewhat from hire firm to hire firm and according to the size of the craft. Some hire firms provide items like soap, washing-up liquid, scouring powder and toilet rolls. In some cases all linen including pillow cases, tea towels, etc., are subject to a supplementary charge. And in all cases life-jackets for youngsters can be hired. The majority of hire cruisers today are fitted with radios and some firms even supply television sets for a supplementary charge.

Do not hesitate to be a bit fussy about the craft you select for the secret of an enjoyable holiday afloat lies basically in the craft rather than in your itinerary. You can, of course, obtain full information on all these points from brochures and correspondence with the hire firm, but for beginners a personal visit to the boatyard will give you and the family a much clearer idea of your mobile holiday home as well as an exciting preview of the fun to come.

As you become better acquainted with the waterways you may be as lucky as we were in finding an all-purpose craft which feels exactly right, which exerts a hold upon you and which comes up to the family concept of the ideal. You will sense this after your first few days of cruising aboard her and as you hire her again the following year, perhaps from a different base, you will come to feel that she almost belongs to you.

In our case, our favourite craft is a 'Toledo' class six to eight berth steel-hulled canal cruiser, 6 ft 10 ins in beam, 43 ft in length, 1 ft 9 ins in draught and with a superstructure clearance of just under 5 ft 9 ins without removing her spot-light or windscreens. She will go anywhere on the waterways network, apart from the isolated sections, and is the closest we have ever come to perfection in a cruiser, superbly laid out and equipped for comfort and efficiency.

You will find the diagrammatic layout of our favourite narrow cruiser, the *Flying Mexican,* at the bottom of page 40.

Hire charges

What do craft of this type cost to hire? The *Flying Mexican* can be hired at rates ranging from £46 per week early in the season, except for the Easter period, to a maximum of £80 per week at peak season (mid-July to the end of August), tailing off to £38 per week in late September and October. Four-berth canal cruisers with similar facilities range in price from £26 to £52 per week according to season. Two-berth craft can be obtained for a weekly charge of between £15 and £36 per week, according to season. Rates for river cruisers of equivalent size and standard are roughly the same. This means the cost per berth for hire craft varies roughly from about £6 to £22 per week, depending on the season and the type of craft. Some hire firms will let craft for shorter periods than a week and when hiring for three days or less the charge is usually half the weekly rate, while hiring for four days or more you will usually pay one-seventh of the weekly rate per day.

Some readers may at first consider these charges rather expensive but will realise that they provide good value for money when compared with hotel accommodation or caravan hire charges. After all, you are getting a comfortable fully equipped mobile home giving you an opportunity to explore and enjoy aspects of your country which can be achieved in no other way.

CHAPTER 3

ON HANDLING BOATS

DON'T BE put off by doubts about your ability to handle a boat as all our craft are designed for easy handling. A short trial run with one of our experienced staff is all you need before you set out on your own.

Steering a cruiser is exceptionally straightforward, but a trial run before finally leaving the boatyard is always arranged to familiarise you with the simple controls.

Generally if you drive a car you will certainly be able to handle a boat; but non-drivers please take heart, you will soon learn the basic requirements of boat handling. Controls are fewer than in a car and much simpler : even the greenest of novices will be away on their first voyage—waving goodbye to the boatyard—within minutes of taking over after the trial run.

These three quotations, taken from the brochures of three hire firms offering craft for hire on rivers, on canals and on both rivers and canals, are representative of comments on boat handling expressed by all hire firm operators. What's more they are perfectly true. I know of no hire firm that will not let their craft to complete novices or who will ask to see a car driving licence. To do this, allowing amateurs with no experience whatsoever to take charge of boats costing thousands of pounds, they must be confident that hirers can cope.

Some hire firms offer advance tuition in boat handling for prospective hirers of nervous temperament but this course of special instruction is generally regarded as unnecessary and hire firms offering these facilities are few and far between.

Trial run

Every hire firm will supply you with a stencilled or printed list of instructions covering the most important points of boat handling and maintenance, or with a comprehensive booklet of cruising hints incorporating basic information on these points. So even if you should forget certain aspects of what you are shown on your trial run you will have a written reminder at hand.

Let us assume you and your crew are stowed away and on board your hire craft ready to cast off. One of the hire firm staff is with you and it will be he who starts up the engine, casts off bow and stern ropes, or 'straps' as they are sometimes called, pushes out the bows or entire craft, and gets you under way. You will find that he will let the engine run for some minutes before untying the boat, and will advise you always to give the engine a chance to warm up. You will also be told if you are aboard a sizeable cruiser that when you are not at a boatyard or designated moorings you should push out the stern first and reverse into mid-stream. This is because cruisers, and particularly long narrow canal cruisers, do not steer easily near the bank because they swing about on their own centres, i.e. the stern must swing into the bank for the bows to go out.

You will be shown that there are only one or two effective controls, a gear lever with forward, reverse and neutral positions, and a throttle. On some craft gear lever and throttle are combined. If there is a separate throttle it must always be closed down before going from forward to reverse and vice versa. If controls are combined you will be told to move the lever to neutral for a moment before changing from forward to reverse gear and vice versa.

Your mentor will show you the ignition switch, which in some cases will incorporate the starter, while in other craft there will be a separate starter button. He will locate the horn button, headlight switch and water pump switch and, in the case of a diesel engine, a control resembling a choke in a car or piece of wire with a loop at the end, which has to be pulled to stop the engine.

While you are cruising along he will show you where the gauges are which register oil pressure, engine temperature and battery charge, and advise you on normal readings. You will be told to check the oil in the sump regularly, just as you would in a car. You will be advised that when engine temperature rises unduly it will probably be due to debris wrapped round your propeller or shaft. You will be told how to clear this, and if your craft has a weed box for easy access from the 'engine room' to the propeller assembly your instructor will advise you always to ensure that bolts are firmly tightened after you replace it.

Even before you leave the boatyard you will have been shown where all of the equipment is stowed, and the positions of fuel and water tanks will have been made known to you too. Simple daily maintenance duties will be explained either before or during the trial run, i.e. checking oil, pumping bilges, turning grease points or pressing the lever of the shaft lubricant container, whichever is applicable, and topping up any header tank that may be aboard. Maintenance of both petrol and diesel engines is simplicity itself and literally takes only a few minutes a day. It's a good idea to take care of these easy but important chores first thing every morning as a matter of routine so that you don't forget them and cause unnecessary complications on your holiday.

Your mentor, in checking the inventory of the craft with you before the trial run, will give you some useful tips. You will be shown where the Calor gas is kept, and, if you are on a long cruise, how to change over the bottles and re-light any refrigerator aboard. If your craft is equipped with a cold box rather than a Calor gas fridge you will be advised to turn off the Calor gas at the bottle each night and turn it back on again in the morning. You will also be shown how to light the Calor gas heater pilot light and operate any levers that may enable you to obtain hot water heated by the engine rather than the gas heater.

More breakdowns are caused by flat batteries than any other single cause. In the great majority of cases where this happens it is simply because hirers don't run their engines every day. This does not mean that you must keep on the move, but it is mandatory to run your engine for at least half an hour every day, whether on the move or not, to maintain a good charge in your batteries.

There is much more equipment using electricity on a boat than in a car. Provided you run your engine daily there is no need to be parsimonious about using lights and electrical equipment aboard a boat.

One point that hire firms rarely if ever cover is use of water aboard a boat. Many hire craft have relatively small freshwater tanks and even on craft with water tanks of 100 gallons or more capacity, fresh water will vanish quickly, even if you do not use the shower or bath aboard. On a boat, you should establish a self-enforced ruling never to wash or wash up under a running tap. If you depart from this ruling you will almost certainly run out of fresh water frequently or have to make sure you reach a watering point every day for topping up. Showers are particularly wasteful of water and we invariably shower only when we are moored near or are approaching a watering point.

Steering

During your trial run you will quickly note that wheel steering on a boat is similar to wheel steering in a car, i.e. your craft turns in the direction that you turn the wheel. Response to the wheel of a boat is not as direct as that in a car, however. Your craft will not turn as quickly or as sharply as a car, and particularly if your boat is a sizeable one. With narrow cruisers in particular, as your mentor will demonstrate, when your bows swing left, your stern will come round to the right. Narrow cruisers steer rather like a pencil floats in a stream. Tiller steering is more direct, and although the craft reacts on the same principle, it reacts differently. To turn left with wheel steering, you turn the wheel to the left, but to turn left with tiller steering you push the tiller to the right. Whatever the type of steering on your craft you will grasp the technique easily during your trial run.

Boating on the inland waterways is quite different from motor-cruising or sailing at sea. Craft at sea can be left to run or drift for long distances, but on inland waterways the steerer must steer all the time that the craft is under way, or go hard ashore very quickly. Mooring and casting off and coming alongside, which happens once or twice a day at sea, is done a few times an hour on the inland waterways.

When steering on inland waterways of any kind you have to keep as alert as you do at the wheel of a car, even though there is comparatively little traffic. When you first take over the wheel or tiller of a boat, try lighting a cigarette, cigar or pipe and you will see what I mean. With practice you will learn to do this safely by hooking an arm over the wheel, or standing astride the tiller.

The usual 'rule of the road' on waterways is to keep to the right. This rule will frequently be broken for many good and bad reasons, but if in any circumstances you intend to veer left you should, if any other craft are about, give two blasts on your horn, or better still hold out your arm horizontally in the direction you intend to go. You can make your intention abundantly clear by a sharpish change of course in that direction. While there are no authentic hand signals on the waterways, you should do your best to indicate any change of course to moving craft around you. There are official sound signals, which you may find useful, but the trouble is that few hirers bother about or understand them. One blast of your horn indicates that you are altering your course to starboard (right); two blasts indicates alteration of course to port (left); three blasts that your engine is going astern, and four blasts followed by a pause and then two more means that you are turning round to port. Whatever methods you use to signal your intentions when other craft are about, always ease off.

Looking at a waterway, even a canal, it will appear to you to be wide enough to permit your craft to wander at will. But you will find on most canals and all rivers that the navigable channel runs down the centre of straight stretches, while the deep water is invariably on the outside of bends. The inside of a bend may be very shallow, even virtually dry, and you will note that long narrow boats usually have trouble on sharp corners. So keep clear of these craft on sharp corners and never moor at such locations.

Thus, although 'keep right' is the rule of the waterways, when no craft are in sight ahead or behind you, and provided you are not approaching a blind corner or angled bridge hole, it is wise practice to keep to the centre of canals and rivers on straight stretches and to the outside of bends. Of course, you must move over to the right for approaching craft or to permit a craft from behind to pass on your left. Normally, you too should pass to the left of craft, but do not overtake a working boat or pair of narrow boats until you are waved on by the steerer. Overtake on the side he indicates and have the courtesy to thank him as you pass. You will find that you will be unable to pass unless the working boat or pair is slowed down, in any case. This is due to the curious water-flow past the hull of a loaded boat.

Grounding

Attempts to cut corners, whether in passing other craft or not, will almost inevitably lead to going on the mud. It is no great tragedy if you run aground. In most cases, as you are moving forward you will only ground your craft at the bows. Your stern will probably be afloat. Immediately you touch bottom, you should put your engine into neutral. The deep water is back where you came from and your craft has almost certainly dug a trough in the mud as it went aground and is now lying in it. If your stern is afloat and your propeller has not churned up mud you may be able to reverse off the mud. If this does not work you should use your boathook or barge pole. There is no point in sending one of the crew to the bows to push off as his weight and thrust will only ground the bows more firmly and so make it more difficult to get off. The crew should push off from the stern and their weight alone will help lift the bows. Always push off backwards along the trough. If you still cannot get off, get a line ashore on the other side of the canal or river, and pull the boat out backwards from there.

Should you go aground at the stern, switch off your engine at once to prevent damage to rudder and propeller. Then lighten the stern by getting the crew forward to the

bows. If the stern does not float free, then use your boathook to push off backwards and to the centre of the waterway. Never use your engine in any gear when your stern
is grounded.

Should your entire craft be aground, and this can
happen, for example, when the wash of a passing commercial craft pushes you to the shallow side of a waterway,
cut your engine, move your crew to the bows and with
your boathook try first to free the stern and then the bows
and gradually edge your craft to the centre of the waterway. If your craft persists in sticking fast, try rolling it
gently from side to side by shifting your crew from catwalk to catwalk. In serious cases of grounding you may as
a last resort have to lighten your craft by getting the crew
over the side, or ask a passing craft to take a line from
your stern and assist you.

Navigating bridge holes

Whatever canal or river you cruise you are bound to
encounter bridge holes. Many are wide and easy to navigate but others will be both narrow and badly angled to
the navigation channel. The easy way to navigate bridge
holes is to line up your craft with the hole as you approach
it so that you pass straight through. Never worry about
the right side of your boat. Whether at wheel or tiller
simply see that your left-hand catwalk will clear the left-
hand side of the hole by a foot and you will invariably
pass under the bridge without difficulty. Do not try to
just clear the left-hand side of the hole, as a bend may
follow and you will need the clearance on either side to
allow your stern to swing when you steer round the bend.
The height of your superstructure must always be taken
into consideration. Your hire firm will advise you if there
are any particularly low bridges or tunnels on your route.
But do not take anything for granted. Ease off before

bridge holes and tunnels to see if your craft will easily pass through. You will quickly be able to judge clearances, just as you become acquainted with the width of a new car. Rivers and canal pounds can be in flood, reducing normal clearance, and it is up to you to exercise due care.

It is bridge holes on blind corners or sharp bends on canals that sometimes cause concern to the inexperienced. Positioning a boat to go through a narrow opening on a bend is largely a question of practice. The most helpful advice I can give is to urge you to think of your craft as being steerable separately from both ends. There is little difficulty in aiming the bows so that the boat will enter the bridge hole. On a sharp turn this will mean steering for a point on the far side of the hole and then gradually bringing the bows round until they enter the gap. This done, you can turn your attention to the stern. If it is coming too close to either side of the bridge hole, you can move your rudder to bring the stern into line. Moving the stern over will have the effect of forcing the bows towards the side of the hole, but you will find that there is time enough to rectify this when the stern is past the danger point. You will find that most bridges on canal bends have bays cut in the outside bank on either side of them, and these are designed to allow for the stern swing of a 70 ft narrow boat. With a shorter craft you should have no difficulty in lining it up for the hole in plenty of time to see and avoid any craft that happens to be coming the other way.

Navigating tunnels

Tunnels are really no more forbidding than bridge holes although longer tunnels, which may stretch for over a mile, are dark. In many cases you will not be able to see the exit and this can be forbidding to the beginner, particularly as few long tunnels are absolutely straight. Ease off and proceed slowly until you are confident of your ability to steer through a tunnel. Use your headlight, of course, and pitch its beam so that it hits the centre of the curved roof of the tunnel about 20 ft ahead of your bows. You will find that this will illuminate both the top and sides of a tunnel. Also if you turn on all the cabin lights you will find that the brightly illuminated sides of the tunnel will make steering much easier. There are one-way tunnels which should be negotiated rather slowly as you may have only feet or inches clearance on each side. But canal tunnels which permit two-way traffic are wide enough for craft to pass each other, however narrow they may appear to you. If you feel a kind of astigmatism developing as you cruise through a long tunnel, reduce your speed. When passing oncoming craft, if you are worried, pull over to the right side and stop to let the approaching craft pass. After navigating a few long tunnels you will get the hang of it and enjoy your subsequent tunnels at normal speed.

Do not worry if you bump the side—your craft can take it. If you continue to veer against the sides, however, ease off for a more comfortable passage. Quite a number of tunnels are wet, even if they drip only at air vents. The helmsman should slip on a waterproof coat and if there is anything on deck that you do not want to get wet, store it below.

Stopping a boat

Boats, unlike cars, have no brakes. Steering in the almost frictionless element of water is only achieved by adding drag to one side of a boat, or applying extra drive to the other. Both forces make the boat turn in the same direction, but it will turn on an imaginary pivot slightly forward of amidships. The bows will therefore move sideways in one direction and the stern sideways in the other.

As the imaginary pivot round which a boat turns is

forward of its central point, its stern will obviously swing wider than its bows. There is therefore more likelihood of hitting something with the stern than with the bows. You will also find that when going full speed ahead a rudder will resist being turned and you will have to exert a good force on tiller or wheel to overcome this resistance, a breaking wake being formed as your craft comes round. But when you are idling along very slowly, rudder action will be light. If drifting with the engine off you will not be able to steer at all, for a boat must be under way to obtain steerage.

The only way of stopping is by going astern. A propeller is far less efficient for this than when going ahead. If you are moving forward, even at only four to six miles per hour, your craft will continue to move forward for some distance even if you put the engine in neutral. You will need considerably more engine to get any worthwhile stopping effect, and even then you will find it seems to take a long time before you lose way. To stop you should first put your engine in neutral and then into reverse—and don't hesitate to 'gun the engine'. Most bumps occur because boat handlers do not allow sufficient space or time to stop. Do practise stopping with your hire craft a few times so that you can see for yourself the distance required before the craft comes to a halt. Once you are aware of this, stopping will cause you no problem. You will find, once you have gone through a lock, that stopping in confined water is a much faster process than stopping in a wide reach of river or canal.

Reversing

While practising stopping it is a good idea also to try going in reverse. You will soon see that when going astern the propeller is the wrong side of the rudder and cannot deflect water off it. Unless you are going hard astern,

which you usually do not want to do, the rudder will
have virtually no effect. In fact, it is difficult, if not
impossible to steer accurately when going astern. One way
to change your heading, that is to come about, is to move
to the right side of the navigational channel and then
give your engine a brief burst ahead with the wheel hard
over to the left. Put your engine in neutral, swing your
rudder the opposite way, then go hard astern briefly. A
few manoeuvres like this and you will be facing the
opposite direction.

Of course, many waterways are wide enough to enable
you to turn your craft simply by putting the rudder hard
over. Canals have winding holes, i.e. turning points or
deep indentations in one bank to permit a 70 ft narrow
boat to turn. Navigational guides to waterways generally
list winding points, and approaches to locks are often
wider than the waterway itself, enabling all but the biggest craft to turn about.

Mooring

You will be mooring your craft several times a day. And
mooring is really very little different from stopping in
midstream. It is a simple matter to come to a halt beside
a designated mooring—a quayside, platform or floating
dock—because there is usually sufficient depth of water
for your craft. You simply ease off and steer to bring your
craft at a 10–15° angle to the mooring, first going into
neutral and then using reverse gear and opposite rudder
to come to a halt.

It is along the banks of rivers and canals, those rural,
isolated or out-of-the-way spots that appeal to you, that
mooring can require a little finesse. This is because many
of the most scenic and desirable moorings have little depth
of water. Whenever attempting to moor at undesignated
moorings always bring your bows in first at about a 45°

angle with a member of your crew armed with a boathook to make soundings of the depth of the water. Even if you go aground, your stern will still be afloat in deeper water and you can reverse safely back into midstream. If your bows come in to the bank without grounding a member of the crew can leap ashore with the bow line and while he or she holds the bows in you can turn your rudder towards the bank and reverse your stern close enough in to enable other members of the crew to jump ashore with the stern line. This is also a useful technique to employ when mooring in a narrow gap between other craft.

It is possible to moor along shallow banks provided you keep your craft a foot or more off the bank and use a gangplank for leaving and boarding the boat. The main thing to remember about mooring is to do it slowly. On canals you can moor craft facing in any direction, but on rivers with a stream running always moor with your bows facing upstream. You will find that the stream will help you come to a halt and your craft will ride more comfortably when facing the stream.

Never moor on bends, in locks, on approaches to locks, in bridge holes or their entrances, or on sites with 'no mooring' signs. Don't run the risk of being rammed or clipped by other craft.

The most common method of mooring is to two points, at bow and stern, and this method is best for overnight mooring or for leaving the boat for any length of time. At recognised moorings you will find mooring rings or stakes to which you can tie your mooring lines. On occasions they may be too far apart for the length of your craft and it may be necessary to use one of your own mooring stakes and mallets or heavy hammers. For safe and comfortable mooring, drive these stakes into the ground at a 45° angle away from the bows and stern, siting the stakes about 6 ft ahead of your bows and 6 ft behind your stern. In a field positioning does not matter but obstructing a canal or river towpath with mooring lines can cause accidents—and it may be your crew who are the victims.

Mooring lines should never be taut with your craft pulled hard against the bank. Allow a little slack so that the boat can cope with the wash of passing craft and/or the natural flow of the stream. If your craft is equipped with fenders rather than rubbing strips do adjust the height of the fenders to take any bumps from quayside, posts, rails or the contour of the bank. The only time you will need knots is when you moor, and two half-hitches are what you should use. Ask your hire firm instructor to show you how to tie a half-hitch. This is simple to tie, is safe in that it cannot work loose and is easy to undo. In fact, if you simply pull the half-hitches down the stake after lifting it they will undo themselves.

Another method of mooring, useful for short stops, for making tea, waiting a turn at a lock, or to let your dog ashore, is to use a 'breast rope'. This is simply a short line from midships to a stake, mooring ring or post in the ground abreast of the centre of the boat. It saves work and is amply secure in waters without tide or stream.

In the brief spell that your hire firm mentor is aboard he will not have sufficient opportunity to advise you on all these aspects of boat handling. As soon as he feels you are unlikely to wreck the boat, or drain pounds or reaches dry, he will wish you a pleasant voyage and leave you to get on with it. When cruising on inland waterways be assured that contacts with banks, lock-sides and even other boats are normal and inevitable. Inland waterway cruisers are designed to take bumps, though this does not mean you should be careless and ram or scrape everything in sight.

Locking

Locking is no doubt the most formidable aspect of inland waterways navigation to the amateur. When the boat-yard is near a lock, which is often the case, your mentor will take you to the lock and demonstrate exactly how it is worked. Even so, you may not take in all his advice and thoroughly understand the function of locks. A lock is simply a device to enable boats to go up or downhill.

Although rivers usually have a constant supply of running water the water would run too fast or be too shallow to float boats if it were not controlled by dams or weirs, and locks to raise or lower boats from one level to another without releasing all the water behind the dams. Canals are more heavily locked, for water in canals has no regular flow and each level is rather like a still lake. To get boats over a hill the next lake, usually called a 'pound', is constructed some feet higher up, and a lock permits the boat to be raised up to it. To make up for the water lost by working the locks, more water has to be fed into the canal on the highest or 'summit' pound. This means tapping reservoirs or other sources of water, is always most expensive, frequently very difficult and some-times virtually impossible. Therefore wasting water while working a lock is the most heinous offence you can commit on a canal.

A lock is really a simple device, first built by the Chinese over a thousand years ago, when rivers were split up into steps for the first time. There are various types and sizes of locks but basically a lock consists of a chamber or box of brick or stone or concrete or iron with gates at either end tough enough to withstand the huge water pressure. It is provided with primitive shutter-like valves called 'paddles' or 'sluices' at either end to allow water to enter or leave it. River locks can be huge, big enough to handle coastal steamers. On broad canals locks will be about 14 to 15 ft across and 72 or more ft long, with double gates at each end pointing towards the higher water level. Narrow canal locks are usually only 7 to 7 ft 6 ins wide and about 72 ft long. Usually they have double bottom gates but only one upper gate, opening in the direction of the higher pound. Many bigger river locks have gates opened by power but the smaller canal lock-gate is usually opened by pushing on a massive 'balance-beam' which projects from the gate over the lock side. The easiest way to manipulate these is by putting your seat against the balance-beam and pushing with your feet on the ground, rather than by pushing it with your hands.

Paddle gear may look very primitive to you but it is effective. A bar is attached to the top of a paddle, which in turn is attached to an iron rack with a double track. A pinion on a shaft with a square end engages this. The only equipment or tool needed to work a paddle is the lock key or 'windlass', an iron handle with one or more square sockets on its end, which fit the square end of the shaft. There are two basic sizes, $1\frac{1}{4}$ ins for gear on rivers and broad canals and 1 in for gear on narrow canals. Windlasses are supplied with hire craft, either double-socketed types or sets of both sizes when required, or

simply the correct size windlass for the particular waterways you are cruising. When fitted to the square end of
the shaft and turned the windlass makes the pinion pull
up the rack and paddle, and so open it. To prevent the
paddle falling back again when the pressure from the
windlass is removed, there is a ratchet and pawl on the
pinion shaft. You should keep this in the 'on' position as
you wind up the paddle so that, should your hand slip

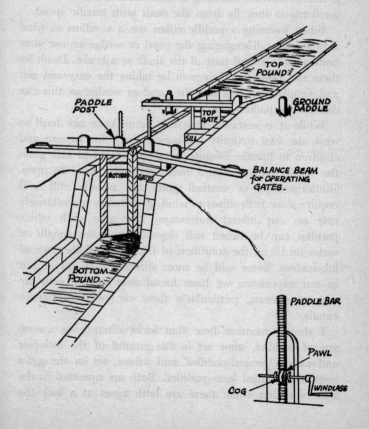

off the windlass for any reason, the weight of the paddle
dropping will not cause the windlass to fly round. If
no pawl is provided there is usually a wedge to place
between the rack and pinion to hold up the paddle, either
attached to a chain or fixed to a hinged stirrup.

When working paddles NEVER let go of the windlass
while it is on the shaft and never leave it on the shaft
while locking through. Always ensure the pawl or wedge
is engaged and then remove the windlass once the paddle
is raised. Careless handling of windlasses can cause serious
accidents as they fly from the shaft with terrific speed.

When lowering a paddle either use a windlass to wind
it down after disengaging the pawl or wedge or use your
hand on the round part of the shaft as a brake. Don't let
them run down on their own by taking the easy way out
and simply knocking out the pawl or wedge as this can
damage the paddle gear.

While it is certainly true that some locks are hard to
work the vast majority are easy enough for women and
children to handle. Despite the great weight of lock gates
the heavy balance-beams make the gates easy to open.
Guillotine-type or vertical gates are usually stiff and
require some little effort to wind up but they are relatively
rare on our inland waterways. The ease with which
paddles can be raised will depend upon the weight of
water on them, the condition of the gear and the state of
lubrication. Some will be more difficult than others but
in our experience we have found over 80 per cent are
easy to operate, particularly those on locks on narrow
canals.

I should mention here that locks often have several
sets of paddles, some set in the ground of the lock-side
and called 'ground-paddles' and others, set in the gates
themselves, called 'gate-paddles'. Both are operated in the
same way but when there are both types at a lock the

ground-paddles should be raised first, quite slowly, as they do not cause such a rush of water as gate-paddles, and then the gate-paddles. It is unwise to open paddles too quickly when your boat is in the lock for the rush of water can throw the boat about.

Some locks, where water is scarce, have 'side-pounds'. These have special paddles of their own and should be used first in both emptying or filling a lock. By using these nearly half a lock-full of water is saved every time a boat comes up or down.

When passing through locks it is essential that the right procedure be used to avoid damage to craft or the locks. The best way for amateur crews to handle locks is to divide the various duties among the crew, so that each crew member knows exactly what he or she has to do.

All waterway guides have specific and detailed instructions on the operation of all types of locks on the waterways they cover and they need not be repeated here. When you come to a complicated lock or those ingenious 'staircase' locks you will find instructions posted and, most likely, a lock-keeper on duty. Proceed with care and you will meet no insurmountable problems.

One of the most pleasant pastimes on a cruise is 'lock-wheeling'. All of our crews, and particularly our dog, enjoy it. If you have sufficient crew members to cope with locking, one crew member can move ahead at flights of locks and consecutively prepare each lock in the flight. This will obviate mooring at each lock before entering it. Some holidaymakers take a bicycle along with them and the lock-wheeler can then cycle ahead along the towpath to prepare locks in advance and perhaps have time to shop or collect beer from a canal-side pub.

By watching others with experience you and your crew will develop a system for locking and you will soon be taking great pride in the speed and efficiency with which you can pass through. You will learn that fenders should be used in wide locks. You will quickly find the easiest way to land or take on crew members close to the lock head and tail, and that you will be able to control your boat on its engine in narrow locks without mooring lines, and in wide locks you will find that a crew member on both bow and stern lines, keeping them taut as your craft moves up or down, using bollards when available, will ensure smooth passage.

Handling boats on inland waterways is within the competence of any amateur who keeps alert, obeys the rules and practises common courtesy. Steering cruisers is great fun for all the family once the 'feel' of your hire craft is acquired and that glow of confidence arrives.

CHAPTER 4

GETTING READY

ONCE YOU have chosen and booked your hire cruiser your appetite for the waterways will have been well whetted and the real fun can begin. You will know your starting date and starting point and you will have a tentative itinerary roughly planned. You and your crew can now start preparing for your holiday in earnest.

Personally I find that much of the enjoyment of any holiday lies in anticipation and preparation and this is particularly true of boating holidays. Different crews can cover the same waterways journey and yet have quite different holidays. There is considerable scope in every cruise for individual choice—each waterway caters for a host of varied interests. You can set off without paying more than lip service to planning, other than reading your joining instructions from the hire firm, and thoroughly enjoy yourself. But the odds are that you will regret it when you run out of water miles from a watering point, when you go out to shop and find it is early closing day or when you discover from other boating holidaymakers that you missed that little antique shop, that marvellous restaurant, that charming pub, that outstanding exhibition or that wonderful view. What is more, you will have wasted a winter and spring of planning pleasure, which I regard as being almost as fascinating as the holiday itself.

Documentation

From the hire firm brochures you will note that most hire firms recommend or offer certain basic maps and booklets, including the Stanford's Inland Cruising map you have used to work out your tentative journey, or Imray, Laurie, Norie & Wilson's map of the Inland Waterways of England and Wales, which is equally well executed and informative.

Among the guides available will usually be a localised navigation booklet or cruising guide. These vary in content but all give an outline of facilities and amenities of waterways within the cruising range of the hire firm and are well worth the few shillings they cost.

Waterways outside the jurisdiction of the British Waterways Board are often covered by local charts and maps or even official guides such as *Gateway to the Avon,* published by The Lower Avon Navigation Trust. Also available for certain waterways like the River Medway and the Rivers Lee and Stort are handy inexpensive Inland Waterways Association illustrated handbooks.

For the nationalised waterways there is an entire series of sixteen invaluable Inland Cruising booklets, selling at between 5s and 6s, and they add enjoyment to your holiday out of all proportion to the cost. If not available from the hire firm they can be obtained from the British Waterways Board or the Inland Waterways Association. Each of these begins with a short but interesting history of the waterway or waterways covered. The courses are inevitably depicted as a perfectly straight blue ribbon running up and down the page. Locks, tunnels, bridges, basins and wharves are all indicated along with mileages and important characteristics of the vicinity. While these diagrammatic maps distort other topical features, they are easy to read and follow. Bridges are always numbered in sequence and as these numbers appear on most of the actual bridges they are constant guides to your exact whereabouts. Locks are also numbered and frequently named, and the booklets show which side of the water-way the towpath is sited. They also indicate the position of watering points, mooring points, winding points, post offices, pubs, public telephones, toilet facilities, garages, railway stations and other services. Along the side of each diagrammatic map is a running narrative describing some of the highlights of the waterway and the country through which it passes.

The one-inch Ordnance Survey Maps, from 6s 6d, showing in great detail just what lies either side of the waterways within striking distance are, I find, a great help in preparing for a boating holiday. And as the various booklets do not incorporate information like early closing days and market days, I have found an *ABC Railway Guide* most useful both for planning a cruise and for work-ing out the most convenient method for picking up and disembarking guest crews.

Obviously you will need only those maps and guides relevant to your proposed journey and your hire firm will either stock these or will tell you what booklets are needed. It is possible that you will discover a certain amount of duplication in the hire firm's booklet and the B.W.B. Inland Cruising booklet. We have found from experience that no guide is fully comprehensive, and in addition to the documentation already mentioned we have added to our planning material by obtaining from the library official guides to certain cities and towns which we intend to visit as well as the so-called county books, such as the *King's England* series, the *County Books* series and the *Companion* series.

The advance log

Most boating holidaymakers tend to keep some sort of
diary or log of the holiday but I believe that an 'advance
log' is of great value. When planning my own boating
holiday I buy a loose-leaf notebook in which to set down
the collated net results of planning. This I keep by me
throughout the holiday as a reminder of potential opportunities and for handy reference. Of course, I also take
the relevant maps, charts, navigational booklets and guides
but one can hardly keep spreading these out to find
exactly what is available round the next bend, particularly
when steering or when it happens to be windy or wet.
This notebook can be kept open by the wheel or tiller and
can be transferred quickly to the pocket in inclement
weather. It will tell you your rate of progress and enable
you to judge whether you can reach a certain place in
time for lunch or whether it is feasible to get through a
flight of locks before dark.

The preparation of this advance log will give you considerable advance knowledge of what lies along the route
and will make for the most enjoyable of holidays.

Tentative schedules

Once I have completed my advance log I select a series
of tentative mooring points for tying up overnight and
even for lunch-time halts. In short, I work out how far I
am likely to cruise each day, taking into consideration
average cruising time on the basis of lock miles and
facilities available along the route. Each day's cruising
will vary in lock miles covered. One day I may plan to
cruise only twenty lock miles because this enables us to
moor overnight at a place with a host of facilities. Another
day I may plan to cover thirty lock miles because there
are long canal pounds with few locks and few apparent

amenities along the waterway, while a particular water-side town would seem ideal for overnight mooring and shopping next morning.

We do not, of course, rigidly adhere to this tentative schedule. Heavy rain, fishing or excursions may upset a particular day's cruise. In making a tentative plan I take into consideration too that the crew may well have had enough in working a couple of long flights of locks in one day, and may want to moor early for the night. It is also necessary to allow for locking times. All river authorities specify the hours of locking. On the Thames where all locks are manned, lock-keepers are on duty from 9 a.m. to sunset, with an hour off for lunch. While there are no specified hours on canals, flights of locks are padlocked at night, usually at 7 p.m. and it is not unusual to find yourself separated from the pub outside which you intended to moor overnight by several miles of padlocked locks. On the Oxford Canal there have been silly experiments in closing locks to craft over certain periods of certain days to allow fishermen to pursue their sport in absolute peace. The literature you receive from your hire craft firm should contain this information as well as information on stoppages. Except for emergencies the waterways authorities do not suddenly close locks for repair but plan these well in advance and publish a list of planned stoppages for many months ahead. You will find that only rarely will a planned stoppage affect your holiday, for most repairs are carried out during the off-season periods.

If you prepare your advance log on the left-hand pages of your notebook, each right-hand page can then be used for an actual log of your holiday cruise. My own logs are very simple, noting time of departure from the overnight mooring each day, times taken through locks or flights of locks, times of passing underneath selected bridges and

aqueducts, times of mooring for lunch, watering, shopping, sightseeing and times of mooring for the night. I
make brief notes when warranted of the condition of locks
or stretches of waterway; comments on moorings, waterside pubs and restaurants; observations of excursions,
shopping facilities, scenic beauty spots, noteworthy items
of waterways architecture or engineering; and I invariably
add such items as unlisted watering points and meetings
with working craft. Each evening after mooring I quickly
calculate and note the actual cruising time for the day
and the number of lock miles covered. Simple division
then provides accurate statistics on average speed per
lock mile.

You will find that keeping a simple log of this kind in
conjunction with your advance log takes very little time,
yet is most useful for the return trip along the same waterways and for planning other holiday cruises. After a few
days you will be in a position to estimate accurately
whether your planned itinerary is practical; whether you
can indeed extend your cruise or whether you will have
to turn round earlier than anticipated to arrive back at
your hire firm's boatyard by the deadline.

Food

Your advance log completed, you can then turn your
attention to what to take with you on your boating
holiday. Storage space on hire craft is usually quite
adequate but it is unwise to burden yourself with non-
essentials. Food is an important consideration but it is
certainly not necessary for you to transport bulk supplies
for the entire holiday from your home. Most hire firms
have arrangements with local shops for the boat hirer's
order to be delivered to the hire craft on the day of
departure and payment is conveniently by cheque. Some
hire firms automatically supply printed order forms from

the shops while others make a small charge for completing your shopping for you.

The idea is not to order stores for the entire cruise as shopping along the waterside and in strange towns and villages, particularly on market days, is all part of the fun of a boating holiday. We usually order through our boat hire firm only enough food and drink to keep us going for three or four days at most. As you usually start your boating holiday at a weekend when few shops are open and as shopping facilities can be few and far between along the waterways, you should start off with at least the essentials.

We take very little in the way of food from home but have learned that a cooked ham, turkey or a couple of chickens are most useful to have over the first weekend when the crew is settling in and cooking aboard is not convenient. It is not always possible to shop for fresh milk every day and indeed fresh milk is not always easy to obtain when wanted. We therefore order a tin of powdered milk and take a few cartons of 'Longlife' milk with us for emergencies. A large easy-pouring plastic container of salt and a pepper mill also goes along with us. Most items of food and drink can be obtained during the boating holiday. If you have noted in your advance log where specific shopping facilities are, it is a simple matter to coordinate shopping so that it does not interfere with your holiday plans. According to what is needed, I arrange to moor near the most appropriate facilities. If it is raining no one will want to walk to a village general store a mile or more away when by cruising on for a few more miles a waterside shop or a town providing all services is available.

Handy items

One of the most useful items on a boating holiday is a

collapsible shopping basket on wheels. We usually take
two and a real boon they are. Another handy item for
shopping convenience is a half-gallon plastic container,
which we use to collect draught beer, draught cider or
milk. It is much easier to carry than a number of bottles.

If you check your hire craft inventory you will see that
it provides for most essentials. However, no inventory will
cater one hundred per cent for everyone's particular wishes.
Few hire firms include a large tray yet this item is invaluable for luncheons eaten under way or for drinks on deck.
When placed on top of the Calor gas stove (unlit!) it
provides an additional draining board for washing up.

We also take our own large cast-iron frying pan or a
large non-stick one as it seems that food almost invariably
sticks to strange frying pans. If a large casserole dish is
not in the inventory, we take one of these, and as we are
partial to salads we take a large salad bowl too. Being
inveterate coffee drinkers one of our twelve-cup coffee pots
is taken also. A knife sharpener or stone can also be invaluable.

Other items we gather in a 'boat box' are a 12–15 ft
length of clothes line or ¾ in nylon or manila rope to use
as a breast rope and to secure the gangplank firmly. We
include a ball of stout cord and a sharp pocket or sheath
knife. We take a ground sheet or tarpaulin, which is easily
stowed under a mattress, to use on picnics ashore or if the
superstructure of the craft is leaking. Another wet weather
aid is a small rubber mat. Borrowed from your car and
placed on the cabin floor just inside the entrance to the
boat it will save a lot of mess and cleaning. A torch or
two, depending upon the size of your crew, is really
essential, as a number of overnight moorings are likely to
be in remote places along a towpath.

A basic first aid kit to cope with headaches, cuts, bruises,
abrasions and burns is a must, and a thermometer is useful

if you have small children with you. We regard insect repellent and sun tan oil as part of our first aid kit.

Cameras and film should not be forgotten and the crew will get a good deal of pleasure from a pair of field glasses. Bird and flower fanciers may want to include suitable reference books, and a pack of playing cards will help to while away rainy spells.

You will see that in your hire craft inventory there are normally three blankets per berth and one pillow; sheets and pillow-cases are either included or provided for a small supplementary payment. On our first boating holiday we discovered that blankets take up a lot of room during the day and that dismantling and making up beds each day seemed an unnecessary chore. We subsequently asked the hire firm to supply one blanket per berth plus pillows and pillow-cases, and took sleeping bags with us. These can be rolled up compactly after airing and are more easily stowed than several blankets.

If you take your dog with you, you will be asked to keep him off berths and boat blankets and you will be warned that you are liable for any damage he may cause. We take a heavy-weight rug for our dog, and this goes on the cabin floor at night and over a lower berth by day.

Linen table cloths and napkins are unsuitable and we find paper napkins more convenient. You will find a heavy-duty floor cloth useful, and also a couple of spare good-sized bath towels.

Jewellery and expensive watches should not be taken; nor should transistor sets unless the boat is not equipped with a radio. For my advance log notebook I take a ball-point pen with a clip and use the back of this notebook to jot down captions for all the photographs taken. You will find it is impossible to identify every one taken unless you caption them at the time.

Clothing

Most boating holidaymakers take far too much clothing with them and then grumble that there is not enough storage space. Of course it is never possible, even with long-range forecasts, to be sure of your holiday weather and boat crews have to be prepared for anything. Informality should be the keynote and above all clothing should be serviceable. Very little tidy clothing is necessary. A drip-dry dress and cardigan or a drip-dry blouse, skirt and cardigan for the ladies and a pair of slacks and sports jacket or blazer for men is all that you will need for social occasions.

Clothing will get dirty and drip-dry material is most suitable in shirts, sports shirts, blouses, sun-tops, and socks. I have a pair of drip-dry lightweight trousers and a pair of jeans for chilly weather. Ladies will find that trousers and shorts are better than skirts for getting about boats and lock-sides, and shorts and jeans are most suitable for youngsters of both sexes.

Everyone will need rubber-soled shoes, which all hire firms insist upon. Tennis shoes will do admirably, or you can buy economically from ships' chandlers proper boating shoes which are much the same style but come with blue canvas uppers. These will inevitably get wet so you will want a spare pair, even though tennis or boating shoes can be dried out reasonably quickly in a Calor gas oven. Every crew member will want a pair of walking shoes, preferably with rubber soles. Ladies would be well advised to leave high-heeled shoes at home.

I always take a pair of short calf-length rubber boots for use in wet weather instead of a second pair of boating shoes. These together with waterproof trousers and jacket enable me to stay at the wheel or work locks in the heaviest of downpours without getting soaked. These boots are ideal for walking along towpaths after rain or in heavy early morning dew. Children will find ordinary Wellingtons useful for towpaths and for walking across fields, but they should not be worn on board. Although it rarely happens, it is possible for a child to fall overboard and these boots are a handicap in such circumstances.

Waterproof jackets and trousers are relatively expensive and an ordinary good raincoat can be substituted. In any case raincoats will be necessary for shopping and sight-seeing, or if cruising in lighter rain or drizzle. Tunnels frequently leak badly and when at the wheel or working locks in the rain, it is a good idea to wear shorts underneath your raincoat or to roll up your trouser legs.

Even when cruising at the height of summer you will want warm clothing, and every crew member should have a heavy pullover, preferably with a roll neck. We have found the most useful garment is the hooded anorak which not only sheds water but is cosily warm. It is much more practical than a smart jacket for men, women and children.

Items like dressing gowns are superfluous. Wear pyjamas and use your raincoat as a dressing gown if you consider one necessary. Provided the crew has anoraks, bulky top-coats or duffle coats take space and are never really needed. The usual underclothing, toilet articles and make-up will be needed and for the ladies a head scarf is useful. While all waterways are not suitable for swimming, there are many swimming pools to be found and in any case you will need swim-wear for sunbathing.

All crew members should make out a clothing list and then ruthlessly prune it to essentials. Mothers will of course allow for the ability of young children to soil clothing rapidly.

Most of the crew's clothing will be stowed away in drawers under bunks. Hanging cupboard space, except

on larger craft, is at a premium and is usually only enough
for the crew's tidy gear, and perhaps raincoats.

You will probably think of other things, such as games
to amuse the children, reading material and so on. Avoid
the temptation to overload your boat. You can easily buy
paperbacks *en route* and children will find more than
enough to keep them amused during the holiday. You
may also find that you make a surprising collection of
souvenirs while shopping in strange places and will take
home with you many items from antiques to clothes.

CHAPTER 5

OUR WATERWAYS STORY

EVER SINCE man discovered that a lóg would float, there
has been boating of a sort. Britain's natural rivers were
the chief means of both transport and communication
from the earliest times until a few centuries ago. The
Romans and other invaders like the Vikings established
their sway in these islands by following the then wild and
perilous tidal courses of the major rivers inland. Building
stone and other necessities were soon moving along the
dangerous rivers as settlements along waterways evolved
into communities and castles, monasteries, churches and
manor houses sprang up. The River Thames became
London's life-line to the sea and in medieval times the
Severn became the busiest river in Europe, apart from the
Meuse. River traffic was erratic, however, for the rivers
were untamed and afflicted with devastating floods in
winter and extended droughts in summer. As industry
slowly developed, and consequently the demand for
reliable transport, the rivers were gradually improved for
navigation, the only alternative being the costly and slow
pack-horse train, for roads capable of accommodating
wagons had yet to be constructed. The muddy tracks of
the time could scarcely be called roads.

Progress in improving river navigation was painfully
slow, for Britain of the sixteenth and seventeenth centuries
was short of capital for such projects and possessed no
engineering talent to speak of, while vested interests like
millers and fishermen did not want their waters tampered

with. The major engineering achievement of this period was the drainage of the Great Level of the Fens, carried out by Holland's Sir Cornelius Vermuyden with the backing of Dutch labour and finance. Even this project was primarily undertaken for the purpose of land drainage and reclamation, with benefits to navigation, the canalised river channels and artificial 'cuts' coming as a by-product.

Artificial waterways were not then completely alien to Britain. The Romans had made a start in East Anglia many centuries earlier. The Fossdyke Canal, for example, from Torksey on the River Trent to the Witham River at Lincoln which flows into the Wash, was dug by the Romans as early as A.D. 120, and Henry I was wise enough to deepen and improve it in 1121. The Exeter Canal from the River Exe estuary to Exeter was completed in 1566 and, although only five miles long, was also demonstrably practical and useful.

It was not, however, until the demands of a mushrooming industrial revolution became urgent in the middle of the eighteenth century, that any serious consideration was given to creating a national network of waterways. Vast areas of the country were still remote from river communication and cried out for an effective means of obtaining cheaper raw materials and distributing manufactured goods.

Although not the first man to build a canal in Britain, Francis Egerton, third Duke of Bridgewater, can fairly be said to have initiated the canal era in Britain. At the age of eighteen, in the course of an educational tour of Europe, he came across and was greatly impressed by Louis XIV's 150-mile Languedoc Canal, now known as the Canal du Midi. With his tutor Robert Wood young Egerton bumped by coach along the course of this unique waterway, which, completed in 1681 and still operational

today, links the Atlantic at Bordeaux with the Mediterranean at Sète.

Within five years of the young duke's 'discovery' of the
Canal du Midi and other canal engineering feats in
Europe, he had obtained in 1759 the first of several Acts
of Parliament authorising him 'to make a navigable Cut
or Canal' in Lancashire. In its way the Duke's canal, first
opened to traffic in 1761 and linking the family coal mines
at Worsley with Manchester, was more revolutionary than
Louis XIV's canal connecting two seas.

When the 'Sun King' built his canal, inland waterway
navigation was already well established in France and
Europe. When the 'Canal Duke' carved out the Bridgewater Canal with the help of his able agent, John Gilbert,
and an almost illiterate millwright imbued with engineering genius, James Brindley, he had few precedents. The
Roman navigable channels of East Anglia were little more
than simple drains, John Trew's Exeter Canal was a
miniature endeavour. One Henry Berry, with the blessing
of the Liverpool Corporation, a few years before the
Bridgewater Canal got underway, had begun the building
of the St Helen's Canal running from Earlestown, near
St Helen's, some eleven miles to the River Mersey
estuary. The Duke no doubt picked up a few tips from
Berry's efforts, but while Berry's canal improved the course
of a stream, the Sankey Brook, the Duke's waterway,
nearly three times as long, was independent of any river
bed and was supplied with water from the soughs. It
combined an underground mining canal and an open
canal, the first of its kind in Britain and the world.

The Duke's canal was an instant success, the foundation
of the famous 'Bridgewater millions'. More important, it
was directly responsible for immediately halving the price
of coal in Manchester, and coal, with water, was the basis
of the Industrial Revolution. Brindley's ingenious Barton

aqueduct, which carried the Bridgewater Canal over the Irwell River, was regarded by many at the time as 'the greatest artificial curiosity in the world' and demonstrated both that canals could be made to travel almost anywhere and that canals were superior to the old river navigations.

By 1767 the Duke's grand design was completed, over twenty-eight miles of main-line canal, several branch canals as well as some forty-two miles of underground canal, and Manchester had been connected with Liverpool and the open sea. But even before all was completed James Brindley had conceived a brilliant idea of a 'cross' of canals to link the Rivers Trent, Mersey, Thames and Severn, and had begun work on the Grand Trunk or Trent & Mersey Canal which was to open up a navigable waterway from the upper Trent via the Duke's canal to the Mersey.

The canals of this country were promoted primarily by local interests and enterprises, manufacturers, mine-owners and merchants. The Trent & Mersey Canal was fostered by a group of pottery manufacturers led by Josiah Wedgwood. These entrepreneurs, and others who followed them, often faced considerable opposition from certain landowners, mill-owners, road turnpike trustees, land carriers, coastal shipping interests and others who feared that their existing prerogatives, trade or livelihood would be adversely affected.

But at the same time the Duke's Bridgewater Canal had fired the imagination of the country and the nation's 'canal mania' was as catching as the 'tulipomania' that swept Holland some 150 years earlier. The press of the day reported on and speculated about canals and what they could contribute to the country and the people. Everywhere there was talk of canals, in inns, offices, manufactories, shops and homes. Of course it was the nobility, the landed gentry and 'big business' of the time that subscribed most of the capital for the construction of canals, but many professional people like doctors and lawyers and clergymen, and many small shopkeepers, tradesmen and craftsmen put what money they could scrape up into canal ventures in the hope of making quick profits from the most exciting projects of the period.

For it had dawned on the country that cheap and dependable transport of coal and raw materials would not only serve mines, supply factories, power steam engines, facilitate the building of houses and roads, enable agricultural land to be improved and bring warmth to the homes of even the poor, but that it would also expedite the distribution of both agricultural produce and manufactured goods to ever widening markets. With canal boats superseding pack-horses and cumbersome wagons, and with steam augmenting and supplanting water power, the whole pattern and pace of life would be changed and the country and its people could come into the greatest prosperity they had ever known.

Over my study desk at home is a framed map of 'the New Intended CANAL to join the Rivers Severn and Trent' with a cutting taken from an eighteenth century issue of the *London Magazine*, which reflects something of the enthusiasm and hopes of the canal age. The cutting describes the proposal for the canal advanced by one Dr Thomas Congreve and claims that although

this navigable communication will cost a very large sum, that the carriage of goods will, thereby, be made vastly cheaper, and that 71 market towns and cities may trade by this canal; to which we shall add, that such inland navigations might be made a support for our seamen in time of peace, if a law was made, that in time of peace, it is hoped it will be agreeable to the people; and having such a supply always ready at command upon a sudden rupture, would encourage the government to engage in every undertaking for increasing and extending our navigable communications.

The Staffordshire & Worcestershire Canal, or the 'Wolverhampton Canal' as it was originally known, was engineered by James Brindley and opened to traffic in 1772. Brindley, in fact, found himself engaged in a number of major canal projects at the same time. He and other engineers like Thomas Telford, John Rennie, William Jessop, Thomas Dadford, Samuel Simcock, Josiah Clowes and James Green designed and drove canals over one watershed after another, in the course of which they put civil engineering on the map with their locks, bridges, aqueducts, tunnels, inclined planes, canal lifts and what Dr Johnson called 'great efforts of human labour and human contrivance'.

So one canal led to another, for as canal mileage increased more industries were launched which in turn created the need for yet more canals. In the hey-day of the canal era, in 1793-4, Parliament authorised the construction of no fewer than thirty canals. Within eighty years of the initiative of the Duke of Bridgewater's canal, by the late 1830s, there were over 4,000 miles of navigable inland waterways, the vast majority of the canals forming a network centred on Birmingham and linking together the rivers and ports of the country. Other canals created time-saving short-cuts across the countryside, or connected other cities and towns directly with the sea. Some 2,600 miles of waterways had been added to the inland navigations of Britain between 1759 and 1840, and few towns were more than 15 miles from a navigable waterway. According to Rennie, craft could safely ply over 2,236 miles of improved river navigation and 2,477 miles of canals in Britain with sixty-nine rivers and eighty-six canals available in England and Wales alone.

Cities, towns, villages, industry, trade grew apace. Then, just as the canals augmented and in many cases superseded the old river navigations, the railways came, first to feed and then to throttle and eventually supersede the canals. Canal mania was quickly converted to railway mania as the success of this new form of transport became apparent. There was bitter rivalry between canal and rail, the effects of which linger with us to this day. The decline of the canal industry, involving in 1840 over 100,000 direct employees alone, was as rapid as its swift rise to prosperity.

The citizen of the 1970s can be forgiven for assuming that it was the steam locomotive that killed commercial transport on the canals. Certainly the locomotive made the transport of passengers by horse-drawn canal boats and, indeed by horse-drawn stage coach, obsolescent almost overnight. But as you cruise the canals and rivers you will see that water transport possessed and still possesses a number of advantage over rail and road as far as the carriage of heavy goods is concerned. That it did not and does not survive except in a few areas was and is due to a number of causes.

When the canals were built they were essentially constructed to meet local needs at different periods and, more often than not, were planned without taking into consideration that they might eventually form key links in a trunk route. This is one reason why they are so interesting to holidaymakers today for there is no uniformity of width, depth or gauge of locks, not only between different canals but even on the same canal. The railway builders were blessed with more foresight; with only one exception Britain's major railways were built to a standard gauge.

The canal companies were handicapped by generations

of neglect of old river navigations with which their canals connected and upon which they often heavily depended for much of their traffic. It was not until the nineteenth and twentieth centuries that badly needed major improvements were carried out on the Thames, Severn and Trent rivers, to name but a few, to advance navigation much beyond archaic medieval standards. Had new locks and other improvements been installed on these rivers before or even when the railways were introduced, the connecting canals could have given the railways a good competitive run for their money on through traffic. While the canal companies had no control over the river navigations, it was certainly their own fault that they exploited their monopoly position by charging often extortionate tolls and so foolishly competed instead of cooperating with each other.

The canal companies were further handicapped because they were merely toll-takers and not carriers like the railways. Carrying on the canals was handled by many canal carrying companies, many of them in a rather small way of business, who operated over particular waterways. This meant that the canals could not effectively speed through traffic along the inland waterways or indeed easily quote through-rates. While the railways first concentrated on passenger and parcels traffic to oust the canal packets and the stage-coach they soon, in the face of competition from each other, moved into the heavy freight field. This precipitated a freight rates war between canals and railways, and with drastically reduced revenue the canals became ripe for what we today would call 'take-over bids' by the railways. Some canals were bought up and converted into railways. Many coming into railway control were, with rare exceptions, run with the deliberate intention of reducing and ultimately killing competition. Every weapon at the railway's command was used to discourage freight carrying on the canals they had taken over—maintenance was neglected, water supplies were diverted, tolls were raised, Sunday and night working prohibited, powered craft banned, and they even stooped to closing waterways for lengthy periods on the pretext of making repairs to locks, bridges or canal sides. Between 1845 and 1847 alone nearly a thousand miles of inland waterways became the property of railway companies, and because these and other waterways subsequently taken over included primary trunk routes the prospect of the remaining canal companies coming together to form a coordinated system of inland waterways to compete with the growing dominance of the railways was most effectively demolished.

In the century that followed the birth of the railways few improvements were made to the canal system. There were many 'committees' and proposals of all kinds and many good intentions but precious few results. Lack of traffic and neglect closed many canals, yet quite a number of independent canal companies continued to carry heavy traffic into the twentieth century and continued to operate at a profit. In 1905 the canals were still carrying over 42 million tons of freight, but by 1924 the figure had fallen to under 17 million tons and by 1938 to under 13 million tons.

Early in our own century a Royal Commission spurred by a revival of interest in canals recommended extensive canal development, but its recommendations were never implemented and the First World War then intervened. Between the wars a number of improvements were put in hand, primarily on the broad canals of the North-East which continue as busy commercial waterways today. Further south a group of canals were amalgamated to form the Grand Union Canal Company and thus to unify routes between London, Birmingham, and Nottingham. The new company then carried out an extensive widening

scheme by constructing no fewer than fifty-one new
broader locks between London and Birmingham.

These were moves in the right direction and prospects
for the canals at last looked a little brighter. But with
road transport added to rail competition canal modernisation was on too small a scale and what was done was,
heavily outweighed by neglect and abandonment on other
routes. Then another war intervened. Wartime controls
were scarcely lifted when in 1948, some 1,600 miles of the
waterways network was nationalised. This 'takeover' was
not as disastrous as the railway takeover a century earlier,
but virtually nothing was done for the canals by a series of
custodians until the British Waterways Board was given
control in 1962 and the Government, jogged by the per-
sistent Inland Waterways Association campaign and clear
evidence that the public was increasingly using the waterways for pleasure, published a White Paper, *British Waterways: Recreation and Amenity*, in September 1967.

Legislation has since created a new charter for the
inland waterways as far as the public is concerned. Over
1,400 miles of nationalised waterways have been designated
'cruiseways' and along them there are literally thousands
of bridges, well over 1,000 locks, more than 275 aqueducts
and upwards of forty tunnels. The system goes from sea
level to a height of 518 feet and forms an interconnected
'grid' stretching from London and Sharpness in the South
to Skipton and Selby in the North and from Wales in the
West to East Anglia. In addition to this network there are
some picturesque lengths away from and separated from
the others, like the Lancaster Canal and the Crinan and
Caledonian Canals in Scotland.

The Government has yet to take action to reclaim
derelict canals and to foster and encourage commercial
traffic on the canals, which if it did nothing more than
relieve road congestion would be worthwhile. All that

recent legislation has done is to designate less than a dozen canals and navigations as commercial waterways. These will add tremendously to your cruising pleasure, for pleasure craft are permitted to join working boats on such fascinating waterways as the Aire & Calder, Calder & Hebble, Caledonian and Crinan, Sheffield & South Yorkshire, New Junction, Trent, Weaver and Weston, Severn, Gloucester and Sharpness and Lee waterways. On some you will encounter traditional narrow boats, on others not only craft large enough for the coastal trade but vessels that venture to and from major European ports.

And quite apart from the waterways under control of the British Waterways Board there are even more miles of waterways open to you which are under the jurisdiction of other authorities. Many are connected with the Board's waterways, like the Bridgewater Canal which inaugurated the canal era, the River Thames, the Lower Trent, Humber and Yorkshire Ouse, the River Nene and River Avon. Still others like the Norfolk Broads, the Great Ouse and its tributaries and the Middle Level of the Fenland waterways and the River Medway provide easy access and additional scope and opportunity for holidays.

CHAPTER 6

THE FETCHING FENS

DURING OUR boating holidays over the years we have met hundreds of first-timers on the waterways and, while there have been some calls for practical assistance or advice, by far the majority of crews brought conversations around to what other waterways had to offer. I make no apologies, therefore, for the boating adventure tales that follow. They are a compilation of experiences on our inland waterways and reflect an enthusiast's determination to make the most of opportunities that both present themselves and must be ferreted out. They are set down in the hope that they will help you cater for the particular interests and tastes of your own crew and encourage you to seek out and exploit others.

There is no doubt that the one aspect of boating holidays which causes concern among beginners is the navigation past weirs and through locks. Yet locks and associated weirs are not difficult to navigate and most first-timers have little or no trouble with them. They can be forbidding and wearying, however, if beginners try to tackle too many in a single holiday.

My advice to those who have never been on our waterways before is to select those that have relatively few locks, and locks that work easily. I can think of no better area for beginners than the South Level of the Fenland waterways of East Anglia.

Fenland is a unique, low-lying district of some 2,500 square miles stretching to the west and south of the Wash, from south of Lincoln to Suffolk and from King's Lynn to St. Ives. There is something for everyone in Fenland, for the explorer, the naturalist, the antiquarian, the angler and for those who just want to relax. Even the history of this seventy-five-mile-long by thirty-five-mile-wide area is reflected in the continuing tenacious opposition to the various drainage schemes in succeeding generations.

Frequent flooding has been caused in the Fens by the coincidence of high spring tides and rivers swollen with water drained off the land. The system of sluices, closed at high tide, keeps the sea water from entering the rivers but likewise prevents the river water from escaping to the sea. The consequent piling up of fresh water strains the banks and flooding follows. There have been a number of disastrous floods since the early drainage works were constructed, but none so terrible as the flood of March 1947 when damage was estimated at over £20 million. On the night of 31 January/1 February 1953, a gigantic North Sea tidal surge caused further trouble and loss of life in King's Lynn and district.

Today, however, nearly half a million acres of the finest agricultural land in England are protected from flooding by the Great Ouse Flood Protection Scheme, completed in 1964, an ingenious £11 million project involving the South Level. This is the area to the east of the Hundred Foot River, through which the rivers are carried high above land level in embanked channels.

With no need to worry about a repetition of the disastrous floods of the past, the idea of boating through Fenland, where little windmills still occasionally dot the flats and where that old English dye-plant, woad, still grows, appealed to us. As it is impossible to cover all the Fens in a single holiday we chose first to do the South Level, comprising the Great Ouse, the Cam, the Little

Ouse, the Old West, the Lark and the Wissey rivers with the Burwell and Reach lodes.

The 300-odd miles of navigable waterways in the South Level will take you to five counties—Bedfordshire, Cambridgeshire, Huntingdonshire, Norfolk and Suffolk— and provide as pleasant cruising on gently meandering non-tidal streams as almost anywhere on Britain's inland waterways. The tributaries probe to within fifty miles of the popular Broads, yet Fenland has remained comparatively undiscovered. You will meet plenty of other craft but you will never feel crowded or rushed, for everywhere there is a predominant mood of peace and tranquillity. Many may imagine that the Fens are flat, dull and monotonous but this is not so. The range of scenery along the rivers is as varied as anywhere in England and there is a kind of medieval attraction about the Fens that is easier to sense than to explain.

Although the authorities, as throughout the Fens, are primarily interested in drainage rather than in navigation, there are few hazards and only fifteen locks, including the tidal lock at Denver, making the South Level a boon to novices, particularly as all but seven of the locks are manned. Boats up to 100 ft in length and 14 ft 6 ins in beam can traverse some sections of the South Level waterways, but the maximum size craft which can navigate the entire system can be no longer than 45 ft, with a beam of 10 ft 3 ins, draught of 2 ft 3 ins and freeboard (fixed height of craft above water level) of 6 ft 6 ins.

Our crew of five with our golden Labrador and current pet hamster boarded our comfortable and well-designed 36 ft x 9 ft 8 ins bridge-deck hire cruiser *Invader* from Banham's boatyard in Cambridge one Saturday afternoon in August. Banham's, who have built many a Cambridge 'eight', can be highly recommended for their hire cruisers. Of course there are other boatyards on the South

Level, among them Elysian Holidays of Ely, whose recently introduced glass fibre craft have particularly impressed us.

It was pouring with rain as we stowed our gear aboard but as we collected our dinghy and set off, the sun burst happily through the clouds. Despite our previous experience we welcomed the short trial run, as every craft we have ever hired has had some differences in controls and instrumentation and the time to become familiar with these is at the start of a cruise.

As my wife's family lived near Cambridge we knew the city well and did not explore it, but those of you who are not familiar with it will find a day reserved for sight-seeing most rewarding. The best mooring for this is below Jesus Lock on the left bank, as power craft are not welcomed above Town Quay at King's Hill.

We were surprised to find the reach of the Cam from Banham's to Baitsbite Lock, half an hour's cruise down-stream, a direct antithesis of the slum-like conditions of the Thames riverside at Oxford. This reach is used by Cambridge University and Town Rowing Clubs and a section of it on either side of the Plough Inn at Ditton is the only one where cruisers are requested to reverse the 'keep right' rule. The notice boards are easy to spot. The Plough Inn, much favoured by undergraduates, offers good moorings, food and drink. It is only one of the scores of pubs, all friendly to the boating fraternity, along the South Level waterways. Half a mile beyond the Plough Inn is Baitsbite Lock and your first lesson in operating locks.

By now you will begin to appreciate having your advance log and chart of the South Level waterways at hand to alert you to points of interest. The Cam is already very pretty. After leaving Baitsbite Lock the river flows through an avenue of trees and osiers, dominated on the right bank by Horningsea's thirteenth-century church. Another half-hour of cruising brings you to Clayhythe

Bridge and the good moorings and food of the Bridge Hotel. The village of Waterbeach is within easy walking distance of the bridge. Watch carefully for sailing craft between the bridge and Bottisham Lock. Once through Bottisham Lock you can cruise for 130 miles if you wish without going through another lock, for the next locks are at Denver on the Ouse, Hermitage on the Old West and Isleham on the Lark.

You will find the scenery changing now to more open Fenland countryside. A few miles along on the right, some eleven miles from Cambridge, at Upware, we would recommend leaving the Cam to pass through the electrically operated lock gates at Burwell Lock to explore the Burwell and Reach lodes. Return passage through the lock will cost 3s, but this investment is small enough for the pleasures it opens up to you and your crew. Although the Lord Nelson Inn at Upware was destroyed by fire many years ago it carried a tablet on its wall with a brief legend all boaters would do well to think upon. It said simply : 'Five miles from anywhere—No hurry'. This is a motto or slogan for all boating holidays everywhere.

After leaving the lock you will come to a wooden bridge on the left bank. You can moor virtually anywhere on either side of this bridge which leads to Wicken Fen, now a National Trust Nature Reserve. It is one of the oldest and in many ways one of the most important in Britain, for it has preserved many of the plants and animals characteristic of the ancient Fenland before drainage and agricultural improvement changed the landscape.

When the drainage of the Cambridgeshire Fenland was begun in the seventeenth century the folk of Wicken managed to keep undrained an area of nearly 250 acres close to the village, which would permit them to continue gathering reed and sedge for thatching and digging peat for fuel. Because of their stubborn insistence on their rights

to take these raw materials they preserved the flora and
fauna which drainage banished from the rest of the Fen-
lands. Wicken Fen today remains the home of over 5,000
species of insects including over 700 kind of butterflies
and moth and nearly 200 kinds of spiders. There is a vast
variety of birds and something like 300 species of flowering
plants as well.

The National Trust acquired the first strip of Sedge
Fen in 1899 and since that time many donors have added
to the original holding so that not only the Sedge Fen but
another 400 acres of St Edmunds Fen and the bordering
North Adventurers Fen on the other side of the lode are
all part of the Trust property. Admission to Wicken Fen
can be obtained from the keeper's house, a pleasant walk
along the narrow Wicken lode beyond the footbridge.

Just past the footbridge you will come to a fork in the
main waterway. Bearing left is the Burwell lode and to
the right the Reach lode. The upper ends of both lodes
are narrow and shallow but we took them gently to visit
the tiny hamlets at the ends of each. The hamlet of Reach,
where the Iceni under Boadicea built the Devil's Dyke, is
perhaps not as attractive as Burwell but you will enjoy
the lovely water-lilies on the Reach lode. We enjoyed
rootling among the antique shops in Burwell, buying some
of the best sausages we ever tasted from the butcher near
the church, and visiting the church itself with its notable
brasses.

Back on the Cam once more, two miles of cruising
below Upware brings you to Pope's Corner. The Fish
and Duck Inn stands on the left at the junction of the
Cam, the Ely Ouse and the Old West. The old white
painted inn has recently been rebuilt with greatly improved
facilities, and remains a popular port of call.

Continuing straight on and using the 215 ft high West
Tower of Ely Cathedral as a landmark you will find the

river now widens. As Ely is approached the high banks give way to meadows and as the course bends to the left there is a low railway bridge and the Cutter Inn comes into view. There is a little ferry here which shunts back and forth across the river. You will get a friendly reception if you moor at the Riverside Boatyard of Elysian Holidays which incorporates the fleet of Appleyard Lincoln & Co., a name well known throughout the South Level. This is a well equipped and handy service centre and the atmosphere of the Cutter Inn is most pleasant. Round the next corner you can moor at the attractive U.D.C. moorings on your left, just a short walk to the shopping centre and cathedral.

Ely, so-called because of the abundance of eels in the river, has a fascinating history which can be traced back to A.D. 673. It ranks as a city because of its cathedral but is really quite a small town, albeit one with particular charm. The splendid cathedral itself dates back to Norman times and is the third largest in England. It stands at the top of a hill and below it is a collection of both ancient and modern buildings. Do not overlook the monastic buildings, the quaint old shops and inns, Steeple Gate, Goldsmith's Tower and Sacrist's Gate, the fifteenth-century Palace and the park known as Ely Porta. Ely queens it over the Fens and rightly so.

Continuing downstream you may meet some barge traffic from the local sugar-beet factory. These barges sweep very close to the banks here and mooring along this section is unwise. Your next landmark is the Queen Adelaide Bridge, the start of the 'Adelaide Course', a three-mile stretch used for the Cambridge trial 'eights'.

You will shortly spot the entrance to the River Lark on the right. This attractive little river is navigable for some ten miles, flowing through the villages of Prickwillow and Mildenhall. There is only one lock near Isleham, with a resident keeper. Prickwillow, which derives its name from the old 'pricks' or skewers which were made from willow, is about four miles above the entrance to the Lark, and the only accessible village on the river. In spite of its pretty name, frankly we found the village disappointing.

The bridge over Isleham Lock is rather low and it may be necessary to lower the canopy and screen. You can cruise on safely for two miles to Judes Ferry, and the inn there marks the site of a useful turning point. It is possible to row a dinghy to Mildenhall but there is too little water to take a cruiser beyond Judes Ferry.

Returning to the main river the next landmark is Sandhill Bridge and there are moorings on the left bank for Littleport. Some $3\frac{1}{2}$ miles downstream you will reach the junction of the Ouse and the Little Ouse or Brandon Creek. On the corner stands the Ship Inn, with a convenient water hose, a well-stocked kiosk, meals, snacks and drinks. There are moorings here, just round the corner on the right by the inn. Hire craft on the South Level are equipped with insulated cold boxes, and ice packs can be changed at all boatyards, stores and inns which you will find listed in the cruising guide. These boxes are most useful for perishables in hot weather. The Ship Inn can usually supply frozen foods and fresh bread and milk.

The Little Ouse is navigable for some twelve miles to Brandon Railway Bridge, and is as attractive as the Lark, with interesting walks to Hockwold cum Wilton and Brandon. Along this river you will find Cross Water Staunch which is no longer used and has but one channel, clearly marked. It looks narrow but there will be no difficulty in getting through. There are a series of meres as you cruise on to Wilton Bridge, with good moorings in the wide pool just before the bridge, and the craft can be turned with ease. The footpath to Hockwold cum Wilton is on the left bank and you can walk along the river to

Brandon which has a good shopping centre; here also is the Flint-Knappers Inn. Until a few years ago the ancient craft of flint-knapping was carried on behind the inn, the last surviving centre of an industry which produced the firing material for flintlock guns. We were fortunate enough to find the last of the flint-knappers still at work but he told us that with the decline of his last substantial trade with Africa he had decided not to continue. The site remains but there are no longer any flint-knappers. The flints themselves came from Grimes Graves, some four miles from Brandon, and this is an excursion you will find fascinating. The mines made by Neolithic Man in excavating flints for making his primitive implements are kept open to the public by the Ministry of Works and both the mines and the countryside surrounding them are more than just interesting.

Turning right out of the Little Ouse and heading north there are few landmarks but conditions are excellent for sailing all the way to Denver. Some four miles downstream of the Ship Inn on the right is the entrance to the Wissey River, the narrowest, wildest and loveliest of the three eastern tributaries of the Ouse. The entrance is deceptively narrow and it is wise to stay in midstream unless you are passing other craft. In less than ten miles of the Wissey there are stretches of open meadowland, bird-filled reeds and wooded country. We were much taken by the little village of Hilgay with its pleasant moorings just beyond the bridge on the right, friendly shops and All Saints Church. In the churchyard is the grave of one of Lord Nelson's school friends, Captain George Manby, inventor of the rocket life-saving apparatus. The idea of developing the rocket lifeline came to Manby at Yarmouth where he saw a seaman die as a result of being stranded on a wreck close to the shore. Local legend has it that he used All Saints Church tower for experiments with his invention.

It was at Hilgay that we met one of those unforgettable characters surprisingly frequently found along the waterways. We first sighted him riding a bicycle along the river bank and it was he who hailed us with an offer of fresh vegetables and fruit from his garden. When he came aboard with the supplies we offered him a drink and learned that his name was Albert Armsby, and that he had been a mole-catcher for over thirty years. He entertained all of us with fascinating tales of the mole's way of life. Little is known of the voracious and restless mole because he lives entirely in the dark in burrows and is one of the few creatures which cannot be kept in captivity. We did not realise at the time that Armsby, who has spent his life trapping moles both for their valuable pelts and to prevent damage done by their tunnellings, is an international authority on moles. Several years ago I read in *The Times* a report that he had been summoned to Holland to advise the Dutch on trapping moles. He presented me with a monogram on the subject written by him and published in 1952. This is among the most treasured of our waterways souvenirs. The text is not only informative and interesting but is filled with delightful sentences such as :

He has vocal chords and can be heard making snuffling noises and slight squeals and purring as he plays moley games with his friends.

The river broadens into a small lake beyond Hilgay and the countryside is wooded all along the upper reaches. The Bull Inn, with good moorings and a friendly landlord, is the limit of navigation. A short walk to the village of Stoke Ferry will supply basic stores, petrol and water.

Returning to the main river again, turn right for Denver

Sluice, a mile away. This is the guardian of the Fens and the key to the drainage of the South Level. It is the limit of navigation for hire craft although boatyards will occasionally permit experienced crews to lock through Denver to make the return trip via the New Bedford or Hundred Foot River. This is as straight as a Roman road and uninteresting, and the depth of water can vary considerably. The river below Denver is tidal, of course, and dangerous for beginners. In any case there is little of interest between Denver and King's Lynn. Even experienced skippers can come to grief on this tideway if they encounter the bore which can produce a fast-moving wall of water up to 3 ft and more high, or if they navigate the tideway at the wrong state of the tide.

While at Denver you can see the new head sluice of the Flood Protection project to the east of the Denver sluice and the junction of the new Cut Off and Relief channels. Perhaps of greater appeal to most of the crew, however, is the Jenyns Arms, just west of Denver Sluice. This pub is reminiscent of a coaching inn and here you can obtain refreshments, stores and water. Downham Market, where Lord Nelson and Captain Manby went to school together, is within walking distance of Denver and from Downham you can take a bus to Hunstanton or to Sandringham.

From Denver we returned to Popes Corner and the Fish and Duck Inn, mooring along the way as fancy dictated. At Popes Corner you can turn right into the Old West river, for eleven miles of delightful cruising. The river is narrow and shallow despite considerable recent dredging and should be taken slowly. There are bridges with blind approaches and it is impossible to see round some bends because of high banks. But the Old West will give the novice no trouble if navigated at reasonable speed.

The scenery along the Old West is all rural and you

may well find cattle straying into the river. The engine
house between the road bridge carrying the B1085 over
the river and the Wooden Bridge contains a most impressive 1837 Boulton and Watt beam-engine still in perfect
working order, a reminder that steam provided the power
to drain the Fens. An inspection can usually be arranged
with the pump-man, who lives in the house adjoining the
engine house.

Little more than a mile beyond the Wooden Bridge
there is a large basin with good moorings hard by the
Royal Oak, a favourite rendezvous of anglers. The bridge
here carries the A10 and as you pass under it there is a
sharp bend to the left and the river becomes narrow as it
flows along for some distance parallel with the highway.
The next road bridge is called 'Twenty Pence Bridge' and
on the right bank stands the Bridge Inn. The river continues to wind its way through pleasant rural countryside
with here and there a glimpse of a farm or pumping
station. As you come within sight of Hermitage Lock, on
the right bank is a recently established boatyard of Elysian
Holidays.

Once you have passed through Hermitage Lock which
was rebuilt in 1968 the river is tidal for the short stretch to
Brownshill Staunch. There is no danger here, but when
mooring do leave the ropes slack enough to allow for a rise
and fall of water of up to 4 ft. The normal summer rise
and fall rarely exceeds 2 ft 6 ins. At low water this reach
is inclined to be shallow, and care should be taken. As
you leave Hermitage Lock you will see the New Bedford
or Hundred Foot River entrance to your right and almost
immediately beyond this the mooring for the Crown Inn
followed by the Quiet Waters Boatyard of F. W. Carrington, which is in a backwater above the Crown. You can
moor at either place. Carrington's provide the usual boatyard services, petrol and water. Earith is a pleasant little

village with good shopping facilities. It is but 20 minutes from Earith to Brownshill Lock and on your right before the lock is Bury Fen, where the National Ice Skating Championships are held. There are shoals at the approach to the lock almost in midstream so check the chart and proceed carefully. The lock-keeper's house is hidden behind a high bank on the left and you may have to tie up to the landing stage for a bit while a member of the crew fetches him to work the lock for you.

From Earith there is another thirty miles of cruising on the Ouse with nine locks to Tempsford Bridge, the current limit of navigation for cruisers, and it is all most attractive. Beyond Brownshill Lock you will find the pretty Pike and Eel Inn on the right bank, set among weeping willows. A little further along the river is the village of Holywell. We found it enchanting with its thatched cottages, one of which housed a poodle parlour, ancient church whose tower was once a beacon for ships, historic well which accounts for the name of the village, and 'Ye Olde Ferry Boat Inn', part of which, like the church, dates back to A.D. 890. Here, where Hereward the Wake fled across the river from William the Conqueror, we dined superbly one evening. Here too, we watched the reed cutters at work. It is wise to book meals in advance at the Ferry Boat Inn (telephone St Ives 3227). When sitting in the bar, enjoying a drink, ask the landlord to tell you the tale of Juliet Tewsly, whose 900-year-old ghost is said to appear at the inn on St Patrick's Day. And ask him to show you the grey granite slab which once marked her grave and which is now incorporated in the bar floor.

From Holywell to St Ives the water is rather shallow in places and careful navigation is required. The approach to the lock should be taken with caution if the sluices are running, for the water from them creates a strong eddy and tends to run a cruiser into the lock. Once through the lock, avoid the piles on the right and turn left into Staunch Haven, the L. H. Jones boatyard, for water if you did not fill up at the lock, or just to visit the ship's chandlers.

St Ives, which appears as Slepe in the Domesday Book, and is named after the Persian bishop Ivo who died at Slepe about A.D. 600, is a picturesque halt, and mooring is available at the town quay on your right before the bridge or at the Waits Quay above the bridge. For overnight mooring the town quay is ideal, and convenient for shopping. The medieval bridge at St Ives is lovely and quite remarkable in that it still retains a chapel built upon the middle of it and dedicated to St Ledger. It is one of the few bridges with chapels now left in Britain. It is interesting to note too that the arches nearer the town are pointed in the Gothic style while the ones on the opposite side are round.

The Dolphin Hotel is at the waterside and the town is good for shopping. There are many old houses and a statue of Oliver Cromwell in the Market Place. Cromwell was born at Huntingdon but farmed at St Ives and lived at Old Slepe Hall, near what is now known as Oliver Cromwell Place. The most interesting place in St Ives, we thought, was a rope factory where our children were shown how ropes were made before modern machinery took over.

The scenery between St Ives and Hemingford Lock is glorious. Hemingford Lock is the first of the unmanned locks and here you will be able to try your hand at operating a lock. The chart will reveal a shoal in the middle of the pool at the approach to the landing stage for the lock. As you leave the lock you will see a boathouse to the left with a licensed restaurant. St James's Church with its peculiar truncated spire stands between the boathouse and the lock. Hemingford Grey is a real beauty-spot with many

lovely timbered houses and thatched cottages. Just round
the bend in the river from Hemingford Grey there is a
backwater to the left. This is only navigable to the Bailey
Bridge but is a pretty diversion, heavily carpeted with
water-lilies. Close to the entrance to this aptly named
Sleeping Waters is Hutsons boatyard and nearby is
Hemingford Abbots.

Houghton Lock and Mill, next upstream, are owned by
the Society for the Protection of Rural England. The mill,
a seventeenth-century timbered building, is used as a
youth hostel. There is a particularly beautiful stretch of
river past ancient Hartford church to Huntingdon, but the
water is shallow in places.

Huntingdon is linked to its neighbour Godmanchester
not only by river but by a raised road known as the
Causeway. To visit Huntingdon, moor at the Huntingdon
boatyard on the right bank, just before the bridge, at
the Old Bridge Hotel hard by the bridge, or above the
bridge on the opposite bank at another Elysian Holidays
boatyard. Godmanchester lock is not far away and on
locking through a backwater round to the left offers excellent moorings from which to explore Godmanchester,
which has the distinction of being the smallest borough in
England. While Huntingdon has two inns of interest,
some ancient churches and chapels, and the house where
the poet Cowper lived for a time, Godmanchester, which
obtained its first charter from King John, boasts many
beautiful old houses and an excellent pub, the Black Bull.
Shopping facilities are adequate.

After Brampton and Offord locks, the latter set in
between wooded banks, you will come to the two villages
of Offord Cluny and Offord D'Arcy, once noted for lace-
making. These are on the left and in Offord Cluny you
will find the Swan Hotel less than 200 yards from the
river. There are several islands in the reach to St Neots

Lock and your chart of the South Level is invaluable here. It is a help to keep the chart in use folded to the relevant section beside you in a plastic envelope, weighted down by something heavy. This keeps it dry and prevents it being blown overboard.

Beyond the lock the approach to St Neots is by several more wooded islands which open up to a very wide stretch of water bounded by pleasant meadows on both banks. There are scores of mooring places on this reach and while our dog dug for moles we tried a little fishing. The Great Ouse is one of the most popular rivers in England for coarse fishing, and bream, chub, dace and many other kinds can be caught, even trout. Fishing from the banks requires a permit from the riparian owners, but fishing from the boat needs only a licence from the Great Ouse River Authority. We did not on this particular occasion fish for very long for our youngest daughter managed to imbed a fish hook in her leg so effectively that she had to be taken to the local doctor in St Neots to get the hook removed. St Neots, named after St Neot, a monk of Glastonbury who, with St Swithun, educated King Alfred of 'burnt cakes' fame, is a charming market town with one of the largest market places in the country and a fine church. Shopping facilities are excellent and we enjoyed the fair held there during our visit.

There is still another hour's cruising to Eaton Socon lock and mill at Tempsford Bridge, the head of navigation until such time as restoration, now well under way, is completed to Bedford. These upper reaches are lovely although there are very few ports of call other than the Kelpie Marine Boatyard and the Anchor Inn near Tempsford Bridge.

We shall never forget our return journey from Tempsford to Cambridge. On the morning of our departure, a heavy mist was hanging over the river so that visibility was similar to that from an aircraft flying through wispy white clouds. As the sun burst through, it created a kind of halo over the river and this peculiar light effect produced yet another perspective of the Fenland waterways.

We cruised over 300 miles on thirty-nine gallons of petrol in a fortnight, which gave us more than adequate time to explore most of the countryside. Yet we feel we scarcely scratched the surface of the beauty, peace and delight the Fenland rivers offer. We remember many of the interesting people we met, the picnic lunch in the meadows near St Ives, the beer gardens at the Three Jolly Butchers at Wyton; indeed, each member of our crew, despite the many boating holidays we have enjoyed since our discovery of the South Level, still occasionally comes out with a 'do you remember' question about the Fetching Fens. You and your crew will experience many of these and other pleasures like the memorable view of Hemingford Grey church from upstream and you will regale your friends with tales and photographs of your adventures, explaining to these landlubbers how, for example, you quickly mastered that guillotine gate at Hemingford Lock.

Like us, you too will have some experiences you will not talk too much about. Although we returned the *Invader* in good condition there was one little bit of damage. One night we put our hamster's cage a little too close to a curtain and in the morning found that he had literally eaten the bottom half of it. Banham's thought this hilariously funny when we showed them the neatly bisected curtain, but perhaps this was due more to my embarrassment than the damage. They did not want to make a charge for the damage but when I insisted upon it they finally accepted the princely sum of 1s 6d.

CHAPTER 7

THE 'LITTLE MED'

WE CALL the River Medway, which separates the Men of Kent from Kentish Men, the 'Little Med' because, like the vast Mediterranean Sea it offers, albeit on a small scale, a great variety of holiday pleasures. The estuary, from the River Thames to the tidal lock at Allington a short distance downstream from Maidstone, is no place for novices, but the Upper Medway Navigation is as perfect a waterway for beginners as can be found anywhere.

From the tidal lock at Allington to Tonbridge Great Bridge, the head of navigation, is little more than eighteen miles, but the Upper Medway Navigation packs more scenic beauty, rustic charm and historic association into its short course than many rivers ten times its length. The countryside through which it flows has appropriately been named 'the Garden of Eden'—a sweeping panorama of meadows, orchards, hopfields and woodlands. Studded sporadically throughout this garden like jewels in a treasure-chest are impressive memorials of Kent history—castles and churches, manor houses and moated homes, ancient bridges and picturesque villages, to say nothing of strangely-shaped oasthouses and charming pubs. We were, in fact, amazed to find that apart from a short stretch of river round the country town of Maidstone this beautiful navigation was almost completely rural. The river tends to lose itself in the countryside and in history.

Our short holiday on the Medway, shared with our

friends, Dr Roger Pilkington of the 'Small Boat' series fame and his wife, Miriam, was squeezed into an already full cruising programme on the *Thames Commodore* on the Continent, and on hired narrow cruisers on Britain's canals.

Yet our first taste of the Medway that May weekend so whetted our appetite for the river that we have subsequently returned for more of the same, and have brought the *Thames Commodore* from Teddington Lock on the Thames through the Medway tideway right up to Maidstone Bridge, which is as far as a craft of her dimensions can venture.

Beginners who have only a week or two to spare will find the Medway an ideal waterway on which to start messing about in boats. And experienced boaters who have overlooked the Medway will find it charmingly different from any other waterway they have explored.

Allington Lock, with its unusual Victorian-Gothic lock house, is located at the end of an attractive, curving reach of river which is under the authority of the Medway Lower Navigation Company as far as the College Garden, Maidstone, little more than a fifth of a mile south of Maidstone Bridge. The remainder of the non-tidal navigation is controlled by the Kent River Authority which deserves to be congratulated on its superb maintenance of the waterway. There are only nine locks on this, the Upper Medway Navigation, each capable of taking craft up to 80 ft long and 18 ft 6 ins beam, and almost any craft drawing 4 ft or less with freeboard of no more than 8 ft 6 ins can cruise right to Tonbridge without a qualm. Unlike the Thames and most other rivers in Britain and abroad, there are refuse disposal arrangements at every single lock and we saw no litter anywhere. All locks were in first-class condition and we found it possible to moor virtually anywhere along the navigation. The London and

Home Counties Branch of the Inland Waterways Association have seen to it that there are landing stages at each lock, fresh water taps, a public mooring at Tonbridge, and they publish a most useful handbook or guide to the river, complete with handy chart of the Upper Medway navigation.

There are a number of hire firms on the Medway, including Hire Cruisers (Maidstone) Ltd at the Tovil Bridge Boatyard where we found an excellent choice of craft. The four-berth, 24 ft x 8 ft *San Diana* with a draught of 2 ft and headroom of 5 ft 11 ins was spotlessly clean and well equipped when we took her over that sunny Friday afternoon in May. Our golden Labrador, Wiggers, who has become a sea-dog of great discrimination, approved of the standard of comfort and found the modest vibration of the Stuart Turner diesel much to his liking. If you take a dog on a boating holiday you may find that he will spend a good deal of time lying directly over the engine. I have never discovered whether it is the vibration or the warmth of the engine that appeals to dogs because Wiggers will lie over the engine both in cool weather and in blazing sunshine.

We cruised first from the boatyard to East Farleigh Lock, some twenty minutes upstream, to collect our lock key as arranged by Derek Salmon. He, as honorary secretary of the London and Home Counties Branch River Medway Sub-committee, also gave us a special I.W.A. lock pass for a fee of £2. This enabled us to pass through all locks between 8 a.m. and one hour before sunset and permitted us to work the locks ourselves. Until recently locks on the Upper Medway Navigation were worked by lock-keepers and the upper six locks, Sluice Weir Lock to Tonbridge Town Lock, could only be navigated at fixed times with craft in convoy unless skippers held an I.W.A. pass. In 1968 the London and Home

Counties Branch succeeded in getting all restrictions on locks lifted and you can now operate them yourself.

Cruising back from East Farleigh to Allington Lock we skipped Maidstone and made directly for the Malta Inn at Allington, an absolute 'must' port of call on the Medway. Originally a bargeman's inn, dating back to the late eighteenth century, it has in recent years been extended and 're-done' and unfortunately nothing now remains of its old character; it can best be described as 'plush popular', but the food, wine and service is of high standard.

We set off next morning for Maidstone, passing cruising clubs and marinas, a string of moored sailing barges converted to houseboats but no moving craft. Through the trees was a glorious view of the moated, medieval Allington Castle, now a retreat centre run by the Carmelite Order. The river all the way to Maidstone is wide and fairly deep and with luck you will meet tugs and lighters carrying paper pulp or coal to the paper works at Tovil or the gas works at Maidstone. Once past Allington Marina you come to industrialised riverside waterworks, engineering works, sweet factories and the like, as well as relics of the old waterside at Maidstone. This industrialised shabbiness lasts for only half a mile to Bazalgette's Victorian Maidstone Bridge with its wide granite arches. Through the bridge you will find moorings at a low wharf beneath the splendid Archbishop's Palace and high-towered All Saints Church, the largest parish church in Kent. The county town of Kent looks little more than an ordinary shopping centre by road, but it is extraordinarily rich in fine old buildings and such treats as the remains of a fascinating eighteenth-century water-pavilion, the Chillington House Museum and Art Gallery and the Coach Museum founded by Sir Garrard Tyrwhitt-Drake. Nearby the moated Leeds Castle stands romantically.

From Maidstone to Tonbridge there is a continuous towing path for those who enjoy pleasant waterside walks. Between Maidstone and Tovil there is a little more industry but above Tovil Bridge the river narrows and winds through woodlands to East Farleigh Lock. Just above the lock you will come to the first of the many superb medieval bridges on the Medway. East Farleigh Bridge, in my view, is the finest of them all and one of the most beautiful in England. Its four rather flat pointed arches are separated by massive cut-waters both up and downstream, and though the roadway is a scant 11 ft wide, there are no recesses for pedestrians. The bridge is also the worst navigational hazard on the Upper Medway, for the navigation arch and lock are well out of line and a dead slow angled approach from the lock to the bridge is essential. Craft have come to minor grief here through excessive speed and carelessness.

On a hill above the bridge on the south bank sprawls a large hopfield with its forest of poles and wires strikingly topped by the broach spire of St Mary's Church. There is a memorable view of the river from the top of the hill. East Farleigh village has a grocery shop and is a quarter-mile from the lock.

The wide two-mile reach to Teston Bridge and Lock is typical of the rural charm of the entire river to Tonbridge. There is the timber-built Kettle Bridge whose piers are encased in concrete, the soaring spire of Barming church rising above green orchards, and hop gardens on sloping hills. We were told that fishing is excellent and we spotted wild mink swimming as we approached the rushing waters of the wide weir beside Teston Lock. Behind it, nestling in the hillside, you will see the ivy-covered remains of an old linseed mill, to add one more delightful touch to one of the most attractive spots on the river. Teston (pronounced Teeson) boasts a bridge that runs East Farleigh's a close second for beautiful simple lines and it does have handy pedestrian recesses.

Kent, of course, is the home of cricket and at Teston village cricket and hockey balls have been made since 1808. We cruised on through open fields and patches of woodland falling gently to the banks, to the distressingly modern Wateringbury Bridge. You can get a bus from the village crossroads at the top of the hill for a visit to nearby Mereworth Castle which is open to the public.

Leaving Wateringbury behind, you will come to a straight reach and will soon see Nettlestead church and the 'big house' on a hillside to starboard. This is Nettlestead Place but is not open for inspection. St Mary's Church can be reached via a narrow footpath from the mooring just below Nettlestead Place. This church is fascinating for the half-dozen great fifteenth-century windows of the nave and similar but smaller windows of the chancel, designed as frames to exhibit the skill of the craftsmen in painted glass of the period. Enough of the glass still remains to make one bemoan the loss to posterity.

From Nettlestead the river bends sharply and there are some high banks where it divides, swinging to port to become the main channel to Twyford Bridge. Although a dead end it fully repays exploration and there is ample room to turn round. There are glorious views along this wide reach bordered by meadows and with the Beult and Teise streams flowing into it. Back at the junction, taking the right-hand channel and moving slowly through the narrow cut will take you to Hampstead Lock, where the towpath changes to the left-hand bank. This lock, built in the eighteenth century at the end of an artificial cut to save travelling round the big Yalding bend in the river, is the second deepest lock on the river and is certainly deep enough to use the hanging chains in the chamber.

At the upstream end of the narrow cut, just round a

bend, is a small drawbridge which is quite simple to
operate with your windlass. You can get water from a
hosepipe here. Immediately beyond the drawbridge you
will find the ancient thatched Anchor Inn with moorings
on the wall opposite.

From the moorings here you can walk half a mile across
the fine Twyford Bridge, with its massive pointed cut-
waters, and the pleasant Lees to Yalding. In this most
attractive village with its ancient cottages, pretty timbered
and Georgian houses, a smithy and at least five pubs, we
discovered in one of these latter a pre-1912 wall pinball
machine which proved great fun and rather profitable.
Medieval Yalding Bridge, a scheduled monument like the
old bridges at Twyford and Laddingford on the Teise,
is distinctly different from all the other ancient bridges on
the Medway, for it is really a stone causeway some
hundred yards long with seven arches and showing signs
of having been widened on the upstream side.

From the Anchor moorings and the big automatic
sluices nearby, the river makes a right-angle turn, an area
popular with swimmers. After two more bends you will be
in pretty open countryside again with trees overhanging
the banks of the river.

The nine locks on the Medway give a total rise of 58 ft
6 ins and the six remaining locks to Tonbridge from
Hampstead Lock were ten until 1914, for in the 8½ miles
of river involved, the rise is well over 30 ft. Extensive
work by the Kent River Authority has made four of these
locks unnecessary. However, you can still see the remains.
There are only two main bridges over this stretch and five
minor ones, so that the entire course to Tonbridge is unspoiled valley and weald. The river above Yalding is
somewhat shallower than below but will accommodate
craft of under 4 ft in draught.

The river, now banked by woodland, narrows above the

angled Branbridges Bridge and becomes shallower with
the banks being noticeably gravelly and high. There are
a number of sharp bends and because of the shallowness
you should steer round the outside of the bends, keeping
well away from the banks. There are more shoals at the
approach to Sluice Weir Lock than anywhere else on this
river, I would say, yet the lock is the deepest on the Upper
Medway. Once through the lock you will note that the
valley begins to open out again and soon you will pass
the mouth of the River Bourne, another of the Medway's
many tributaries, to reach Oak Weir Lock, beautifully
situated in a setting of trees.

Above the lock the banks are wooded for a short stretch
but you will reach open countryside again before Ford
Green Bridge. There is a pleasant picnic mooring spot
where the river widens into a pool below the bridge. More
hop-gardens and meadows appear as the scenery almost
constantly changes. Where the river divides you should
take the left-hand channel to East Lock about a quarter of
a mile further on. There are many footpaths leading to
little hamlets like Tudely Hale and Golden Green, and
such inviting names made us regret we had so little time
on the Medway.

The towpath changes from the left to the right bank at
East Lock and at Porter's Lock you will find a most beautiful and peaceful setting. Below it, beside the towpath,
you can search for a weathered milestone marking the
distance up from Maidstone. The next reach, a mile long,
with woodlands to port and meadows to starboard, will
seem so isolated and quiet that time almost stands still.
From this reach you can see 'May's Folly', a peculiar
Victorian-Gothic erection some 150 ft high, dominating
the countryside. It was built at Hadlow in 1810 by a
Barton May, ostensibly to permit him to see the sea, but

it was not quite tall enough and later the slender top storey was added.

At Eldridge's Lock in surroundings of open fields and orchards, we saw some youths clowning with a canoe, which we later discovered had been stolen. This is the only instance of theft we have encountered on the waterways in over a decade, either in Britain or on the Continent. Although you are now only little more than a mile and a half from Tonbridge, you will find the river bordered by farmlands, water meadows and willow trees. We reluctantly ignored the many tempting moorings along this reach which twists and turns on its way to Cannon Bridge, where the gasholder inevitably blots the horizon, and Tonbridge Town Lock, nearly 60 ft above Maidstone. It is not wise to moor on the high brick wall below the lock. Lives have been lost scrambling between boats and the top of the wall. There is another drawbridge at Town Lock, from which you can see the excellent I.W.A. mooring on the left.

The Great Bridge just beyond the I.W.A. moorings is the official head of navigation, but smaller powered craft which require only about 5 ft clearance can cruise slowly for another two miles upstream to Lucifer Bridge.

Tonbridge, a Medway crossing from pre-Saxon times, home of an ancient public school, a centre of printing and a bustling market town, is rich in history. You will enjoy viewing the ruins of the moated castle high on a 60 ft mound beside the Great Bridge. The gardens are particularly colourful. There are fine half-timbered houses in the High Street, not least of these The Chequers, the oldest pub in Tonbridge, which has very pleasant bars.

Tonbridge, perhaps more than any other town on the river, was transformed by the opening of the Medway to commercial traffic. It was King Charles who started the move to make the Medway navigable in the 1660s, but

nothing was achieved for some seventy-five years and the
river was not opened for traffic to Tonbridge until 1741.
The then unimportant town, so poorly served by roads,
quickly became a thriving commercial centre. Coal, timber,
stone, iron, lime and other cargoes were first bow-hauled
by men and then drawn by horses in increasing quantities.
The town's whole appearance changed as imported building materials replaced the local timber and the new
Georgian-style architecture became fashionable.

Monopoly of carriage on the river coupled with the
coming of the railways affected trade from the 1850s and
the conditions on the river progressively worsened. Despite
the establishment of a new authority and the complete
remodelling of the navigation above Maidstone to enable
the reopening of the river to commercial traffic in 1915,
this traffic never returned. We mused sadly on this as we
cruised peacefully back to the Tovil Boatyard in the warm
sunshine. Commercial traffic will never conceivably return
in force to the Upper Medway but Kent and England has
a grand and beautiful waterway that must be preserved
at all costs.

We find ourselves returning again and again to the
'Little Med', sometimes by boat, sometimes by car for
lunch at a waterside inn and sometimes just to walk along
a stretch of towpath to exercise our dog and feast our
eyes. There remains much more for us to see and we
want to delve one day into the story of the oasts. A complete stranger I met on the towpath was telling me only
the other day that hops were reputedly cultivated in Kent
in the 1520s to provide beer for Flemish weavers who had
settled there. The secret of success in processing hops is
apparently in the drying, and the picturesque Kentish oast
gradually evolved into its present form from replicas of
oasts used in Flanders. Circular oasts with revolving

draught cowls were the brain-child of one John Read in the 1830s and are still in use today. It is boating holidays with towpath encounters like these that rouse one's curiosity and open up new fields of interest. You cannot help but enjoy such a beautiful little river as the Medway remains to this day.

CHAPTER 8

THE NOWHITHER NENE

IT WOULD be misleading and unfair to suggest that it is mandatory to introduce yourself, your family or friends to boating holidays on navigationally easy waterways with only a few locks. There is no reason why more active and energetic first-timers on the waterways should not holiday on our many artificial cuts or canals, or indeed on a combination of rivers and canals, as long as excessive ambition in respect of locks is curbed and ample time is allowed.

While holidaying on the South Level of the Fenland waterways we had met a craft from the River Nene which had come from Peterborough to Hilgay via the Middle Level, and the owner of the converted lifeboat and his wife had raved over the beauty of the Nene. While the Nene had certainly caught our fancy we also had a yen to try out tiller steering and after some debate the vote was to try to combine the two. We were fortunate to find very quickly at Bletchley on the Grand Union Canal the tiller-equipped *Suzybelle S.3*, a comfortable and suitable 6-8 berth 41 ft x 6 ft 10 ins narrow cruiser with a draught of 1 ft 10 ins, which would take us anywhere on the waterway network. It was a simple matter to work out the lock mileage from Bletchley to Peterborough and return, and to calculate that the 180 miles and 128 locks of the round voyage could be covered in a fortnight by averaging an easy 22 lock miles per day.

By early February we had booked the *Suzybelle S.3* and

completed an advance log based on available charts and
relevant literature.

Until modern engineering brought it under control in
this century, the Nene was a terrible rogue of a river,
dealing out death and destruction after heavy rain or
quick thaw. The fear in which the Nene was held for
centuries is reflected today in the way towns and villages
were defensively built on spurs of high land at the sides
of the broad valley, two miles wide in places. The sites
chosen were close enough to the river to use it for transport and power but high enough and distant enough to
avoid the floods, damp and fog of bygone days. The
history of the Nene is a fascinating story worth delving
into, but you will be more interested in what it is like
today. The Nene rises in the Northamptonshire uplands,
one branch near the battlefield of Naseby, the other from
a spring near Borough Hill, the site of the B.B.C. Daventry
station. The streams join forces and then the Nene proper
flows through the outskirts of industrial Northampton
and back into open country at Midsummer Meadow,
where some 500 years ago thousands fleeing from the battle
of Northampton were drowned.

The valley broadens out almost immediately into a flat
expanse of lovely meadows which continue to the outskirts of Peterborough. Northampton is only forty miles
from Peterborough as the crow flies, but what we have
dubbed the 'nowhither Nene' loops so much that there are
some seventy miles of wild and unspoiled river between
these two towns. This is referred to as the Middle Nene,
for it only becomes a big tidal river in the lower reaches
stretching a further twenty-odd miles from the Dog-in-a-
Doublet lock to the Wash.

We all hoped there was a little madness left in the Nene
as we took over the *Suzybelle S.3* from the Bletchley
boatyard one Saturday afternoon. It took a few miles as

we cruised north along the pleasant and rural Grand Union for all the crew to get the feel of tiller steering, much more direct than the wheel steering we were accustomed to. It was strange standing at the tiller instead of sitting on a high stool by a wheel. A folding deck chair did not quite provide comfortable steering as the tiller arm was too high and the frame of the chair got in the way every time a sharp turn had to be made. It took us some little time to discover that the most comfortable way to steer with a tiller for any length of time is to straddle the arm. This enables you to steer with the inside of your legs and to shift your weight from one leg to another. This is useful on long pounds, but when approaching badly angled narrow bridge holes and locks it is wise to return one hand to the tiller arm and use the other to manipulate the throttle and gear lever.

You will enjoy the gentle lock at Fenny Stratford on the Grand Union with its swing bridge and a fall of only a few inches.

The lock marks the beginning of the eleven-mile Fenny pound, nearly three hours cruising without having to work a lock, and goes through the pretty valley of the Ouzel. Canals are like this. You will find pounds unobstructed by locks for twenty miles and more, and then on the same canal there is a succession of locks or even flights of locks within a distance of a few miles. Most canals take full advantage of the contours of the land but many have to be taken over watersheds and through hills, thus the necessity for locks and tunnels.

The Grand Union Canal was built only after the completion of the Midlands canals made a direct link by water with London imperative. The thriving Oxford Canal was not really satisfactory because it connected the Midlands waterways with London via Oxford and the Thames, a roundabout route which meant higher shipping costs. Several schemes for new canals were mooted and in 1793 the Grand Junction Canal, stretching from Braunston high up on the Oxford Canal to Brentford on the Thames, was authorised by Parliament, today the longest section on the Grand Union system.

The Grand Junction took twelve years to complete and must have nearly driven the noted canal engineer, William Jessop, to distraction. By the time it was finished in 1805 Jessop had successfully locked over the Chilterns and had driven two long tunnels through the tough ironstone outcrops at Braunston and Blisworth. The latter, the longest navigable tunnel on our waterways today, was a particular problem and delayed completion of the Grand Junction for all of five years. Between 1800, when the rest of the waterway was opened to traffic, and 1805, goods had to be transhipped into horse-drawn wagons and hauled over Blisworth hill on a plate railway.

Despite setbacks, the Grand Junction was an immediate success, substantially speeding up and reducing the cost of shipping goods between the South and the Midlands. It was even used for troop movements, and as the newspapers of the day reported that this not only saved time but made for the arrival of troops in fresh condition, you can imagine how dreadful the roads must have been at the beginning of the nineteenth century.

As you cruise along the Fenny pound, with luck meeting a few working narrow boats, it will be difficult for you to imagine that this quiet canal was once the waterways equivalent of the M1 motorway. Only over a relatively few miles will you hear or catch glimpses of roaring road traffic, and you will be smugly satisfied that you are idling along on the water while so many others are cursing congestion and delays on the roads.

Work on the Grand Junction continued sporadically over the years until 1883 when the last of eight arms or branches was completed. It was not until 1929, however, that the present name of Grand Union Canal was adopted after amalgamations. In 1948 the Grand Union was included in the nationalised waterways and has been operated by the British Waterways Board since January 1963.

On the Grand Union there are certainly more pubs than service areas along our motorways. Near Bridge 83 the Barge Inn at Little Woolstone specialises in country wine and chicken on the spit. By Bridge 77 you will find the Old Wharf Inn and still another pub in Lindford village, a short walk along the road to the left. And at the next bridge, No. 76, stands the Black Horse Inn and a café. The bridges along the Grand Union are eye-openers. You will find, quite apart from the marks of old tow lines, graceful architecture to admire and beauty of line.

Cosgrove Lock and the end of the eleven-mile Fenny pound comes almost immediately after the short Wolverton aqueduct. The derelict Buckingham Arm is on the left above the lock, which takes you up a bare 3¼ ft to the next pound, some five miles long. There is a watering point and moorings at the lock, but to visit the village you should moor by the Barley Mow Inn, which sits back from the left bank of the canal in a little hollow. The church repays a visit if only for the lovely view from the tower. There is a good grocer near the church.

The Stoke Bruerne flight of seven locks, like most flights on our canals, is padlocked at 7 p.m. While there is good mooring below the bottom lock, Stoke Bruerne is a long walk up the flight, which raises your craft some 56 ft to the Boat Inn. It is advisable therefore to time your arrival before 7 p.m. With the locks against us we have taken as long as an hour and a half to lock through this flight. By lock-wheeling, however, you can easily do it in under an hour. Unless there are pressing reasons it is foolish to rush through locks and smart and steady winding is the least tiring; windlasses with sleeves on the handles are more efficient than the old type of lock handle without a revolving sleeve.

The Stoke Bruerne flight is itself very pleasing to the eye but the scene at the top is a gem lifted as it were from centuries past. The village of Stoke Bruerne with its Norman church and thatched cottages nestles snugly by the canal, and the canalside itself—with the Waterways Museum depicting over two centuries of canal history, the Old Boat Inn, the cottages of canal employees with their gaily painted doors, an early traditional narrow boat, boat-weighing machine and a pair of cast-iron lock gates among outside exhibits in a natural setting—is the showplace of British Waterways.

The Museum, which is open daily including Sundays from 10 a.m. to 8 p.m. except for meal breaks, is a treasure trove of relics of a most colourful industry. There is a model of a giant brush with which tunnels were cleaned, traditional boaters' clothing and cabinware, paintings, brasses, documents, photographs, a full-size reconstruction of a decorated and fitted out butty boat cabin, and even 'legging' boards on which boatmen lay to propel their craft with their legs through nearby Blisworth Tunnel.

Blisworth and Braunston Tunnels on the Grand Union, like many other canal tunnels, were constructed without towing paths. In the early days when commercial craft were bowhauled by their crews or towed by horses or pairs of mules, an alternative method of propulsion was necessary in these tunnels. The solution was 'legging' and teams of 'leggers' were based at the tunnels. From 1805, when Blisworth Tunnel was opened to traffic, to 1850, when steam tugs took over, 'leggers' took craft through the 3,075 yard long tunnel. 'Legging' boards were placed across the bows of craft and two 'leggers' positioned head to head on the boards with their feet projecting over the

sides of the boat literally walked or 'legged' along the
sides of the tunnel. It was a dark, cold, wet, tiring job and
long tunnels like Blisworth must have seemed endless. The
'leggers' reigned at Blisworth for forty-five years while the
tugs maintained their sway for eighty-four years, until
1934, by which time virtually all craft were motorised and
able to navigate the tunnel unaided.

There is picturesque mooring for scores of craft at Stoke
Bruerne and you will certainly decide to linger here to
water, replenish stores, refresh yourself, do some sightseeing, take photographs and obtain items of 'canalia'
from the little souvenir shop beyond the inn. You'll find
retired boaters here too and both the lock-keeper and
attendant at the museum enjoy chatting and filling you in
on Stoke Bruerne's way of life in its hey-day.

Blisworth Tunnel is just round the bend from Stoke
Bruerne. Although it looks very narrow and gives delusions
of curving away, it is actually fairly straight with good
headroom and ample space for two narrow boats to pass
with care. The tunnel is in good repair and there are seven
air shafts, five original shafts and two added later, all of
which drip and in a wet season provide free showers. This
was our first canal tunnel and we took over an hour getting
through. On subsequent journeys, after discovering the
advantage of turning on all cabin lights as well as our
searchlight, we have navigated the tunnel in under twenty-
five minutes.

You will blink as you leave Blisworth Tunnel and reach
bright light once again. Woodland, cottages and rose
gardens are in strong contrast to the darkness and clammy
atmosphere you have left behind. Another mile along and
some 23½ miles out of Bletchley boatyard, you can swing
90° to starboard into the narrow, somewhat weedy Northampton Arm, leading to the River Nene.

We are early risers and when cruising there is normally

someone astir by 6.30 a.m. We use all the daylight available and are generally tucked in our sleeping bags by 10.30 p.m. Of course it is quite possible to lie abed in perfect peace and quiet and I suppose most people do, judging by the number of craft we pass in the mornings still moored with no sign of life; lying-in undisturbed may be one of the advantages of boating holidays that I have failed to point out.

As you gain experience you will acquire a remarkable knack of estimating accurately how long it will take you to travel from one place to another. My wife had become accustomed to accurate forecasts and when we moored above the Top Lock on the Northampton Arm for lunch on this cruise, I recall being nicely chided for being ten minutes late and responsible for the fact that the roast beef was slightly overdone.

Not a single craft was moving on the Northampton Arm and we could well believe that only two boats had passed through in the fortnight before our arrival. The lock paddles were so stiff that only my son Paul was strong enough for the role of lock-wheeler and he was therefore pleased when the lock-keeper appeared on his bicycle at the seventh lock and kindly took over. No charts exist to my knowledge of this short Arm. There are seventeen narrow 7 ft wide locks in five miles as well as a number of drawbridges providing just as tight a squeeze. We found five broken or malfunctioning paddles and one balance-beam rather less than 18 ins long, but fortunately not on one of the single top gates. The Arm is rather hard work and understandably frustrating and wearying for beginners. But it need not be. More extensive use by boats would ease the stiffness of the paddles and lead to better maintenance. The views from the top of the locks are glorious, the surrounding countryside is unmarred except for one major road bridge, and passing through is great sport, especially

when a heavy dog and heavier crew leap off the bows
with a flourish as you enter locks two inches wider than
the beam of your craft.

We were through the Arm in under three hours, thanks
to noble work by the lock-keeper who, when we thanked
him in approved fashion, tipped us off as to the hazards
on the approach to Northampton Lock No. 1. The stretch
immediately after the Arm's bottom lock is a disgrace to
the city of Northampton, which has conversely done so
much to make Midsummer Meadow so appealing. The
river is badly silted here and chock-a-block with weed
and debris, while the banks look rather like a slum. Once
under the road-bridge we were greeted by a splendid
stretch of quayside to port but we had to avoid weeds
and debris and run on for several hundred yards past the
toll house before we found enough water to moor safely.
This is a typical example of the wisdom of obtaining and
paying attention to the advice of local lock-keepers, for
we could easily have gone aground in a dozen places.

Our keys to the Nene locks were awaiting us at the toll
house as previously arranged with the Welland and Nene
River Authority at Oundle. If you hire a craft on the
Nene these keys are available from the boatyard and you
need not concern yourself with navigation tolls. But as
we had come from the nationalised waterways and our
craft was not licensed for the Nene we had to pay
£2 17s plus £2 returnable deposit on the two keys to
navigate the thirty-seven unmanned locks between
Northampton and Peterborough. There was also a small
insurance premium of 10s to cover possible damage to
river controls. On writing to the Engineer's Office at North
Street, Oundle, you will receive an application form with
several sheets of instructions regarding navigation of the
Nene. These instructions include directions for operating
what I must frankly admit are the stiffest series of locks on

any inland waterway in Britain. The operation of the locks is simple enough but they are hard work, despite the fact that they are modern and in good condition. All the locks are fitted with timber pointing doors upstream similar to those on most canals and rivers but have vertical steel 'guillotine' gates at the lower end. Unless otherwise instructed you must leave locks with the pointing doors closed and the vertical gate raised, and it is the raising of these gates that sets every muscle in your body grumbling. These gates have to be operated with care. There may have been unauthorised interference with the balance weights and at the first operation you will always have to take the weight of the gate carefully, using both hands. Nor can you get away with only partially raising the gate. The river foremen insist that gates be left raised to the fullest extent to ensure that the next craft entering the lock does not sustain damage. I am told, incidentally, that the gearing on these vertical steel gates has been purposely made stiff to prevent rapid opening of the gate and possible damage to craft, but that does not account for the fact that gates supplied by one manufacturer are much harder to work than those supplied by the other.

Once you have your keys to the padlocks on the vertical gates and paddles on the pointed doors of each lock, put them on a long cord and carry them round your neck, as they are so easily dropped into the river. The locks are all 83 ft 6 ins long and 15 ft wide and we calculated a total fall of 189 ft in the sixty-nine miles of the non-tidal Nene. The River Board do not guarantee any fixed water levels and care must be taken when approaching river controls with a rapid flow on the river. The river foremen are quick to come to your aid if you experience any difficulty due to lack of water or in operating locks but they can become justifiably annoyed when someone sabotages their vital water levels. We had no difficulty at all in navigating the Nene and found plenty of headroom under all but half a dozen of the sixty-six fixed bridges. You may find more adverse conditions in times of flooding but they are unlikely to worry you, for craft up to 78 ft long 13 ft in beam, with a draught of 4 ft and headroom of 7 ft 3 ins are always permitted on the river.

Your lock keys will not, however, fit the padlocks on Northampton No. 1 lock, which is set in a lovely park superbly equipped with sports facilities. The lock-keeper who lives in the toll house on the quayside will operate this lock for you and guide you to the best moorings for your visit to Northampton. This is a sizeable community of over 100,000 people and the shopping centre is within minutes of the moorings. You will find a gem of a market square and a host of friendly shops like the specialists in leather we discovered with the finest collection of leather goods we have seen anywhere in the world. Places like St John's Catholic Church, built as a hospice in 1140, are delightful and the parks of the city are an eye-opener. A chatty park superintendent proudly told us that North-ampton has more parks than any other town in Britain and we did not doubt him for a moment.

The whole of the Nene lay before us, shimmering in the sun. No river anywhere presents such a winding course through such pleasant pastoral countryside. Apart from short industrialised stretches at Northampton and Peter-borough and the rather 'niffy' sewage farm at Irthling-borough the Nene presents an almost uninterrupted panorama of meadows, woodlands, lovely stone and thatched villages and picturesque mills and parklands. Although you will find remarkably few inns along the riverside, there are more than enough within a short distance of the banks to keep the thirstiest of crews well fortified.

The river winds through large bends out of Northamp-

Holywell   *Here, where Hereward the Wake fled across the river from William the Conqueror . . . we watched the reed cutters at work*

Holywell   *We found it enchanting with its thatched cottages . . . and reeds hung up to dry*

Stoke Bruerne *The village nestles snugly by the canal and the canalside itself . . . is the showplace of British Waterways*

White Mills *You will find pleasant and peaceful scenery as you cruise to Whiston and White Mills locks*

Lilford Lock   *We believe it is the prettiest on the river, with a background of a charming stone flying bridge*

Braunston   *There is a flight of six locks, descending to Braunston village, a centre of boatbuilding and decoration for many years*

Banbury   *From Banbury the canal continues to be very shallow ... all the locks now have single gates in contrast to those above Banbury*

Foxton Flight   *The flight of ten locks, which has a rise of 75 ft ... is one of the outstanding engineering triumphs of the nineteenth century*

Anderton Lift
*The only boat lift
in Britain . . .
raises boats in
massive caissons
from the level of
the Weaver some
50 ft to the canal
above*

River Weaver *We were surprised to see round the first bend . . .
a big Danish coaster bearing down on us at about 10 knots*

Chirk Aqueduct *This 701 ft long aqueduct over the River Ceiriog was completed in 1801 by Telford . . . and is some 70 ft high*

Norbury Junction *One of our favourite overnight moorings . . . the company one meets at the Junction Inn is invariably good fun*

Stratford-on-Avon Canal   *A split bridge with a narrow gap in the centre, built this way to allow tow lines to pass through when horses crossed the bridges in the days of horse-drawn craft*

King's Norton   *An imposing open guillotine stop lock, once used to preserve water rights, leads to the Worcester & Birmingham Canal*

Stourport   *The lock-keeper will help you through the two pairs of staircase locks to the four basins 42 ft above the Severn on the Staffordshire & Worcestershire Canal*

Bratch Locks   *The unique Bratch Locks need particular care ... but the flight is most attractive with its white bridges and octagonal lock house*

ton to Rush Mills Lock, which is one of the three on the river with radial shutters instead of guillotine gates. A great variety of wild flowers and wild life decorate the river. With the help of a reference book we identified over thirty different types of birds and I am sure we missed many others. Abington Lock is only a mile from Rush Mills, indeed in the fourteen miles of river between Northampton and Wellingborough, the next sizeable town, there are twelve locks.

The countryside becomes more glorious as you go on through Rush Mills and Weston Favel locks to Clifford Hill Lock and charming backwater moorings. A footpath from the right bank can be followed for a pleasant one-mile walk to Little Houghton, a village of unspoiled stone dwellings.

Billing Lock, under a mile away, has little to commend it as a scenic attraction, but just beyond the lock on the left is the entrance to Billing Aquadrome with moorings for visitors who want to have a meal or to entertain the younger members of the crew at a fun-fair and other attractions available here. There is more than a mile of lovely countryside before Cogenhoe Lock is reached. Moor well below the lock, as there is a rather dirty camp site and chalet village almost on top of the lock-side. The little village of Cogenhoe is reached by climbing half a mile up the steep hill on the right. Shopping is good here and your shopping basket on wheels will be a help.

You will find pleasant and peaceful scenery as you cruise to Whiston and White Mills locks. There is an inn a few hundred yards along the road to the right which also leads to Castle Ashby village and Castle Ashby House, the seat of the Marquis of Northampton. The house is open to the public on Thursday and Saturday afternoons and on Sundays in June, July and August. It is reached by a path through a mile of park, containing big lakes, and the stone houses of the village are tucked away below the terraces of this stately home.

This ornate and beautiful sixteenth- to eighteenth-century house is famed as being the scene of the 'bride in a basket' legend. The first Earl of Northampton having been refused the hand of Elizabeth Spencer, daughter of the wealthy Lord Mayor of London, posed as a baker's boy and carried his bride-to-be from her father's home in a bread basket. They married against the will of Sir John Spencer and Elizabeth was disinherited. Queen Elizabeth intervened and 'ordered' Sir John to adopt a child in place of his disinherited daughter. As the baby proved to be his grandson the tale has a happy ending. As you will have to walk nearly two miles from the lock if you visit Castle Ashby, it is worth stopping to see the handsome fourteenth- to fifteenth-century church as well, with its unique brass in the chancel floor.

Following the road from the lock in the opposite direction for a mile will bring you to Earls Barton, a large village, so called because it was the site of the Earl of Huntingdon's barley farm. The church here is still as it was over a thousand years ago, richly ornamented.

Bird lovers will admire a water-fowl sanctuary to port along the reach to Barton Lock, an excellent use for old gravel workings. Doddington Lock quickly follows. You may think it worth taking pictures here for the lock is beautifully situated and the Mill House is charming. The Mill House at Wollaston Lock is occupied and the boating enthusiasts who live here will provide water if you need it, and we found them very friendly.

The navigation deteriorates beyond Wollaston Lock and the run to Irthlingborough is rather less interesting than the previous countryside. From Upper Welling-borough Lock you are likely to run into weeds. Weed-cutting is normally in progress on the Nene from spring until the autumn and an eye should be kept open for the weedcutters. The weeds cut during each day are allowed to float downstream to a rope or line of timbers across the river, prior to removal. These obstructions are visible some distance ahead, and at times are indicated by floating red markers. The cutters will always release the ropes or timbers on request to permit the passage of your craft but they need a little time to clear a way for you.

Shortly above the lock you will come to the low Wellingborough bridge and pleasant boulevard moorings to port for Little Irchester. If you cross the river bridge and old railway crossing, a few minutes walk will bring you to the Cottage Inn where you may well meet barge crews who deliver grain to the nearby mills. You can get a bus to Wellingborough, a mile away on the other side of the river, for excellent shopping, a visit to the zoo, the famous public school or perhaps a meal in the handsome old Hind Hotel overlooking the market square. The parish church with its medieval tower and a vast fifteenth-century tithe barn are among the other worthwhile sights in this town which is so clearly fond of trees.

Bridges are all rather low in this area and there are a number of shoals at the approach to Lower Wellingborough Lock, and also in the next few reaches. Ditchford Lock is another of the radial-type locks, and is just fifteen miles by river from Northampton. Higham Ferrers bridge, about half-way to Higham Lock some two miles distant, is one of the most dangerous on the river, not only because of low headroom but because it straddles a bend in the river and there are timber baulks jutting up under both sides of the arch. The best moorings are above the bridge for Higham Ferrers, which stands high on a hill to your right. This is a delightful small town which should not be missed despite the uphill walk. The ancient church with its lovely spire has a cluster of ecclesiastical buildings round it that are reminiscent of corners of Oxford and Cambridge. You will not want to moor for the night near Higham Ferrers bridge, however, as the town apparently holds the record for polluting the Nene.

The next bridge on the river is the lowest of the entire sixty-six and should be navigated with great care. After passing through Higham Lock you will quickly come to a railway bridge and viaduct after which you will find moorings for Irthlingborough. This sprawling village has little noteworthy to commend it to the visitor except for its church and the Railway Inn, which can be reached from your moorings across a couple of footbridges. It is a tiny inn which may not be rated highly among the most picturesque inns of England but it is the home of the 'Irthlingburger'. This is an inexpensive, tasty and filling concoction consisting of fried bread and a hamburger topped with a fried egg, worth every penny the landlord charges. Since our discovery of this simple local dish we have duplicated it both at home and aboard our holiday cruisers time and time again.

Once past the tannery and sewage farm nearby you will notice that the locks are more widely spaced and it is over two miles from Irthlingborough Lock to Upper Ringstead Lock. There is a path here leading from the left bank to the village of Great Addington, which stands proudly on a hill dominated by a fourteenth-century church.

From Lower Ringstead Lock the Nene now loops back on itself as you cruise on to Woodford Lock. At the sharp bend before the lock a footpath leads over the fields to Woodford village and the Duke's Arms. Keep clear of the piers of the railway bridge as you leave the lock as there are a number of underwater stakes. Where the river forks at the approach to Denford Lock keep to the left hand channel.

You will probably not want to visit every village along the way, particularly those which involve longer walks, for some have little of special interest to offer. We have found that if neither shopping nor visiting a particular place is contemplated, it is pleasant to moor as fancy dictates and then explore along one bank on an outward journey and on the other on the return trip. We have discovered many charming spots not mentioned at all in guide or reference books, and there must be many more. Sometimes disappointment is inevitable, but footpaths and country roads make pleasant walks and if you take a dog he will welcome the exercise.

By all means, however, moor above the bridge on the next reach between Islip and Thrapston. Islip is a pretty village of stone houses and cottages on the left, and the Woolpack Inn close to the river serves excellent meals. This is one of the Washington villages and as an American I was, of course, drawn to the elegant fifteenth-century church with its monument to Mary Washington, a great-grandmother of the first American President. We also walked nearly a mile into the market town of Thrapston, which despite the loss of its castle and with its modernised church we found most attractive, with good shopping and a well-stocked antique shop. The rector of the parish church of St James kindly took us over the church and showed us the arms of Sir John Washington on a stone tablet in the church. From the stars and stripes in the arms, the American flag stems.

After another two miles of pretty river you will reach Titchmarsh Lock and the new headquarters of the Middle Nene Cruising Club, which used to be located just above the bridge at Islip. Members are most hospitable and helpful and we learned a good deal about the Nene from a talk with two of them.

You will find the Imray, Laurie, Norie and Wilson chart

of the Nene most useful. It includes public footpaths which enabled us to visit the twin-churched village of Aldwincle, little more than half a mile from the river. Aldwincle All Saints and Aldwincle St Peter's are linked by a long street with delightful groups of grey houses set among trees. The poet John Dryden is said to have been baptised at the 600-year old font in All Saints Church and St Peter's Church is claimed to have the finest broach spire in all of Northamptonshire. You will like the 450-year old Rose and Crown too, and find it worth the walk. The footpath leads surprisingly through vast fields of grain and meadows, one of which happened to be stocked with bullocks. Catching sight of Wiggers they mounted a charge, but our crew must have been more frightening than frightened for we all shouted at the top of our voices and waved our walking sticks with such ferocity that the herd turned aside a dozen yards from us. Since that day we have always made a point of looking into fields before striking across them.

Thorpe Waterville, once a Danish settlement, lies on the right bank of the river, just five minutes from the bridge. It once had a fine castle built in 1300 but the walls were destroyed in the Wars of the Roses and all that remains is the great banqueting hall with a kingpost roof, which today serves as a barn. Good grills can be obtained at the attractive Fox Inn.

The Nene now takes on a new beauty in a rather weedy narrow reach to Wadenhoe where there are moorings at the King's Head. The lovely village with its ancient mill lies near the river and a steep winding footpath leads to its saddleback-towered church standing on a lonely knoll. From Wadenhoe it is little more than two miles to Lilford Lock, which we believe is the prettiest on the river, with a background of a charming stone flying bridge, woodlands, Lilford Hall farm and deer park.

A few miles of idyllic river will bring you to the first of the Barnwell Locks. After the lock on the left is a sharply angled channel into Oundle Marina, created from old gravel pits by J. T. Newington. This marina is splendidly laid out and set in woodland with the noble spire of Oundle's church in the background. A well-stocked chandlery can be found here and a fleet of hire craft. Until Newington introduced hire craft to the Nene in 1963, none were available on this river. He has shown how it can be used for holidays and his hire craft can be recommended wholeheartedly to anyone who wishes to explore the Nene.

Beyond Lower Barnwell Lock the river winds and curves back on itself once again *en route* to Ashton Lock and pleasant backwater moorings. Once through the lock there is a footbridge with a path leading on the right to Ashton, a village owned by the Rothschilds, and noted as the venue for the annual All England Conker Championships. The footpath to the left leads to Oundle with its famous public school, and to one of the most interesting churches along the river, and the old Talbot Hotel. While shopping and sightseeing in Oundle my wife discovered that she had left her purse in Thrapston's antique shop. By telephone we learned it was being held for us, so we hired a taxi whose driver insisted on giving us a free tour round Barnwell Castle, home of the Duke of Gloucester. Although it is not open to the public, our driver knew his way about and we much enjoyed the drive.

Cruising on through looping river you will come to Cotterstock Lock and Mill with a grand view of Cotterstock Hall from the distance. The attractive village of Tansor follows on the right but moorings are difficult to find as the water near the bank is very shallow. After another mile of open country the oddly named Perio Lock is reached. It has been impossible to find out how this lock came by its name for no one seems to know. From the lock the splendid tower of the Collegiate Church of Fotheringay can be seen. Good moorings can be found here and the church and bridge both merit inspection. Two booklets can be bought at the church giving historical notes; Richard III was born in a castle of which only a grassy mound remains, and Mary Queen of Scots was imprisoned and executed here. There are many delightful buildings in the village, a good shop, and the friendly Falcon Inn.

Beautiful as Fotheringay Bridge is, make sure you strip your decks and take the centre arch, as many craft have been damaged here.

We found people along the Nene very friendly and helpful. At Elton a householder invited us in for tea, the publican at the Crown delivered supplies to our craft, we were shown over Elton Hall although it was not officially open, the couple who run the general shop and post office provided us with produce from their garden and even cashed cheques. Fishermen use this village a good deal and fishing is very good indeed. Many sizeable fish are frequently caught, we were told, and there are pike, tench, chub and many other kinds for those with patience and skill. It is not noteworthy for trout but it holds so many different kinds that few but the trout specialists will mind. It can be fished in most places and day tickets are available from local angling clubs.

From Elton there is a long three-mile reach past the village of Nassington on the left with backwater moorings by the Queens Head, to Yarwell Lock which has a low guillotine gate worth watching. Yarwell is only a wide loop of river away from Wansford Lock and then in a few minutes you will be in Wansford-in-England. The river itself is not so beautiful here but the village is charming despite the nearby highway. It reminds one that the Nene valley is rich both in history and folklore. We enjoyed our stay because we knew one version at least of the legend of 'Drunken Barnaby', and how the village obtained its name. This genial character was sleeping off the effects of too much drink in a haycock one evening when the river rose in flood and carried haycock and Barnaby to Wansford. On waking up, he was fearful that he had been washed out to sea. Even on being told he was at Wansford, he shouted, 'Wansford where?' The reply was 'In England', hence the present-day name.

The lovely old Haycock Inn at Wansford-in-England serves a good country tea. We happened to arrive in the midst of a wedding celebration, and one chap, who reminded us somewhat of Barnaby, insisted on giving the entire crew, including our dog, champagne.

After Wansford there is nearly four miles of cruising through wooded countryside and past the villages of Stibbington and Sutton, facing each other across the river, to Water Newton Lock. Here there is a mill and a church surprisingly close to the river banks. You will cruise now past the site of Roman potteries and indeed the old Roman town of Durobrivae, and a footpath from the left bank will lead you into the village of Castor, one of the most important of all our Roman settlements. There are still Roman remains to be seen; the church is one of the most beautiful ever built by the Normans who used stones from an earlier Saxon church and convent; there are two pleasing inns, and two lovely old houses. Milton Hall is a handsome Elizabethan house in a park of some thousand acres, one of the seats of the Fitzwilliam family.

Further along the river on the right is Peterborough Cruising Club, with good moorings and a watering point. We found our I.W.A. pennant was a kind of passport on the Nene to the four motorboat, cruising and yacht clubs on the river. A warm welcome, ready assistance, and yarn swapping was automatic as soon as the pennant was spotted. While moored for the night at pretty Alwalton Lock just beyond the Peterborough Cruising Club—the sunsets here are glorious—we were hailed by the commodore of the Cruising Club who was on his way to evensong at Alwalton church. He stopped to chat and missed the service and indeed the licensing hours at the Wheatsheaf Inn as well. This kind of thing happens frequently and we revel in the little parties we give aboard our hire cruisers. The commodore had led fifty to sixty craft through the Middle Level navigation from Peterborough in 1965 in a bid to keep this little used system of waterways open, and we were interested in his experiences. The system consists of some ninety miles of almost lock-free 'navigable drains' lying between the Nene and the Great Ouse. The area is for the most part below sea level and the channels run between high banks and pass through or near the towns of Chatteris, March, Whittlesea and Ramsey. Cruising here is not what one would describe as gloriously scenic and there are few villages to be found on Middle Level drains, but I can confirm that they have a charm of their own. The countryside is wild and remote, nature in the raw so to speak, and the most peaceful and quiet you will find anywhere. Coarse fishing is reputedly excellent here, and bird watchers will have many a rewarding day. It is not possible to enter the system much after mid-June because of heavy weed accumulating in the approach channel, but for an off-beat spring cruise really to get away from it all, the Middle Level is the answer to a prayer.

One more huge loop and the river at last reaches Orton Lock and the approaches to Peterborough. Despite its proximity to the cathedral city, this reach is glorious with delightful 'lynches' or wooded banks. Orton Lock is the last on the non-tidal Nene and you are soon in Peter-

borough, which sprawls across the river. There is a town
quay, a good shopping centre, a fine Guildhall and busy
market place, to say nothing of the impressive cathedral
which is considered to be among the grandest in Europe.
Care should be taken when mooring, for there is little
water by the quays and often quite a number of barges
about. The banks opposite are shallow and stony too.
Just beyond Peterborough there is a channel which goes
under a railway bridge to the right, past two boatyards
to the lock leading into the Middle Level. By taking the
left-hand channel there is some five miles of Fenland
cruising to the electrically operated Dog-in-a-Doublet sea
lock, worth inspecting if you have never seen one, but
you will not be permitted to take your craft into the tideway and The Wash. If you visit one of the local inns and
watch the antics of the tide, the flotsam and jetsam and
the mud banks, it makes you appreciate all the more the
beauty of the non-tidal Nene which you will explore
further on the return to your boatyard.

CHAPTER 9

ON TO THE 'GRAND CIRCLE'

To COMBINE both river and canal on a boating holiday and thus to enjoy the different beauties of both and the varying pleasures which each affords is rather like having your cake and eating it too. Even though, as on our River Nene holiday, you spend but a few days on relatively short sections of the Grand Union Canal, you become vividly aware of the contrasts.

The first holiday on which we felt we had broken out of the rank of beginners was our cruise round the 'Grand Circle' in the brand new narrow cruiser *Aylesbury Golden Eye,* recently re-named the *Flying Mexican.* In twenty-one days we chalked up no less than 367 miles and 235 locks from the canal basin at Aylesbury to the Grand Union at Marsworth, to Napton at the junction of the Oxford Canal, to Oxford on the Thames and thence to Lechlade before returning downstream to Teddington, out on the tideway to Greenwich Pier, into the Regent's Canal Dock, through London to Uxbridge and back along the Grand Union and Aylesbury Arm to the canal basin. We averaged just under 29 lock miles per day over the total 602 lock miles at an average speed of 4·77 miles per hour. Our total cruising time was 126 hours or approximately six hours a day.

Having stowed away our stores, our own gear from home, a 56 lb anchor for use if necessary on the Thames tideway, and checked to see that we had all the appropriate maps and booklets, we left Aylesbury one Saturday afternoon late in July. The Aylesbury Arm is rather shallow and one has to go slowly, which gives a good opportunity to get the feel of the boat. As all locks have to be emptied after locking through and you are locking up on this Arm, it takes about four hours to cover the $6\frac{1}{4}$ miles and sixteen narrow locks to the junction with the Grand Union Canal main line at Marsworth. No chart exists of the Arm, the locks are fairly well spread out and preclude lock-wheeling, and although narrow and shallow the canal is surprisingly weed-free and passes through pleasant farming country for most of its length.

The Arm was so attractive and isolated that we have subsequently walked its towpath from Marsworth to Aylesbury with our dog on a number of occasions in the spring, enjoying a good lunch at the Bell or Bull's Head in the market square.

Passing by a working pair moored at Marsworth we picked up speed in the Grand Union, despite occasionally churning up mud from time to time. We were quite content to moor at Ivinghoe Bridge at 8 p.m. as it was raining hard, having covered ten miles and twenty-one locks.

With bright sunshine next day we were all astir early and underway before 7 p.m., having breakfast while on the move. Everyone was in a gay mood and we negotiated one lock after another to reach the twin towns of Leighton Buzzard and Linslade before 9 a.m.

As my wife and I had frequently joined Dr and Mrs Roger Pilkington both on the *Commodore* and the *Thames Commodore* on Continental waterways, we invited them to join us on this voyage. We arranged to meet 'any time on Sunday on the Grand Union north of Marsworth' and agreed that I would chalk our locking-out time on one of the balance beams. The lock-keeper wondered what it was all about when I wrote '1038' on the balance beam but grinned when I explained. The

Grand Union in this area is very rural. There is a delightful towpath walk between the Globe Inn with its unusual bar on the canal side near Linslade and the inn beside the Three Locks. The villages near the canal are worth exploration as all have some attractive features. From Bridge 106 you can walk half a mile into Stoke Hammond and then four miles through hilly Bedfordshire landscape to the Duke of Bedford's scenic and amusing Woburn Park.

Topping up our water tanks at Fenny Stratford gave us an excuse for a pre-lunch drink at the canal-side Rose and Crown. During the afternoon the heavens suddenly opened and as we locked damply through Cosgrove Lock, I had some difficulty in chalking our time on the wet balance beam. It was pelting so hard as we approached Bridge 57, near Grafton Regis, that we could hardly see our friends who were huddled under the bridge. We found the *Golden Eye* a marvellous craft for entertaining and after a pleasant meal we heard Dr Pilkington's hilarious description of their attempts to find us. He was able to estimate exactly where he could encounter us on the canal but the road system in this area is confusing. However, they had waited only five minutes for us at the bridge. Normally the best way of arranging for guests to join you *en route* is to work out when you will reach a convenient railhead near the waterway on the day agreed and set a tentative meeting place and time. It is usually easy to telephone the day before and confirm existing arrangements. One of the great joys of boating holidays is the mere fact that you do not have to keep to a timetable but can dawdle along as you will. We often get a day or two ahead or behind our planned voyage. Some stretches may be less interesting and we cruise on with few halts, or we may decide to moor for the better part of a day to laze about, or to visit a place nearby.

It was great fun for us all to revisit Stoke Bruerne, and the Waterways Museum never fails to provide new interest and new people to chat to. We had the pleasure of leading a convoy of six craft through Blisworth Tunnel, all of which had waited for a boat to lead them through. Just after passing the Northampton Arm leading to the Nene river, the wash of three working pairs of hurrying narrow boats put us temporarily aground.

You will see the radio masts of Daventry on the horizon as the Grand Union sweeps wide round the town. As you come to the Weedon Beck aqueduct over the Nene, on your left is an enchanting view of what we call the 'church-in-the-hollow' standing well below the canal. There is a farm beyond the aqueduct with fresh eggs for sale. You will find many pleasant moorings from which to explore pretty villages like Everdon, Fawsley, Nether Heyford and others, some immortalised by Gray and Dryden and also those associated with the Washington family.

The seven Buckby locks mark the end of the long sixteen-mile pound from Stoke Bruerne, and Buckby top lock provides splendid overnight moorings. There is a well stocked shop and a useful grocery store beside the New Inn on the canal side. We were amused when the grocer locked his store, walked to a door at the back, stepped into the pub and then, functioning as the publican, opened for business. Here we met a family of boaters, who rarely talk to amateurs, but this family was an exception. They told us that they always started at first light and kept on the move until dark, but despite the meagre living, hard work and long hours, and living in cramped conditions they would not wish to live on land. The Grand Union, they said, is not what it used to be. Now they could only carry 20 tons in the boat and 25 tons in the butty, because the canal was no longer kept dredged to its normal depth as in the old days. Their young daughter, just in her teens, did not approve of the life and wanted a 'proper house' and 'fun'.

The Leicester Arm branches off to the right and the route to Braunston is straight on from Buckby along the two miles of the Braunston Summit on the great divide of the Midlands, rising to over 600 ft. Braunston Tunnel, like Blisworth, has no towpath but it is much shorter, 2,049 yards, and not quite as wet. There is a flight of six locks, descending to Braunston village, a centre of boat-building and decoration for many years. There are watering points at both top and bottom locks, and moorings at the Blue Line boatyard and marina. Full marks must be given to Michael P. Streat, managing director of Blue Line Cruisers, for what he has done not only to develop Braunston boatyard into one of the finest in England, but to popularise pleasure cruising and to maintain commercial carrying on the canals.

After shopping in the village we lunched at the Rose and Castle on the canal side and then took the wooded five-mile reach to Napton Junction. Dozens of traditional narrow boats, gaily painted, are usually moored at Braunston Junction, which marks the southern end of the Northern Section of the Oxford Canal. You are on the Oxford Canal rather than the Grand Union until you reach Napton Junction and the northern end of the southern section of the Oxford Canal. It is unusual to find that such an essential link in a main line canal route is actually part of another canal. This entire reach is a haven of peace and beauty.

At Napton Junction turn left into the southern section of the Oxford Canal, one of the earliest to be built. By 1790 this canal, with the Coventry Canal, linked the Thames with the Trent and Mersey, and for fifteen years saw very heavy traffic. However, in 1805 when the more direct route was opened between Braunston and Brentford via the Grand Junction, which also connected to Napton and Birmingham and the Warwick canals, the southern section below Napton lost the bulk of its traffic and was not improved or straightened like the northern section between Napton and Hawkesbury. Thus the southern section is still the original contour canal planned by the famous James Brindley. It is this which gives it its river-like character and the well-deserved reputation of being one of the loveliest of our English canals. Its entire fifty-mile course from Napton to the Thames is virtually un-spoiled and rural, truly idyllic. Its thirty-eight locks (thirty-nine including the lock in Duke's Cut leading to the Thames) will take craft no larger than 7 ft in beam and 70 ft in length, and because of the many low bridges and lift-bridges will take craft with no more than 7 ft headroom. It is also very narrow and shallow and it is wise to keep dead centre while under way. Even so we went aground twice. We noticed workmen hedging and ditching, thus keeping the towpath clear, but dredging is all too infrequent as a single dredger has to be shared with the Northampton Arm.

Two miles from Napton Junction there is a sharp 90° bend, an attractive bridge, and Napton Bottom Lock, the first of a flight of nine. Although the locks on the Oxford Canal are operated by users, there is a lock-keeper on duty at Napton Bottom Lock, but his major task seems to be issuing warnings about the proper use of the locks. A fortnight before our arrival a working pair had slammed through the flight, twisting two lock gate rails, breaking two paddles and cracking a balance beam. This is all lovely countryside and after passing Napton on the Hill you will see very few dwellings and will hardly believe that throughout its length the canal is within easy reach of so many attractive villages, parks and interesting churches. This is Civil War country, rich in the history of the Cavaliers and Roundheads.

There will inevitably be days when the weather and everything else seems to go wrong, and our next day was dark and overcast, cheered only by a few bursts of sunshine. The water pump failed to switch itself off but a one-notch adjustment put that right. Then the sink became blocked. However, we found that by taking our coil of water hose, inserting it in the sink drain outlet just above the water line and giving a few hearty blows it was cleared. This is a very simple method and most effective. A 60 ft length is not necessary, a yard-long piece being sufficient, and should be taken as useful equipment.

Soon you will cross the Warwickshire-Oxfordshire border where the local brownstone gives villages a Cotswold-like appearance. From Bridge 135 a three-quarter-mile walk will bring you to Wormleighton and into Tudor England, with a lovely manor house, a 700-year-old church, and thatched cottages. This is a delightful hilltop village where stands the great gateway, gatehouse and cottages built for John Spencer in the reign of Henry VIII.

Fenny Compton is a little over a mile beyond the canalside George and Dragon but we found its name more attractive than the village itself. The canal now enters a cutting, still called the 'Tunnel', although the former tunnel was opened out as long ago as 1868 to save its being rebuilt. This is the longest straight stretch on the southern section and very pretty.

We were down the five Clayton Locks in under half an hour and in the next two miles went quickly through Elkington's, Varney's, Broadmoor and Cropredy Locks. There are many pleasant villages near the canal, including ancient Chipping Warden with its Roman remains and a church containing a 'leper squint'. Cropredy must be seen, however, and you can fill up your stores at the pretty village shop, obtain water at the coal yard, and wander through the village to look at the church which commemorates the Civil War battle of 1644 by displaying a collection of relics such as suits of armour and weapons. It also has a fine brass globe and eagle lectern.

The channel from Cropredy to Banbury is extremely shallow and although we eased off to almost crawling speed we went aground just above Bridge 157. However, some energetic poling soon had us off.

We arrived in Banbury by dinner time and found rather miserable moorings. What a pity that the town council filled in the canal basin to make a parking place, for it could have become the most attractive feature of the town. We felt that the once lovely town square had been ruined by modern shop fronts and that the local authorities made a mess of a town long famous for its Cross and its cakes. In 1790 the town blew up its ancient church rather than repair it and replaced it with a sombre substitute. Even the famous Cross was destroyed and the present one dates only from 1858. British Waterways is trying to improve facilities at Banbury by the construction of a marina there, part of the new Amenity Service Division's plans to develop the canals for pleasure in conjunction with private enterprise.

From Banbury the canal continues to be very shallow and we grounded above Grant's Lock. All the locks now have single gates in contrast to those above Banbury which have single top gates and double bottom ones. From Tarver's Lock a footpath leads to pretty Adderbury, a village with a sturdy church and a large medieval tithe barn close by. The Cherwell flows along the canal for miles south of Banbury and the countryside is mostly lovely meadows.

Aynho Weir Lock is an unusual diamond shape. We had

come across this type of lock before on the Lower Avon
Navigation. The width is double that of the narrow boat
lock and is built only where the rise or fall is small. The
object of such a shape is to equate the amount of water
passed with that of the ordinary deeper locks above it.
Aynho Weir Lock has a fall of little more than 8 ins while
Nell Bridge Lock above it falls 8 ft 8 ins and Somerton
Deep Lock below it has a fall of 12 ft, the second deepest
canal lock in this country.

The village of Aynho is most attractive with its typical
Oxfordshire cottages and there is a beautiful view of the
surrounding countryside from the church tower. We ran
into weed beyond Aynho Weir Lock, near Somerton.
This village keeps its church constantly locked and to get
in you have to collect a huge key fastened to a massive
truncheon from the local shop-cum-post-office opposite
the church.

The thirteen miles from Somerton to Bridge 220 hard
by Hampton Gay are the most beautiful along the entire
canal with pleasant pastures and fields which were ripe
with grain. There are delightful villages set back from the
canal with fascinating names such as Steeple Aston, Frit-
well and Duns Tew. At drawbridge 205, the only iron
drawbridge in England, stands Heyford Mill, mentioned
in the Domesday Book. Rebuilt in 1800, it stopped milling
only after the Second World War. Eel-traps can still be
seen here, for it once supplied the local manor with
hundreds of eels. Both Upper and Lower Heyford are
worth visiting for photography and shopping alike.
Rousham House and Park, the gardens laid out by William
Kent, and Blenheim Palace and Park, which needs no
recommendation, are the next features of real merit along
the canal.

Almost immediately after Baker's Lock, the Cherwell
joins the canal for about half a mile and here the water

is deep indeed. All too soon you will come to Shipton Weir Lock, another diamond-shaped one with a fall of little more than 2 ft.

Hampton Gay has a lonely church set in a field of buttercups, lit by candles and containing one of the few real barrel organs in the world. On the final stretch to Oxford, the canal is lovely right up to the British Waterways Juxton Road Wharf, where we reluctantly had to disembark the Pilkingtons who were going off to continue their cruise on *Thames Commodore* on the Moselle.

There are two ways to enter the Thames from the Oxford Canal. The shortest, easiest and prettiest is via Duke's Cut below Bridge 231, which brings you into the river above King's Lock; the other is the more difficult and exciting route via Isis or 'Louse' Lock, and a railway swing bridge below Fiddler's Island. This latter entry is three miles further on, may involve some delay and is little used, but there is a right of navigation which we, as a matter of principle, usually decide to exercise.

The Thames is broad and beautiful as you pass from the railway swing bridge into this once royal river at its downstream junction with the Oxford Canal. To traverse one of the loveliest of England's canals and one of the loveliest of her rivers in one cruise is perhaps the single most delightful aspect of the Grand Circle Tour.

The beauty and charm of the Thames, navigable for over 215 miles from Lechlade to the sea, lies in the eye of the beholder. This truly national river has a claim on the affections of the English everywhere as it has on all visitors and expatriates like myself who inevitably succumb to its lure. The Thames is all things to all men, its appeal is many-sided for it serves the varied interests of artists and writers, antiquarians and historians, naturalists and anglers, boaters and ramblers, swimmers and campers and others involved in specialised sports as well as those who, far from being marine-minded, nevertheless obtain enjoyment from just sitting in their cars along its banks.

We cruised briskly up to Godstow Lock and bought a return lock pass from Godstow to St John's Lock, near Lechlade. Next to the Norfolk Broads, more pleasure craft ply the Thames than any body of water in Britain, and as this was the high season we had decided to spend our weekend on the little used upper reaches. These lie above the ugly steel Osney Bridge, the lowest bridge anywhere on the Thames, with a headway of only 7 ft 7 ins at summer water level, thus precluding many craft from these lovely waters.

There are excellent moorings for the night just above the mellow stone Godstow bridge to port, almost opposite the Trout Inn with its peacocks and its fish leaping for tit-bits in the weir stream, and only a few steps from the ruins of Godstow nunnery. There is no point in casting off until shortly before 9 a.m. in the mornings for the manned locks do not open until then. We greatly enjoyed our run along the twenty-eight miles of rural Thames and ten locks to Lechlade, despite an incessant downpour. We stopped only once—for lunch at one of our favourite pubs, the Rose Revived, just downstream of Newbridge. Above King's Lock the river narrows considerably, is very winding with a number of horseshoe bends, and completely rural with only a few houses and pubs in view from the water. Its beauty is beyond description even through misty fog-like conditions. We had the river almost to ourselves for we passed fewer than half a dozen craft on the move and all under 25 ft. There are good and extensive moorings at Lechlade. Apart from its dominating church spire there is little of interest other than 'Halfpenny Bridge', an attractive stone structure built by an Act of Parliament in 1792, and so-called because of the toll levied here.

Although barges once made their way to Waterhay

Bridge the stream is now navigable only for canoes and skiffs as far as Cricklade. Experts still argue over whether the true source of the Thames is Seven Springs, at the head of the Churn, or the spring at the base of an ash tree in a pleasant meadow some three miles from Cirencester. Be that as it may, the willow-fringed rustic stream that is the Thames above Lechlade is well worth exploring on foot to find charming spots like Ashton Keynes with its host of little bridges.

It was a gloomy Sunday morning when we began our 155-mile cruise down the Thames to Greenwich Pier. Half a mile downstream we came to St John's Lock and Bridge, hard by an old riverside inn, the Trout, whose garden is constantly under attack from the weir stream. Soon we had bright sunshine, giving quite a different look to the pastoral scenes stretching for miles beyond each bank. Fishermen were more numerous than cattle and from the number of fish we saw landed it must have been a most successful day for them too. The next lock, Buscot, is one of the deepest on the river, some 9 ft with a charming Cotswold cottage for a lock house, leased to the Thames Conservancy by the National Trust. The river meanders peacefully along, scarcely 30 ft wide, through winding reaches, continually building up shoals which are more or less marked by floating buoys. Lonely isolated Grafton Lock stands amid flat green fields, the only sign of civilisation being the lock-keeper's house.

After another mile of lovely river on which stands Kelmscot Manor, the home of William Morris, Radcot Bridge appears, spanning two arms of the river. This is actually two bridges, the one over the former main stream built in 1200 being the oldest on the Thames, and the second over the current navigational course built in 1787 to span the newly dug channel. Alongside the newer bridge is the delightfully unspoiled Swan Inn, noted for its fine collection of fish decorating the bars, all caught locally, and for its beautiful garden.

At Radcot Lock, half a mile below the bridges, is the first of the Thames Conservancy Sanitary Stations. Many locks and some boathouses have these facilities, which are largely responsible for the absence of flotsam and jetsam and litter on the non-tidal Thames. The Thames Conservancy which is responsible for over 135 miles of river from Cricklade to Teddington and its catchment area (nearly 2,500 miles of tributaries and subsidiary streams) does an excellent job. The waters within their jurisdiction are beautifully clean. Boaters are not allowed to use flush toilets or even drain washing-up water into the river. While slightly inconvenient this is a splendid measure appreciated by all who live beside the Thames or use it in any way.

Below Radcot Lock the gaunt Old Man's footbridge straddles the stream, marking the site of a former flash weir of the same name. At Rushey Lock there is a splendid garden kept by the lock-keeper. The lock garden competition, with the Sir Reginald Hanson Challenge Cup as the prize, is indeed an inspiration contributing greatly to the natural beauty of the river. You will soon pass Tenfoot Footbridge, which apparently leads to nowhere in particular, and the village of Chimney on the left bank, once called Chimley, which explains why some country folk still mispronounce the word. There are suitable lunch-time moorings in the lovely cut leading to Shifford Lock. Although the lock and cut were built comparatively recently, in 1896, nature has healed all the scars and created worthy scenes to admire. Newbridge, actually one of the oldest, dating back with its name to the thirteenth century, is the next identifiable spot, site of the attractively named The Rose Revived, and boasting a second inn, the Maybush, on the opposite bank. Find a bridge on the

Thames and you will usually find a pub, sometimes two or more. Just above Newbridge the River Windrush adds its waters, and scarcely a mile away is Ridge's footbridge, marking the site of Hart's Weir. In the upper reaches, we are told, footbridges inevitably indicate that weirs once existed on the site.

At the next lock, Northmoor, the weir adjoins the lock and provides a unique opportunity to look at the construction and operation of a weir. A weir is an artificial dam built across the river to maintain its water at a certain minimum height, known as head water level. This is done by means of weir tackle at the top of the dam, regulated according to the flow of water. Some two pretty winding miles beyond Northmoor Lock stands the Chequers Inn and here is the last ferry on the Thames, Bablockhythe Ferry, big enough to transport cars and yet operated by chain, pulled by hand. This chain stretches taut across the river when in use and is lowered to the bed of the river when the ferry is not working.

The scenery now is hilly as the river curves to Eynsham (Swinford) Bridge, with Whitchurch, one of the last two toll bridges remaining on the Thames, and Eynsham Lock. There are excellent moorings here for the Swan Hotel and Talbot Inn and shopping in Eynsham. For a modest fee the Thames Conservancy allows camping on the lock island here and at four other lock sites, Pinkhill, King's, Godstow and Day's Lock. With extensive woodland on your right you will soon reach an island, and the Thames has more lovely islands than any other river in the country. Mooring once again above Godstow Bridge we calculated actual cruising time from Lechlade to be just under seven hours, every moment of it thoroughly enjoyable.

From Godstow Lock, where we bought a lock pass to Teddington, there is a lovely view of the spires of Oxford across Port Meadow, which is seemingly oblivious of time.

This broad reach is a favourite one for sailing and rowing. As you come to the little village of Binsey and the Perch Inn you now follow the main stream to the right of Fiddler's Island, the left branch leading to the main entrance of the Oxford Canal. Beyond the low Osney Bridge there are moorings convenient to the market and the railway station, and from here you can easily explore the many famous sights of Oxford. Between Osney and Folly Bridges the Thames is undoubtedly sordid. Oxford, one of the most interesting and beautiful cities in Britain, should be ashamed of its treatment of the Thames, which is frankly disgraceful.

Once Folly Bridge is passed, the river comes to life again. From the remaining wharf and boathouses it is evident that commercial traffic once heavily plied the Thames. Salter Brothers boatyard and offices are here and have run a seasonal river steamer service between Oxford and Kingston since 1888. The new university boat houses are splendid and the river looks lovelier than ever as you cruise on past Christ Church Meadow, the entrance of the Cherwell river, and past the remaining college barges to Iffley Lock.

Hire cruiser yards now appear on every reach. After Sandford Lock, the deepest on the river with its paper mill and nearby King's Arms Hotel, you will come once again into open country. You can ease off as you pass Nuneham Park to watch the deer. There are pleasant moorings between two willows on the right bank above Abingdon Bridge, hard by the municipal swimming pools and the remains of Abingdon Abbey. The delicate spire of St Helen's Church and the surrounding almshouses are beautiful and you will find Abingdon well worth the hours you spend there. The Crown and Thistle, dating back to 1605, is an enchanting creeper-covered hotel with a delightful courtyard in which to enjoy a tankard.

A little further downstream the River Ock joins the Thames very near the one-time entrance to the derelict Wilts & Berks canal, which once passed by Wantage, Swindon and Calne to join the Kennet & Avon some twelve miles east of Bradford. The short Culham reach soon branches left into the long and narrow Culham Cut leading to the lock, while the weir stream, well worth visiting, flows along to the pretty village of Sutton Courtenay to fall over a series of modernised weirs into beautiful Sutton Pools. At Clifton there is a similar long lock cut and the reaches become increasingly lovely. Beyond Clifton Lock, a red brick bridge, once a toll bridge for the old toll house which can still be seen on the right, leads to Clifton Hampden and the Plough Inn on the left, and to the half-timbered, thatched-roof Barley Mow Inn of *Three Men in a Boat* fame.

There are now open meadows and woodlands as you pass Burcot. The wide sweep of the river as it approaches Day's Lock make the Sinodun Hills, or Wittenham Clumps as they are called locally, look as if they are on the move. From Day's Lock there is a pleasant mile-long track skirting the ancient Dyke Hills to Dorchester, a delightful town with an Abbey church as interesting as its coaching inns. The lovely reach between Benson's and Cleeve locks is the longest on the Thames, some $6\frac{1}{2}$ miles, and then the first really attractive Thames-side houses appear on the short half-mile reach between Cleeve and Goring, one of our favourite stretches of river with lovely wooded islands. Goring and Streatley are twin villages, joined by a bridge, with the attractive Swan Inn on one side and the historic Miller of Mansfield on the other. The Lower Hartslock woods are decidedly impressive on their hilly site and Whitchurch Lock is very pretty indeed, looking much as it did in etchings in books published over a century ago. The second toll bridge on the Thames just below the lock

links Whitchurch and Pangbourne, the former peaceful
and picturesque, the latter bustlingly commercial. The
little islands in the next 2½ miles long reach are clearly
popular with campers. Mapledurham Lock, the first to be
mechanised on the upper reaches, is electrically operated
and we were through in less than three minutes, compared with an average of eight minutes for the locks upstream. Historic Mapledurham House, the mill and a
church used for both Protestant and Roman Catholic
services, are the highlights of the area. After more pleasant
riverside houses and gardens, industrial Reading rears its
ugly head, as if to vie with Oxford.

However, the beauty of Sonning makes you quickly
forget Reading and the lock garden backed by trees is
enchanting. Sonning is almost invisible from the river
and a charming port of call. The path to the Bull Hotel
leads through a churchyard, the best kept we have seen
anywhere, and the church itself has a lovely carved
wooden entrance porch. The reach to Shiplake is like an
oasis of peace with views of pleasant fields and gentle hills.
Near Shiplake a series of wooded islands adds to the charm.
This lock works hydraulically, a system which is proving
superior to electricity. Moorings can be found at the
George and Dragon at Wargrave, whose inn sign is surprisingly the work of two Royal Academicians.

Another chain of attractive eyots lies in the reach to
pretty Marsh Lock, and it is only a fifteen-minute run to
Henley on a wide reach dotted with more islands. There
are good Council moorings above the five-arched Henley
Bridge with its two sculptured heads of Isis and Father
Thames and also at the Angel Hotel which, with the
church tower, dominates the left bank by the bridge. The
town's long main street is almost as attractive as the river
here and useful for shopping.

The famous Henley Regatta course, dead straight for

a mile and a half between Phyllis Court and Temple Island, was deserted except for Canadian geese as we cruised by in the early morning. After a very sharp right hand bend we were at lovely Hambleden Lock with its beautiful weir stretching back to the white mill in a wonderful play of falling water. The 3½ mile reach to Hurley Lock is also one of our favourites, beautifully wooded, dotted with islands with overhanging trees and crowned by the picturesque Medmenham Abbey. What an ideal spot Sir Francis Dashwood and his Hell Fire Club chose for their orgies. There is a glimpse of chalk cliffs before the entrance to Hurley Lock cut and another typical Thames view unchanged in over a century. Here half a dozen islands provide peaceful moorings from which to visit the famous Olde Belle.

Twenty minutes more of blissful cruising brings you to Marlow with its recently rebuilt suspension bridge. This bridge with the tall spire of Marlow's church on one side and the Compleat Angler and vast curving weir on the other, makes Marlow one of the most delightful spots on the Thames. Just above the bridge is Meakes Boatyard and chandlery, one of the best in the country. There are now a succession of delightful reaches and locks, Marlow, Cookham, Boulters, Bray, Boveney, Romney and Old Windsor, to good overnight moorings at the Bells of Ouzeley. Cliveden reach, between Cookham and Boulter's locks, is the loveliest of them all.

We felt inclined to carry on and did so, feeling that this is one of the nice things about a boating holiday. We by-passed Maidenhead which we have never found particularly interesting, and even Windsor, which we decided to reserve for a return visit next morning. Windsor has unfortunately become a 'tourist trap' with only the castle and park attractive. There were far too many shoddy souvenir shops for our liking.

Beyond the Bells of Ouzeley, whose original bells were thrown into the river at the Dissolution and eventually replaced with bells of Bristol glass now on view in the bar, is Magna Carta island and Runnymede with its hill-top R.A.F. memorial and, at the foot of Cooper's Hill, the American memorial to the signing of the Magna Carta and the British Memorial to President Kennedy. Factories straddle the riverside through Staines, but just before Rennie's bridge, on the left bank in a recreation ground a few yards from the river, stands the famous London Stone, surrounded by railings, and marking what was once the upstream limit of jurisdiction of the City of London before the Thames Conservators took over in 1857. This most historic stone bears a worn inscription— 'God preserve the City of London A.D. 1280.' It functions today as a mark for the upstream limit of free fishing. From Staines into London the river becomes rather heavily populated with houses and bungalows in almost every conceivable type of architecture. Penton Hook Yacht Basin on the right bank is without doubt one of the finest and best equipped inland harbours in Britain. Over 500 craft can be moored in its eighty acres of sheltered water connected to the river by a deep channel. Good use is made of the islands on the pleasant reach to Shepperton Lock for there are communities of bungalows and weekend cottages here, all tidily kept and clearly enjoyed. This lock and the entrance to the pretty little River Wey below it delights the eye and makes an ideal overnight mooring.

The river now is not as scenic or appealing as the upper reaches but there are some rather charming spots, such as Sunbury, and also Hampton Court. The run through Kingston brings civilisation but in contrast a regatta was under way as we approached Teddington Lock, the end of the non-tidal Thames and snug overnight moorings.

CHAPTER 10

LONDON'S WATERWAYS

TEDDINGTON LOCK is something of a misnomer for there
are actually three locks—a large barge lock, 650 ft x 24 ft
9 ins, a launch lock, 177 ft 11 ins x 24 ft 4 ins and
similar in size to the upriver locks, and a 'coffin' lock,
49 ft 6 ins x 5 ft 10 ins for small craft.

Teddington marks the limit of the tidal waters of the
Thames. Above the locks the river is placid and quiet,
while below the locks tides are as relentless as time and it
is evident that anyone who ventures on to a tideway in
a small boat must have his wits about him.

Hire firms will normally allow amateurs to take hire
craft through Teddington Lock for some four miles to
Brentford, opposite Kew Palace, where locks lead into the
Grand Union Canal. The use of the lock at Brentford
Dock is regulated by the state of the tide and you should
consult the lock-keeper at Teddington or the British
Waterways Board at Brentford (01 560 8941) to ensure
that you arrive at this lock at the right state of the tide.
High water here is one hour later than at London Bridge
and the locks operate a few hours before and after high
water.

If you buy Stanford's Chart of the Lower Thames
and follow the course duly marked on it carefully, you
should have no difficulty with this stretch of the tideway.
On your first experience of a tideway, never attempt to
moor. A wall which looks perfect for mooring when
you see it at high water may have 20 ft less water beside

it when the tide goes out. Always give a wide berth to
other craft on the move or at anchor as well as to bridge
arches, for you can be sucked against them if you go too
close. A good rule for beginners on a tideway is to keep
six feet away from everything except when entering or
leaving a lock.

Passing through Brentford Lock, the Grand Union
will take you through eleven more locks, including the
Hanwell flight for six miles to the Bulls Bridge junction
with the Paddington Arm which in turn gives access to
the Regent's Canal. This is the simplest and easiest way
to explore London's own canal from the Thames. We had
special permission to take the *Golden Eye* through the
heart of London and into the Regent's Canal from its
other end at Regent's Canal Dock, some eighteen miles
downstream of Teddington. We can strongly recommend
this itinerary to any enthusiast with sufficient practical
experience.

However, there are complications in using this route.
The distance between Teddington and Brentford is so
short that you can leave Teddington on the tide and have
ample time to get into Thames Lock No. 101 before it
closes. Even if you have to cruise the four miles against
the tide it is no problem. But as Regent's Canal Dock is
much further than this and high water is over an hour
earlier than at Teddington, it is impossible for a slow-
moving small craft to catch the tide and arrive at the
Dock in time to use the tidal lock there. In order to arrive
when the lock is in operation means bucking the tide and
making a much slower journey with greater fuel consumption.

To benefit from the tide involves arranging overnight
moorings at Greenwich Pier (which are very bumpy) and
passing through both Regent's Dock Lock and Regent's

Canal next morning; intricate calculations are necessary to make sure timings are accurate.

On the Brentford route the best time to leave Teddington is shortly after high water there, which will enable you to by-pass the half-tidal Richmond Lock, used only between half-ebb and full flood. Soon after the water reaches the half-tide mark patent sluices stretching across the river beside the lock are drawn and boats can pass freely until about two hours after high water. The tide will increase your speed by two to three knots and you will be exhilarated by the surge before you pass the obelisk on the Surrey shore, 300 yards below Teddington Lock, which marks the beginning of the jurisdiction of the Port of London Authority, stretching ninety miles to the sea. Here, 136 miles from the source of the Thames, the Port of London somewhat surprisingly encroaches. We had always assumed it began at London Docks, near Tower Bridge, the furthest upstream of the five great dock systems owned by the P.L.A. But this body controls the whole of the tidal reaches, handles all matters relating to navigation on the tideway, the licensing of wharves and structures extending into the river below high water mark, and the maintenance of the broad approach channel from the estuary into the heart of the port.

It is Britain's premier port and one of the busiest in the world with something like 100 million tons of shipping passing through annually, with cargoes totalling upwards of 60 million tons. Apart from the five great dock systems on both sides of the river, there are many hundreds of privately owned wharves and factories, power stations, gas works, oil depots, sugar refineries, cold stores, granaries, barge building yards, dry-docking facilities and so on, which play an important part in the trade of the port. It is constantly changing, indeed facilities are moving closer and closer to the sea, as the use of large containers and other modern developments alter the pattern and nature of water transport. However, in spite of modernisation, the river banks through London remain overcrowded with history.

The water is dirty and brown as compared with the upper reaches and vast quantities of debris drift along at the whim of the tide. Evasive action must frequently be taken to avoid damage to propellers. But the river has a stark beauty of its own. You will notice that the Surrey shore is still pleasantly rural while attractive gardens and houses can be seen on the left bank. Past Eel Pie Island, once famous for its eel pies, you will see yacht clubs, cruiser clubs and boatyards as you approach Richmond Bridge and the open sluices under the narrow footbridge. Past Isleworth Eyot you may get waves from cheerful crowds taking the sun by the old London Apprentice, one of London's most charming riverside pubs. Syon Reach is as beautiful as any upstream with the gardens of Kew stretching almost to Kew Bridge, while on the left Syon House still stands majestically in its park, followed all too quickly by the Brentford entrance to the Grand Union Canal. Turning left here brings you to new locks which were mechanised and enlarged in 1962 to take barges of up to 175 tons. It is wise to keep an eye open for commercial traffic and the lock-keeper will tell you what to do.

The Thames down river of this point is a tremendous thrill which you can look forward to seeing another time. Every reach and bend provides a unique glimpse of what London once was and what it is today. The blending of old and new along the river is by no means incongruous and provides an unusual history lesson. We were surprised to find that London's bridges varied so much, being built of stone, iron, steel or concrete, some with only three arches and others with seven, some ornate and colourful and others plain, and with clearances at high water ranging from 14 ft 3 ins at Hammersmith to 140 ft 9 ins at Tower Bridge with the bascules up.

Towering concrete and glass skyscrapers vie with the Gothic Houses of Parliament and ancient Lambeth Palace; pleasure gardens compete with power plants; modern Festival Hall and the South Bank contrast strangely with ageing warehouses beyond Blackfriars. Cleopatra's Needle, St Paul's, the Tower of London and Tower Bridge stand out in all their splendour from the river while picturesque Wapping Old Stairs, the Angel and the Prospect of Whitby can really be appreciated only from the water. And then there is the clutter of shipping of all kinds from all parts of the world, dashing trip boats and ferries, fast-moving P.L.A. and police launches along with tooting tugs towing nests of lighters. Dockland with its batteries of cranes is nothing short of spectacular, an education in itself. From Teddington to the dry-docked *Cutty Sark* at Greenwich Pier took us just $3\frac{1}{2}$ hours at one-third throttle, an afternoon one can never forget.

The Thames was as busy as Hyde Park Corner at rush hour with scores of tugs and lighters on the move, huge freighters and even a Wilson Line ocean-going vessel when we left Greenwich Pier as *Gipsy Moth IV* arrived that August Monday. We bobbed about like a tiny cork in the cross wash over the two-mile run and after twenty exciting minutes we swung to starboard up to Regent's Canal Dock and heaved lines over our heads to the bollards on the quayside. The dockmaster, Mr McLean, gave us priority treatment and we locked through with a timber barge in under fifteen minutes. Few people are aware of the huge basin inside the locks which will take craft up to 300 ft in length, 45 ft beam and 16 ft draught. From the basin there was, until recently, a regular service of ships to and from the Continent.

We had to wait for about fifteen minutes while two workmen pushed and shoved half a dozen timber barges out of the way so that we could lock into the Regent's Canal. The lock-keeper quickly ushered us through and as we thanked him a colleague set out along the towpath on a miniature tractor to prepare the next locks for us. This was a most unusual and unexpected service, performed most cheerfully. Beyond the first four locks, on the starboard side, is one of the shortest canals in the world, the Hertford Union, only 1½ miles long. Also known as Duckett's Canal, after a previous owner, it was completed in 1830 to link the Lee Navigation and the Regent's Canal, which technically is an arm of the Grand Union. Duckett's Canal has three locks and for most of its length borders on Victoria Park, one of the East End's largest public parks. It is inevitably filled with timber barges. For this reason we had chosen the Regent's Dock entrance instead of the adjacent Limehouse Cut or Bow Creek entrance, 2½ miles downstream. Today Limehouse Cut is abandoned but a new arm leads from Regent's Dock basin into the Lee Navigation.

The East End and City sections of the Regent's Canal are like something out of another age, comparable to entering a familiar home through an untidy and unfamiliar back door. It has to be seen to be believed for even Londoners are largely unaware of its existence. After City Road Basin comes Islington tunnel, which passes under the Angel at Islington. This is a narrow tunnel without a towpath, just 960 yards long, and the first of four on the run to Braunston from the Thames. Just beyond St Pancras Lock—and how different this part of London looks from the water—is British Waterways' St Pancras Yacht Basin, on the port side and skirting the marshalling yards. Once used for unloading coal it was allowed to become derelict and then wisely, in 1958, was reconstructed as a permanent harbour for pleasure craft.

Kentish Town and Hawley Locks follow, both original examples of the double locks on this canal. The narrow boat *Jenny Wren*, which takes both adults and school children on educational cruises, is moored below Chalk Farm Road bridge. At Hampstead Lock, the last on the canal, the original lock-keeper's house still stands in proud and arrogant neglect. Beyond it a green cast-iron tow-horse bridge swinging diagonally across the canal is yet another tribute to the elegance of canal architecture. Then at a sharp right turn under a bridge lies Cumberland Basin, near the Regent's Park Zoo. The manager of the Barque and Bite, an excellent floating restaurant permanently moored in the basin, was most helpful in hauling on ropes to enable us to berth in the space normally used by a 15 ft launch.

That night we had a party with some seventeen friends joining us for cocktails aboard the *Golden Eye* in the basin. As the party warmed up everyone insisted on a short cruise, so we had a hilarious three-mile run past the Zoo to Little Venice and back during which we passed the famous *Jason* and the Zoo waterbuses, and explained to our guests why the iron bridge at North Gate, Regent's Park, is called 'Blow-up Bridge'. Fifty-four years after the canal was completed in 1820, a boat laden with gunpowder blew up under the bridge. The tree at the south-east corner of the bridge still bears the marks of the explosion. The original bridge, together with the boat and boatmen, was destroyed by the explosion, but the iron stanchions were salvaged and used again, and were erected back to front. Towline marks are still visible on the 'wrong' sides of the stanchions. Since 1874 boatmen have always called this 'Blow-up Bridge'.

The Regent's Canal is only a little over eight miles long and it is the last mile to Little Venice that is the most attractive, taking you through the Zoo and under Maida Hill tunnel, unexpectedly topped by houses. The canal in its present state is hardly a holiday venue but in recent years a number of voluntary bodies, local authorities and groups of enthusiasts have been campaigning for a 'face-lift' for the Regent's Canal and the Paddington Arm. More recently still, the London Chamber of Commerce, in its official journal, added its influential voice to the demand for urgent action to improve these waterways, insisting that London could have stretches of canal as beautiful as those in Amsterdam if only more attention was paid to them. Westminster City Council and the G.L.C. have taken some steps to improve some areas of the canal but there is tremendous scope for further action. A Thames barrage to exclude the tide and danger from flooding has now been suggested and this would transform the Thames through London. Welcome as piecemeal improvements are, it is, however, high time that London began seriously to consider the needs that increasing leisure will demand. Our London waterways taken together offer most promising and rewarding prospects for meeting at least a part of these needs.

Swinging hard to starboard at Little Venice you enter the Paddington Arm of the Grand Union, 13¾ miles long without a single lock to Bulls Bridge, where it joins the main line of the Grand Union Canal. This stretch is dingy, dirty, and bordered by slum housing, coal and timber yards, rubbish dumps and run-down factories relieved only by Sudbury Golf Course and the odd pub like the Black Horse at Old Field Lane Bridge.

There is a completely different atmosphere after you pass under a humped towpath bridge and turn sharp to starboard at Bulls Bridge into the Grand Union main line. From Denham Lock it is well worth visiting the delightful old-world village here, with its fine fourteenth-century church, pleasant inn and lovely houses. The canal side becomes attractive once more and along these pounds you will come across names like Benbow Way and Black Jack's Lock, inexplicable links with the sea. Black Jack's is pretty but the next lock, Copper Mill, is lovelier still for here the River Colne makes one of its junctions with the canal.

Through a weedy section of canal to Rickmansworth, and then comes Cassiobury Park. Here Watford maintains some 900 acres of enchanting parkland. The park was once the home of the Earls of Essex and has long been a beauty spot on the banks of the River Gade, which flows alongside the canal. There are children's playgrounds, a paddling pool and miniature railway in the park and in fine weather this is a superb place for a picnic. The Gade flows into or alongside the canal all the way to Hemel Hempstead and there seems to be a glut of weirs. The locks become more numerous as they form a long flight of steps carrying the canal over the Chiltern Hills. The Fishery Inn at Bridge 149 near Boxmoor is a good place to stop for a 'bargee sandwich', a triple decker filled with bacon, egg, cheese, tomato, lettuce, mayonnaise and pickle. This inn combines beauty with good service and reasonable prices.

The canal then goes through pleasant countryside to the swing bridge hard by the Three Horseshoes, and then the pounds become shorter and shorter as the ascent through the Chilterns grows steeper. There are in fact eighteen locks in under seven miles but the hard work has its compensation in the beauty of the wooded rolling countryside, and pleasant moorings at the Cowroast at Lock 46. From here it is only a five-minute bus ride to Tring for shopping and sightseeing. The Rothschild collection of crustacea, reptiles, fish, moths, butterflies and rare insects at Tring is one of the finest in the world and is open to the public. There are interesting medieval earthworks at Berkhamstead near the castle, as well as ancient inns and homes dating from the fifteenth century. At Northchurch, a mile from Berkhamstead and connected to the town by the ancient and mysterious rampart known as Grims Dyke, is one of the oldest and most delightful churches in the world, dating from Saxon times. A walk into the countryside from here will give you splendid views of the Chilterns.

This is one of the three summit levels, some 400 ft above the level at Brentford. There are now very pretty tree-shaded stretches and within an hour you will reach the disused Wendover Arm and the Marsworth Seven, the last of the locks before the junction with the Aylesbury Arm. The Marsworth Seven is a place for bird watchers for all along on the left are reservoirs populated by many rare species. From here Ivinghoe Beacon can be visited where you will find some of the most beautiful views in the country.

Next morning we reached the *Golden Eye*'s base at Aylesbury and the crew all agreed that the 367 miles and 235 locks of the 'Grand Circle' had been a wonderful experience.

CHAPTER 11

LOOPING THE MIDLANDS LOOP

THE COTSWOLD glass swing door between the dining room and kitchen of our new home in Highgate has on the dining room side a huge wooden handle into which has been carefully embedded and covered with plexiglass an irregularly rectangular piece of slate about 12 ins x 3½ ins. It is one of the most unusual door handles in the world, for this particular piece of slate was picked up high in the Welsh hills near the magnificent Pontcysyllte Aqueduct on the Llangollen Canal about dawn one morning a few years ago by Dr Roger Pilkington in the course of a pre-breakfast walk. On this piece of slate he inscribed:

> MS Aylesbury Golden Eye
> Captain—Fred Doerflinger
> July—August 1967
>
> Market Harboro'
> Anderton
> Ellesmere Port
> Pontcysyllte
> Autherley
> Leicester
> Market Harboro'
>   RP

This slate briefly outlines a wonderful 700-lock-mile holiday cruise which we refer to as looping the Midlands loop of waterways. Your inland waterways map will show you that this journey forms a massive irregular figure '8' over the Midlands on to which is added the wide sweeping curve of the Llangollen Canal probing into Wales. It embraces eight canals and three river navigations in no less than ten counties and covers 428½ miles of waterway with 268 locks, the only waterways lift in the country, as well as the most spectacular aqueducts and tunnels anywhere in the world. The enthusiast could happily plan three to four separate holidays over this journey, yet the full itinerary is a realistic target with three weeks to a month to spend on it. Our total cruising time was 176 hours and 51 minutes and we averaged 3·93 lock miles per hour for a normal cruising day of 8 hours and 25 minutes.

As we did not want to repeat the familiar Grand Union run from Aylesbury to Braunston, we arranged to board the *Golden Eye* at the basin boatyard at Market Harborough instead of its then home port of Aylesbury Basin. The pretty little town of Market Harborough lies at the end of a completely rural 5½-mile long canal arm with no locks. At first the tortuously winding arm is shallow and a bit weedy but it widens after Bridge 13 and you can cruise at normal speed past glowing fields of grain and along quiet wooded stretches of waterway.

There is pleasant mooring above Bridge 3 at Foxton for a visit to the village where John of Gaunt was once lord of the manor. A hillside church commands a view of cottages and orchards but the village has only one claim to fame, the nearby Foxton Flight, one of the outstanding engineering triumphs of the nineteenth century. We moored for the night in the large basin below Foxton Bottom Lock as we wanted to pass through the flight of ten locks, which has a rise of 75 ft, in daylight. Built on the Brindley pattern, arranged in two staircase formations, and numbered 8-17, each 7 ft wide lock has its own side pond and there is a meeting pond between locks 12 and 13 which allows craft to pass each other. It normally takes about ninety minutes to lock up, but if the lock-keeper helps, you can, as we did, navigate the flight in under the hour. This is admittedly tiring and because of this in 1900 an ingenious lift was constructed alongside the locks on an inclined plane to reduce passage time to only twenty minutes. This inclined plane was 300 ft long with a rise of 75 ft, having twin tanks or caissons running on rails. The two tanks, connected by a wire rope, each taking two narrow boats or a barge, ran sideways on eight sets of wheels carried on four pairs of rails. It cost just under £40,000 with the land and was of the counter-balanced type, using a steam-driven winch to overcome friction. Opened for traffic in July 1900, it was sound enough in principle but was built before its time in the sense that only steam power was then available to operate the winch. This meant keeping steam up on the boiler continuously, and with commercial traffic falling off, this soon proved uneconomic. By November 1908 it was decided to reinstate the locks, originally built in 1812, to pass traffic at night when the inclined plane was not working. Two years later it ceased operation and all traffic has since used the locks. The machinery of the inclined plane was allowed to rust away until 1926 when it was dismantled and sold in 1928 for only £250. Nature was then allowed to reclaim the site and today you would never dream that one of the wonders of the canal system ever stood here. The Foxton Flight is as attractive a sight today as can be found on canals anywhere. The view from the top is one that you will never forget.

Once up the flight you are on the summit pound 412 ft above sea level. The Leicester section of the Grand Union Canal looks down on valleys dotted with farm houses, barns and grazing cattle in meadows between rolling hills. There is a wealth of bird life from hawks to warblers and finches. The reed-lined canal is rather weedy but there is ample water to maintain normal cruising speed. It takes a wide and gentle sweep around the hills, giving view after view, all unspoilt, for no villages lie on the canal at all, although many are within easy walking distance.

It is two hours' cruising with panoramic views all the way before you reach the 1,166 yard long Husband's Bosworth tunnel. Although completed in 1813 it has not a single drip to dampen your quarter of an hour passage through. The nearby village has both religion and witch-craft to commend it to history. It is the birthplace of Henry 'Silver-tongued' Smith, that most eloquent of Elizabethan preachers, and the home of John Duport, a local rector who was one of the makers of the Authorised Version of the Bible. At the same time the village is notorious for one of the cruellest and most tragic stories of witchcraft in English history. One morning in 1616 nine women were executed as witches because some poor boy had a series of epileptic fits. Six more women were convicted of being 'hostages to Satan' and provoking these fits, sentenced to death, but later fortunately reprieved.

Between Husband's Bosworth and the 1,528 yard long Crick Tunnel is another beautiful stretch as you pass the derelict Welford Arm and along an aqueduct over the River Avon. There are hours of peaceful chugging along, each bend bringing yet more delightful views. The first few hundred yards of Crick Tunnel leak very badly, and it has always been a problem. When the engineer, Benjamin Bevan, completed the Foxton Flight he found that the line of his proposed tunnel at Crick went through unfavourable strata including quicksand. A new line had to be adopted and the present tunnel was built at an extra cost of over £7,000.

Crick village and the Red Lion are within easy walking distance. This was the home for the last fourteen years of his life of George Smith of Coalville, a brickworker, born in poverty at Clayhills in Staffordshire in 1831. Smith did more for canal folk than any man in history. After little more than a year's schooling he was put in the brick-fields, working thirteen to fifteen hours a day for a meagre wage of 6d. His biographer, Edwin Hodder, describes his youth and early manhood as 'commonplace'. He married twice, had two sons, managed several small brickyards and made the first blue bricks and sanitary ware in his part of the country. This would have been George Smith's story had he not begun the series of one-man crusades to help under-privileged children. In 1868 he wrote his first letter to the newspapers about the plight of brickyard children. He kept up a constant bombardment of letters to the press and by 1871 had published *Cry of the Children from the Brickyards of England*. This forced Parliament to pass regulations concerning the employment of children in the nation's brickyards. He then turned his attention to the plight of gypsies and again got the government to take remedial action.

Smith's movement to aid the canal population began with a letter to the London and provincial press in October 1873. By this time he knew how to whip up public opinion and waged a nation-wide 'Letters to the Editor' campaign which he adroitly followed up by lobbying Members of Parliament and ministers. He alone was responsible for the Canal Boats Act of 1877 regulating boat-life and securing some education for the waterways children. In his fascinating book *Our Canal Population* he ruthlessly exposed the dreadful plight of canal folk, emphasising that in the 1870s over 100,000 men, women and children lived and worked on the 4,170 miles of river and canal network in a state of wretchedness, misery, immorality and cruelty. There were some 22,400 men, some working in threes and operating the fast non-stop 'flyboats', others who were traditional boatmen, and still others known as 'Rodneys' or 'loafers', that is helpers. There were over 22,000 women, of whom 13,000 were living with but were not married to the men whose life they shared on the waterways. Of the 72,000 canal children, some 40,000 were illegitimate and fewer than 2,000 went to school. Smith's figures may not have been completely accurate but they certainly represented the most intelligent estimate made at the time. None of these canal families had homes on land. The average family of four or five, and often as many as twelve, shared a narrow boat cabin only 6 ft x 7 ft 6 ins x 4 ft 6 ins or some 202 cubic feet in size. The cabins were 'damp, hot, stuffy, buggy, filthy and stinking holes', according to Smith, who walked and went on the boats on many stretches of canals in his investigations. One canal woman told him she had not slept on land for twenty years, another was quoted as admitting to giving birth to twenty-one children in the same cabin.

At that time a 70 ft narrow or 'monkey' boat cost between £100 and £130, could carry 30 tons and could be expected to last about twenty years. The average speed for these horse-drawn craft was a mere 2 miles per hour, and there were some 25,000 on the waterways network. Wages were low. The men earned between sixteen and twenty shillings per week and with his entire family hard at work they might get as much as twenty-three to twenty-four shillings. Over 95 per cent of the boatmen could not read or write, some 90 per cent could be classed as drunk-ards, and less than 2 per cent were members of a Christian church. In short, boatmen and their families lived and behaved almost like animals until Smith, a

pioneer of social welfare, succeeded in getting legislation
to improve their miserable and unhappy lot.

It is only a mile from Crick Tunnel to the graceful
Watford Flight. Here, within sight of the M1, are seven
narrow locks in under half a mile with a total fall of 52 ft
6 ins. Like those of the Foxton Flight they have side ponds.
Numbers 7, 2 and 1 are the usual type of locks with
individual top and bottom gates. Numbers 3 to 6 are
staircase locks which, it should be pointed out, share gates
so that the top gate of one lock is the bottom gate of the
lock above.

After leaving the long and lovely twenty-mile pound
between Foxton and Watford Flights, one of the highest
stretches of navigable waterway in Britain, you will be
360 ft above sea level for the final two-mile run to the
swing bridge at Norton Junction and the deeper water of
the Grand Union main line.

It is less than half an hour's cruise along the
Northamptonshire heights to the 2,042 yard, bat-
occupied Braunston Tunnel, another difficult feat of
engineering for the canal builders. Quicksand caused
delays and extra expenditure here too, added to which a
contractor made a miscalculation in direction so that the
tunnel, which was opened in June 1796, has a slight S
bend in it. I never travel through Braunston Tunnel without recalling 'Ben the Legger'. He was discovered by
George Smith in 1880, at which time Ben was in his
seventies. Smith reported that Ben had been legging boats
through the tunnel for over fifty years. 'He legged—lay
on his back upon a narrow board about 12 in wide and 3 ft
long, overhanging the side of the deck, called a "wing",
and worked a boat along with his feet between 50,000
and 60,000 miles, or twice round the world, through this
watery and ghastly cavern of black midnight darkness',
is how Smith succinctly summed up Ben's career.

It is six locks to Braunston Junction, the Blue Line Marina and the Rose and Castle. Here you turn right into the Northern Arm of the Oxford Canal and an important chapter of canal history. It took over twenty-five years to create the vast network of canals linking the major rivers of the country, of which the Oxford Canal is an integral part, and that great canal engineer, James Brindley, master-minded most of them, laying out no less than 523 miles of waterway.

But built over such a long period of time by different companies, employing different engineers, frequently hampered by lack of funds, subjected to alterations in line as still more canals mushroomed in the wake of changing trade patterns, the canals of the 'cross' were not uniform in gauge and some canals even varied in architecture from section to section.

As you cruise along the Northern Arm of the Oxford you will find it quite different from the idyllic, narrow and twisting Southern Arm. The canal is much wider and straighter for between 1829 and 1834 the contour route was shortened by $12\frac{1}{2}$ miles at a cost of nearly £200,000, while the declining Southern Arm which carried less traffic was left virtually untouched.

It is little more than twenty-two miles from Braunston to Hawkesbury Junction and the end of the Oxford Canal, but the landscape consists of hills and rolling fields and a few farm houses. Most villages, like feudal Barby, are well over a mile from the waterway. The first six miles to Hillmorton Locks crosses and recrosses the Warwickshire-Northamptonshire county boundary. There are three pairs of locks at Hillmorton for they were duplicated in 1840 in order to speed up traffic. You can moor at Bridge 59 for Rugby, three-quarters of a mile to the left. Rugby is a pleasant town for sightseeing and shopping and is, of

LOOPING THE MIDLANDS LOOP

course, the home of the famous school founded by a grocer,
Lawrence Sheriff.

Less than half a mile further on you will find pleasant
moorings for Newbold on Avon, which stands on a hill
between the canal and the looping River Avon. There
is excellent shopping here and on the hill above the river
you will see beautiful cottages, many of them centuries old,
farms and a fifteenth-century church with very lovely
porches. Near the church can be found the old tunnel
through which the canal originally ran.

Newbold Tunnel beyond Bridge 50 is only 205 yards
long, is bone dry and rather unusual in that it has two
towpaths. There is a swing gate across the canal at the
Maid Line Cruiser headquarters at Brinklow and a watering point. The manager of the yard advised against using
the Coventry Arm which runs for 5½ miles from Hawkesbury Junction to Bishop Street, only a few minutes' walk
from the new cathedral and shopping centre. The short
arm is virtually lined along its entire length with industrial
eyesores and is frequently used as a dumping ground for
everything from old prams to parts of car bodies. To visit
Coventry you can take a bus from Binley, not far along
the canal from Brinklow.

There is now fairly flat country to Hawkesbury Junction
along rather fine cuttings and embankments on the four-
teen-mile pound from Hillmorton Locks. Near the junction
you come into the sprawling outskirts of Coventry and
the junction itself is rather dirty and neglected. After
Lock No. 1, open at both ends, there is a 90° turn hard
to starboard under a statuesque cast-iron towpath bridge,
and once again a sharp 90° turn again to starboard—a
virtual doubling back on your course—and you are in the
Coventry Canal. This is not a canal on which to linger
and because of the state of the navigation some hire firms
no longer allow holidaymakers to take their craft on it.

There is little scenery to speak of and few interesting places at which to stop, but we found it both frustrating and fascinating. Immediately after Hawkesbury you pass the collieries of Bedworth and Nuneaton, and after about two miles you will reach Marston Junction. Here on the right is one of the loveliest little canals in the country, the Ashby-de-la-Zouche Canal. Although there is a stop lock beyond the bridge at the entrance, the canal has no other locks, and is the only lockless canal in Britain. It was completed in 1805 and was originally some thirty miles long, intended for carrying coal from the Leicestershire coalfields at Ashby-de-la-Zouche and Moira to the canal network. Severe mining subsidence long ago forced the draining of the last seven miles and it is now navigable only as far as Ilott wharf, some twenty-three miles from the Coventry Canal. The canal-side scenery is exquisite along almost its entire length and you can spend a pleasant day or two on a side-trip along the Ashby Canal. About a mile beyond the entrance is the opening to the Griff Arm, a private canal built in 1787 by Sir Roger Newdigate to link his colliery, about half a mile distant, with the Coventry Canal. Coal has been carried on this short canal for nearly 175 years and traffic ceased only when Griff colliery closed down in 1961.

You will now notice that the water in the canal is red and dirty and that there are effluent pipes discharging constantly into the canal as you approach Nuneaton. Between Bridges 23 and 30 the canal is not only dirty and smelly but exceptionally shallow. We had great difficulty in navigating this stretch although we slowed down to tick-over speed to give our propeller the greatest possible clearance. Even so our rudder frequently bumped the bottom and on occasions we were literally ploughing our way along.

Typical of the attractive canal architecture are the

old workshops of the Coventry Canal Company at Harts-
hill by Bridge 32. Now part of British Waterways' maintenance yard here, they have a splendid clock turret. It
is only a few miles now to the Atherstone Flight of eleven
locks with a total fall of 80 ft, and as you near them the
water becomes cleaner and deeper. You will also notice
stone quarries near the canal from which roadstone was
shipped by water for many years. There are good moorings
and a watering point beside the King's Head five locks
down. Watling Street or the A5 crosses the canal a little
further on and it is only a short walk into Atherstone
from the bridge. There is a milestone in the town which
calls attention to the fact that Atherstone is 100 miles
from London, Lincoln and Liverpool. Although the canal
is shallow the surroundings suddenly become attractive.
As you approach Lock No. 6 you can see the turrets of
Merevale Hall on the left, jutting out of wooded hill-
sides. The remaining locks are now somewhat further
apart and soon you are at Bridge 52 at Polesworth. This
is a good centre for exploration of the North Warwickshire
countryside with is squat-towered churches and old
villages like Appleby Parva and Appleby Magna. The
canal continues to be shallow and there are vast tips along
the banks, some huge and so old that they are now screened
by trees and undergrowth, others startlingly red with
truncated tops.

At Fazeley Junction, you turn right into the Birmingham & Fazeley Canal to join the detached portion of
the Coventry Canal to Whittington Brook for the Trent
& Mersey Canal at Fradley. The whole of this stretch,
which is 209 ft above sea level, is quite attractive and
winds a great deal. There are no locks but we counted
over thirty bridges, about three per mile. Fradley Junction
is one of the most picturesque canal junctions in the
country and the Swan Inn just opposite the swing bridge

is a gem and is managed by Wilfred Bolley, an enthusiastic boater who cruised for many years off the Norfolk coast. He is very proud of the Swan, where he has been since 1961, and showed us over the old stables, built in 1763, where at one time as many as twenty-two towing horses were stabled. The inn, of white-painted brick, is as old as the stables, with relics of the days when it catered for working boaters and their horses. It has old canal maps and handwritten lists of subscribers to the Coventry Navigation dated 1767. There are several bars and even a basement bar which Bolley claims was once used by smugglers. You will find mooring rings on the quayside in front of the inn.

This section of the Trent & Mersey between Trent Lock and Great Haywood was the first to be built and was completed before Brindley died in 1772. There are three narrow locks in quick succession with woodland all along the left bank and the hills of Cannock Chase in the distance. At Bridge 54, some two miles from Fradley Junction, you can moor if you wish to visit Lady Godiva's home at pretty King's Bromley.

On the left as you approach Armitage Tunnel is a handsome collection of waterside buildings; the entrance to the tunnel is carved out of solid red rock, making it one of the most unusual anywhere on the canals. This tunnel was probably the first to be built with a towpath through it. The Trent & Mersey provides a series of con-trasts. The attractive scene at Armitage Tunnel follows a factory-lined section of canal where peeping through the windows you can get a glimpse of the wide range of sanitary ware manufactured locally. Our youngsters nearly went into hysterics as window after window revealed lavatory pans of every shape and colour. Once through the tunnel you pass through massive coalfields with huge pithead structures competing with a new electricity generating station for attention. This panorama of power development may bring out the cameras for the massive wheels and huge towers make good subjects for photography. The River Trent twists its way along the canal and you cross over it at Brindleys Bank aqueduct a mile beyond Rugely, which lies on the edge of Cannock Chase.

Past Wolseley Park and Hall on the left, you will quickly come to Colwich Lock with hills soaring to over 500 ft in the distance. Haywood Lock follows and from here there are views of a conglomeration of bridges spanning the Trent & Mersey, the Staffordshire & Worcestershire as well as the Trent and Sow rivers. The marshy land around Great Haywood Junction is a haunt of wild birds and you will see many herons both here and for miles along this canal. Between Hoo Mill and Weston Locks stands Ingestre Hall in a majestic park designed by 'Capability' Brown. From Haywood Lock you are gradually rising with locks getting deeper and deeper as you go, with the River Trent rarely more than a few hundred yards away and the rolling countryside dotted with great houses and parks. The views across the Trent Valley are magnificent, particularly round Sandon. From here you can spot five hills, each decked with structures of one kind or another. One boasts a church, another a house, another a ruined tower and the other two monuments to Parliamentarians. A long straight stretch of canal brings you to Aston Lock, which we voted the prettiest of the seventy-six on the 93½ miles of the Trent & Mersey Canal.

The old and interesting town of Stone is little more than a mile further on, and both canal and river flow through it. The big basin at the bottom lock is shallow and there is better mooring above the first lock beside the Star Inn. The four locks of the Stone Flight take you up nearly 40 ft and there are a few more miles of lovely scenery before you begin to notice the potteries and power stations beyond the Meaford Flight of four locks. After Bridge 103 there are moorings for a visit to the famous Wedgwood Factory which can be seen from the canal. Josiah Wedgwood, who was born at nearby Burslem in 1730 and started his first works there, was a great canal enthusiast. It was a pamphlet of his published in 1765 which pointed out the advantages of a canal to link the Trent and Mersey rivers and thus the ports of Liverpool and Hull that sparked off the construction of the Trent & Mersey Canal, originally called the Grand Trunk. He even contributed handsomely to the cost of Brindley's survey of the line and actually cut the first sod of the new waterway at Burslem in July 1766.

Three more pottery-lined miles and the five locks of the Stoke Flight appear. The canal gradually gets dirty and rusty looking and we encountered considerable floating weed. Despite the museum at Stoke-on-Trent with its fine exhibition of pottery, the town from the canal is ugly, lined with factories and slums, and we hurried up the 50 ft flight to the summit pound above. The entire six miles of this pound is shallow, weedy and dirty as it wends its way through the heart of the potteries, but the exciting passage through the 2,919-yard Harecastle Tunnel is more than adequate compensation. The first tunnel which was 2,897 yards long was designed by Brindley and completed in 1777 and was the first tunnel over a mile in length to be constructed anywhere in the world, but it had no towing path and was subject to subsidence. The present tunnel beside it was built by Thomas Telford between 1824 and 1827 and is much larger and with a towpath. Mining subsidence made this towpath impassable at the turn of the century and electric haulage had to be introduced, a tug towing as many as twenty craft through at a time. Powered craft put the tug out of business and today boats move through the tunnel individually after first reporting to the tunnel keeper. You will see a gauge over the entrance as you approach and the keeper will insist that your craft clears this gauge before you are permitted to navigate it. This is simply because the walls of the tunnel have shifted from subsidence, making the tightest squeeze for craft of any tunnel on the inland waterways network. Most hire craft will go through but it is wise to check in advance that the boat you hire will meet the 5 ft 9 ins headroom specification of the gauge. This is, of course, one-way traffic only and it takes a good forty-five minutes to navigate. Many sections leak, there are numerous stalactites, and the walls appear to be buckling inwards in many places. Progress can be checked by the large painted numbers on the walls and the lowest part of the tunnel is from 15 for about 250 yards. Our handrail scraped on one occasion and you will have to be careful of sunken towpath sections, but your passage should cause no problem if you go cautiously.

The canal continues to be shallow and weedy for another mile to the Red Bull Flight of six locks which now take you down over 54½ ft. Just before these locks is the entrance to the Macclesfield Canal on your left, which will seem odd as the canal is actually on your right. This canal, 26½ miles long, connects the Trent & Mersey with the Peak Forest Canal high in the Pennines near Marple and the entrance to it is most unusual. It was designed by Telford, famous for his road and harbour engineering, and he devised a three-quarter mile branch canal to run parallel with the Trent & Mersey and then swung it over the latter on an aqueduct, the first 'fly-over' canal crossing in the world. Incidentally, the Macclesfield Canal together with the few miles of the Peak Forest Canal between Marple Junction and Whaley Bridge is still open and provides some of the most wonderful canal scenery anywhere. A whole week can be spent dawdling along, exploring these two almost forgotten waterways, an experience never forgotten.

We continued along the Trent & Mersey, through the Red Bull Flight and into rural countryside once more. From Harecastle Tunnel twenty-four of the twenty-six locks to Wheelock are in pairs but some are derelict. Shortly after the Lawton Flight of six you will come to Upper Thurlwood Lock, one of the most unusual on our canals, a high and imposing steel structure. Special instructions on the site do not advise users to slide the long bar which releases the lower gate. We found three craft with very puzzled crews waiting to get through.

After Hassal Green with the Romping Donkey near Bridge 147 the Wheelock Flight of eight locks carries you down nearly 80 ft, and you will find there is steam over the canal all the way to King's Lock near the junction with the Shropshire Union Canal. The salt and chemical works here even turn Rumps Lock into a warm bath. However, from Crows Nest Lock there are delightful country walks to well-favoured villages like Warmingham. For overnight moorings we recommend the British Waterways hire cruiser base just beyond the junction with the Middlewich Branch of the Shropshire Union which links the north with the Midlands. Middlewich grew to prosperity on salt and the canals which carried it away to markets all over the country. The town is agreeable and excellent for shopping. The old stocks still stand outside the local church but of course have not been used for some long time.

After passing through the Middlewich Flight you will find Lock No. 75 which has double gates and is wider than the locks already navigated from Fradley. Both this lock and No. 76 are 9 ft wide. Lock No. 76 is near the top end of the Trent & Mersey before it flows through Preston Brook tunnel and links with the Bridgewater Canal. The

Trent & Mersey therefore has three different widths in its locks. From Middlewich to Dallow Lane Lock just beyond Burton-on-Trent the locks are 7 ft wide, their size being governed by problems of water supply and the width of the Harecastle Tunnel which would have cost a fortune to make wider. But the six locks below Dallow Lane Lock are all wide enough to take Trent river barges. When the canals were being constructed their builders had good reason for making narrow locks, such as water supply or lack of money, but eventually the variations in gauges from one canal to another made it much easier for the railways to supersede water transport.

The Trent & Mersey goes through lovely countryside all the way to the outskirts of Anderton, some nine miles from Middlewich. There are woodlands and meadows, wild flowers and birds, and from time to time the canal widens into large lakes, the biggest one being after Bridge 180 near Billinge Green. At Bridge 184 there is a handsome black and white pub called The Old Broken Cross, and there is a useful canal-side shop.

We had arranged to meet Dr and Mrs Pilkington at Anderton one afternoon for what we promised would be an incomparable adventure. This was to enter the Shropshire Union Canal from the top end at Ellesmere Port via the Anderton Lift, River Weaver Navigation and Manchester Ship Canal. While there is no reason why beginners should not navigate the Anderton Lift and even venture into the Bridgewater Canal, some experience in handling a boat would be useful before cruising on the Manchester Ship Canal and into Ellesmere Port. It is only a short run back to Middlewich and the convenient Middlewich Arm entry into the Shropshire Union Canal.

While waiting at Anderton we talked to the Fleet Superintendent of what was then the Willow Wren carrying company who bemoaned the decline of commercial traffic on the waterways. Since our visit the former North Western fleets of Willow Wren and British Waterways have merged into a single narrow boat fleet, operated by the Anderton Canal Carrying Company, which is now the largest in the country. Even so, this company began 1970 with only ten craft, and except for the transport of concrete piles, the company's activities are conducted solely between Preston Brook on the Trent & Mersey and Weston Point Docks. Much of their cargo is salt for export and the boats are often used as floating warehouses to save double handling. The reason for the company's survival in the difficult business of commercial narrow boats seems to be their ability to load or unload direct into ships, thus avoiding paying dock dues.

The seven-mile elevated run to the Bridgewater Canal through the crooked Saltersford, Barton and Preston Brook Tunnels, the first to carry canals through hills, is a delightful diversion. From Anderton you may also wish to visit nearby Marston, where salt has been mined for centuries. The village is built on pillars of salt which are slowly dissolving and much of it has been lost in the old brine pits. In 1958 a new half-mile section of canal had to be built and was opened within weeks of part of the old section of the canal collapsing into a mine shaft. In 1844 the Tsar of Russia came to visit Marston's famous Old Mine, one of the biggest in England, and dined in it with the Royal Society. Ten thousand lamps were used to illuminate the ancient mine, which is 360 ft deep and covers thirty-five acres.

CHAPTER 12

SENSATIONS AND SPECTACULARS

You will find many opportunities on inland waterways holidays to make gala occasions of certain runs. For our voyage from Anderton to Chester via the Manchester Ship Canal we arranged a little party, and our guest crew on this occasion included not only Dr and Mrs Roger Pilkington but also Dr and Mrs Lawrence Pilkington and the Lord Bishop of Chester, who had not yet seen his diocese by water, he said, and his son.

The River Weaver lies some 50 ft 4 ins below the Trent & Mersey Canal at Anderton and transhipment of cargoes from one waterway to the other was an expensive and time-consuming business until the massive Anderton Lift was opened in 1875. Although there are even bigger lifts on Continental waterways today, the Anderton Lift is the only one in use in Britain. Situated on an island in the river basin, this unusual structure is connected to the canal by a two channel aqueduct some 162 ft 6 ins long, each channel being 17 ft 2 ins wide. These lead to the two 75 ft x 15 ft 6 ins x 5 ft wrought iron tanks of the lift itself, each tank when full of water weighing 252 tons. For the first thirty years these tanks carried boats up and down hydraulically but in 1907 the main rams were renewed and the lift was electrified. Each tank is now suspended by means of wire ropes passing round large overhead pulleys. Counterweights consisting of 252 tons of cast iron hang from the free ends of the wire ropes, so that comparatively little power is needed to raise a tank, although the total weight moved is about 570 tons. Power is supplied direct to the pulleys by an electric motor of only 30 h.p.

It is a strange sensation to cross the aqueduct, enter the open water-tight doors of a tank, see them close behind you and then float almost silently in the tank as it moves slowly down between a vast network of girders, wire ropes and weights while pulleys whirr overhead, being lowered to the river over 50 ft below. The whole operation takes under 15 minutes and costs £2 single or £3 return. British Waterways supplies an illustrated souvenir ticket with pertinent statistics. Initially the lift cost £26,302 and modification costs were £25,000. An attendant is on duty from 8 to 5 on weekdays, 8 to 11 on Saturdays and occasionally on Sundays in summer. He will take you on a conducted tour of this enormous structure and its mechanics and you may be as lucky as we were in meeting a pair of narrow boats coming up from the river as you descend from the canal.

As you leave the lift a vast I.C.I. complex towers dead ahead. Turning left into the Weaver you can cruise for a few miles through two locks to the pretty Winsford Flashes, large lakes beside the river with access just above to Winsford Bridge. A right turn takes you to the Manchester Ship Canal. You soon come to lovely tree-covered hills and glorious views. The river is wide and deep and there are only five locks on the twenty-mile long navigation, each taking craft up to 130 ft long, 35 ft in beam and up to 10 ft in draught. Even so, we were surprised to see round the first bend after leaving Saltersford Lock a big Danish coaster bearing down on us at about 10 knots.

Despite some major industrial plants, there is magnificent scenery all along the Weaver. At Weston, some nineteen miles from Winsford, Marsh Lock gives access to the Manchester Ship Canal. This is a busy commercial waterway and pleasure craft must obtain written permission to use it from the Manchester Ship Canal Company. Our brief excursion on it cost us £5, involving us in obtaining £50,000 insurance cover and a certificate of seaworthiness for our craft, the acquisition of extra gear including a 56 lb anchor, and a fair amount of letter-writing to arrange a Saturday passage timed to fit in with the operation of the Anderton Lift and entry into Ellesmere Port.

The Ship Canal, which runs from Eastham Locks some thirty-six miles to Manchester, is not what one can describe as scenic for it has high banks depriving anyone on a boat of all but rare glimpses of the surrounding countryside. It is nearly as broad as the Thames through central London and considerably deeper. There are lights and signposts all along the canal, and Ince Low and High Cuttings are clearly cut out of solid rock. We saw many huge tankers discharging, and two of them pulled out of their berths within a hundred yards of us, swinging across the canal seemingly oblivious of our presence.

All boating enthusiasts have their favourite spots on the waterways. One that comes most frequently to my mind is Ellesmere Port, which links the Manchester Ship Canal to the former Ellesmere, now the Shropshire Union Canal. Ellesmere Port has both striking beauty and repulsive dilapidation. It recalls bygone architectural and engineering genius and reflects current regrettable negligence. It tells the whole tragic story of the rise and fall of this country's canal system. The modern and mechanised facilities for the Ship Canal here are excellent, but the nearby 'Shroppie' Cut facilities which brought growth and prosperity to the former group of tiny villages, are by comparison an incongruous island of decay.

As we swung up to the large tidal lock we noted on the

north pier a gem of a miniature red brick lighthouse, 35 ft tall with a graceful lantern. Dating back to the opening of the Ellesmere Canal or Wirral Line from Chester in 1795, it guided vessels coming to the port from the Mersey tideway before the Ship Canal was completed in 1894. The vast outer basin here contained a motley collection of shabby craft and as there were at that moment dark skies overhead, it gave the atmosphere of a 'ghost port'. We turned under a warehouse arch to zig-zag our way through obstructions jutting out of the water into an inner basin, filled with a mass of floating rubbish. The narrow locks were derelict and the water in the wide locks, in the short pound between them and in the canal above was a bleak panorama of duckweed and floating clumps of reed filled with old oil drums and an appalling collection of flotsam and jetsam as far as the eye could see. The padlock on the lock gates had to be sawn off after the lock-keeper dropped the keys in the lock, either by accident or threw them away in disgust. As the locks filled a great cascade of green descended and we went ahead very cautiously indeed. Then we had to hook the biggest and heaviest of the debris away from the top gates. Even then there was so much left on the 4 ins thick bed of duckweed along with wriggling elvers that we had to plot a course out of the lock. Although the weed thinned gradually the waterway was almost totally green with it to Stoke Bridge, some three miles distant. Never before in all of Europe's waterways had any of us encountered so much weed that our wake was completely undetectable. There is only one thing to be done under such conditions, other than turning back, and that is to proceed gently. Attempts to get through quickly will only damage your craft.

The first real development of Ellesmere Port was inspired by my favourite canal engineer, Thomas Telford, whom I have already mentioned. The Wirral Line was Telford's first canal enterprise and the transformation of Ellesmere Port his last. When in 1835 he began the construction of new sea and canal locks, docks and warehousing, Ellesmere Port consisted only of a pub and a few small cottages. He died before his last great contribution to the nation's canal system was opened with great ceremony and noisy celebrations in September 1843. After an expenditure of some £100,000 Ellesmere Port was now geared to deal with any coastal trade and canal traffic and could boast over seventy houses, a church and church school, and three inns. The crowning glory then, as today, is the unique main warehouse to his design to facilitate transhipment from river to canal. This warehouse, standing in mellowed beauty today, is four storeys high. The bottom floor is level with the docks and the third floor on the canal side is on a level with the canal. Adjoining this are three wings of two storeys each, resting on handsome arches, which form a passage for craft between the big outer dock and the smaller inner basin. If the little lighthouse at Ellesmere Port is worth preserving, Telford's warehouses are a masterpiece in canal architecture and a heritage that must be saved at all costs. It is worth bringing your craft up from Chester to Ellesmere Port to have a look for yourself—the navigation has been improved since our cruise. One can spend a long time in quiet admiration of this product of genius and it is no wonder that the Lord Bishop of Chester who was with us, spontaneously appealed in his Diocesan leaflet for the restoration of 'these fine buildings and waterways to full use'. Adding that the 'brick and stone buildings have a Venetian touch about them, and the craftsmanship is splendid', the Lord Bishop suggested that the warehouses would make ideal youth club premises.

However, Telford's warehouses and the connection with

the Ship Canal have been threatened with demolition since
1967. The Manchester Ship Canal Company, which hold
the lease of the area, wants to redevelop it to provide new
berthing and other facilities for the Ship Canal. Ellesmere
Port Council, local interests and canal enthusiasts have
indicated that they would like to preserve the group and
convert it into a marina and canal museum. To seal off
the exit of the Shropshire Union into the Ship Canal
would be disastrous, making a dead end of the Wirral
Line and a mockery of the Government's declared intentions to retain the Shropshire Union main line and all its
branches as amenity waterways. The area is too small to
provide substantial facilities for the Ship Canal, yet
Ellesmere Port is a natural focal point for the creation of
new leisure amenities. Despite the recent fire Telford's
warehouses should certainly be declared an historic monument, thus preventing their destruction, and then they
should be adapted to provide both a youth club and canal
museum. Below them one can easily visualise a great marina
with boatyards, a restaurant and other amenities.

The nine-mile cruise from Ellesmere Port to Tower
Wharf in Chester has no locks and after two miles of
industry it is all unspoiled countryside with herds of dairy
cattle grazing in valley pastures. There are a number of
interesting little villages along the winding course and a
visit can be made to Chester Zoo at Upton from Caughall
Bridge, easily identified by its number, 134, and its iron
arch and parapet. As you get nearer to Chester the Welsh
hills loom on your right and for such a large cathedral
city, the waterways entrance is surprisingly open with
only a short stretch of canal with houses backing on to
it. Tower Wharf, just beyond the short branch leading
through three locks to the River Dee, is a good overnight
mooring. The Dee is tidal to Chester but those with some

experience can cruise safely for ten miles along this pretty river to Almeree Ferry.

We cannot praise Chester too highly as a port of call. A guide book is a great help in exploring the city and no one should miss the panoramic walk round the city walls. The wide curving approach to Northgate Locks, three of the staircase type carved out of solid rock and carrying you up 33 ft, is very shallow and you should stay in mid-channel. The canal goes through a beautiful deep rock chasm for a quarter of a mile along the outside of the city walls and there are memorable views of King Charles's Tower and Chester Cathedral. The exit from Chester is industrialised for a couple of miles but from Chrisleton Bridge it is all beautiful countryside. After passing over the River Gowy there is a favourite mooring spot at Bates Mill Bridge, from which you can visit the ruins of thirteenth-century Beeston Castle with its famous 370 ft deep well in which Richard II is reputed to have concealed a vast treasure, the old mill and the Old Shady Oak Inn. There are picturesque hills all round as you cruise along to Wharton Lock and the two Beeston Locks. The first is known as Beeston Iron Lock and is unique, built entirely of bolted iron plates instead of stone because this was the only way to cope with the running sand at the site.

In the next five miles to Barbridge Junction and the southern end of the ten-mile-long Middlewich Arm there are five hire cruiser yards including that of Ladyline Cruisers at the junction, complete with chandlery, groceries and souvenirs, all available from sunrise to sunset. Above the junction stands the Jolly Tar which we found rather grand for a canal-side pub. It is only a wide sweeping mile to the mammoth Hurleston reservoir and junction. Immediately beside the reservoir on the right is the flight of four Hurleston Locks which will carry you over 34 ft up into what is widely regarded as the most beautiful canal in this country. The first lock is a tight squeeze and you should ensure when you hire the craft for your holidays that you can get into this canal. Of course, hire craft are available on the canal itself.

The Llangollen Canal, originally known as the Ellesmere Canal, runs for forty-six miles from Hurleston Junction to Llantisilio in Wales with twenty-one locks, the breathtaking Pontcysyllte and Chirk aqueducts, three tunnels and well over 100 bridges, and these include some of the most picturesque lifting bridges on the waterways network. It also has an inimitable inland harbour at Ellesmere and, in fact, it owes its origin to a group of industrialists and business men from the Ellesmere area who promoted a parliamentary Bill which authorised the construction of a system of canals radiating from Ellesmere and linking the Rivers Severn, Dee and Mersey. They engaged Telford in 1793 to build the system and the first section to be completed was the Wirral Line, the only section with broad locks. There were modifications to the original plans but what is now known as the Llangollen Canal was opened all the way to Llantisilio by 1808.

Once through the Hurleston Locks the canal, with its low banks, looks out on prosperous farming country with brick farmhouses and outbuildings. The canal is lined with flowers and there are many birds, including king-fishers, and so beautiful you may be tempted not to go far from the water, even to visit the occasional nearby village. After two miles you will reach the two Swanley Locks, closely followed by the Baddiley three and the wooded park of Wrenbury Hall, now a training college. Wrenbury with its mill and charming lifting bridge is reminiscent of Holland, although the Cotton Arms here is entirely British. We found amateur artists at work; indeed, one had hired a cruiser just to paint along the Llangollen Canal. From the next lock at Marbury it is just under half a mile to the village. This village is worth a visit to see the black and white, or magpie, style of architecture which is striking, and Marbury Mere is not only pretty but has a plentiful supply of coarse fish. The countryside is now flatter as you lock up the oddly named Quoisley, Willeymoor and Povey's Locks and approach the Grindley Brook Flight. The first three are orthodox locks but the top three are staircase locks with only four gates between them. Care must be taken at the latter for the bridge is out of line with the lock chambers. You will find a convenient canal-side pub here, a post office and general stores.

The canal is full of turns and twists after Grindley Brook but soon after Platts Lane Bridge, No. 43, it becomes wider and straighter and the scenery rapidly changes. The Prees Branch of the canal is on the left and although it is officially closed, craft drawing under 2 ft can cruise for about a mile and a half to Waterloo Bridge. This is peat country and Whixall Moss is still worked. The waterway now goes briefly into and out of Wales as it winds through wooded countryside and into what the locals call the 'Lake District'. Cole Mere and Blake Mere are beautiful and unspoiled lakes beside the canal. Near Cole Mere we saw the only 'no mooring' signs on the entire length of the Llangollen Canal and indeed mooring is possible virtually anywhere. Through the short, straight 87-yard-long Ellesmere Tunnel you reach a junction with the quarter-mile Ellesmere Arm. The route to Llantisilio is round to the left but if you venture under the pretty rustic wooden bridge into the arm you will find moorings in the neatest little inland harbour in all Britain. This gives easy access to the amenities of the town. The local castle has long since disappeared but the heights on which it stood have been converted into a bowling green and there are fine views over lovely countryside. The Ellesmere area is claimed to be the most prolific milk-producing area in the world.

As you return to the junction you will see a fully equipped British Waterways maintenance yard, well worth inspecting. There are unfortunately heaps of junk about but it was while we were nosing through these that we discovered and bought some rusty old canal signs which, refurbished and repainted, we took home to decorate a part of the exterior of the house, and also a heavy balance beam cap which, now repainted, we have placed at the curve in our drive.

The canal is broad and deep for a short stretch beyond Ellesmere and then narrows and winds through fields of grain and pastures with grazing cattle. Once past Bridge 65 you will begin to get magnificent views of the Welsh hills on the left. Passing under Bridge 69 there is a useful mooring near the entrance to the abandoned Montgomeryshire Canal which once led to Welshpool and Newton. The first bridge beyond the junction is not No. 70 as might be expected but is No. 1; the bridges from here to Llantisilio are numbered 1 to 49A. At Bridge 5 there are shops at the village of Maesterfyn. If you feel energetic it is 2½ miles to Whittington with its nineteenth-century castle ruins.

The countryside is more hilly and broken now and at Newmarton are the last two locks on the canal with thirty-four miles of lock-free cruising beyond. There is a canal-side bakery at Bridge 13 which is useful for delicious cakes and bread, and local butter and eggs can be bought. Beyond the Lion Inn at Bridge 17 the canal sweeps into the beautiful Ceiriog Valley for a good mile before reaching Chirk aqueduct over the River Ceiriog. This 701-ft-long aqueduct is 9 ft wide and formed of cast-iron plates

flanged and bolted together. It was completed on masonry
arched piers in 1801 by Telford at a cost of over £20,000
and is some 70 ft high. The railway bridge alongside it,
from which you can get good photographs of your craft
crossing the aqueduct, is much higher but was not built
until forty years later. This is the first of the major
aqueducts on the canal and is closely followed by Chirk
Tunnel, 459 yards long, which is dry and has a well-
fendered towpath. You can moor in the basin before the
tunnel and follow a path on the right up an incline into
Chirk. This is an appealing little town with good shops, a
hotel, and an amusing antique shop. Chirk Castle, with
its handsome wrought-iron gates, has a collection of paintings, armour and antiques and lies about a mile from the
town. The 191-yard-long Whitehurst Tunnel is little more
than a mile from Chirk and you emerge into the beautiful Dee Valley. The canal passes through wooded hill-
sides for another mile before sweeping round to the right
to the highlight of the canal, the Pontcysyllte aqueduct.
The views on the long approach to this astonishing
memorial to Telford's genius are really glorious. The
1,007-ft-long aqueduct soars 120 ft over the surging River
Dee below. Although it was completed in 1805 the
eighteen massive masonry arches carrying the 7 ft 2 ins-
wide trough of bolted cast-iron flanged plates are in superb
condition. Along the right hand side of the trough runs a
4 ft 8 ins towpath at the same level as the base of the
trough. The aqueduct is scheduled as an ancient monument and the towpath railings when they were renewed
in 1964 were made to Telford's original design. There is
no need to have any qualms about taking your craft across
under power unless there is a strong wind blowing. In
these circumstances it can be somewhat alarming as we
discovered, for on the occasion of our crossing strong
winds were blowing and the *Golden Eye* was being pushed

against the edge on the left with a sheer drop into the valley below. It is possible to walk your boat across from the recessed towpath should your crew wish to do this, but whichever way you cross I am perfectly certain you will never have a more thrilling experience on the waterways. This structure, which cost only £47,000 when it was built 165 years ago, would cost millions today and is, without doubt, the finest example of canal engineering in this country.

You will find good moorings just across the aqueduct at the Anglo Welsh Canal Cruisers' base at Trevor. The remaining six miles of canal to Llangollen and Llantisilio follows the contours of the hills along the course of the Dee but for the most part is shallow and narrow. Craft with over 2 ft draught should not attempt passage, which will take a good four hours one way. You can take a bus from Trevor to Llangollen and then travel a couple of miles by horse-drawn lifeboat to the end of the canal and Horseshoe Falls. Llangollen is packed with visitors during the summer months. However, the town is worth exploring for here the River Dee tumbles over rocks and below the fourteenth-century bridge is a lovely salmon leap. There is a modern pottery, offering a wide range of hand-made earthenware; nearby are the ruins of Valle Crucis Abbey with its famous mutilated cross, the Pillar of Eliseg, and wishing well, and the eighteenth-century Plas Newydd which the local council keeps open to the public.

On turning round you have the whole of the beautiful Llangollen Canal to cruise once again and even rain on the journey will not diminish the wild beauty of this waterway. As you join the main line of the Shropshire Union again you will notice the relative tameness of the agricultural countryside to Nantwich. You can moor at the basin for a visit to the old salt town. The old English

word for salt-rock was 'wych', and thus the names Nantwich, Middlewich, Northwich, etc. Nantwich Junction
Bridge marks the end of the broad Chester Canal completed in 1779, and the remaining twenty-nine locks on
the thirty-nine mile run to Autherley Junction are narrow.
After the bridge the canal enters a long and high embankment, the first of many earthworks built by Telford
on the route south to Autherley, each providing excellent
views of the peaceful countryside. The canal goes up and
up through Hack Green Locks and then through the long
and delightful flight of fifteen Audlem locks stretching
over two miles and taking your craft a further 93 ft higher.
You can moor, water and shop at Lock 13, the third of
the flight, for the old coaching town of Audlem has good
shopping facilities.

A peaceful wooded cutting starts immediately above
the locks and then comes the Adderley Flight of five locks
taking you up another 31 ft as you cruise from Cheshire
into Shropshire. Only another couple of miles now to the
graceful Betton Coppice Bridge which takes the towpath to the opposite side of the canal in a handsome sweep.
Shortly afterwards there is a canal basin on your left and
the headquarters of Ladyline Cruisers and Holidays
Afloat. From moorings here you can visit Market Drayton
with its many charming old buildings, inns and churches.
Wednesday is still market day and a visit to the open-air
swimming pool, followed by a call at the Corbet Arms, will
refresh your crew after working so many locks.

You now cross the 'Forty Steps' aqueduct over the Tern
to enter a wonderful cutting hewn through sandstone
with trees forming an arch over the canal. This approach
to the Tyrley Flight of five locks is unforgettable. The
rise of 33 ft is immediately followed by another tree-lined
rock cutting over 1½ miles long before you come into open
countryside again. Once you are through Tyrley Locks

you are on a seventeen-mile pound which is 333 ft above sea level, and from the many cuttings, embankments, aqueducts and even a short tunnel you will appreciate even more the true genius of Telford, who had none of today's mechanical aids to help him create this waterways route; he had only hardworking navigators or 'navvies' with simple tools.

The canal now wends its way into Staffordshire with no noticeable change in scenery. The high Shebdon embankment is followed by a lovely wooded cutting with an enormously high canal bridge which is unlike any other in the world. About half-way up you can see a buttress upon which stands a telegraph pole and wires, directly underneath the road bridge itself. Another two miles will bring you to Norbury Junction, one of our favourite overnight moorings. The Junction Inn has been spruced up but the company one meets here is invariably good fun. Horse-drawn canal day boats operate from the wharf at the pub.

The valley of the Meese with its open fields and pastures nestling between the hills is never more beautiful than in the early morning. The ancient village of Gnosall is quite charming, not least for its church of St Lawrence and its various inns. There are good shopping facilities near the bridge. Cowley Tunnel, wide and carved out of rock, bores through a wooded cutting for 87 yards, and for the next few miles the canal passes along on more embankments and aqueducts and through still more wooded cuttings to Dirty Lane Bridge and then Tavern Bridge with the Hartley Arms and Wheaton Aston Locks close by. The canal then goes up again for 7 ft to the last pound on the main line, some seven miles from Autherley Lock and Junction, with almost continuous cuttings, heavily wooded or narrowly cut from rock. The bridges here have odd names like 'Skew' and 'Turnover' and for nearly half a mile before Autherley Junction you will see an enormous collection of moored pleasure craft, almost up to the old Stop Lock with its very small rise of 6 ins. This lock dates back to the days when rival canal companies jealously sought to maintain control over their own waters. What was once the toll office is now manned by British Waterways to give advice to holidaymakers and to sell souvenirs.

After locking out, turn sharply to the left for the twenty-mile run back to the Trent & Mersey Canal at Great Haywood Junction. The Staffordshire & Worcestershire Canal north of Autherley Junction is in complete contrast to the twenty-six miles south of the Junction and nothing like as beautiful. Only eleven of the forty-three locks between the Trent & Mersey and the Severn are on the canal north of Autherley but it does possess some interesting features. As you leave Autherley on the outskirts of Wolverhampton you are on the summit pound and after an unexpectedly wide stretch there is a cutting so narrow and overhung with long grass and shrubbery that your craft will rub against the banks from time to time. But soon there is open country with farmhouses and stretches of parkland.

One fascinating feature of the 'Staffs & Worcs', as we call it, is that the majority of the bridges are not only numbered but are also named, and some amusing names there are. Passing through wooded country, at Gailey Lock you begin your descent to the Trent & Mersey. There are now six locks quite close together, the last being Penkridge, which, because of the low bridge above the lock, appears at first sight to be a dead end. From the Boat Inn by the bridge the canal follows the course of the river Penk and there are four more locks in the next three miles, a humdrum stretch with only Teddesley Park providing pleasant views up to Stafford. There are good moorings at Radford Bridge, No. 98, by the headquarters of Radford Marine Ltd, and the nearby Trumpet Inn. From here you can visit Stafford by bus and this is also a convenient place to embark or disembark guest crew.

Just beyond Stafford the River Sow joins the River Penk and the two streams pass under the canal at Tixall. Beyond the aqueduct is Tixall Lock and then the lovely Tixall Broad, a small canal lake about a mile long with pleasant views to Tixall Park, where Mary Queen of Scots was once held prisoner. Fishing in this area is said to be very good indeed, particularly in the Penk. Once out of the Broad you are at Great Haywood Junction and the beautiful wide-span bridge that carries the Trent & Mersey towpath over the Staffs & Worcs canal.

The thirteen-mile cruise to Fradley Junction and The Swan was even prettier than the earlier cruise in the opposite direction. From Fradley there are four locks to Bridge 46 and one of our favourite waterways villages, Alrewas, once famous for its basket making. There is an old mill here, the friendly George and Dragon Inn and some delightful thatched cottages. We also found that the butcher makes delicious home-made sausages.

After Alrewas Lock the canal joins the Trent river for a short stretch. You will pass a heronry here. Once through Wychnor Lock the canal narrows, and becomes shallow and weedy. After Branston Lock the wooded Sinai Ridge is on the left as you enter Burton-on-Trent, famous for its beer. There are moorings at Bridge 13 from which you can catch a bus for the town for shopping or possibly for a visit to one of the many breweries. It is said that as early as the thirteenth century the monks used water from the local wells for brewing ale but certainly Burton has been world-famous for its beer since the eighteenth century. The suburbs of Burton to the last of the narrow locks at Dallow Lane are hardly impressive but you soon reach open countryside again. There are good British

Waterways moorings above Bridge 23 at Willington and you will find a friendly welcome at the Green Dragon nearby. The local railway station which serves both Repton and Willington is a gem right out of Victorian days.

Stenson, the first of the wide locks, is noticeably difficult to operate after the narrow locks. Beyond the abandoned Derby Canal, Swarkestone Bridge carries the road for a mile over the river and the expanse of meadows which have been subject to flooding from the earliest times. A pretty wooded cutting leads to Weston Lock with its watering point and nearby shopping facilities. It is now a mixture of pastures and power plants as you cruise on to Aston and Shardlow Locks. You can moor beside the Malt Shovel, an old-time canal pub with a snack bar, or you can visit the Lady in Grey for hot meals.

To lock out of Derwent Mouth Lock is a blissful experience for your boat will surge ahead in the wide deep waters at the junction of the rivers Trent and Derwent, but it is important to keep straight ahead and avoid the dangerous weirs. Sawley Flood Lock will be open at both ends and after going through you will be in one of the biggest and most modern boating centres in Britain, Sawley Bridge Marina. There are usually hundreds of craft moored in the Sawley Cut and you will find every conceivable facility here from new and used craft to fuel and chandlery, and a fleet of hire cruisers.

This is actually part of the River Trent and all too quickly you will pass through Sawley Locks and into Trent Junction, a kind of Scotch Corner of the waterways system. On your left you will see almost tucked away Trent Lock leading into the 11¾-mile Erewash section of the Grand Union Canal, still navigable as far as Ilkeston. Straight ahead is the rather narrow Cranfleet Cut and the water highway of the River Trent to the north. To the right of the yacht club on the island is a broad channel flowing under a railway bridge, and then over Thrumpton Weir. This branches sharply off to the right into the River Soar Navigation. The junction is well sign-posted and once you pass the yacht club on the left turn into the River Soar, keeping close to the right-hand corner and well clear of the weir stream.

Having already cruised the narrow and shallow twenty-mile summit pound between Foxton and Norton Junction this end of the Leicester line will come as a surprise to you, for the Soar is wide and deep and very unlike a canal. A lovely sweep of river will carry your craft to pretty Red-hill Lock, with its little shop. Wooded hills and slender church spires demand your attention as you cruise on. There are pleasant moorings on the right about half a mile beyond Kegworth Top Lock, beside the Whitehouse Inn and the Soar Boating Club. Despite the nearness of road and railway along the canal, the only traffic to be heard are aircraft flying high over the wooded hills and woodlands. All along the canal on this stretch there are sleepy villages like Zouch and Normanton-on-Soar which will probably appeal to those who have to live in a town. There is a wharf and boatyard and shopping facilities in Loughborough, the town of the bells. Bells from the foundry here ring out round the world, and from here came Great Paul of St Paul's Cathedral, the biggest bell in England. You should visit the 151-ft-tall Grand Caril-lon in Queen's Park, the first to be built in England in 1923. The chamber houses forty-seven bells, the heaviest being over 4 tons and the lightest just over 20 lb.

The canal rejoins the Soar again after Pilling's Lock, in lovely Quorn hunting country. The village of Barrow-on-Soar is hard by Barrow Deep Lock with an amusement park on the right. As you approach Mountsorrel, famous for its granite, there are huge boatyards and hire cruiser bases on the right. Beside the lock stands the Waterside Inn which is to be highly recommended. The Soar continues to flow in and out of the canal like a writhing snake. Charnwood Forest is not far off and there are many delightful walks to nearby villages like Rothley, Cossington, and Newton Lindford with its thatched and timbered dwellings and cedar-shaded inn. Nearby is beautiful Bradgate Park, one of the homes of the ill-fated Lady Jane Grey, with a thousand acres of natural forest which have become almost a shrine to the nine-day queen.

To the right from Bridge 19 lies the Roman settlement of Wanlip whose secluded fourteenth-century church contains admirable brasses, including one dated 1393 of Sir Thomas Walsh and his wife, with the earliest prose inscription in English on any brass in the country.

It is now but three miles and three locks to Leicester and the last, Belgrave Lock, has a lovely weir with hundreds of swans. The best moorings for shopping and sightseeing are by the North Bridge Inn, Frog Island. The navigation out of Leicester is rather weedy and sordid but you soon reach pastures and fields of waving grain. From Bridge 87, which leads to Wigston Magna, once called Wigston Two Steeples, the countryside is glorious and the waterway one of utter peace.

The locks now take on most amusing names, such as 'Bumble Bee' and 'Turnover' lock. After nine more locks, all with an average rise of about 6 ft in the next four miles to Saddington Tunnel, the total is forty from the Trent. After the first four, Bridge 80 leads to Newton Harcourt and in the shady churchyard stands a miniature church with spire, porch, windows and battlements, perfect in every detail and of undoubted craftsmanship, set up in memory of a boy of eight. Saddington Tunnel is only 880 yards long, wide and in good condition, with no sign of the headless ghost said still to haunt it.

There are three more miles of winding and wild canal between Saddington Tunnel and Foxton with no locks and only one swing bridge. I had asked special permission to take the *Golden Eye* along this stretch in the dark. We turned on the spotlight and rigged our portable navigation lights and got through without mishap. It was a wonderful but eerie experience and one we have seldom repeated, but it made a perfect ending to looping the loop of the Midlands waterways when we put in to Market Harborough the next morning.

CHAPTER 13

INTO SHAKESPEARE'S COUNTRY

THE RECENT restoration of the southern section of the Stratford-on-Avon Canal from its junction with the Grand Union Canal at Kingswood in Warwickshire makes it possible once again to visit Shakespeare's Stratford-on-Avon by water. The £300,000 Stratford Canal which runs for twenty-five miles from King's Norton on the Worcester & Birmingham Canal via Lapworth was begun in November 1793, but owing to financial problems and canal politics, was not completed until June 1816. It was difficult to construct for it involved building fifty-six locks, a 352-yard-long tunnel at Brandwood, near King's Norton, one brick aqueduct and three iron ones. It was not a money spinner as unfortunately it was completed less than thirty years before the railway mania year of 1845. Intended as an alternative route between Birmingham and the Severn by way of the River Avon, it never captured substantial through traffic and was used primarily to carry coal to Stratford.

The southern section between Lapworth and Stratford ceased to be navigable about the end of the Second World War and in 1958 Warwickshire County Council announced that it was applying for a warrant of abandonment. This led to many public protests and sparked off a British Transport Commission Act of 1960 authorising a lease of the waterway to the National Trust with a government subsidy of £27,500, and the southern section was restored and reopened in 1964.

Our fortuitous discovery of the *Golden Eye* under the name of the *Flying Mexican* at Warwick meant that we had only a few pretty rural miles of the Grand Union, the Cape Flight of two, the Hatton Flight of twenty-one wide locks and the 443-yard Shrewley Tunnel to navigate before joining the short arm leading to the Stratford Canal.

Passing through Lock 20 at the end of the arm you enter a large basin. On the left are locks leading into both the northern and southern sections. Your course is 180 degrees to port into Lock 21 under an unusual type of bridge—a split bridge with a narrow gap in the centre. This, and other bridges, were built this way to allow tow lines to pass through when horses crossed the bridges in the days of horse-drawn craft.

Beside the lock is the National Trust canal office where for a toll of £1 2s 6d you can cruise for a week on the southern section. For a 10s deposit you can obtain a key which opens the padlock on the locks into the River Avon at Stratford and you will certainly want the 3s guide to the canal. It is wise to paste your licence in a window of your craft and to read the sheet of navigation notes which insist that all lock gates and paddles are closed after passage.

The Stratford-on-Avon Canal is a gem in the waterways system. You will find it somewhat narrow, but lined with wild flowers, shrubs, trees and fields of grain. The first ten locks to Lowsonford and the Fleur de Lys pub are within easy walking distance of each other and a very pleasant walk for one or two of the crew, moving ahead and preparing the locks. Beyond Lock 29 you will come to the outskirts of Lowsonford village, passing a demolished railway bridge which once carried the first railway to Henley-in-Arden, which is as beautiful as its name and contains a number of architectural gems. There are grassy

moorings beside the towpath just before Lock 31 and
nearly opposite the waterside gardens of the Fleur de
Lys. These are convenient for visiting the pub and for
going to the village of Lowsonford which has at least
one shop which is open on a Sunday.

The pub is the home of the famous Fleur de Lys pies.
The story is that the original chicken and mushroom
pies were made here from mushrooms grown in the
cellar. Today the pies are made in a factory but can be
bought at the pub, either hot or cold, along with steak
and kidney pies and a wide selection of sandwiches. It
will take some searching to find the watering point at
Lock 31, but it is in a shed abutting the lock cottage.
Beyond Lock 31, the banks are green fields and meadows,
grazed by sheep or cattle. Below Lock 36 the towpath
mysteriously changes sides away from the small stream
which parallels this winding contour canal from just
beyond Lapworth Junction. Why this was done is a puzzle,
for in so doing the canal builders created the biggest single
cause of flooding on the southern section of this canal.
Had they put the towing path embankment on the opposite side, between the canal and the stream, this would
have prevented any flooding.

At Lock 37 you will notice an unusual type of lock
cottage, owned by Mr and Mrs Wagstaffe. This 'barrel'
type cottage is in effect the replica of a 14 ft wide canal
tunnel above the surface, and was erected by the canal
builders about 1812. The occupants have modernised the
cottage in a most charming way and have turned it into
a cosy residence. We were told that the tunnel-like brick-
work can still be seen in their airing cupboard. They will
be pleased to show you over their home on request but
they do ask you to make a donation to the Stratford-on-
Avon Society for the restoration of the Avon between
Stratford and Evesham. Restoration of this navigation is

already under way and will complete the waterways ring,
as the waterways map will show you, and provide easy
direct access between the River Severn and the Midlands
canals. You will hear some interesting stories about Lock
Cottage, about the days when tow-horses were stabled at
the cottage for 6*d* a night and a bag of beans, or about
the lock-keeper's wife who brewed beer for the boatmen.

There is good mooring between Locks 37 and 38 and
it is wiser to moor here than at Bridge 47 where there is
no ready access. Henley-in-Arden is little more than a mile
along the road on your right. The Crab Mill Inn, 400
yards from the bridge, and the Manor House tea garden
nearby are convenient for meals. Some two-thirds of the
way along the pound between Locks 38 and 39, just after
Bridge 53, you reach a long concrete quay by the attractive pink Navigation Inn. At the time of writing, Harborough Marine Ltd are building a new hire cruiser base
here with full facilities.

From the moorings here the road under the nearby
aqueduct leads to the oddly-named village of Wootton
Wawen, one of the most charming little villages in
Warwickshire, with a timbered inn, delightful old cottages,
a fine hall in lovely grounds and the oldest church in
the county.

Once over the aqueduct the scenery changes as the
canal no longer follows the tributary stream of the River
Alne which now joins the canal. The canal builders had to
cut through higher ground to reach the side of the Avon
valley. There are a number of cuttings with bushes hanging over the canal and from time to time an embankment
giving pretty views across the countryside. One such cutting carries the Bearley or Edstone aqueduct over a road
and railway. This early nineteenth-century aqueduct with
a sunken towpath is exceedingly narrow and must be
navigated at a very low speed. You are now in the lovely

Forest of Arden, not as thick as it was in Shakespeare's day for the trees were used to feed the iron works of the Midlands before the Industrial Revolution developed. The area is still more heavily wooded, however, than many other so-called wooded parts of Britain.

Bridge 59 is a new concrete bridge, so obviously stark after the graceful brick arches and split bridges you have passed. If you wish to visit Wilmcote you can moor at the watering point beyond the bridge. Pass through a gate and turn right on the road for Shakespeare's mother's house. Mary Arden's house is open daily from 9 a.m. to 6 p.m. and on Sundays from 2 p.m. to 6 p.m. A collection of antique agricultural tools is on exhibition. To the left of the bridge, at the road junction, you will find shopping facilities and also the Mason's Arms which sells paintings.

Moving along towards Bridge 60 you will get your first glimpse of the Cotswolds, about a dozen miles away on the other side of the Avon valley. Having now passed over a watershed you will now reach a flight of eleven locks, numbers 40 to 50, in three groups of three, five and three. There are wonderful views going down this flight of locks, Warwickshire being the most typically English of all English shires, and all the locks are easy to operate. There is a mile-long pound between locks 50 and 51 and after the latter you will be in the outskirts of Stratford. Some 300 yards beyond twin railway bridges there is a wooden wharf on the right, the base of the recently established Western Cruisers Ltd. There are two useful watering points with hoses on the wharf and a souvenir shop with canal books and various items connected with the canals. The entry to Stratford via the canal is shabby, but points of interest include the strange right-angled or cranked balance beam on the lower gate of Lock 53, constructed so that leverage can be obtained despite the close proximity of the bridge.

You may possibly find that wading is necessary at Lock 55 because water often flows over the top of the upper gate and floods the sides of the lock. All you have to do is to ensure that your craft is well away from the top gates when in the lock so that it is not caught in the 'falls' when the lock empties. You will also have to guide your boat down as you empty the lock slowly, so that the hull is not caught on the lock-side.

A sharp bend brings you to the lowest bridge on the canal and care should be taken to see that the super-structure will clear the underside of the bridge. If it will not, walk beyond the bridge past the basin to Lock 56 on the River Avon. Use your special key on the padlock, open a paddle and let some water run out into the river. This will lower the level of the pound and let your boat pass beneath the bridge. Keep left as you go under as there are submerged remains of a towpath on the right.

The Bancroft Gardens basin, once an ornamental pond with a fountain and masses of water lilies, has been cleared to make moorings near the Royal Shakespeare Memorial Theatre. This is convenient for shopping up Bridge Street or Sheep Street, both of which lead to more shops in the High Street. There are beautiful alternative moorings on the river, one north of Lock 56 and one to the right opposite the theatre along a line of poplars. There is easy access to the town across the old tramway bridge. River mooring can be uncomfortable and should be avoided if the river is in flood.

Stratford-on-Avon is such a popular holiday centre with so many guides and books describing it in great detail that no full description is needed here. The official guide costs a shilling and the inside cover has a useful town map. The theatre is open from April to December and it would be a pity to miss going at least once. Shakespeare's birthplace is in Henley Street, and many other places are well worth a visit. There is old Holy Trinity church where he is buried, medieval Clopton Bridge over the Avon, Shakespeare's statue at the canal basin, the classic town hall, Harvard House and the neighbouring Garrick Inn, the Shrieve's House and Emms Court, the Guild Chapel, Guildhall, the Grammar School and almshouses, and many old timbered houses and inns. Anne Hathaway's thatched cottage at Shottery is a mile from the town and there are buses running there frequently. Stratford is like the hub of a wheel with roads stretching in all directions, offering sights everyone should see at least once in a lifetime. The surrounding country-side is dotted with farms, market gardens, woodlands, parks and orchards, stretching into the Cotswolds, the Vale of Evesham and the Edgehills, and delightful villages like Henley-in-Arden, Shipston-on-Stour, Chipping Camp-den and many others are within reasonable distance.

There are many interesting items to note on the return journey such as the fact that the balance beams carry an iron plaque with the words 'Built from English oak by Wyckham Blackwell Ltd., Hampton-in-Arden 1961-5', or that the reconstructed lock sides often show the oak leaf emblem of the National Trust. The tops of the bollards at some locks have inscriptions on them and there are beautifully restored lock cottages at Lock 25. The tow-paths are sound and easy and give an opportunity for some lock-wheeling. There are a great number of different grasses, reeds, cat-tails, ferns and wild flowers, and in the hedgerows and along the banks scores of many species of birds, and even dragonflies. Fishing along the southern section is private, however, and no guns are allowed along the canal according to the notices. At several locks there are useful white square signs with black symbols showing, for example, a telephone, a farmhouse loaf, or a mug of beer.

We had another talk with Mr Bannister, the National Trust representative, when collecting the deposit on our key for Lock 56. He has been on the waterways all his life and lived in the cottage now occupied by Mr and Mrs Wagstaffe for twenty-two years as the lock-keeper. We found the southern section of the canal very pretty and a relaxing interlude. As regards scenery, the thirteen-mile southern section, in our opinion, comes very close to the longer Llangollen Canal and the southern section of the Oxford Canal.

The northern section of the canal, a little over twelve miles long and under the control of the British Waterways Board, was something of a surprise. We had been told that it was scarcely worth navigating. The Lapworth Flight of nineteen locks is admittedly hard going, but as they have to be emptied after locking through, they will all be with you and the bottom gate can be gently pushed open with your bows. There is mooring on the curving concrete wall below Lock 14 and the Boot Inn is a few steps along the road to the left, giving easy access to the little village of Lapworth with its varied shops. Within a few miles of Lapworth are some of the finest country houses in England, Chadwick Manor, Knowle, Broom and Bushwood Halls and Wroxall Abbey.

Working your way some 120 ft up the Lapworth Flight will be all the more rewarding if you stop at Bridge 31 to visit fifteenth-century Packwood House whose gardens contain a magnificent yew hedge clipped to represent the Sermon on the Mount. Nearby is moated Packwood Hall.

Beyond the Lapworth Flight the canal turns into a shady tree-lined cut with lifting bridges to Hockley Heath. There are moorings at Swallow Cruisers beside the Wharf Inn, which shows a 'R U 18' licence plate beside the bar.

There is now more open countryside with distant views and then miles of shady cruising past the Bluebell, a cider house, and Earlswood Marina. You can moor here if you wish to visit the Roman remains and moated manors in the countryside round Waring's Green and Earlswood. The canal side then becomes rather built up before the 352 yard long Brandwood Tunnel, then a swing bridge and an imposing open guillotine stop lock. This is two massive gates operated by huge pulleys once used to preserve water rights, and leads to a short cut and the junction with the Worcester & Birmingham Canal at King's Norton.

This latter canal, built between 1791 and 1815 after constant battling with rival canal companies, is a wide waterway running for thirty miles from Worcester Bar junction, Birmingham (within half a mile of the city centre) to the River Severn at Worcester, with five tunnels totalling some 4,260 yards in length and fifty-eight narrow 7 ft-wide locks with a total fall of nearly 450 ft. You join it some 5½ miles from Worcester Bar.

While famous for the longest flight of locks in the country, the Tardebigge Flight, it is particularly remembered by us because of an incident above the tunnel at Wast Hill. My wife spotted a plaid carrier bag in the water and hoisted it aboard. When the bag suddenly emitted an extraordinary noise she dropped it back into the canal and shouted 'Cat ... cat ... cat', urging me to reverse and retrieve the bag. As it was pulled aboard we could all hear mewing. Inside, wrapped in a scarf, was a tiny marmalade kitten, yelling for the very last of its nine lives. The sodden little creature was shorter than my hand and looked more like a rat than a cat as we rushed it down below where my wife dried it and gave it a little whisky in warm milk and then held it to dry off completely in the gas oven. He was immediately named 'Worcester' and allocated a cardboard box and a soft towel in the shower. I may add that no one used the shower while he

was there, but his escapes were so numerous we had to
put a lead on him. He has since grown into a handsome
ginger cat with a tail like a fox's brush and a temper to
match.

Once through Wast Hill Tunnel you are in Worcestershire and the countryside is one of rolling hills and woodland. Ahead are the Lickey Hills and in the far distance
the Malverns and the Cotswolds. All along the canal are
black and white country houses and charming villages.
This part of the country is crossed by old Roman roads.
Beyond Hopwood and the Bittel Arm lies Bittel reservoir,
a bird watcher's paradise.

The waterway goes through wonderful scenery to the
613-yard-long Shortwood Tunnel and a mile beyond lies
the first glimpse of big orchards, the Tardebigge Boat
Company hire base and the Tardebigge Tunnel. This tunnel has been hewn largely from stone and both the width
and height vary considerably. Outside the tunnel and past
a British Waterways yard is the top of the famous Tardebigge Flight. In $2\frac{1}{2}$ winding miles there are thirty easily-
worked locks with a total fall of 217 ft, but the views from
the flight are magnificent throughout the $2\frac{1}{2}$ hours it will
take to go through.

Here George Bate made friends with us and we found
in him a fountain of local knowledge. He lockwheeled
with me down a dozen locks and I learned that he had
started work on the Worcester & Birmingham Canal at
fourteen, eventually becoming a lock-gate maker. He
retired in 1968 at the age of sixty-seven, with a British
Empire Medal, but had returned to oversee the Tardebigge Flight for the 1969 season. His father had been a
maintenance man on the canal all his working life. His
grandfather had been a trader on the canal and had been
the innkeeper at the Queen's Head between Locks 29
and 28 and also the local blacksmith. His great-grand-

father was the blacksmith who founded the smithy behind the Queen's Head when the canal was being built. In this smithy the first horses and donkeys which towed the boats along the canal had been shod.

The Tardebigge Flight is followed almost immediately by the Stoke Flight of six locks with a total fall of 42 ft. Along this flight are signs of old canal arms which once carried boats to the salt workings at Stoke Prior. Brine was first brought up from great depths here by the inventor, John Corbett, who devised the most perfect system of salt manufacture in the world. Near the bottom lock is an unusual shop with canal souvenirs for sale and rare 'pie crust' plates recovered from working narrow boats, and the clever woodcraft of R. G. Sherwin. This shop also has authentically designed working boatmen's corduroy and moleskin front-flapped trousers.

Through the Astwood Flight of six locks dropping 42 ft you will find that the canal is higher than the surrounding land, with long views of rolling wooded hills. Next comes Hanbury Wharf and Marina, all that remains of the disused Droitwich Arm, built by James Brindley along the Roman road of Salt Way to Droitwich. This town, one of the oldest in England, is famous both for its salt and as a spa. The springs are so impregnated with brine that the water is reputed to be over eleven times the strength of sea water and with a greater density than that of the Dead Sea.

After the weir at Hadzor you will reach Dunhampstead Tunnel, the last and lowest of the five on the canal, and only 275 yards long, and as you emerge the Malvern Hills loom ahead. Then follows the Offerton and Tolladine Flight of eight locks, falling a further 56 ft into open countryside with the spires of Worcester Cathedral in sight some four miles away. From here you can visit Hindlip Hall and Park, which is less than a mile from the canal.

The approach to Diglis Yacht Basin is built up and the water becomes literally black. Entry into the River Severn is through two barge locks operated by a lock-keeper.

You will find excellent moorings at Worcester, below the railway bridge to the right. The town is hardly impressive, but the cathedral, which took 500 years to complete, and the Royal Porcelain works are worth visiting.

From Worcester it is only a four-hour run down the Severn to Tewkesbury and the beautiful River Avon. You will certainly want to make the few stops possible on the fast-flowing stream. As you leave Worcester you will pass once more under the main bridge and will notice high brick walls on the left with mooring rings in them. These were put there long ago but there is now little water beneath them and the town has done no dredging. Leaving the cathedral and the entrance to the Worcester & Birmingham Canal on the left, you come to a river junction. Keep to the left here as the right-hand stream leads to a dangerous weir. Diglis Locks nearby are electrically operated, one being over 93 ft long and 17 ft 9 ins wide and the other 142 ft long and 30 ft wide, both controlled by 'traffic lights'. The banks of the Severn are some 15 ft high with huge boulders to prevent erosion piled along the right-hand bank, and trees on the left.

There are few landmarks but you will soon see the narrow mouth of the River Teme, which rises in Wales. The countryside is now heavily wooded and the Malvern Hills dominate the landscape. Despite the high banks, there are many lovely views. Moorings for the charming village of Kempsey are on an old barge. You can explore the Malvern Hills and visit the town of Malvern from appropriately named 'Cliffey Wood' on the right.

The Severn along the next few reaches is rather like a miniature Rhine. There are manors and churches perched high above the river, as are the Rhineland castles, on the approach to Upton-on-Severn. This town, once a flourishing port for two shires, is pure delight, but not at weekends. There are moorings on the stone steps at the foot of the bridge on the right. Most of the pubs in this fishing town are above average, and offer superb meals, particularly at the Old Swan, and excellent rough cider or 'scrumpy' at the Plough. Giving the little town a kind of French air is a national monument, the remains of a church on whose thirteenth-century tower a copper cupola, which is now blue, was erected in 1780.

Beyond Upton there are more wooded banks and after rounding Sandy Point and abreast of Uckinghall Meadow the spires of Tewkesbury Abbey can be seen. There are many pretty villages in this part of the country but mooring on the Severn is not easy. The chart of the river must be consulted, coupled with probing with the boathook, to find suitable moorings along the wild banks. Twenty minutes after the M50 bridge, and it is wise to note that the Severn speed limits are 6 m.p.h. upstream and 8 m.p.h. downstream, you will pass under Wythe Bridge and it is then only five minutes to the mouth of the Avon on the left. This is a hazardous spot, with shoals extending well out into the main river and you must pass the junction before turning wide to enter the Avon from downstream of its mouth. Keep to the right once you enter the Avon as far as the lock gates and the unusual new lock cottage, on stilts. Lock charges vary according to the size of your craft and length of stay, but with our boat of over 40 ft long, through all eight Avon locks over a seven-day period, it cost us £2. The official handbook on navigation of the Lower Avon is on sale at the lock house. There are also various souvenirs for sale here. To the right are public moorings by Healing's Mill, or you can moor just upstream of the 800-year-old King John's Bridge on the left as you leave the lock.

Tewkesbury is a pleasant blending of old with new, and the town is laid out in three main streets in the form of the letter Y, the stem leading to the splendid Norman abbey church at the southern end of the town. The handsome water mill close by the abbey is twelfth-century. Shopping is a pleasure here and the High Street has ancient shop fronts and signs. Fowler and Sons supply sherry from casks by the gallon. The white timbered The Ancient Grudge restaurant and delightful alleys are reminiscent of medieval times. The inns of the town are good value too, including the Bell, associated with the book *John Halifax, Gentleman,* the Hop Pole Hotel, mentioned in *Pickwick Papers,* and Ye Olde Black Bear, reputedly 'Gloster's Oldest Inn'.

CHAPTER 14

BACK THROUGH BIRMINGHAM

THE AVON is undoubtedly one of England's most beautiful and peaceful rivers. You owe your holiday on it to a number of people, not least the Lower Avon Navigation Trust, a charitable organisation formed in 1950 which restored the navigation between Tewkesbury and Evesham after twelve years of arduous labour. Today, although a few locks leak, the navigation is maintained in good condition by voluntary private subscriptions without any help from the government, and it is the first successful restoration of its kind in the world. Craft up to 70 ft long, 13 ft 6 ins in beam and 4 ft draught can now safely cruise on the twenty-seven miles from the River Severn to Bridge Inn above Evesham Lock.

For some strange reason the speed limit on the Lower Avon Navigation is 10 m.p.h., which we consider is too fast and should be brought into line with the River Severn limits. After passing under the biggest but angled arch of King John's Bridge, you enter a broad and deep reach with a great many sailing craft about. You must give way to these boats, even if they cut right across your bows. Some 2½ miles out of Tewkesbury you will come to Twyning Fleet on the left with moorings by the Fleet Inn. Tewkesbury has virtually no outskirts along the river and you are at once in a rural setting with cattle grazing in the fields, pretty woodland and lovely hills ahead.

Bredon, little more than a mile from Twyning Fleet, has a lovely fourteenth-century Tithe Barn and a little church

with an almost needle spire. You will find the lock-keeper
at Strensham Lock most helpful. He is treasurer of the
Staffordshire & Worcestershire Canal Society and can tell
you much about the waterways in the area. He owns and
runs a little and useful shop there. From this lock the
river winds its way through beautiful countryside to the
charming sixteenth-century red sandstone Eckington
Bridge, the most perfect of all the old bridges surviving in
the county. As you cruise along the Avon you will see not
only meadows and hills, fields with sheep and cattle and
many orchards, but countless willow trees lining the banks.
The unspoilt beauty is broken only by a few villages and
houses, some almost as large as 'stately homes'. The settings
of the locks cannot be bettered on any waterway. It is only
three-quarters of a mile from Eckington Bridge to Swan's
Neck bend where the river narrows and twists with a bend
of 180°, and it is wise to reduce speed here. There is a
swing bridge over Nafford Lock which should be closed
again after going through. If you follow the path leading
off from the left of the lock to the road, you will come to
the old-world village of Birlingham with its orchards and
cottages. Here is the Swan Inn, and a shop. St James's
Church can be found through a gateway, once the twelfth-
century chancel arch of the church.

You are now coming into the supreme beauty of the
River Avon. Swans will come close to your boat for food
and you may see graceful terns and marauding hawks, as
we did. Near Pershore you will pass under the centre of
two bridges almost side by side, one relatively modern,
and the other a thing of beauty built for wayfarers of the
fourteenth century. The lock here is an unusual one,
having shallow diamond-shaped sides and a deep centre
portion which is parallel-sided. Put your boat up against
the planks instead of on the sloping beams on the right. It
is only two minutes from moorings at the foot of the rec-

reation grounds to the small market town of Pershore, said
to have derived its name from the pear trees that once
grew on the 'shores' of the Avon here. Some parts of the
lovely abbey with its delightful lantern tower date from
1090, but work was not completed until the fourteenth
century. It is the only church I know of which has a lock
key or windlass on its interior walls, with a plaque reading :
'To the Glory of God as a symbol of Thanksgiving for the
completion of the work of restoration this lock key was
placed here by the Lower Avon Navigation Trust—1962'.

Pershore and Wyre locks are only just over a mile apart
and sailing dinghies often use this short reach. At the lock
there is an old grist mill converted into a social club. There
are moorings here for water. Beyond Wyre Lock the river
twists and turns through orchards and beautiful countryside with superb views of Bredon Hill. You may notice that
there is no towpath along the Lower Avon. This is due to
the fact that horse-drawn traffic was unknown on this river.
Early craft using the navigation were sailing barges carrying grain and flour and coal, and when necessary, these
35 ft barges were bow-hauled by men.

Standing high on the left bank beyond Wyre Lock is
the little village of Wyre Piddle with gardens coming right
down to the waterfront. The Anchor Inn serves really
good food and you can have your meal brought to you on
board if you wish. There is little sign of habitation on the
three-mile winding reach to the 1887 Jubilee Bridge, carrying the road between the villages of Fladbury and Crop-
thorne. There is a very narrow navigation with a blind
corner leading to Fladbury Lock. If I had to choose one
lock as the loveliest in England I would have to choose
Fladbury, with its impressive weir and two picturesque old
mills.

As you reach the undulating Evesham golf course, you
will find big loops in the river with delightful water

meadows below the Woodnorton hills. Chadbury Mill and Lock, the last lock before Evesham, follow and soon you will see Abbey Manor through the trees. An obelisk in the grounds marks the site of the Battle of Evesham in 1265 in which Simon de Montfort, Earl of Leicester and reputed to be the founder of English parliamentary government, was slain. Closer to the river is the Leicester tower, built in 1840.

A huge horseshoe bend makes the prosperous market-garden town of Evesham into a peninsula. At the warning sign for Hampton Ferry blow three blasts on your horn to have the ferry rope lowered, and when passing over it put the engine in neutral as a safeguard against propeller fouling. Evesham Borough moorings are on the right, near a watering point in the little park. The handsome bridge ahead is Workman Bridge, about a hundred years old. Navigation is possible as far upstream as the Boat Inn, beyond Evesham Lock, but the Lower Avon Navigation Trust's control ends at Evesham Lock, and until the entire river from Stratford is made navigable again the shoals above this lock are likely to remain and cruising is inadvisable.

Opposite the moorings are lovely gardens sloping to the river and behind them Evesham's Bell Tower, dating from 1539, with its famous peal of twelve bells. There was once a massive abbey church here, founded on the basis of a vision of the Virgin by a swineherd, but little remains of it now, but the parish church of All Saints and the Pilgrims' church of St Lawrence with their noble spires still stand proudly. The abbey gateway is a memorable corner and the Almonery Museum in the fourteenth-century Almonery of the former Benedictine monastery, has exhibits on view which tell the story of Evesham from prehistoric times.

Heavy rains in the Midlands for several days before our

arrival at Evesham caused the river to flood and shortened our stay. As the water rose we hastily returned to Tewkesbury to make sure that we could get under King John's Bridge, the lowest on the navigation, before the floodwaters marooned us on the Lower Avon. In spite of the dark and glowering skies, mist hanging over the hills and for a time a torrential downpour, the return cruise of about twenty seven miles with six locks in under six hours was a happy one. It was very peaceful as no other craft were moving, the cattle were lying huddled in their pastures and the willows along the banks were literally weeping.

Locking out of Avon Lock for the River Severn we were tempted to run down once more to Gloucester and Sharpness, and on to the Bristol Avon. However, I have deliberately excluded detailing such a cruise from this book; although Gloucester, Bristol and Bath, the pleasant riverside and canal-side pubs, and the prospect of visiting the Wildfowl Trust at Slimbridge were all very inviting, this is a cruise filled with dangers for the inexperienced. The Severn is one of the oldest navigations in Europe and tidal effects increase as it nears Gloucester. However, the spectacular and famous Severn bore, that peculiar formation of a tidal wave rising at times to as much as 10 ft, which sweeps up the river at the head of each spring tide, will not affect your cruising above Tewkesbury.

Although you have already cruised from Worcester to Tewkesbury you will find that the wide river is more beautiful than ever when travelling upstream. The river runs fast too, so it will take you somewhat longer to cruise back to Worcester. Above Worcester you are quickly into wooded banks and open fields. Three miles from Worcester is Bevere Lock, operated by lock-keepers as are all locks on the Severn, and three hoots on the horn will get you through between 6 a.m. and 7.15 p.m. You now go past the silted entry to the derelict Droitwich Barge Canal. On this 'Wich Barges', sailing craft similar to those on the Severn, used to travel to Droitwich for cargoes of salt.

The river now goes through meadowlands to Grimley. As wooded hills rise on the right you will see tiny chalets in rows on the right bank with freshly painted fences and miniature gardens. The turrets of Holt Castle are visible on the left and Holt Lock follows with moorings for the Lenchford Hotel, an old and attractive building. We had here the most hilarious meal we have ever had on this kind of holiday. Silver salvers were topped by tins of baked beans and slices of toast, there were French mustard pots with leaping jacks-in-the-box, coffee cups the size of chamber pots and hinged spoons which had us all in hysterics. This kind of service would perhaps not always be welcomed but we were in the mood to appreciate the fun.

I have not mentioned all the inns and pubs on the banks of the Severn, of which there are many, as your chart will show, but the names are fascinating. Many have nautical ones, Ship, Sloop, Barge and Jolly Waterman, and others are named after animals, birds and fish, such as Lion, Hart, Bull, Dog and Duck, Bird-in-Hand, Salmon and even Plate of Elvers. As might be expected there is a Shakespeare. Virtually all were once navigation inns, catering for river men. Many carried on 'sidelines', trading in coal, fodder, bricks or general merchandise, and some were possibly engaged in smuggling.

Lincomb Lock is a mile below Stourport where the banks are lined with timber yards, factories and oil depots. On the left is the cliff knows as Redstone Rock with a great labyrinth of chambers. The British Waterways moorings are disgraceful and it is advisable to go on past the big barge locks of the Staffordshire & Worcester Canal on the right to the humpbacked bridge entry to the narrow locks,

installed in 1781 to save water, a few dozen yards further
on. The lock-keeper will help you through the two pairs of
staircase locks to the four basins 42 ft above the Severn
where there are good moorings and facilities.

The Staffordshire & Worcestershire Canal, which was
opened in 1772, is linked to the Severn by these locks and
basins, all interconnected and criss-crossed by pathways
and bridges. The old Tontine Hotel, which stands here,
was named after Lorenzo Tonti, the originator of a 'life
assurance' scheme whereby a number of people contributed to a fund and the last survivor took the lot. The
ancient warehouse with the white-painted clock tower is a
masterpiece of its kind and fortunately has been declared
an 'ancient monument', being used by the Stourport Yacht
Club.

Stourport is an example of a canal town which still
retains its old-time character with its waterway attractions
which are happily under a Conservation Order. It owes
its very existence to Brindley for he brought the canal here
only after the nearby town of Bewdley had rejected the
scheme. The views from Areley Kings church on a nearby
hill are memorable and the churchyard shows many amusing epitaphs.

The narrow York Street Lock, with its nearby 'Boat
Shop', has excellent souvenirs of the canal and delightful
watercolours of waterside scenes. Once past the 60 ft weir
and Upper Minton Bridge (No. 8) you will be in open
countryside. Most bridges appear to be sited on blind
corners but are distinctly numbered and named on pleasant
iron plaques. The canal runs high above meadowland with
hills rising gently beyond, through many one-sided red
sandstone cuttings with bracken-covered banks and profuse
growth of trees, vying for the sun. You cruise past Olding
Woods to Falling Sands Lock with a cast iron split bridge,
similar to those on the Stratford-on-Avon canal. From here

you can see the factory chimneys of carpet-making Kidderminster. Mooring is a problem here for there are several
miles of industrialised canalside before you reach Wolverley Court Lock and open countryside once again. There
are lovely flowers here and flowering weeds amidst cat-
tails; the pound is one of the most delightful on any
canal, with low-lying meadows on one side and wooded
sandstone cliffs on the other. Near Wolverley Lock is the
Lock Inn with one of the finest collections of horse trappings ever seen outside a museum. If you walk along the
road on the other side of the canal you will come to the top
of the hill and will find the unique 'Wolverley Pound', an
open-topped cavern of sandstone with an iron gate once
used to impound straying animals until they were
claimed. Down the one-way road, past the red brick eighteenth-century Italianate church, is the enchanting 'lost
village' of Wolverley. It nestles beside a little stream, with
ancient stone cottages and the former Sebright Grammar
School, which was built in 1620 by Sir William Sebright
and has unexpectedly noble proportions. It is no longer a
school but is used to some extent by the local council.
Were it not for the Kidderminster factories this canal
would challenge the Oxford and Llangollen for being the
most beautiful. Beyond Wolverley Forge Bridge it narrows
and passes through a rock-hewn bed and creeper-covered
sandstone cliffs. At Debdale Lock with its rock cliff and
cave you will find a circular weir, one of many built when
the canal was constructed to save space, and possibly the
first you have ever seen.

After the sixty-five-yard-long Cookley Tunnel the canal
is bordered by ferns and wild balsam and many kinds of
trees flourish along the banks. Past aptly named 'Hanging
Rock' you enter Staffordshire. The narrow Whittington
Horse Bridge is the place to moor if you wish to visit the

famous oak-timbered Whittington Inn, dating back to 1300 and reputed to be haunted by Lady Jane Grey.

Beyond the Horse Bridge you will see more cave dwellings amidst the trees. Until the turn of the century they were inhabited by boating families and this particular area became known as 'Gibraltar'. From Kinver Lock you can visit the town of that name and also nearby Kinver Edge, a wild area of woodland gorse, once the home of prehistoric men. The National Trust now preserves the ancient cave dwellings. A narrow cut soon brings you to small Dunsley Tunnel and Stewponey Lock, with a pub, a modern steak bar, a shop and garage. There are buses from here to Stourbridge where the famous crystal glassware is made. Then comes the entrance to the Stourbridge Canal, which links with the Birmingham Canal Navigations. It is only just over five miles long with twenty narrow locks through pleasant agricultural country and is a boon to those who wish to 'pub-crawl' for it has at least two pubs for every mile of waterway.

You now go on past an area known as Devil's Den and through six more locks, bordered by pubs ancient and modern, under Giggety Bridge to moorings for beautiful Wimbourn. From Bumble Hole Lock modern housing estates begin to encroach but there are pleasant views of the Orton hills. The unique Bratch Locks need particular care. They are not staircase locks but three individual ones separated by very short pounds fed from side ponds. Locking instructions must be followed to the letter or you may ground your boat on a flooded lockside. There is normally a lock-keeper on duty to help you. The flight is most attractive with its white bridges and white octagonal toll house.

After seven more locks at the rate of one a mile you are on the summit level, 294 ft above the Severn at Stourport, having navigated 33 locks and one of the loveliest stretches

of canal anywhere. It is less than two miles to Aldersley
Junction and the Birmingham Canal Navigations.

Today all but sixty-eight miles of the vast complex of
canals on three levels round Birmingham, known as the
Birmingham Canal Navigations, are navigable, a total of
112 miles having been adopted as official 'cruiseways'.
Cruising these waterways, for the most part running
through heavily industrialised areas, may seem dull, sordid and uninteresting but unless you go through at least
some of them you will have missed the very heart and soul
of our inland waterways. The Inland Waterways Association held a special rally at Farmer's Bridge on the B.C.N.
in July 1969 in a publicity bid to save the remaining sixty-
eight miles of these fascinating canals. Birmingham is the
centre of the country's canal system and the focal point of
the St Andrew's Cross which forms the rough layout of the
network and connects the main rivers of the country. If you
count the currently unnavigable canals, this large city is
said to have more miles of canals than Venice. The 7 ft lock
(many are a little wider) is standard throughout the system
which is fed by drainage pumped from the many disused
mine shafts and other pumping wells in the vicinity. The
Wolverhampton level is the highest of the three levels on
the system, being 473 ft above sea level, the Birmingham
level is 453 ft and the Walsall level is 408 ft above sea
level.

From the Staffordshire & Worcestershire Canal the
'Wolverhampton 21' flight carries you up to the Wolverhampton level, and into the city of Wolverhampton. The
countryside is quickly taken over by industry and there is
virtually nothing to stop for through this flight of locks.
Factories standing cheek by jowl along the canal side are
not such eyesores as the countless arms and basins leading
from the canal, now largely dumps or graveyards for rotting narrow boats. As you go along you can watch hot steel

rods like long flares coming from the blast furnaces, or penetrate deep into the Black Country by taking the Wednesbury Oak loop for the two mile run into Bradley. The main line continues through the wide Coseley Tunnel, 360 yards long and with railed towpaths on both sides. At Factory Junction you can turn right through Tipton and follow the Wolverhampton Level to Smethwick 6 miles ahead via Oldbury, which is Brindley's original line, or, as we did, lock through the three Tipton Factory Locks on to Telford's Birmingham Level.

We had no choice, for the M5 motorway was under construction when we were cruising here and huge signs warned us to use the Birmingham Level. We had planned to explore Dudley Tunnel on the nearby Dudley Canal, an unusual 3,172-yard tunnel built in the 1790s with a complete system of basins, branches to old workings and limestone caverns.

By the locks you will find the first of the former gauging stations where commercial craft were measured for displacement in order to make life easier for the toll clerks on the B.C.N. Below the locks is the first of a number of twin-arched bridges. Always take the left-hand arches into Birmingham at each of these bridges as only the left hand channels have been dredged. Also pass to the left of the 'toll islands' you will meet.

The canal now runs straight as a Roman road through Dudley Port past the junction for the Netherton Tunnel branch to the Dudley Canal. Netherton Tunnel was completed in 1858, is some 2,027 yards long and was the last canal tunnel built and is the biggest in circumference. Two boats can pass inside, it has twin towpaths and is actually lit, first by gas and later by electricity.

Now on a high embankment the canal soars past junction after junction to Spon Lane locks, the oldest working canal locks in the country, and the new M5 motorway

with only a 7 ft 3 ins gap left for navigation. It was somewhat harrowing passing by the tall steel girders of the
motorway with the clanging of work going on high overhead. Brindley's old line also shortly passed overhead on
the Stewart Aqueduct.

The Main Line now lies in a valley some 40 ft deep,
Telford's famous Galton Cutting, the sides being most
attractive with gorse and wild flowers. Next comes the magnificent arch of Telford's Galton Bridge, one handsome
span of cast iron across the 150 ft gap. From all the loops
you have passed since Deepfield's Junction you will
appreciate the scope of Telford's canal-straightening project
here.

At Farmer's Bridge there is a round island with signs
pointing to Coventry, Worcester and Wolverhampton. By
following the sign to Worcester, a few hundred yards will
bring you to Worcester Bar and Gas Street Basin with
excellent overnight moorings, only five minutes from the
centre of Birmingham. There are alternative overnight
moorings along the route to Coventry, just above Farmer's
Bridge Locks. We moored here where the city of Birmingham and British Waterways have restored the canal to its
former glory. A lovely marina has been built by the shining
white lock cottages and the British Waterways Board has
opened an information centre and a canal shop. An old
30 cwt crane stands beside the marina, and a new pub, the
Longboat, was being constructed when we were there. The
lane from the marina to the British Waterways Board
centre has been appropriately named 'James Brindley
Walk' to mark the exemplary cooperation between the
city and waterways authorities.

We found Farmer's Bridge most attractive. The flight
of thirteen locks, with L-shaped pounds and freshly painted
black and white balance beams, falls sharply to disappear
after half a dozen locks under a bridge. After leaving

the flight there is a short factory-lined pound with the Birmingham & Fazeley Canal continuing to the left at Aston Junction through the 11 Aston Locks. Keep right here into the Digbeth Branch, almost a mile long, and after two bridges you will reach the six Ashted Locks, which are in rather sordid surroundings. You have to make a sharp left turn under Bridge 96 into the narrow Warwick Bar and it is easy to miss. The Birmingham Canal Navigations will appeal to the enthusiast much more than to the novice who must remember that weekend passage is restricted and that pleasant overnight moorings are very limited indeed.

Although now out of the B.C.N. through Camp Hill Locks the Grand Union flows past factory after factory with only a few glades of overhanging trees for some six miles to Bridge 79. Here you now reach open countryside again. You will find pleasant moorings just beyond Bridge 78 or Catherine de Barnes Bridge. The attractive village of the same name lies sprawled on either side of the canal. The Grand Union now wends its way through prosperous farming country to the first of the wide locks on the long route to London. Knowle Locks, a pretty flight of five, falling 42 ft from the summit level of 379 ft, provide splendid views of Warwickshire. The delightful village of Knowle is less than half a mile away and not far from Knowle is the Forest of Arden and the Tudor Grimshaw Hall.

Beyond the locks the canal runs high above the meadows and fields. Then comes the Black Buoy Cruising Club on the right with the Black Boy Inn on the left by Bridge 69. The front door of this tiny plain pub is on the canal side and, according to the present publican, has been for over 200 years, making it older than the canal itself which was completed in 1799.

Here we met Mr Neville Bent, Commodore of the Black Buoy Cruising Club, and owner of the *Iron Duke* narrow cruiser moored in front of the pub. It boasts two original paintings of the Duke of Wellington and is a unique craft, the 35 ft hull coming from a British Waterways steam pump boat, formerly used to clean out locks. Mr Bent built the superstructure and fitted her out himself in well-planned comfort to sleep six. The unique feature of the *Iron Duke*, apart from her specially commissioned portraits, is that she has twin screws, something we had never come across before in a narrow canal cruiser. One is powered by a small Enfield diesel and the other by an electric motor and batteries.

Three bridges beyond the Black Boy is Rising Bridge, No. 66, and from here you are within easy reach of Baddesley Clinton, one of the best examples of Tudor architecture anywhere in Warwickshire. The village is charming and a fine centre for pleasant country walks. One more bridge and you are back at Kingswood Junction and the short cut to the Stratford-on-Avon Canal. There remains only the dripping Shrewley Tunnel, the Hatton Flight and Cape Locks with its boaters' pub and you are at Warwick, having covered, if you have done the entire trip, 244½ miles and 300 locks, or 544½ lock miles. Our actual cruising time was 103 hours and 28 minutes which means an average speed of just a fraction over five lock miles per hour.

With time in hand you can tour beautiful Warwick, with its magnificent castle, or continue along the canal for a couple of miles and take in gracious Leamington Spa. Your cruise has taken you through the very heart of England—Shakespeare's country. You have been exposed to history and heritage, to the works of many craftsmen both on and off the canals and rivers in the four counties of Warwickshire, Worcestershire, Staffordshire and Gloucestershire. It is, along with the adventure of the canals of the Black Country, a voyage of enchantment.

CHAPTER 15

ADVENTURES TO COME

THE INLAND waterways already described will keep any boating convert happily in holidays for a decade or more. Apart from the River Thames, which could not possibly be excluded, all these ribbons of water are still remarkably unpublicised and still largely empty of pleasure craft, even in the height of summer. The amateur can cruise any of them with complete confidence and, escaping from noisy crowds, find a forgotten heritage in perfect peace. They offer such endless variety and extensive choice that boredom is impossible, however discriminating or eccentric the tastes of the skipper or crew may be.

There are more inland waterways, of course, many hundreds of miles of them. They are not less interesting, exciting or beautiful but if I am to follow my own advice to the novice of not attempting to travel too far too soon I must leave you with the expectation and anticipation of more thrilling boating adventures to come.

The short River Wey and Lee & Stort navigations have not been described for they are more suited to weekend outings or brief excursions from cruises on major waterways. Nor have I dealt with the Kennet & Avon Canal and the two short river navigations which once formed a broad water route across the south of England to link the Thames and the Severn. There are a few isolated navigable sections but the vast majority of this waterway is derelict and through navigation is impossible. The Kennet & Avon Canal Association, formed in 1951, was transformed in 1962 into the Kennet & Avon Canal Trust and restoration work has been undertaken and is continuing in many places. The pace is slow, the problems formidable and the finance hard to come by but one day with luck we may yet cruise from Reading to Bristol.

I must confess to some slight prejudice in giving the Broads so little space. The Broads, however, are the most popular and most publicised of all our inland waterways and today boats per mile on these waters are more dense than vehicles per mile on our roads, with one reliable source estimating over eighty as compared with seventy-four. The navigational areas are being extended but after holidaying on the cuts where there are only about four boats per mile, the Broads have less appeal to one seeking essentially to escape from the hustle and bustle, the noise and stress of everyday life.

I am in no way suggesting that you ignore the Broads, particularly if you want to be in on what is called 'the scene'. But unless you want lots of company and prefer socialising to privacy I would recommend that you book your hire craft for either early or late in the season. If the popular resort type of holiday appeals to you, you will greatly enjoy the Broads and its many amenities. You will find many reports on the Broads when holiday supplements are published in newspapers, magazines and other mass media. Any of the three Broads hire craft associations will provide copious literature about these pleasant waterways.

You will have noticed that while the waterways of the South, East, West and the Midlands have been explored in this book, the waterways system of the North has not. There are many good reasons for this. The Trent, Humber and Yorkshire Ouse tideways are no places for beginners to learn the rudiments of navigation and boat handling.

In any case, special permission is necessary to take hire craft on these tideways.

The Trent, of course, is the waterways artery to the North, linking up not only with the Humber, Yorkshire Ouse, Ancholme, Don and Hull rivers but with a vast network of navigations that join Rotherham, Doncaster and Sheffield, Wakefield, Huddersfield and Sowerby Bridge, Goole, Leeds, Burnley, Wigan, Leigh, Manchester, Runcorn and Liverpool by water and sprawl across the north of England. On the way to the North the Trent picks up the ancient Fossdyke and Witham Navigations and the semi-derelict Chesterfield Canal. Beyond these junctions bows can be pointed west to Hull and Grimsby, north to Goole, Selby, York and Ripon, and west into a canal network that encompasses the Aire & Calder, Calder & Hebble, Huddersfield, Stainforth & Keadby, Selby, New Junction, Sheffield and South Yorkshire, all of which still throb to commercial traffic, some surprisingly heavy. Some experience is desirable in order to obtain maximum enjoyment from these waterways. The remote and isolated Lancaster Canal must be included in the canals of the North on geographical grounds and, of course, that pride of the North, the cross-country Leeds & Liverpool Canal, which is he very heart of the system.

Although the Lancaster and the Leeds & Liverpool Canals are eminently suitable for beginners and are among the wildest and most beautiful in the country, they cannot be divorced from an appreciation of the waterways of the North which deserve a book of their own to do them justice. I and most of my boating friends tend to reserve the Leeds & Liverpool for that last great fling, holding holidays upon it in abeyance so as to have one last prize to enjoy.

This explains why I am reserving the waterways of the North for a sequel to this book which has been written essentially for those who have never enjoyed a holiday on

our inland waterways. The novices going for their first
venture on skis wisely head for the nursery slopes rather
than risk their limbs on terrain that gladdens the hearts of
the experts. There is challenge and scope and excitement
enough for the beginner and convert alike on the inland
waterways described in previous chapters. Taking on more
than you can handle, exposing your crew of family or
friends to unnecessary risks, defeats the whole purpose of
carefree, peaceful holidays on the water. If you have no
confidence in your ability to cope and worse still if your
crew suffers from anxiety because you are clearly out of
your depth, the boating holiday will be spoiled for everyone.

From experience I can assure you that you and your
crew will get so much more out of holidays on the waterways of the North if you reserve them for later adventures.
I still get a thrill every time I recall locking out of Keadby
and taking the tide to Trent Falls, arriving just after low
water to catch the tide there all the way to Naburn Locks
just below York, particularly as I had worked out the
precise timings for myself. I remember with some chagrin
grounding momentarily in the rushing Trent off Torksey
and the entrance to the Fossdyke Navigation in the glowering dusk. The sudden meeting of a long train of 'Tom
Puddings', those coal-laden compartment boats linked in a
convoy of nineteen and towed by a tug, as we swung into
the Aire & Calder from the Selby Canal is stamped indel-
ibly in the minds of our crew and none of them will forget
the exciting navigation of the Linton 'clay huts' on the
Ouse above York. Many memories come back sharply :
roaring down the New Junction with half a dozen massive
barges and locking through the Sheffield & South Yorkshire with craft that made our cruiser look like a lifeboat in
comparison; shooting the fast flowing Ouse current under
the battered wooden bridge at Selby; the sight of mount-

ains of detergent foam on the dangerous Don; manoeuvering with ocean-going shipping at Goole and slithering smoothly across the tide past the tall open lock gates at West Stockwith. When eventually you go on the waterways of the North you will find a completely different kind of boating holiday, and get supreme satisfaction from mastering the tides, the shifting sands, the obstructions to navigation and even from little things like countering the high wake of passing barges without allowing your bows to move off course.

I would emphasise that your craft is the most important element in your boating holiday and time spent in ensuring that the craft you hire suits your particular needs is never wasted, indeed pays you handsomely in the enjoyment of your holiday. We have tried broad and narrow-beamed cruisers from only a few of the many hire firms now operating and with regret have not had the time diligently to inspect every boatyard and the craft they offer for hire, although we have covered quite a few. We have for the most part travelled with a sizeable crew on combinations of waterways and therefore craft that have suited us perfectly may not be your particular cup of tea. No one can supply you with a list of 'best boats' or classify hire firms in order of importance, convenience or value for money, although I stand by my comments on those already mentioned. If you neglect the basic 'homework' described in earlier chapters you will only have yourself to blame for unnecessary disappointments on your boating holiday. You may feel that you wish to have the minimum of planning, but to make sure of the greatest possible enjoyment of your holiday on the waterways do give yourself plenty of time to choose your hire craft carefully.

The following list gives the names of firms in many parts of the country who can offer you a choice of craft which can be hired for a week or more on our rivers and canals. The list has been arbitrarily divided into areas for your convenience, but bases should be regarded as starting points only. The permitted cruising range beyond home waters for any craft should be ascertained from the firm in each case, for the dimensions of the boat, facilities aboard or the barriers of tideways may limit the cruising range. Obviously, craft based on waterways which are disconnected from the network are restricted to their home waters.

No undertaking or guarantee about the craft or services offered can be given although every effort has been made to check the accuracy of all information provided. Most of the firms listed here issue free brochures giving details of their craft, services and charges, and often considerable extra information to help you in planning your particular holiday. Enquiries about craft and services offered should be addressed to individual firms or booking associations, and hirers should check all detailed arrangements and conditions of hire carefully with the firm from whom they will be hiring the craft of their choice.

APPENDIX

Firms with Northern Bases

Adventure Cruisers, The Jolly Roger Boating Station, Catforth, near Preston, Lancashire. Telephone: Catforth 232
2-6 berth craft. (Lancaster Canal only)

Beetham Cruisers, 10 Greendale Road, Liverpool, 25. Telephone: 051-428 2039
4-6 berth craft. (Leeds & Liverpool Canal)

Bradford Boat Services Ltd, Yacht Station, Apperley Bridge, Bradford, Yorkshire. Telephone: Bradford 612827
4-7 berth craft. (Leeds & Liverpool Canal and connecting waterways)*

Canal Boats Ltd, The Ship Inn, Rosemary Lane, Haskayne, near Ormskirk, Lancashire. Telephone: Halsall 446
2-6 berth craft. (Leeds & Liverpool Canal and connecting waterways)*

Inland Waterway Holiday Cruises Ltd, Preston Brook, Warrington, Lancashire. Telephone: Aston (Runcorn) 376
4 berth craft and 12 berth camping barge. (Bridgewater Canal, Leeds & Liverpool Canal)*

Key Line Cruisers Ltd, Timperley, Cheshire. Telephone: Sale 8962
2-10 berth craft. (Based on Bridgewater Canal)*

Nor'west Holiday Cruisers, Canal Wharf, Galgate, near Lancaster. Telephone: Galgate 368
2-7 berth craft. (Lancaster Canal only)*

Pennine Boats of Silsden, The Wharf, Silsden, Keighley, Yorkshire. Telephone: Ilkley 3444
4-6 berth craft. (Based on Leeds & Liverpool Canal)*

Preston Hire Cruisers, 4 Beech Avenue, Warton, near Preston, Lancashire. Telephone: Freckleton 823
2-6 berth craft. (Lancaster Canal only)

Summit Boat Services Ltd, Finsley Gate Marina, Burnley, Lancashire. Telephone: Padiham 71175
2-6 berth craft. (Based on Leeds & Liverpool Canal)*

Firms with Midlands Bases (including bases in North for
Midlands waterways)

Alsop, Stokes & Co Ltd, 2 Sandown Road, Toton, Beeston,
Nottinghamshire. Telephone: Long Eaton 2260
2-8 berth craft. (Erewash, Grand Union and Trent &
Mersey Canals)*

Anglo-Welsh Canal Cruisers, The Canal Basin, Leicester Road,
Market Harborough, Leicestershire. Telephone: Market Harborough 2594 and 4326
4-8 berth craft. (For canal network)
and at The Canal Wharf, Trevor, near Llangollen, Denbighshire. Telephone: Ruabon 2337
(For Llangollen Canal)*

Ashby Canal Cruisers, Station House, Shackerstone, Nuneaton,
Warwickshire.
4-6 berth craft. (Based on Ashby Canal)

Beeston Castle Cruisers Ltd, Beeston Wharf, near Tarporley,
Cheshire. Telephone: Tarporley 595
4-8 berth craft. (Based on Shropshire Union Canal)*

The Bijou Line Cruiser Co, Penkridge Wharf, Penkridge, Staffordshire. Telephone: Penkridge 2732
2-6 berth craft. (Based on Staffordshire & Worcestershire
Canal)

Blue Line Cruisers (Hire) Ltd, The Boatyard, Braunston, near
Rugby, Warwickshire. Telephone: Braunston 325 or 216
2-8 berth craft. (Based on Grand Union-Oxford and Strat-
ford-upon-Avon Canals)*

Boats (Warwick), 146 Coventry Road, Warwick. Telephone:
Warwick 42968
4-8 berth craft. (Based on Grand Union Canal)*

Bridge Canal Cruisers, Bridge Farm, Wrexham Road, Whitchurch, Shropshire. Telephone: Whitchurch 2012
4-6 berth craft. (Based on Llangollen Canal)

British Waterways Board, Hire Cruiser Office, Chester Road,
Nantwich, Cheshire. Telephone: Nantwich 65122
4-8 berth craft. (Based at Oxford on the Oxford Canal and
Nantwich on the Shropshire Union Canal)

Canal Cruising Co Ltd, Stone, Staffordshire. Telephone: Stone
2620
2-6 berth craft. (Based on Trent & Mersey Canal)*

Coltwood Hire Cruisers, Soar Valley Boatyard, Mountsorrel,

Leicestershire. Telephone: Weedon 739
2-6 berth craft. (Specialise in circular cruises on Grand Union and Oxford Canals and River Thames)*

Cruiseways (Hire) Company, Sawley Bridge Marina, Long Eaton, Nottinghamshire. Telephone: Long Eaton 4643 or 4278
4-8 berth craft. (Based on River Trent)*

S. C. Cummins Ltd, Nantwich Pleasure Craft, Basin End, Nantwich, Cheshire. Telephone: Crewe 55302
4-6 berth craft. (Based on Shropshire Union Canal)*

Dartline Cruisers, Bunbury Wharf, Bunbury, Cheshire. Telephone: Bunbury 638
4-6 berth craft. (Based on Shropshire Union Canal)

Dawncraft Cruisers, The Paddock, Kinver, Staffordshire. Telephone: Kinver 2368
2-8 berth craft. (Based on the Staffordshire & Worcestershire Canal)

Double Pennant Cruisers, Hordern Road, Wolverhampton, Staffordshire. Telephone: Wolverhampton 752771
2-6 berth craft. (Based on Staffordshire & Worcestershire Canal)*

Enterprise Cruisers Ltd, Wardle, Cheshire. Telephone: Wettenhall 666
2-4 berth craft. (Based on Shropshire Union near entrance to Llangollen Canal)

Farrow Marine Ltd, Kilworth Marina, North Kilworth, Rugby, Warwickshire. Telephone: Husbands Bosworth 484
2-8 berth craft. (Based on Grand Union Canal)

Foxton Boat Services Ltd, Foxton Bottom Lock, Foxton, near Market Harborough, Leicestershire. Telephone: Kibworth 285
Traditional narrow boats for hire. (Based on Grand Union Canal)

Gailey Canal Cruisers, Calf Heath Marina, Hatherton Junction, Walsall, Staffordshire. Telephone: Walsall 27137
2-6 berth craft. (Based on Staffordshire & Worcestershire Canal)*

G. T. G. Marine, Canal Bank, Derby Road, Loughborough, Leicestershire. Telephone: Loughborough 2019
2-6 berth craft. (Based on Grand Union Canal)*

Holidays Afloat Ltd, The Boatyard, Market Drayton, Shropshire. Telephone: Market Drayton 3181
2-7 berth craft. (Based on Shropshire Union Canal)*

Hopwood Craft Limited, Birmingham Road, Hopwood, near Alvechurch, Worcestershire. Telephone: 021-445 2592
2-18 berth craft. (Based on Worcester & Birmingham Canal)

Inland Hire Cruisers Ltd, Rowton Bridge, Christleton, Chester, Cheshire. Telephone: Chester 35180
2-6 berth craft. (Based on Shropshire Union near Llangollen Canal)*

The Kingfisher Line, Hoo Mill Lock, Great Haywood, Staffordshire. Telephone: Little Haywood 384
2-6 berth craft. (Based on Trent & Mersey Canal)*

Ladyline Cruisers Ltd, Wardle, Nantwich, Cheshire. Telephone: Wettenhall 682
2-8 berth craft. (Based at Barbridge on Shropshire Union near Llangollen Canal)*

Maidboats (Midlands) Ltd, Brinklow Marina, Stretton-under-Fosse, Warwickshire. Telephone: Pailton 449
4-9 berth craft. (Based on Oxford Canal)*

Mid-England Narrow Boats, 221/223 Belgrave Gate, Leicester. Telephone: Leicester 24181
4-6 berth craft. (Based on Trent & Mersey Canal)*

Midland Luxury Cruisers, Newcastle Road, Stone, Staffordshire. Telephone: Stone 2688
2-7 berth craft. (Based on Trent & Mersey Canal)*

Nautocraft Ltd, Boot Wharf, Nuneaton, Warwickshire. Telephone: Nuneaton 5833
2-6 berth craft. (Based on Coventry Canal)*

Poly Marine, 65 Queniborough Road, Queniborough, Leicestershire. Telephone: Syston 4935
2-5 berth craft. (Based on Grand Union Canal)

Shropshire Union Cruises Ltd, The Wharf, Norbury, Staffordshire. Telephone: Woodseaves 292
2-8 berth craft. (Based on Shropshire Union Canal)*

Solaris Hire, Hanbury Boat Marina, Droitwich, Worcestershire. Telephone: Droitwich 3002 or 3017
2-6 berth craft. (Based on the Worcester & Birmingham Canal)

Stafford Cruisers, Radford Wharf, Radford Bank, Stafford. Telephone: Stafford 3519
2-6 berth craft. (Based on Staffordshire & Worcestershire Canal)

Swallow Cruisers, Rear of Wharf Inn, Hockley Heath, Warwickshire. Telephone: Lapworth 2418

2-6 berth craft. (Based on Stratford-on-Avon Canal)

Swan Line Cruisers Ltd, Fradley Junction, Alrewas, Staffordshire. Telephone: Alrewas 332
2-6 berth craft. (Based on Trent & Mersey Canal)*

Tardebigge Boat Co Ltd, The Old Wharf, Tardebigge, Bromsgrove, Worcestershire. Telephone: Bromsgrove 3898
2-11 berth craft. (Based on Worcester & Birmingham Canal)*

Venetia Pleasure Boat Centre Ltd, Calveley, Tarporley, Cheshire. Telephone: Bunbury 279
2-6 berth craft. (Based on Shropshire Union Canal)*

Warwickshire Cruisers Ltd, Scarfield Wharf, Alvechurch, Worcestershire. Telephone: 021-445 2909
4-6 berth craft. (Based on Worcester & Birmingham Canal)

Water Gipsy Cruisers, The Globe Inn, Stowe Hill, Weedon, Northamptonshire. Telephone: Weedon 763
4-6 berth craft. (Based on Grand Union Canal)

Welsh Canal Holiday Craft, The Wharf, Llangollen, Denbighshire. Telephone: Llangollen 3302
4-6 berth craft. (Based on Llangollen and Shropshire Union Canals)*

Western Cruisers Ltd, Western Road, Stratford-on-Avon, Warwickshire. Telephone: Stratford-on-Avon 3878
3-6 berth craft. (Based on Stratford-on-Avon Canal)*

Willow Wren Hire Cruisers Ltd, Rugby Wharf, Forum Drive, Rugby, Warwickshire. Telephone: Rugby 4520
2-12 berth craft. (Based on Oxford Canal)*

Winsome Luxury Cruises, Lindenfels, Birmingham Road, Shenstone, Lichfield, Staffordshire. Telephone: Shenstone 226 or 658
2-5 berth craft. (Based on Trent & Mersey Canal)*

Wyvern Shipping Co Ltd, Leighton Buzzard, Bedfordshire. Telephone: Leighton Buzzard 2355
4-10 berth craft. (Based on Grand Union Canal)*

Firms with Southern Bases

Abingdon Boat Centre, Nag's Head Island, Abingdon-on-Thames, Berkshire. Telephone: Abingdon 1125
3-5 berth craft. (Based on River Thames)

T. W. Allen & Son (Yachts) Ltd, Ash Island Slipway, East Molesey, Surrey. Telephone: 01-979 1997
2-9 berth craft. (Based on River Thames)†

Allington Marina Ltd, Allington, Maidstone, Kent. Telephone:
Maidstone 52057
2-6 berth craft. (Based on River Medway)

Brian Ambrose & Co, Bert Bushnell Ltd, Raymead Road,
Maidenhead, Berkshire. Telephone: Maidenhead 24061
4-5 berth craft. (Based on River Thames)†

Andrews Boathouses Ltd, Bourne End, Buckinghamshire. Telephone: Bourne End 22314
2-10 berth craft. (Based on River Thames)†

Andrews Bros, Boat Builders (Maidenhead) Ltd, Ray Mead
Road, Maidenhead, Berkshire. Telephone: Maidenhead 24056
2-6 berth craft. (Based on River Thames)†

W. Bates & Son, Bridge Wharf, Chertsey, Surrey. Telephone:
Chertsey 2255
2-9 berth craft. (Based on River Thames)†

Benson Cruiser Station Ltd, Benson, Oxfordshire. Telephone:
Benson 304
3-7 berth craft. (Based on River Thames)

The Boatyard Iver, 200 Mansion Lane, Iver, Buckinghamshire.
Telephone: Iver 1496
4-8 berth craft. (Based on River Thames)

British Waterways Board, Hire Cruiser Office, Chester Road,
Nantwich, Cheshire. Telephone: Nantwich 65122
4-8 berth craft. (Based at Oxford on Oxford Canal)

John Bushnell Ltd, Wargrave, Berkshire. Telephone: Wargrave 2161
2-7 berth craft. (Based on River Thames)†

Horace Clark & Son Ltd, Clarks Wharf, Thames Street, Sunbury, Middlesex. Telephone: Sunbury 82028
2-8 berth craft. (Based on River Thames)†

Clifton's Holiday Cruiser Co, Orchard Farm, Sheepcote Lane,
Wheathampstead, Hertfordshire. Telephone: Wheathampstead
2202 or Maidenhead 20896
4-6 berth craft. Associated with Red Rose Cruisers Ltd.
(Based on River Thames)

Concoform Marine, The Boatyard, High Street, Weedon,
Northamptonshire. Telephone: Weedon 739
2-6 berth craft. (Based on River Thames)*

Morgan Giles Ltd, Aynho Wharf, Aynho, near Banbury, Oxfordshire. Telephone: Deddington 483
5-8 berth craft. (Based on Oxford Canal)

John Hicks Boatyard Ltd, The Waterfront, Datchet, Slough,
Buckinghamshire. Telephone: Slough 43930
4-6 berth craft. (Based on River Thames)†

Hire Cruisers (Maidstone) Ltd, Tovil Bridge Boat Yard, Maidstone, Kent. Telephone: Maidstone 54889
2-8 berth craft. (Based on River Medway)

Hobbs & Son Ltd, Station Road, Henley-on-Thames, Oxfordshire. Telephone: Henley 2035
2-7 berth craft. (Based on River Thames)†

Maidboats Ltd, Ferry Yacht Station, Thames Ditton, Surrey.
Telephone: 01-398 0271
2-10 berth craft. (Based on River Thames)*†
also at Wallingford Yacht Station, Wallingford, Berkshire.
Telephone: Wallingford 2163
2-8 berth craft. (Based on River Thames)*†

Maidenhead Court Boathouse Ltd, Boulters Lock, Maidenhead.
Berkshire. Telephone: Maidenhead 20723
2-6 berth craft. (Based on River Thames)†

Maple Line Cruisers, Symonds Farm House, Childrey, near
Wantage, Berkshire. Telephone: Childrey 285
2-6 berth craft. (Based on River Thames)

Pearl Line Ltd, Eyot House, D'Oyly Carte Island, Weybridge,
Surrey. Telephone: Weybridge 48586
3-6 berth craft. (Based on River Thames)†

Popular Boats Ltd, The Boat Centre, Caversham Bridge, Reading, Berkshire. Telephone: Reading 75777
4-6 berth craft. (Based on River Thames)*

Red Line Cruisers,, Wilsham Road, Abingdon, Berkshire. Telephone: Abingdon 1562 or 1760
2-6 berth craft. (Based on River Thames)

Red Rose Cruisers Ltd, Towpath, Station Road, Berkhamsted,
Hertfordshire. Telephone: Berkhamsted 6383
2-10 berth craft. (Based on Grand Union and Oxford Canals
and River Thames)*

Salter Bros Ltd, Folly Bridge, Oxford. Telephone: Oxford
43421
2-6 berth craft. (Based on River Thames)†

J. Tims & Sons Ltd, The Boat House, Staines, Middlesex. Telephone: Staines 52093
2-7 berth craft. (Based on River Thames)†

Weybridge Marine Ltd, Thames Street, Weybridge, Surrey.
Telephone: Weybridge 47453

3-6 berth craft. (Based on River Thames)†

Firms with Western Bases

Canal Pleasurecraft (Stourport) Ltd, Stourport-on-Severn, Worcestershire. Telephone: Stourport 2970
2-6 berth craft. (Based on Staffordshire & Worcestershire Canal)*

Combe Fleet Ltd, The Fountain Grill, Stourport, Worcestershire. Telephone: Stourport 3313
4-7 berth craft. (Severn and Avon Rivers only)

Kim Line Cruisers, Strensham Marine Ltd, Mill Lane, Strensham, Worcestershire. Telephone: Tewkesbury 3596
2-6 berth craft. (Severn and Avon Rivers only)

Killside Boatyard, 37 Bridge Street, Pershore, Worcestershire. Telephone: Pershore 249
2-4 berth craft. (Severn and Avon Rivers only)

D. M. Phillips, 11 Finchcroft Lane, Prestbury, near Cheltenham, Gloucestershire. Telephone: Cheltenham 7378
4 berth craft. (Based at Tewkesbury for Severn and Avon Rivers and adjoining canals)

Tewkesbury Marine Services Ltd, 'Gay Boat' Yard, St Mary's Lane, Tewkesbury, Gloucestershire. Telephone: Tewkesbury 2187
2-6 berth craft. (Severn and Avon Rivers and adjoining canals)*

Firms with Eastern Bases

H. C. Banham Ltd, Riverside Works, Cam Road, Cambridge. Telephone: Cambridge 59486
2-6 berth craft. (South Level of the Fenland waterways only)‡

Blakes (Norfolk Broads Holidays) Ltd, Wroxham, Norwich, NOR 41Z. Telephone: Wroxham 2141
2-10 berth craft of various types. (Broads only)

R. B. Bradbeer Ltd, 7 Battery Green Road, Lowestoft, Suffolk. Telephone: Lowestoft 3172
2-12 berth craft of various types. (Broads or canals)

Broads Holidays, Port of Yarmouth Marine, Great Yarmouth, Norfolk. Telephone: Great Yarmouth 56531/2
2-10 berth craft. (Broads only)

F. W. Carrington, Quiet Waters Boatyard, Earith, Huntindonshire. Telephone: Earith 400

APPENDIX 249

2-6 berth craft. (South Level of the Fenland waterways only)‡

Elysian Holidays Ltd, 5 Annesdale, Ely, Cambridgeshire. Telephone: Ely 2244/5 or Earith 555 or Huntingdon 3060
2-6 berth craft. (South Level of the Fenland waterways only)‡

Fleming Holidays Afloat Ltd, Cruiser Hire, 10 Laxton Close, St Neots, Huntingdonshire
2-6 berth craft. (South Level of the Fenland Waterways only)

Hoseasons Sunshine Holidays, Sunway House, Bridge Road, Oulton Broad, Lowestoft, Suffolk. Telephone: Lowestoft 62181
2-8 berth craft. (Based on Broads, Thames, South Level of Fenland waterways and canals)*

L. H. Jones & Son, The Boathaven, St Ives, Huntingdonshire. Telephone: St Ives 3463
2-6 berth craft. (South Level of the Fenland waterways only)‡

R. Moore & Sons Ltd, Wroxham, Norfolk. Telephone: Wroxham 2293
2-7 berth craft. (Broads only)

Oundle Marina, Oundle, near Peterborough, Northamptonshire. Telephone: Oundle 3311
2-6 berth craft. (Nene River only)

Rentacruiser, The Anchor, Tempsford, Bedfordshire.
2-4 berth craft. (South Level of the Fenland waterways only)

Robinsons (Yacht Builders) Ltd, Oulton Broad, Suffolk. Telephone: Lowestoft 5028
3-8 berth craft. (Broads only)

Waveney Yacht Station, Burgh St Peter, Beccles, Suffolk. Telephone: Aldeby 217
4-6 berth craft. (Broads only)

Hotel boats and Hostel craft

Horsebarge Hotels Limited, Towpath, Berkhamsted, Hertfordshire. Telephone: Berkhamsted 6383
1-2 week cruises of Grand Union Canal in horse-drawn broad barges

Hostelcraft Ltd, 2 Waverley Road, Fordingbridge, Hampshire. Telephone: Fordingbridge 2150
Weekly cruises over much of canal system in horse-drawn traditional narrow boat

Inland Cruising Co. Ltd, The Boatyard, Braunston, Rugby, Warwickshire. Telephone: Braunston 216

Regular cruises in pair of converted traditional narrow boats over many canals

Inland Waterway Holiday Cruises Ltd, Preston Brook, Warrington, Lancashire. Telephone: Aston (Runcorn) 376

Regular cruises in converted traditional narrow boats over wide choice of canals*

*   Member of the Association of Pleasure Craft Operators on Inland Waterways

†   Member of the Thames Hire Cruiser Association

‡   Member of Great Ouse Boatbuilders and Operators Association

INDEX

Non-fiction in Tandem editions

Best-selling fiction in Tandem editions

Edith Pargeter's memorable trilogy
of medieval England and Wales
The Heaven Tree 7/–
The Green Branch 6/–
The Scarlet Seed 6/–

Romance and history combine in a swift-moving story of
border warfare, power politics and private feuds on the
Welsh border in the reign of King John.

"A highly dramatic and intense story, beautifully written"
Glasgow Evening Times

Elizabeth Lemarchand
Death of an Old Girl 5/–
The Affacombe Affair 5/–

Two first-class detective stories featuring Chief Detective-
Inspector Tom Pollard of Scotland Yard, and sure to
appeal to anyone who enjoys Agatha Christie.

"A superbly told tale of blackmail and terror"
Manchester Evening News

"A real genuine police detection story . . . a hundred
per cent winner"
Sunday Times

Catherine Cookson
Hannah Massey 5/–
The Garment 5/–
Slinky Jane 5/–

Compelling and moving novels, set in the North Country
which Catherine Cookson has made famous.

"In an age when so much rubbish is published and writers
are two a penny, Mrs Cookson comes as a boon and a
blessing. She tells a good story. Her characters live"
Yorkshire Post

Name..

Address ....

Titles required ....

....

- -

The publishers hope that you enjoyed this book and invite you to write for the full list of Tandem titles which is available free of charge.

If you find any difficulty in obtaining these books from your usual retailer we shall be pleased to supply the titles of your choice — packing and postage 9d — upon receipt of your remittance.

WRITE NOW TO:
       Universal-Tandem Publishing Co. Ltd.,
       14 Gloucester Road,
       London SW7

SOFTNESS
of the
LIME

MAXINE CASE

UMUZI

Published in 2017 by Umuzi
an imprint of Penguin Random House South Africa (Pty) Ltd
Company Reg No 1953/000441/07
The Estuaries No 4, Oxbow Crescent, Century Avenue, Century City, 7441,
South Africa
PO Box 1144, Cape Town, 8000, South Africa
umuzi@penguinrandomhouse.co.za

First edition, first printing 2017
1 3 5 7 9 8 6 4 2

ISBN 978-1-4152-0933-2 (Print)
ISBN 978-1-4152-0911-0 (ePub)

Cover design by publicide
Text design by Fahiema Hallam
Set in Adobe Caslon

Printed and bound by Replika Press Pvt. Ltd.

In memory of Barbara Ellen Michael, my Ma
6 November 1927–12 December 2016

'It is the softness of the lime that is fatal to the bird.'
– Malagasy proverb

Geert, 1782

My father's funeral has gone off splendidly, so splendidly that I think if he himself had been in attendance, he would have not faulted the proceedings and might even have been pleased. Most gratifying, I am sure, would have been the multitude of mourners who arrived to see him off. My father had been of the opinion that nothing speaks more to a man's stature than the number of his fellows – the *bloedvrienden* – who accompany his body to the grave. Indeed, as I recall, my father rarely passed on an opportunity to join the funeral processions of the Cape's foremost citizens.

When the old governor Ryk Tulbagh passed away after long months of ill health, only to be dispatched by the gout, my father had taken up a prominent place in the cortège. I was not yet thirteen years old at the time, a lad. Nevertheless, I remember it well. On the morning of Governor Tulbagh's funeral, the bells of the Castle and those of the church had begun their toll early in the morning and had continued to do so on and off until the procession left the Castle for the church sometime in the afternoon.

The cortège made a great impression upon me as I watched it go by from the front stoep of our house. It was headed by soldiers wearing bands of a black material around their hats and on their guns. They were followed by bearers carrying the governor's effects – his insignia, his standard, his arms – and his stablemen leading his horses. Eight undertakers in full funeral dress trooped behind. Then, draped in mourning cloth, came the coffin. A merchant held up each corner of the cloth, while the coffin itself was carried by Company officials with their relievers marching alongside. Tulbagh's *bloedvrienden*, my father among them, walked behind his coffin. Mounted cavalry brought up the rear. What I most recall was the noise – the clanging of the church bells and the firing of the guns to honour the dead man. I counted nineteen shots fired from the Castle's distinctive main battery alone, which were answered by the other batteries, there being no ships in the waters of Table Bay to reciprocate at that time of year. On his return home, my father had patted my head and remarked to one of his associates who'd accompanied him that it was unfortunate that a man like Tulbagh had not had sons to carry on his name. I beamed.

Less than two years after Governor Tulbagh's death, his successor, Baron Pieter van Reede van Oudtshoorn, was laid to rest in the same church and in a likewise fashion. The replacement governor had been newly appointed in Holland and was travelling to the Cape aboard the *Asia* to take up his post. Weeks after the ship departed Dutch shores, Van Oudtshoorn succumbed to death at sea. His body was placed in a leaden coffin with which he'd so happened to be sailing, and in this manner completed the remaining four months' journey to the Cape. Imprudent men mocked that the governor's body had been preserved in a barrel of brandy instead of a box. But when I asked my father whether this was true, he'd merely smiled and shaken his head, complaining about men who had nothing better to do than make up untruths about their betters.

I heard said that it was a lavish funeral – Van Oudtshoorn had first arrived at the Cape in 1741 and had held high office before leaving for the United Provinces on personal business. I had been ill with a fever at the time and thus had not been able to watch the spectacle, nor accompany my father to pay my respects. The following morning, my father stridently derided the ostentatious display, but we all knew that he was proud to have once more taken up his place as one of the Cape's eminent burghers.

Now, on the day of his own funeral, my father's high standing at the Cape was without question. As his oldest and sole surviving son, it had fallen upon me to adjure the funeral arrangements. In the Cape, it is customary to engage the services of a funeral director to ensure the contrivance of the matter. The man whom I engaged had been responsible for all the important funerals and I had no complaints regarding the execution of his duties. In addition to the invited guests, he had procured the services of a group of *huilebalken* or professional mourners to lead the column. A troop of *tropsluiters* walked at the back in order to swell the already great number of mourners, and because of the old superstition that whomsoever fell last in line would be next to perish, the director justified. We paid them a rix-dollar each.

The procession that set off from my father's house was larger than most, but not so large as to be considered improper or above his station. His coffin, draped in a rich cloth of black velveteen, was drawn by wagon. We followed behind, a grave file of men mourning a man known for his solemnity.

My father was a man much admired, although I dare not venture that he was much loved beyond the bounds of his household. He was a hard man, given to few displays of warmth, particularly to my sisters and myself. 'If a man spareth his rod, he hateth his son,' he quoted daily. The Bible commands one to honour one's father and mother so your days may be long on earth, and honour him we did. Every morning, my father would gather his family and his chattel together to hear him read from the Good Book and to pray. We were all well versed in the ways of the Lord.

The eulogy was blessedly short. The minister advised the mourners that my father had been a man of humble beginnings who, by dint of hard work and enterprise, had risen to the position of one of the Cape's richest and most respected citizens. 'Nor did he forget his mean background,' the minister said. 'The deceased was a good Christian man, one who regularly gave alms to the poor and succour to the widowed and orphaned in his personal capacity and as erstwhile Orphan Master and Trustee of the Poor Fund.'

As to the living, we were reminded that man is of the earth and that death comes without warning to all. 'Let those among us who have sinned repent of our ways before it is too late,' the minister cautioned.

With the sermon concluded, my father's body was interred in a place of honour in the churchyard. I had had to pay a steep sum for this situation, but it was as he would have wished.

We then repaired to my father's house for the ritual repast; all those mourners had to be fed, and fed well. The kitchen had been occupied preparing the mourning feast for days; the entire household had been in an uproar readying the house for its guests. My sisters were too young to be of much use, and once more it had fallen upon me to ensure that all was as it should be. My various duties left me with but a small measure of time to ponder the significance of my father's demise.

I had arranged to buy the barrels of Bordeaux and brandy that mourners have come to expect at the best funerals, despite the fact that my father had been a rather temperate man in life. There was plenty of tobacco too. Men filled their pipes and their bowls liberally, as if at a fashionable gathering instead of a funeral. The vast numbers of cakes provided were almost untouched, but the mourners made quick dispatch of the roasted legs of beef and mutton and the corned meats that had been prepared and served cold. My father's household was known for the quality of its meats and we did not disappoint. Before long, the front room of the house, with its view of Town and the harbour in the distance, was filled with the fog of tobacco smoke and loud voices.

I sat listening to the men talk, but did not participate in the conversations around me with any vigour. At my age, I was yet uncomfortable in the company of grown men. From time to time, someone would mention my father's munificence, his magnanimity and all would look in my direction, questioningly. The question, I imagined, was whether I was fit to step into his shoes. I nodded in recognition of their words and smiled politely. One is raised to respect one's elders.

Although my father had the reputation around Town for being taciturn, a man of few words and chary of conversing with his inferiors in too free a fashion, he'd enjoyed regaling his children with the stories of his life in order that we could consider his ways and be wise.

'I arrived at the Cape during a time of pestilence and peril,' he'd begin. 'An inauspicious start to my new life in a new land, though it had not been my intention to stay.'

Then, as now, the Cape was a mere, but imperative, stop along the way for ships journeying between Europe and the East. Within days of landing, however, he had taken sick and remained so for a number of weeks, jettisoned in that uncertain domain between life and death. The widow woman with whom he had sought lodgings had tended him reluctantly but thoroughly. She had taken fright at his deteriorating condition and had endeavoured to have him committed to the Company Hospital, yet even in his delirium, my father's will had prevailed.

It was a stroke of providence that my father had found such a pliant landlady, or perhaps the hand of fortune had directed him there. When he recovered his health, the good lady apprised him of the goings-on in Town. More than a thousand souls had already succumbed to the scourge that did not distinguish between freeman and slave, the wealthy or the destitute.

'Most of the Cape's burghers blamed the contagion on a ship returning to the United Provinces from Ceylon,' my father said, years after the fact. 'As a result, all travellers were viewed with mistrust. Nor did locals escape the taint of suspicion,' he qualified. 'Neighbours slammed their doors and windows shut against each other, and a house where the plague had laid waste to entire families, including slaves, was to be avoided at all costs.'

By the time he was well enough to travel, the ship on which he had sailed had already left for the next stage of its journey and my father's intended destination of Batavia. He was marooned at the Cape.

At the age of two-and-twenty years, my father had left his own father's home in Zaanstreek and signed up with the Vereenigde Oost-Indische Compagnie for the requisite five-year term. Despite upheavals in the financial fortunes of both the Dutch Republic and the Company itself, enlisting with the latter promised a respectable occupation and was one of the few places for men of adventurous spirits and limited means. Being a man of some learning, my father was appointed a lower merchant within the organisation when the Cape officials learned this fact – a promotion of sorts.

'Although the Company paid poorly, the post came with certain perquisites,' my father recalled. As a lower merchant, he was permitted to wear shoe buckles of gold or silver under the rules recently introduced in Batavia 'to control the pomp and preening of Company servants and the burghers under its control'. My father had always been peacock-like about his person. This had been one of his few conceits, though he deplored vanity in others.

At the time of my father's joining the Company, his father owned one of Zaanstreek's few thriving shipyards. The district, once the most industrious in all of Europe, according to my father, had been hard hit by the economic troubles bedevilling the rest of the land. 'Its substantial shipbuilding industry had been particularly impaired since fewer vessels were required for trade. Workers began deserting the cities for farms, where they could still coax a living from the soil or from raising livestock for the export market; the fat Dutch livestock were renowned for their quality,' he'd say with no small degree of pride, even as he expounded on the hardships facing his birthplace.

My father's background was thus not as mean as the minister had supposed in his eulogy. As my grandfather's only heir, my father had been expected to take over the running of the shipyard when the time came. For my father, however, sailing the seas aboard ships he'd helped build presented greater temptation than that offered by dry land. He'd always planned to return, he said. He'd never expected to make a home for himself at the Cape, nor at any of the Company's other outposts, for that matter. Yet once he struck land at the Cape, he'd remained land-bound, resigned to his fate. 'My dreams of sailing the seven seas amounted to nothing more than the journey from Amsterdam to the Cape,' he'd said.

Of his arrival at the Cape, my father could not recall much – he was already suffering the first ravages of the fever – save for the shimmering white houses with their green shutters that rose into view as the ship approached Table Bay, and the Castle of Good Hope that loomed above the jetty by which he came ashore. 'This boded well,' he'd ventured. 'I'd expected savagery, a wilderness of a town.'

Once he recovered his health and began his perambulations, he realised that although the Cape bore traces of gentility, on closer inspection it was more akin to a village than a bustling city. True, there was the sprawling five-pointed Castle, 'but it was surrounded by a fairly ineffectual moat and rather crudely constructed from the unattractive blue-grey stone quarried nearby,' he'd said.

Having grown up in this town and having no great European or Eastern cities with which to form my own comparisons, I myself find the Castle rather pleasing, but since these were my father's impressions, my own thoughts on the matter are of no account. This building, home to the governor and several senior officials, as well as housing the garrison, the bakery and other workshops and offices, was the same one in which my father would toil, in an office, going over the Company accounts. Sentries were ever on duty at the entrance built from yellow stone bricks but, being my father's son, I always passed through unmolested from the time I was old enough to visit there on my own. During my childhood, I spent many a happy hour within those stone walls, playing with friends who lived there and catching frogs in the moat.

Then, like now, the Heerengracht was the main road in Town. It is here that the Great Church is located, its spire rising above the buildings. Opposite the church is the Company Hospital. It's the same one within which my father managed to avoid being housed upon his arrival, although it's unlikely that he would have found accommodation there if his widowed landlady had had her way: 'With so many people sick, there were no beds to be had at the time.' My father had not been afflicted by the plague but was suffering from some other, more benign, malady. 'Had I been admitted to the hospital, no doubt my already weakened constitution would have succumbed with ease.'

Privately, I doubted that; my father had always been a bull of a man.

The Slave Lodge lay across from the hospital. It was a place we were told to avoid as children, a sordid place. When I was older, I discovered what my father meant by disreputable; it was a den of iniquity, but as a child I merely followed his injunction as I did in all matters. The Company's Garden lay further eastwards, a short distance from the Slave Lodge. The gardens were where Jan van Riebeeck and his men had begun planting vegetables and fruit for the ships that sailed in to replenish their stores and drop off their sick. By the time I was a child, it was less of a working garden; exotic plants were collected here and it was a fascinating place to explore on a pleasant day.

When he'd first arrived, my father had found walking about anything but pleasant. 'The streets, of which there were but a few, were not in good condition; hither and thither they were rutted with holes and strewn with filth.' On the slopes of Table Mountain, which even my father had to concede was majestic, many of the townspeople kept small plots where they grew vegetables. 'But the mountain was already denuded by the haphazard cutting of wood,' he decried. 'In the rainy months, layers of topsoil silted down into the town and were carried by channels into the bay.'

As a man used to the order and civility of the United Provinces, my father had blamed the locals for the poor state of affairs. Though he was a Company man, he held no high opinion of the burghers living at the Cape. He judged them indolent, relying on others to do all the work.

The plague continued unabated during the first few months of my father's tenure. Like many Dutchmen, he'd blamed the course of the disease on the unsanitary living conditions that distinguished the Cape and made unflattering comparisons with the land of his birth. Zaanstreek was not only a place of industry, but of beauty. It was named for the Zaan River that flows throughout the area – from Zaanstad in the north to Zaandam in the south – on which my father had spent many a happy hour sailing as a boy.

'Hundreds of windmills could be found along the river,' he claimed. 'When the winds blew, the sails of the windmills turned merrily. The grass was of the most verdant green and many of the houses were green too. Wooden houses painted green.

'Despite the economic troubles, it was an orderly place, a cultured place that was in many ways dissimilar to the filth and decrepitude of the Cape. Even the factories, many of which could be found along the banks of the Zaan, were attractive,' he said. 'Nor were the shipyards mean, but a place where men from all over Europe could be found working side by side.'

Listening to my father describe the many superior qualities of the Dutch Republic – as the United Provinces, or the Republic of the Seven United Netherlands, to name it in full, was more commonly known – I imagined that no country could live up to this image he'd painted. I've longed to visit so I can see for myself whether he was speaking the truth or merely being fanciful, nostalgic.

Yet, for all the esteem that my father had bestowed on the country of his birth, he had never once to my knowledge attempted to return. And for all the awe in which he held the funerals of the Cape's finest burghers, he did not return to Zaanstreek when his own father passed on. He had received word that his father was ailing months beforehand, but he had found reasons for remaining at the Cape. I was angry at my father for not going to my grandfather's bedside; he had instilled in me a sense of propriety and it was not proper that he should stay away. More than once, I girded myself to ask him why he had not embarked upon the first ship returning to the old country when he'd heard that my grandfather's life was fading, but never had I summoned the nerve to do so.

The next letter that arrived notified him of his father's death. In the time it took the letter to cross the ocean, this grandfather whom I had never known had already been buried, and by strangers, as he had no family still living in the land. 'It is the Lord's will this was so,' I heard my father tell one of his acquaintances who called at the house to condole with him. Years after this, I learned that my grandfather had lost his shipyard and would have died in penury but for the regular remittances my father sent home. Had I learned this earlier, I might have been less quick to call him an unfaithful son, not that I did so to his face.

In those first months, my father set to work for the Company, earning a meagre forty guilders per year, an insufficient sum for someone who yearned for the finer things in life. All the while, he continued to lodge in the widow's home. She was sixteen years my father's senior and soon became enamoured of him, as certain older women are inclined to be of young men. He must have returned her opinion of him because before the year was out, the two were betrothed. Shortly thereafter, my father bought his way out of his contract since Company officials were not allowed to own farms, and his fiancée possessed a rather large farm in Swellendam in addition to her house and holdings in Town. The Cape was indeed a land of milk and honey for an ambitious young man with an attractive visage and pleasing mannerisms.

With his service period ended, my father set about making his fortune. His new wife – he married her as soon as his service came to an end – owned a share of a meat *pacht*, a lease to provide the Company with meat for its ships that called at the Cape and to satisfy its domestic requirements. Whoever owned shares in a *pacht* was assured of a regular income, despite the fact that the Company set the purchase price, and competition to acquire a *pacht* on auction was thus high. My father managed his wife's interests, but this was not enough for him. He purchased a share of another meat *pacht* on credit, repaying the loan within the year, while, at the same time, he added to his wife's herd in Swellendam. The area was wetter, the grass lusher: the butter from the cows raised there was considered sweeter and the cattle reared there were prized as trek-oxen.

Although he diversified his holdings, breeding sheep and investing in properties in Town and several more farms, including a grain farm in Drakenstein and a wine farm in Stellenbosch, my father always had a particular affinity for cattle. One of his favourite stories to relate was that of a family who had lived in Zaandam many years before he was born.

'The little boy was playing with a kite in his father's fields when one of the family's bulls took offence to this and made as if to charge the boy. When his parents saw this, they immediately ran to their son's aid. In his rage, the animal turned on the parents instead, goring the father with its fearsome horns and butting the mother so that she was tossed into the air.'

'What happened next, Father?' I would ask, though of course I knew the answer from previous recitals of the tale.

'Well, the mother was increasing, due to deliver any day. The baby was born on the very ground she landed. She died soon after, though the baby lived for a few months, it was said.'

'And the boy?'

My father would shake his head woefully, making it clear that there was a warning for me in the story. 'Only the boy whose sport had caused the catastrophe survived to tell the tale,' he said.

As I grew older, I realised that it was a most gruesome story to tell a young child and was not sure that I wholly believed it. I expressed my distrust to my father.

'One day I will show you the church named for the Zaandam bull,' he promised each time, and each time he would remind me: 'The good Lord has given man dominion over all beasts, this is true, but one should never underestimate an animal's strength. Furthermore,' he would add, 'it is due to the humble bovine that we may live so lavishly. Never forget this.'

People who wished to sully my father's name said that it was not by meat, but by marriage that he had made his way. It is true that my father was a well-married man. He had married four times, each time taking a wife of means within the burgeoning hierarchy of Town. My mother had been his second wife, a younger woman, taken in marriage a year after his first wife had died – of natural causes, I hasten to add. His first wife having died without issue, my father had inherited her entire estate. My mother was Cape-born, the eldest daughter of one of the oldest and most respected burgher families. I did not have the privilege of knowing her, for she died giving birth to me, a fact which to this day causes me much grief, as if by virtue of being born, I was responsible for her death.

My father remarried soon after my mother's death, not waiting out the year, but this I cannot condemn. He was a young man with a child, and infants require mothering. I called her 'Mother', my new stepmother, and loved her like a son would his natural mother. She had been younger even than my mother when they married. My new mother's name was Jacoba.

Jacoba was a gentlewoman; her father had been a senior official in the Company and my father had done well to marry her. Indeed, marriage to a woman of her pedigree would have been impossible for him in earlier years, but by the time of the marriage he'd already built the reputation for being a steady man, one of considerable wealth and a growing status.

In short succession, Jacoba produced two daughters, my sisters Dorothea and Johanna, but my father wanted another son. This was Jacoba's undoing. She bore a son, a pitiful thing that died after two days. They called him Stefaans.

I was eight years old at the time. I remember Jacoba's grief after the baby died – ceaseless sobbing that woke me in the morning and accompanied me to sleep at night. My father up-braided me when I asked when he thought she would stop. His eyes had been reddened then, I remember, although I never witnessed him shed a tear.

It had been our cook, Barbetje, who comforted Dorothea and me when Jacoba died, Johanna being too young to comprehend the cause of the sorrow in our house. They were buried together, Jacoba and Stefaans, since his body had not yet been interred in the ground before she followed him. Dorothea and I had been sitting at the table in the kitchen so that Barbetje could watch us while she prepared the evening meal when Jacoba took her last breath. My father came into the room, spoke a few words to Barbetje that I did not hear and then went outside, calling for his horse. Barbetje looked at the two of us, sighed and shook her head. Dorothea began to wail; it was a most piteous sight to behold. '*Troos haar*. Comfort your sister,' Barbetje told me. 'The missus is gone; it's time for you to be a big boy now.'

Dorothea cried even harder at the words; I took her tiny hand in mine and held it close. I only let go once Barbetje placed our food on the table before us and we were forced to eat.

My father married one more time, this time several years after Jacoba's death, and once more was widowed. Although I was older, I don't remember her much. She'd died within a year of their marriage and had not been able to leave a lasting impression on our household. I was seventeen at the time and all I remember is that Catharina, my last stepmother, was young, not much older than I, and very alluring to a lad that age. I am ashamed to say that I was envious of my father when he took her as his wife.

I often wondered what it had been like for my father to bury four wives, but dared not ask him. I thought about this considerably on the day of his funeral. Even though I'd lost so many mothers as well as my baby brother, one never becomes inured to death.

Horse breeding had been the pastime of my father's later years. 'The equine stock found at the Cape are puny things, no more than ponies in comparison to the hardy Dutch draught horses of my youth,' he would tell whomever would listen.

In truth, the horses *were* little more than ponies: standing no more than thirteen hands high, they were insubstantial and most feeble in appearance.

'Hardier horses might be bred by intermingling the Cape horses with imported stock. Should I succeed, instead of allowing scores of oxen to serve first as beasts of burden, the animals could be sold younger, and the beef would certainly be more tender, not toughened from years of hauling ploughs and pulling carts,' my father had explained.

He'd heard of a farmer in the Tijgerberg area who had crossed his horses with a stallion acquired from an English sailor travelling to the East. 'The resulting breeds are reputed to stand fifteen hands high and are said to be healthy and strong,' he'd marvelled.

So my father journeyed to the Tijgerberg himself, returning with a yearling black as pitch but, to my eyes, only slightly larger than the mounts we had known, though I'd kept my own counsel.

For two years, my father coddled that horse, travelling almost daily to his farm in Rondebosch to check on its progress. Mindful of the old Company ruling that limited the riding of colts and fillies under a certain age, he rode that horse only to train it. No one else was allowed to mount it.

During this time, my father grew fond of the horse and decided that, in addition to its stud duties, it would make an excellent hunting horse when it was fit to ride. When the horse was three years old, he removed it to stabling in Town. His plan was to take the horse for a tripple around Town, not long rides, just so the horse could become inured to being ridden.

Witnesses say that the horse had shied when it came across a large crowd of revellers on the square. The fleet was in and the town was busier than usual with sailors and their cohorts drinking and carousing at all times of the day. Moreover, it was a country horse, unused to noise and cobbled city streets. They said that my father had tried to right the reins, but he was distracted, or taken unawares. He fell in the middle of the square, his back broken and one of his legs bent beneath his weight. The horse landed on top of him, breaking its forelegs in the process. An unknown person or persons shot it. It was gone by the time we sent a servant to look for the carcass.

Men of the Town carried my father home. They knew there was nothing that could be done for him, other than attempt to palliate his pain. By the grace of God, he was unconscious throughout his transport home. For days my father had lain abed, and although he did not cry out, from the stifled moans that escaped him once the soporifics fed him wore off, I knew he must have been in agony. The leg on which he had landed had broken in two places; there was no way to staunch the bleeding. Even after they were laundered, the bright, white bedclothes remained that orange-pink colour when water is added to bloodstained linen.

His wounds smelled putrid, but we tried to ignore the malodour, my sisters and I. We took turns to sit with him, wiping his brow with a wet cloth and giving him broth to drink. Thankfully, he slept. He was alert when he woke and more's the pity. The surgeon suggested that amputating my father's leg would save his life, but my sire was a proud man and refused. 'I want to meet my maker whole,' he insisted. Resigned, he added with difficulty that he knew that few people survived a broken back 'and I do not wish to be a cripple'. Instead, we dosed him with copious quantities of tincture of opium for the pain.

Considering the pandemonium in his household, it was a good thing I was home at the time, even if there was little I could do other than manage arrangements once my father passed. I'd left home the previous year, for my father held the belief that a home could not have more than one rooster and in his estimation I had come of age, even if not in fact. The plan had been that I'd decamp to one of his farms to learn the meat business, since I would have to take over when the time came.

My father would brook no argument, but meat is not my métier. If I'd had my way, I would have become a schoolmaster – I loved learning, no matter the low regard accorded to the teaching class at the Cape. Despite having little schooling himself, my father had been a strong proponent of learning. This was abundantly clear from his telling and retelling of stories and his readings from the Good Book. Although there were several schools at the Cape, my father had insisted on engaging the services of a private tutor to school his children, believing that the church-run schools provided little more than a rudimentary education, which he deemed inadequate if we were to assume our rightful place in the world.

Mijneer Bok was a young man fresh from Groningen; he'd attended university there until personal circumstances of which he did not deign to speak forced him to seek his way elsewhere. He too filled my head with the glories of the United Provinces and the Golden Age of its art and culture. He spoke of painters – Rembrandt van Rijn and Johannes Vermeer – and a great lawmaker, Hugo Grotius, and how a man called Jan Leeghwater had determined a way to convert large lakes into *polders* for cultivation by using windmills to pump out the water.

Upon receiving a small inheritance, Mijneer Bok left my father's employ to return to the Republic. I was sixteen years old. I begged my father to allow me to accompany him so that I could take up a place at one of the universities there, but when your father's fortune is based on meat, then that is what you too must become: a meat man.

When I departed from my father's home, I took along with me the small sea chest that he'd brought with him from *his* father's home as his only luggage. I'd become resigned to my fate. In my grandiose moments, I imagined that I was striking off on my own, much like he had all those years ago, but my notions were vainglorious and false.

We set off at dawn. My party consisted of the farm's overseer and a retinue of servants who had lately come to the Cape to deliver the beasts and butter. Slaughtering was a messy business and was, therefore, done at my father's farm in the Drakenstein or the beasts were handed over live. The by-products of slaughtering – the heads, the hooves and intestines – possessing no utility and there being no place to dispose of these, were often dumped by unscrupulous butchers into the sea. When the tide came in, the debris would wash ashore where it corrupted and befouled the air. It was for this reason that my father insisted that any slaughtering that he was responsible for take place far from the built environment, on the outskirts of Town, where it could do the least amount of harm.

Our mode of transport was a large wooden wagon pulled by five teams of two oxen. The top of the wagon was formed by a double layer of sailcloth. This served more to protect me from the sun than the elements, since it had not rained in weeks. Five boxes were fitted into the bottom of the carriage; a mattress was rolled upon the extreme box. This could be unfurled so I could enjoy a restful sleep when we stopped overnight should our party not find accommodation at a farmhouse along the way. The overseer brought along a tent in which to sleep, while the servants slept beneath the wagon or under the skies, as was their wont.

The wagons were heavily laden with provisions for the trip and to last the homestead the many months until the next visit to Town. We set in pounds of tea, coffee, sugar, chocolate and tobacco, the latter item an expectation of the Hottentot servants accompanying me, although I eschewed to provide them with strong spirits. For use along the way and to augment the farm's kitchen on my arrival, my cooking equipment consisted of a frying pan, kettle, a gridiron and cauldron as well as a few porcelain plates, cups and bowls. We took along with us implements to melt lead and repair the wagons as well as supplies such as candles, tinder boxes, blankets, linens, stuffed pillows, measures of rope, iron, a quantity of nails, and tools such as needles and thread should we need to mend the sailcloth covering of the wagon or stitch skins acquired along the way.

Of paramount importance was my weapons store: several guns, including a pair of double-barrelled pistols and four flintlock rifles, knives, long and short, hundreds of bullets and flints, a number of explosive fuses, and three bottles, each holding six pounds of gunpowder. I planned to do much hunting along the way for the pot; I'd heard the country teemed with game. Furthermore, our band required protection against the wild animals that I believed still roamed the area. The overseer had his own arsenal, which he kept in his saddle bags. I stored mine in one of the boxes in the wagon, although I made sure always to carry a small pistol on my person as a precaution.

In addition to the overseer's mount and the ten oxen that pulled the wagon, our train consisted of two more pairs of oxen to relieve the principals; my own horse that I would saddle to hunt and reconnoitre the area; and in the wagon itself, Juko, my dog. Juko proved a most placid travelling companion – content to make the journey in the relative ease of the wagon instead of snapping at the heels and hooves of the men and beasts that made up our small party.

Swellendam lies a distance of some forty leagues east of the Cape. There is but one road out of Town in this direction and thus we headed for the Hottentots Holland Mountains. Throwing up dust as we passed, the road leading towards the mountains had been stamped flat by the thousands of sheep and cattle that traversed upon it. Everywhere I looked was burnished and browned. Low-lying scrubland abutted the road and from the wagon I could espy an abundance of pheasants and here and there an oblivious buck that scattered into the bushes as we approached. Otherwise, it was an empty expanse with no large settlements of which to speak – save for a house or two appearing phantom-like in the panorama. We did not stop to make the owners' acquaintance but pressed on to reach the foot of the mountains before dark. It was here that we set up camp. Exhausted from the day's travel, we sought an early night's sleep: we would require all our strength to attempt the ascent of the steep mountains when the sun came up.

We rose before daybreak, ate and fed the beasts before yoking the oxen to the wagon in pairs. I sat in the wagon, with several of the servants hitching a ride. The overseer led the train on horseback, while a servant more familiar with the steep incline mounted my horse. Two others walked with the rest of the oxen.

The path was of a narrow aspect, and treacherous rocks lay in wait of the unsuspecting traveller. Wagons that had passed here previously had gouged deep welts into the road's surface and left their mark on the overhanging boulders and cliffs. The ascent was long – nearly a league's distance from bottom to top. I was most relieved when we reached the crest.

From this vantage point, the aspect was of a more verdant hue. True, there were patches of dry grass and seared trees, but overall, the picture presented was more green than brown, signifying the imminent change of season. Or perhaps the sea stretching out below us, the thin ribbons of rivers that glimmered dully and the chain of mountains unfolding ahead of us contributed to this impression. Here we rested as the sun beat down at the height of its heat.

A few hours later, we began our descent, driving for several hours until the day darkened. It had been arranged beforehand that we would stop the night at the homestead belonging to one of my father's friends. I hoped that I was not impolite to the farmer and his family, a wife and two comely daughters, by retiring soon after partaking of their dinner. I was grateful for the hot meal, the bed and a proper roof over my head.

Though I rose early, the women of the house were already up, bustling in the kitchen. I accepted a cup of coffee before heading out to check on the animals. My men were sitting around a fire idling.

'Have the beasts been fed?' I asked.

'*Ja, baas*,' one answered.

'Prepare to leave shortly, then,' I instructed. 'As soon as I've broken my fast. There's no good reason to squander the morning's cool.'

The sun was at its highest point by the time we crossed the Palmiet River. We stopped to allow the animals to drink, but did not tarry long. There was much ground to cover and we would encounter further rivers along the way. I found sitting in the wagon tedious, so switched to the saddle, often riding ahead to better survey the terrain.

The farther we drove from Town, the more game and wild animals we encountered: ostriches, zebra and a variety of buck. The buck came closer than the rest but skittered away as if sensing danger. I determined to shoot a few for our evening meal, but the overseer pointed out that it would be best if I waited until we settled for the night.

'We'll camp at the Bot River,' he reminded me, 'there'll be plenty of game there. Animals too need to drink.'

Once we arrived, well before nightfall, I saw that the sport was as good as promised.

The next day, we crossed the Bot River and overnighted at the house of a farmer we'd met as we passed through Oude Hoek. Otherwise, we set up camp along the way. Days passed without event. The journey was settling into a stifling same-ness. Only the landscape changed, and the species of buck we spotted or shot.

On the sixth day, we experienced our first catastrophe. We had left the Steenbok River behind and were aiming to reach the Zoetemelk Valley before evening. The plan was to once again stay with friends and I was anxious to arrive before the dinner hour or the family would be forced to wait for me. We were making good time until one of the animals leading the span fell lame, upsetting the rest in the train, and very nearly toppling the wagon, but for the acute reflexes of the driver who halted all before much damage could be done. It was patent that nothing could be done for the poor creature; the correct thing was to put it out of its misery. I am a meat *pachter*'s son, and as such have no squeamishness when it comes to killing an ox, but there had been a certain nobility about the beast and I felt an odd sense of gratitude and awe that it had borne us thus far. I requested that the overseer shoot the animal, claiming a desire to explore the veld while we were stopped. By the time I returned, the workers had already flayed the skin and were cutting steaks and strips of meat. That night we ate well.

An unpaired ox meant that one of the servants had to be in charge of the single animal in addition to the man in charge of the relief pairs. This impeded our progress as the boy entrusted with this task was young and unseasoned, dragging the journey out due to his inexperience. Furthermore, the unforeseen stop had caused us to lose time and we hastened to make up what we'd lost. I felt ashamed of my cowardice the previous day and scanned the horizon for animals to hunt. We had plenty of meat, but there was a recklessness in me then. I yearned to outrun the feeling of lassitude that had overcome me a few days into the trip, in spite of my intentions to set an example for the men.

The following morning, we called in at my would-be host's home to pay my respects and explain my late arrival. He was a good friend of my father's and no matter how much time we had lost, I could not refuse his invitation to go hunting. The Zoetemelk Valley is renowned for the *bloubok* or blue antelope that is indigenous to the area. These creatures are rather rare and mysterious – I'd never seen one before and longed to do so. The vista abounded with antelope of all stripes, but I kept my eyes alert for the sight of the mythical beast. I was too embarrassed to ask the farmer about the *bloubok*, although as if sensing my interest, he volunteered that he had made a trophy of many a one.

By the time we strode off in search of our quarry, the sun was blazing. There were several flocks of buck, some hundreds of them, but they scurried away as soon as we neared. They were fleet of foot and, at one stage, I myself was forced into a trot to pursue them. It was while I was walking slowly in order to catch my breath that I saw it. Alabaster-skinned and as still as a statue, it sniffed the air as if to isolate the danger occasioned by the flocks' flight. I stopped and stood still too, hidden behind a capacious tree.

In the stillness of the veld, a calm descended upon me. It was just me and the buck. I spotted it with my rifle, careful not to make a sound. I squeezed the trigger and then, nothing. I saw nothing; felt nothing, just that odd mixture of peace and exhilaration that overcomes me when I am on the hunt. It took Juko, who had been constrained and twitching next to me, to find where the beastie fell.

The farmer insisted on skinning the beast himself lest damage come to the pale-blue pelt. It was soft and musky smelling. The horns, curved back in an almost straight line, were blue too. Immediately afterwards, I had felt a sense of shame for killing such a magnificent animal, but the farmer assured me that there were plenty more where it had come from.

We pushed on, travelling far into the night, resting for a few hours and then setting out once more. It was two more days before we reached Swellendam. All told, our journey had taken ten days.

The Swellendam farm had originally belonged to my father's first wife, who had inherited it from her first husband. I had heard, although I cannot rightly say from whom – I doubt it would have been my father – that this man had been one of the men at the Cape who, earlier in the century, had trekked to the south-western parts in order to make a living. Sufficient grazing was in short supply at the Cape. Over the mountains, they discovered, were areas particularly suited to raising sheep and cattle, and these Trekboers, as they were called, were granted tracts of land, some six thousand acres each, for which they paid an annual fee. A timely inheritance had allowed the couple to return to the Cape, but they'd retained the farm, as it had developed into a profitable source of income.

Before I set forth, my father had warned me of the basic nature of the homestead. It was much smaller than his Cape house, but not as rude as I'd expected. The house itself was little more than a large room divided into three: a sleeping area, kitchen and reception room. It was made of brick, had real windows and doors, with a working fireplace and chimney, but no ceiling. I recognised the furniture as cast-offs from the Cape house. There were several Hottentot structures on the farm: simple beehive-shaped dwellings made of wood and straw. The overseer occupied a separate mud-built house some yards away.

The best bed in the house had been readied for me. The overseer had ridden ahead of the party the day prior to our arrival to ensure that this was so. Like the prodigal son, a fatted calf had been prepared for my arrival. They called me *Kleinbaas* – young master – on the farm, but I was master in name only. There was not much more for me to do than stand by and watch. Though I noted that the overseer was overly strict with the Hottentots on the farm, I did not intervene. I had been instructed by my father not to undermine the man's authority, for he had been with him for a number of years and I was there to learn. I comforted myself with the knowledge that unlike many of the farmers in the district (one hears stories) my father paid his workers well: in coin, food and clothing, and for the most part, they were fat and healthy in appearance. Besides the thousands of heads of cattle and sheep, a section of the demesne had been set aside to grow wheat and vegetables for our own consumption. An acreage that size required scores of workers; we hired more during the harvesting time.

I shadowed the overseer as he went about his daily routine, but I soon felt superfluous and chose to let the man continue his work unhampered by my constant presence and questioning, though I essayed to learn from him what I could. Every now and then we'd hear about a farmer in difficulty and would offer to buy up their livestock, which would then be rebranded with our mark. Smaller farmers who were unable to make the journey to the Cape would also sell us their cattle and sheep and we'd resell them with the others. In this time, I travelled up and down the area looking for other farmers interested in selling their stock. Farmers who declined to sell at the prices we offered were forced to drive the animals to Town themselves; I heard that some traded in elephant ivory too, supplementing their activities by nefarious means.

There were few amusements to be had in the village, scant opportunities for uplifting conversation and the sharing of thoughts. The overseer was a busy man; we never mixed much. In any case, his talk revolved around the sheep and cattle, the servants. I imagined him a rather lacklustre person of little imagination and no learning. Doubtless he found me a foolish young man for not caring about those things, but I was not too concerned of his opinion of me. I spent my leisure hours reading the Good Book and composing histories for myself and others – my father and the great men my tutor had spoken to me about. Men who'd left their imprint upon the world. I welcomed the travellers who passed by on occasion, eager for news from farther afield. As is the habit, I would offer them my hospitality, but even if they did spend the night, they never remained for long and I would once again be forced to draw upon my own wits.

I slept in my father's bed, under his roof. Every morning upon waking, after the first rooster crowed, but before the bell rang, signalling the start of the working day, I could not help but expect him to arrive and claim his rightful place.

When the time came to drive the cattle to Town and procure fresh provisions, I was thankful to leave. I wanted new diversions and cultured congress. I'd missed the friendship of my sisters, and my father's guidance. I thought of asking him to allow me to stay.

The route back did not make much of an impression on me, but perhaps I was not looking for diversions. I was looking ahead. We stopped at one of the Company's repositories in the area, a journey four days from the farm, to offload half our cargo. It was here that they fed the cattle that supplied their ships.

Half of the remainder we took to the Company's shambles on the outskirts of Town. Thanks to an enforced delay, occasioned by intermittent thundershowers that sent the cattle into frenzies, we arrived at the slaughter at night. The hysterical laughter of the hyenas guided us there in the dark. Once we were near enough, we witnessed those horrible creatures gorging on the offal, bones and skin – the cast-off waste of the beasts killed there. Clearly the Company too was remiss in the manner in which it disposed of its animals' remains. After handing over the cattle, we drove the remaining quarter to my father's farm, but a short distance away in the Drakenstein. We rested there overnight before journeying to my father's home in Town.

My father's accident took place a few days later. We'd had little chance for conversation of any depth – save for the price the sheep and cattle fetched, the goings-on of the French troops who'd landed at the Cape two years ago when we were under the menace of a British attack, the success of his horse-breeding efforts. It was preposterous to think that the man who had survived the arduous journey by sea from Amsterdam to the Cape, who had withstood the plague that had decimated the town on his arrival here, who had outlived four wives and at least one child, should be bested by a horse. There was almost something ignominious in this fact.

Mindful once more of where I was, and my reasons for being there, I stole a quick look around the room. Still filled with guests, the room, as were all in the house, was a study in gentility. The furnishings had all been imported at great cost. Once my father had risen in standing, Cape-made furniture would not do for him. Sundry mirrors and paintings adorned the walls as did a barometer, an ebony hooded clock with brass mounts, candlesticks and shelves displaying the finest porcelain from England and the daily pewterware that was no less fine.

The hour was growing late. A young girl, seventeen years or thereabouts, came in to light the lamps and position several burning candles about the room, casting a dull glow over the gloom. Her face was not known to me. She was a curiosity: slim and dark, wearing the mourning dress of the house, but bare-footed. I surprised myself by finding her oddly attractive, a sentiment out of place given the circumstances. Or maybe it was because of the dim light that I thought so, or my fatigue. I watched her as she went about her business, oblivious not only to me but to all the guests. It was as if she did not see them and they did not see her. She left the room only to return with a bronze tray; arranged upon it was a fresh pot of coffee, a milk jug and the light-blue porcelain cups and saucers embossed with a pattern of white feathers that had formed part of my mother's dowry. The girl set the tray down on one of the tables and hesitated. I motioned that she should pour.

Coffee imbibed, the Company officials were the first to leave. Only once they left did the stragglers begin saying aloud the words they had previously uttered under their breath. Like many burghers at the Cape, my father had half-detested the Company that in many ways was the source of his newfound wealth. I knew all about the secret meetings and the pamphlet that had been disseminated in Town a few years ago calling for the rights and powers of citizens to be upheld in the face of the Company's abuses at the Cape. It was an incendiary tract in which the authors claimed the right to change government – by violent means if necessary.

'Remember Mijneer Buytendacht,' one of the men present warned. 'The Company can be brutal towards those who dare challenge its authority.'

'Spare a thought for Mewrouw Buytendacht and her children,' another cut in. 'The man was a sot and a wife-beater.'

They were speaking of Carel Buytendacht, a known instigator and troublemaker, who had been arrested and pressganged back into the Company's service and sent to Batavia, forcibly parting him from his family.

This show of power had had the opposite effect to what the Company might have desired. Rather than quelling dissatisfaction, Mijneer Buytendacht's handling served as a call to action for disaffected burghers. Four hundred, my father among them, signed a memorandum addressed to the *Heren* XVII, the Company's directors in Holland. This document detailed the problems at the Cape and the Company officials' hand in them.

'All the recommendations we put forward ...' one of the Town's elders began. 'What became of them?'

'All for naught,' another elderly burgher answered, as if this were a conversation that they'd had many times before.

Without allowing anyone else to interject or contribute to the conversation, the two men spoke of the list of recommendations several burghers had drafted with the aim of improving conditions in the Colony. To my knowledge, these included a call for stronger checks on the private dealings of Company officials and a clearer classification of laws. Economic proposals included the right to trade freely with foreign ships and a betterment of the prices paid by the Company, and a demand that the Company loosen its monopoly on the wine and wheat market. (I am not sure whether it was my father's influence or not, but the memorandum contained no mention of the meat *pacht* in its list of markets requiring reform.) It would not surprise me. When hotter heads prevailed, my father stressed caution. It was for this reason that he had managed to straddle the world of the Company and the interests of the burghers and why both groups mourned his passing.

—

It was dark outside by the time the last mourners departed. Though the leftover coffee had gone cold, and the wine and brandy given out long ago, the men had lingered, smoking their pipes, as if trying to draw out the visit, as if reluctant to close the book on my father's life.

Alone at last, I sat in my chair, weary. I'd been so busy arranging matters that I hadn't had time to ponder the weight of my father's departure from this life and how it would affect me. A cough disturbed me from my reflections. Titus, my father's personal slave, had entered the room. He was still dressed in his funeral clothes and was clutching a wide-brimmed hat decked out with black ribbon. His eyes were red and he reeked of spirits, but I deigned not to notice.

'*Wat is dit?*'

'*Ekskuus, Mijneer.*'

'It's all right,' I said. 'Say what you've come to say.'

Titus stammered over his words. It was obvious that he was overcome, whether by the spirits or the sombreness of the occasion.

'Your father, he was a good man, a good *baas.*'

I thanked him as if he were one of the mourners who'd just departed. The slaves had mourned my father apart from the rest of us, as is proper. I had made sure that they were provided with food and drink, but not too much of the latter; one should not encourage intemperance in one's servants.

'Now go and get some sleep; you're bound to have a sore head in the morning,' I told Titus as he bid me goodnight.

If there was anyone who knew all my father's secrets, I was sure it was he. They were as close as a master and servant could be. Titus had stood behind my father's chair when he'd eaten his meals, held my father's long pipe when he smoked, washed his feet every evening without complaint (one hears stories about the recalcitrant nature of certain slaves, believing themselves to be above such duties) and accompanied him on all his journeys. I found his sincerity oddly more touching than any of the number of condolences I'd received from my father's equals.

My father's slave holdings were immense – scores of men and women, though I warrant less than one hundred in total. I had never owned a slave myself, although we grew up with them in my father's house. Indeed, I had never considered that they too would become my responsibility, along with the welfare of my sisters and my father's properties and businesses. I felt awed and unequal to the task. If I'd learned anything during my year in Swellendam, it was that authority did not come easily to me. I will have to learn ...

We had shared a name, my father and I. He had made the name one that meant something, a name to be reckoned with. Rather than freeing me, his death had added to my burden, but I would not abnegate his legacy. I would take up the reins. Many were reliant on me and I could not disappoint. At two and twenty years, it was time for me to become a man.

Lena, 1854

All the old man's death meant was that I had to get up
earlier to help with the cooking. At that stage, I hadn't
been there long and, as such, my tasks were of a baser nature –
tending the garden, fetching water, carrying in the wood, lighting the fires and so on. It was heavy work, but I was young, my
body was capable, and in any event, who would pay me any
heed had I thought to complain? Some days I helped knead the
bread or churn the butter if one of the other girls was busy
elsewhere. I didn't mind that, it was better than being outside
in the wind and the cold, but Barbetje, who was in charge of
the kitchen, didn't trust that I knew what I was doing. 'She's
not yet used to our ways of doing,' Barbetje pronounced, which
was true, but I learned soon enough.

He had been dying for days, the old man. He'd fallen off

that horse of his, the one he was always showing off with, like he was full of sap and not an old man with grey hair and big children, and even before they brought his broken body home, we all knew he was going to die, only no one knew when. After a while, two, maybe three days, we all began wishing that it would be sooner rather than later, because of the way his wounds stank and the way he whimpered in his sleep like a horse, but that's not a nice thing to say and so maybe I should say that he moaned like a puppy or like someone who'd been whipped, except it was a different kind of sound. And he was like a horse, that old man, all teeth and smiles. Just like a horse can be all teeth and smiles, but nasty too, that old man was like that. Knowing this, we made sure never to turn our backs on him, just like you should never turn your back on a horse that is not yet properly schooled.

For days, we lived with that noise and that smell while the old man clung to his life. He was still alive when we began to prepare for his funeral. I do not know who had given the order, but it would have been his son, I think. I spent most of my time in the kitchen after that: lighting the fire, fanning the fire, scouring the bronze pots with sand until they shone, washing the eggs before they could be used. I cracked eggs and beat eggs, I grated bread and kneaded the dough, I strained the cream off the milk and shooed the *muggies* away. I plucked the feathers off the chickens and pheasants, collecting their blood in the big enamel *bakkie* beforehand so that Barbetje could fry it with onions for our evening meal, which was a treat since no one was watching what food went where. I removed the lacy caul fat surrounding the organ meats and the thicker clods of lard. We used the caul fat for sausages and melted the lard to make *kaiings*, those tiny pieces of meat that stay behind when you render mutton or beef fat. This we ate on thick slabs of fresh bread with or without butter. Oh, in the days it took that old man to die, all of us ate like kings. It was almost enough to forget his smell.

At long last, he died. It was night time. I was on my bed on the floor in the kitchen – all the girls slept there, with the exception of Barbetje, who had a cot with a kapok mattress in a small room off the kitchen. But before bed that night, Barbetje dragged her mattress into the kitchen. She said she was afraid of spooks, Barbetje. A big woman like that, scared of ghosts, and the old man not yet dead. I wanted to say that she should have more fear of the living, but I did not. There was no use trying to tell Barbetje anything.

We all knew how that old man used her body, and we all knew that that was why Barbetje was in charge of the kitchen and the whole house, you could say. We all knew this was why she slept in the small room off the kitchen and not on the floor like we did.

We used to hear him going to her room late at night when he thought we were all asleep. We heard them grunting and squealing like pigs at the trough. Sometimes we saw him leave, adjusting his night trousers with a satisfied smirk. But in the morning there'd be no smirk, no smiles, just hymns and prayers and him reading from his Bible while we all stood there listening to him, his children and we, his other children, he called us. '*De Here is goed, ja*,' we proclaimed after him, even if some of our tongues struggled with the words.

So sometimes Barbetje acted like she was the madam of the house, and it was not so hard for her to do so because the young misses were young and silly and not interested in running things, only in the French soldiers and the French fashions and doing their hair in the French style ... and there was no woman there at the time. One of the other girls told me the old man had been married four times and each time he had sent his wife to an early grave because of carrying his children, but that's just how men are, and Barbetje had no children from the man, none to speak about, and it was better that way. Someone else said that if Barbetje had borne him a child then he would have freed her and the child, but shame, maybe he would free her anyway because he had promised, if what Barbetje said was true. That's all they talked about in the days the old man lay dying – freedom and that big word 'manumission'.

When Titus came to the kitchen, he was always in and out there, fetching boiling water, rags, tea with herbs, I'd listen as he and Barbetje spoke. From their talk, I knew that Barbetje had been there for many years, since before the old man's son was born. Afterwards, she tended the boy when he was a baby and his mother died. She thought all this made her part of the family.

'Me and that boy's mother grew up together,' I heard her tell Titus. 'I was a house-child. Born in the house. Madelijn was such a dear friend to me, I slept at the foot of her bed and when her dresses became too tight for her, they became mine. So close we were!'

'Close, my foot,' I thought to myself, even though there was no way of knowing the truth of her words.

'*Foeitog*,' Barbetje continued, 'she died so young, so all of a sudden; she didn't have time to draw up the papers or even to tell the master to free me when she died, like she always said she would, us being nearly like sisters and all.'

They were both so foolish those two, Titus and Barbetje, always counting leaves of how things would be. I had been disappointed too many times to let my imagination run away from me like that.

Anyways, where was I? Later that night, the night Barbetje brought her bed in with us, I was jerked awake as if someone had shoved me. I opened my eyes, but no one was there. The others were all fast asleep. I checked to see that they were breathing normally – they used to play terrible tricks on me, the other girls, mainly because I was new – but when I looked around, they really were all sleeping and no one else was there.

The room was cold; the fire had burned out long ago and I was freezing. I tried to shift on the mat, gather a larger share of the blanket for myself, but I couldn't move – neither my arms nor my legs. My body felt as trapped and as heavy as a rolled-up carpet when you carry it outside to beat out the dust. All of a sudden, I felt very sad, even though I had not liked him – it's not nice when someone dies – and I knew, I just knew, that death had finally come for that old man.

Inside, the house was still and quiet, even with the breathing and snores of the others next to me. The grandfather clock in the other room kept time, tick, tick, tick …

Listening to that clock, I thought how strange it was that the closing of the man's life made me think of beginnings. Where were his beginnings, the old man? Had he been born here, or had he too come by ship? What did I care? Yet I knew one thing; we all had our own beginnings – beginnings I did not want to think about.

I wanted to sleep.

Tick, tick, tick. I listened as the minutes marked off on the clock, the sound faint but definite, like a heartbeat. Eventually, I fell back to sleep.

When I woke again, the darkness was softening. My body was stiff and tight. Had it really happened, was the old man dead, or had I dreamed it all? Not that it mattered. You should never disregard your dreams. They tell you the truth. I knew that.

Someone lit a lamp; the flare of the tinder sparked and I knew that soon I would be pushed off the mat. Not long thereafter, I heard the cry we'd been anticipating all these days. Something, possibly the lamp – it sounded like the lamp – dropped and rolled onto the floor and then I heard what sounded like a hiss or a gasp that's not let out completely. Like when you see a snake, but you don't make a noise because you don't want it to notice you, and that old man was sometimes like a snake that lay in wait for you if you weren't careful or you weren't paying attention. It was then that I knew the old man's death had been discovered and that I had not been imagining things earlier when I got the feeling that he had died.

The noise made Barbetje rush up off her mattress. She grabbed her shawl and ran out of the room, still in her night-clothes. We heard her cry out loud. When she returned some minutes later, her face was wet.

'Get up,' she shouted. 'The master's dead! Wake up, you lazy girl,' she shrieked, prodding me with those bony fingers of hers. 'Get up, why you want to sleep so long? We have a lot to do if they're to bury him tomorrow.'

All my sleeping companions had already risen upon hearing Barbetje's cries – I was the last one abed, since I was tired on account of waking up in the night and thinking all those thoughts. I got up from the floor at once and gathered the blanket from the floor, folded it, and pushed it together with the straw mat under Barbetje's cot in her room. Then I hurried outside to wash my face.

The young misses were already sitting at the kitchen table when I returned – early for them. One of us usually took them their coffee and biscuits in bed. Barbetje too was sitting, all soft-voiced for the young misses.

'Lena, bring coffee for the young madams. Why you just stand there, girl?'

Both the young misses paid me no mind. Their light eyes were watery and reddened from sobbing. Every now and then, Barbetje would raise an old lace-trimmed hanky to their faces, like they were babies and she their mother.

I poured the coffee, bubbling over the fire, stirred in extra sugar and added lots of milk to lighten it before handing it to the misses.

I listened to what Barbetje was telling them about their father. 'He was a good man, kind master …'

'He always treated me like part of the family,' Barbetje had said when she and Titus discussed their freedom. 'He promised …'

I wondered if the young misses knew about Barbetje and

their father. They were so innocent and sheltered, the young misses. For all their pining for the French soldiers, I could see that they were still ignorant of the ways of the world. Maybe they were older than me in years, those young misses, I don't know. But I was wiser.

'You're so good to us, Barbetje,' they said. 'What would we do without you?'

Barbetje smiled thinly.

She buttered slices of bread for the young misses and chided them to eat. 'You'll weaken, my dears, if you don't take in some nourishment. You need your strength for the days ahead.'

They nibbled on their bread dutifully, like little children wishing to please their mother. I watched as Barbetje carefully dipped clean rags in vinegar, wrung them out and then gave one to each of the young misses to place on their brows. 'Try to get some rest,' she told them. 'You will feel better when you wake up.'

She waited before the young misses had been gone a while before she turned on me: 'Why didn't you say something? Why didn't you tell them you were sorry about Master?'

I said nothing. Barbetje was the one who had told me to speak only when I was spoken to – I greeted the young misses, I helped serve them their meals, their coffee and their tea and washed their dirty dishes once they were done – nothing more than that.

We worked from morning until late that night preparing the house for the funeral. Titus went around to the houses with a card notifying people of the old man's death. I received a dress made of black material so I could show my respects. It was one good thing that came out of the old man's dying, a new dress, and I am not ashamed to say so.

The morning of the funeral, Barbetje handed me a sack of rice. 'Sort it for stones,' she said.

I picked the small black stones from the white rice and washed it before giving it back to her.

'Fetch the *borrie*,' Barbetje said, 'and the raisins.'

This is funeral rice. First you add the *borrie* to turn the rice yellow and then you cook it over a low fire. When it is nearly done, you add the raisins, but you must make sure there is enough water left in the pot. Otherwise, the raisins won't get juicy and soft.

'Watch the rice,' Barbetje said. She was busy roasting the mutton and beef. Meat is more important than rice. That's why she was doing the meat and not the rice. 'Stir it and add more water if it starts to stick.'

Stirring the rice like that made me think of another funeral. That day, we made rice too, but then again, we were always making rice. The day of my father's funeral was the day the trouble all started. Or maybe before then. Maybe the trouble started on the day he died, except we were not sure of the exact day he died, so it was easy to think of his funeral as the day it all fell apart. Until then, life, I would say, was sweet.

I was in my fifth or sixth year when my father died – I reached to his legs, so I must have been thereabouts in age. I do not recall much of him, but I remember that he was slender with dark skin like mine. Also, he had the long ears the men of our area were renowned for, and which you sometimes still see here with other men from there, which is how I can tell they are. Even to this day, whenever I see a man with long ears like that, I am reminded of my father and wonder whether the stranger is my clansman and if he has news of my family and of home.

I was born near the town of A— in a village in a valley bounded by the towering green mountains of the land beneath the sky. My father's name was Rampola; my mother's name was Rafotsibe. I had an older brother by name of Rakota. Two girl children were born after me, but the first died within a few days of her birth and the other had not long been walking by the time I left. She, we called Raketaka. I recollect my brother well but have little memory of my sister. Raketaka's face had been constantly changing as she grew, and just as I set it in my memory, it would be altered in large and small ways. This saddens me sometimes, but perhaps it is also a good thing as I cannot ache for my sister the way I do when I picture my mother's face or my brother's and wonder where they are, or when I see my father's face before me and I think about how he died. When I think of Raketaka, all I miss is the idea of having a sister, a family. I lie. Sometimes when I think of her, I envy her.

We lived on a piece of land neither large nor small; it was adequate for our needs. In the rainy season, my father cultivated rice. Our family owned a few cattle, which made the planting easier. I remember how my father and brother would drive those beasts through the fields before planting the seedlings in the ground. This made a fine mud for the young plants. Afterwards, my father, my brother and the beasts would come back blackened and with lighter patches where the mud had dried. It was a sight to see; it was as if they had painted themselves for battle.

And just like he was going into battle, my brother would come at me, with his soiled arms outstretched as if he were going to smear me with the dirt. I'd run away before he could catch me, screaming and laughing, but I knew he was just playing because he would never have dared sully me while my father was around.

My mother would come see what the noise was about, or maybe she was watching for my father and brother's return from the field, because she'd come out of the hut with a basin of water for my father to wash his face and his hands. And then my brother would wash his face and his hands and someone would put the cattle away before they went to rinse the mud off their legs and bodies in the little stream near our house. While the men washed, my mother would prepare the meal – rice, maybe some fish, vegetables: manioc, sweet potatoes, beans – while I watched.

Oh, it was a sweet life, I tell you, to have a family like that.

My mother at that time did not work in the fields. When she wasn't cooking, she spent her time making cloth out of the bark of the banana tree or spinning silken threads into the finest material. I watched her as she worked, and it is by this picture I have in my mind, of my mother sitting on her heels as she spun the glossy thread for my father's burial shroud, that I can recall the time he died.

Even from a young age, I had been warned about the *dahalo*, the bandits who roamed from village to village stealing cattle. Children were taught to report strangers to our elders. We knew that only bad things could come from foreign men. But these *dahalo* were crafty, creeping and hiding in the hills until they ventured out under cover of night, like cowards.

My family's cattle had been safe, being too few in number to present much of a bounty. They were housed in a hut right in front of the one in which we all slept – too close to be an easy target for thieves. Our homestead was surrounded by a low mud wall; our animals would have alerted us to any intrusion. At night, the men of our village served as sentries against the raiders, yet these particular bandits must have possessed some powerful kind of magic because, one night, they managed to spirit away several hundred heads of our chief's cattle.

So it was that my father was called upon to assist the village men to retrieve the cattle or exact retribution. It was a matter of honour: the honour of our chief, our village and our men. My father left before the sun rose the next morning and there was no time for long farewells if they were to stay on the *dahalo*'s spoor. I did not see him leave. I woke to the news that he had gone and that he would be back soon. I accepted this, for what did I know? I had no reason to think then that anything bad would happen. Why would I? I was so young. I did not yet know what a wicked place this world is, or the evil that dwells in the hearts of men.

Years later, when I walked the tracks worn by cattle that led from our area, I thought that I was following in my father's footsteps somehow, but it was not the same, not really. I remember how we marched: linked arm to arm through the paths where once men drove cattle to the coast. They drove cattle still. Donkeys carried sacks of rice …

I'm getting ahead of myself.

Where was I?

My father, yes. My father had been of the habit, whenever

he set off for other parts, to scoop a handful of earth into a piece of cloth. This he secured fast with string and carried with him. When he returned, he would open the package and empty the soil on the ground. I remember this.

'Father, why do you do this?' I asked him when I first became aware of the practice. 'Why are you throwing the sand into the wind?'

'I'm returning it from where it came,' was his answer. 'I carried it with me so it could remind me of home. It is to ensure that I return safely.'

I wondered whether my father had had time to pick up the soil, and whether he carried it with him wherever he was. My mother could not tell me.

Days passed and we didn't hear anything, not of the men, not of the cattle. My mother was worried; I remember that. Rakota, my brother, was worried too. He was older and more aware of the cruelties that men could inflict upon one another. He nagged my mother, asking: 'When will he be back? When will he be back? When will he be back?' I picked up the refrain. We were so stupid then. In desperation, or maybe to get us to stop asking, our mother slapped us and the baby cried.

Eventually, the chief had to send more men out in search of my father's party. They encountered them a few days' distance away. No cattle had been recovered, but many men had fallen, my father among them. I remember the jubilations and salutations of the women and children welcoming their men back home, while my mother, along with the other widows and orphaned children, had rent her garments and lamented loudly. My brother and I and even little Raketaka, then only a few weeks old, had joined in her wailing and despair. It was no consolation to us that our father had died bravely, as the men who had accompanied him said.

They had had to leave his body behind. For my family, the worst thing about my dear father's death was that he'd fallen in a foreign place. Our enemies refused to hand over his body until we could come up with a sum in silver in return for his body. Twenty *piasters*, the price set, was well beyond my mother's means. Our rice had not yet been harvested and she had no cloth to sell. My mother was forced to borrow the ransom money from my uncle so that she could redeem my father's main bones, the eight bones necessary for a proper burial.

Once the ransom was paid, my father's bones were returned and carried back home by his comrades, who had a sworn duty to protect them. My mother, having no one else to confide her sorrows in, explained the custom to me. If the men went to battle, even if only to reclaim lost cattle or exact revenge against our enemies, those leaving swore to retrieve the bones of their fellows if they died.

My father's bones were placed in the small underground chamber located close to the rice fields where the body of our baby sister was buried. A canopy of stone and clay marks where it is exactly. When my mother dies – if she is not dead yet – her bones will join his there. That's how things are where I am from; a family is buried together on their land. Now my brother, my sister and I are like grains of rice scattered in the dust for the chickens to feed on. Our mother also, I think. Who knows where our bones will lie? It makes me sore just to think about it.

—

Thinking about my family like that made me forget where I was and what I was doing and it was only when Barbetje shouted at me, pulling my ear in that way she did, that I looked down and saw that I had burned the rice. I had to throw the pot out to the dogs, scrape it clean and start all over again. The men would be there soon and would want feeding.

Geert, 1784

In the beginning, I'd regarded myself as the mere steward of my father's fortune, but in my own way I prospered too, adding to his success the fruits of my own endeavours. Before instituting any drastic changes to his estate, I visited each of his farms for protracted periods so I could best determine the health and working of each.

'Why did our father have to acquire so many farms?' Joanna pestered. I'd coerced my sisters into accompanying me on my travels.

'Perhaps to vex you,' I teased, mindful of the fact that my sisters were Town misses and regarded everywhere and everything else as hopelessly staid.

A more accurate answer would have been to point out that our father had inherited two farms – the Swellendam farm on which I'd spent a few months and the Drakenstein grain farm, which had formed part of his third wife's dowry – but I did not want to rekindle talk about our father having made fortuitous marriages, especially not with two impressionable young ladies prone to gossip and speculation. The others had been disparate purchases, scattered across the Cape, which with its ruinous roads made travelling from one to the other arduous in the extreme.

My father had visited his various farms only sporadically, when the weather was clement, and even less so when it was not. His overseers and *knechts* had thus been left to their own devices, running my father's farms as if they and not he were its true masters. I had seen this in Swellendam during my time there, and my opinions were bolstered by my visits to the other farms. On the Stellenbosch and Drakenstein farms I witnessed the meting out of draconian punishments for the slightest of infractions. Although my father had not been one to spare the rod, his punishments had been just. I was a more moderate man, but took pains not to appear overly soft. One cannot demonstrate weakness if one seeks the respect of one's workers.

These visits left me feeling ever more out of my depth. To a man, I found my father's overseers surly, almost combative. Perhaps they'd expected me to be disinterested and therefore more amenable; perhaps my reputation at the Cape had spread: my bookishness and lack of enthusiasm for all things agricultural. I became convinced that they were of the impression that I was a dilettante, undeserving of my good fortune.

It would have been easier had my father employed a manager to look over all aspects of his sprawling interests, in the manner of the more prosperous farmers. Yet deep down, I knew the thought would have been anathema to him – a man who'd seemed determined to live forever and never relinquish the reins of power. Had my character been a disappointment to him? The thought gnawed at my gut constantly, but I tamped it down whenever it surfaced. There was no use in dwelling on all that.

At each of my father's farms, I tried to determine the rhyme or reason behind his interest. He'd always stressed to me the importance of meat, and it was true that the bulk of his revenues had flowed from his contracts to supply the Company with meat, and from sales to foreign ships and private citizens when there was a surfeit thereof. I was also well aware that my father had circumvented the Company when it suited his purposes to do so, claiming to hold less stock than in reality, and how he'd often scrupled to negotiate and renegotiate terms with the Company, even before the contracts were due for review. If one discounted the farmers I'd encountered in the interior when first learning the meat business, men who were willing to sell their animals at low prices if it saved on the expense of sending them to market, one could make a prosperous living through stock farming. However, as evinced by my father's spectacular success, I concluded that possessing a meat *pacht* was the key to true prosperity from meat.

Likewise, the larger wine farmers and those who owned wine *pachten* were guaranteed a good living from the fruits of the vine. I assumed that this must have been my father's reasoning when first he'd purchased the wine farm in Stellenbosch. My father was a temperate man who seldom lifted his elbow, but there was a certain prestige to be gained if one possessed a wine farm. The owners of the Constantia wine farms were among the most esteemed (and wealthy) at the Cape. It was common knowledge that their reds and whites were enjoyed at the finest tables around the world.

Although he visited it infrequently, the farm in Stellenbosch had been a source of no little pride to my father. He'd served his own wines at table for guests, along with the imported Moselle and Bordeaux wines so popular here. Privately, it humoured me to see his guests fawning over his mediocre wine, which was not to my taste, being rather harsh in character, almost sulphuric, while eschewing the fine French wines. Nor had my father succeeded in bidding for a wine contract – the incumbents ensured that potential competitors were hampered at every juncture, as no doubt my father himself had done by placing obstacles in the way of those seeking to gain a meat concession. Nevertheless, I duly made the trip there after passing the months following my father's death at our Rondebosch summerhouse with my sisters. The close quarters of our family farmhouse had become cloying, and at that stage I had still been trying to resist the temptation embodied by a certain female.

Stellenbosch, a distance of some nine leagues from Town, was founded by and named for Simon van der Stel, the commander of the Cape in the year 1679. Later, the name Van der Stel would become ill-famed when his son Willem Adriaan assumed the mantle of governor and the ownership of Vergelegen, arguably the best estate in the district, if not the entire Cape Colony. Vergelegen was so well favoured that, during his rule, and contrary to Company dictate, Van der Stel and his cohorts, among them scores of Company officials, had enjoyed a near monopoly on supplying the Company's food and wine requirements. Willem's governorship was such an unpopular one that more than a century later, burghers still spoke of his excesses when discussing abuses of Company power.

Zeelust, my father's farm in Stellenbosch, had been named after his youthful hankering for the sea and lay in the shadow of the Hottentot's Holland Mountain. The soil was known to be good for grapes, although many in the area used their lands for grazing instead. It was a sizeable property – greater than thirty *morgen* – with an imposing main house built in the popular gabled style that my father said had much in common with the gabled houses to be found along his beloved Zaan River. The only exception was that the gables, instead of occupying the entire front as they did with the narrow houses in Zaan, formed the centrepiece of the façade, rising grandly above the roof, which in this instance was made up of reed thatch.

The vineyards sloped towards the lower reaches of the mountain and, at the time of my visit, were laden with fat globes of green, shining translucently in the February sun. On closer inspection, one could discern the veins, filaments and seeds of the grapes. Harvest time was near – the occasion of my visit, since I intended to witness all aspects that went into producing the wine that bore my father's crest.

I assisted with the picking of the grapes; all hands were needed to bring in the fruits. February is the hottest month at the Cape and the soil in the vineyard was dusty and dry. It was believed that the less water it received, the sweeter the grape. I couldn't resist sampling while I picked, wiping the grapes on my trousers or cleaning the skin with my fingers before popping them into my mouth, and could therefore attest to their sweetness.

Once filled, the baskets were collected and carried to the cellar for pressing. I'd heard that forward-thinking farmers had begun using wooden presses to crush the grapes, but at Zeelust the grapes were crushed in the traditional manner – by foot. The must, that is, the pressings, were then placed into sulphur-smoked barrels to control the fermentation process. The barrels were not filled to the brim lest they explode, and they were kept unstoppered in order to allow the dregs to be drained. After a few days of fermentation, the wine was drawn and placed into freshly sulphured barrels. The drawing and fresh barrelling continued apace until the wine settled, the fermentation process drew to a halt and the sediment, the lees, sunk to the bottom of the barrels – a process that on my father's farm took approximately ten days.

Since the settled wine had to be rested for a few weeks before fining, I decided we should remove to our father's grain farm in the Drakenstein. This was also where he had routinely kept cattle brought from the interior for resale in Town. My sisters and I arrived at the farm within a matter of hours, stopping once along the way to take tea with neighbours who'd been on close terms with our family.

Contiguous to Stellenbosch, Drakenstein was established in 1687, eight years after the former. This is the area where the Company had settled the Huguenots, Protestant refugees from France, when they arrived at the Cape seeking solace from the persecution they'd faced in their home country. Though she'd spoken not a word of French, Catharina, my father's third wife, had been descended from these refugees.

Like the Stellenbosch main house, the farmhouse at Draken-stein was gabled and outfitted to my father's taste for costly and rare furnishings. The kitchen in particular had a munificence of copper kettles and iron pots, and we dined off the finest porcelain using spoons and forks of silver. Plaster numbers set into the gable proclaimed the year the house had been erected: 1780. A few years earlier, my father had caused the original dwelling to be razed and this one to be built in its place. In his more whimsical moments, he used to speak of one day retiring here once my sisters and I were married and off his hands. He would breed horses here, he had told us, when the Cape became too constricting for his liking. The farmland had all the things he loved best: a flowing river and room enough for horses, cattle and sheep to graze freely. It was a truly beautiful place.

Attending church one Sunday, I remembered my father telling me that it was here, upon the door of the church in Drakenstein, that scores ago, one Estienne Barbier, leader of a rebellious group of burghers, had nailed their grievances against the Company.

'Barbier had risen to the rank of sergeant in the Company within a short period,' my father had scoffed. 'But instead of enjoying the perquisites of his position, he'd grown belligerent, accusing the commander of the Castle of Good Hope of thiev-ery and other misdeeds – accusations which were subsequently deemed to be unfounded. He was ordered to apologise publicly to the commander, and upon refusing, was incarcerated in the *Donker Gat*.'

The deep reaches of the Castle of Good Hope housed its dungeons, among them the infamous dark hole of which my father spoke.

'Somehow Mijneer Barbier managed to escape these confines, no doubt due to collusion on the part of a sympathetic captor. He successfully sought refuge in the Drakenstein. It was while he was ensconced there, harboured in a widow's house, that he heard of a group of would-be rebels simmering against the Company's rules and offered them his fraternity and expertise.'

Upon mentioning the story to one of my fellow churchgoers, a neighbouring farmer by the name of Jan van der Bijl, the man took up the story of the hapless Mijneer Barbier with bloodthirsty glee: 'The rebels' grievances stemmed from a bartering expedition certain of them had conducted, venturing beyond the Orange River to trade with Hottentot tribes for cattle.'

He paused to gauge my reaction. There were many who supported such actions, but having no deep-seated notions on the matter, I remained silent, allowing Mijneer van der Bijl to have his say. 'After receiving complaints from several Hottentot members of the expedition as well as from the tribes with whom they'd bartered – and some said attacked – the burghers' cattle were confiscated.'

From my father's telling of the story, I knew what had eventually befallen Mijneer Barbier. Upon meeting up with the rebels, Barbier's intervention was to write the letter that caused the great ado and branded him an outlaw – to be captured alive or dead.

Years later, I recalled my father's words: 'Though he'd evaded capture for more than six months, Barbier surrendered to the authorities under the mistaken belief that he would be pardoned. Instead he was executed, beheaded, one hand dismembered and the remainder of his body quartered. The various parts of his body were then displayed in the most gruesome fashion alongside one of the Colony's busiest roads.' Or so my father had insisted.

All this had taken place so long ago, before my father had even set foot in the Colony, but it was a story he would revisit from time to time. Thinking about it again, I realised that, unlike with my opinionated and biased neighbour, who believed Mijneer Barbier a hero, I never knew whether my father had admired or despised the man.

My sisters were relieved when we returned to Zeelust to participate in the fining and bottling of our wine before returning to Town. The clarifying of the wine was done by adding dried goats' blood. I had not known this and was interested to see for myself how the black and gritty blood could alter its nature, changing it from cloudy to clear. The logic behind this, I was informed, was that the lees would adhere to the particles of dried blood, so creating larger solids that sunk to the bottom of the barrels, which could then be racked, and siphoned off upon bottling. It took a week for the solids to settle before the wine could be separated from its sediment. Despite my scepticism, I can vouch for the efficacy of this method as the resultant wine was clear and crisp, without a hint of the blood that had made it so.

Altogether, my sisters and I spent three months out in the country after my father's death, but we needed to return to Town before the winter rains arrived, as they would make travelling hard, if not impossible, along the poor roads. Also, the Berg River, which originated in the Drakenstein Mountains, had a tendency to overflow during the stormy months, which further impeded travel between parts of Drakenstein and Stellenbosch. I'd enjoyed my time in Stellenbosch. The wine-making had been a revelation, so much so that I was most readily convinced that this was the path I should take, my own path. I could quite see myself as an affable farmer of the grape, puffing on my pipe at leisure. With learning and the right winemaker, perhaps a Frenchman, maybe even one of those new presses, the flavour of the wine could only be improved.

Since the farms in Swellendam, Drakenstein and Stellenbosch were working farms and, as such, self-sustaining, I decided to maintain the status quo on each. The Rondebosch farm was not as sustainable, but it was our respite from the heat and pressures of the sweltering Town during the summer months, and whether out of sentiment or practicality, I could not bring myself to part with it.

While I was learning all I could about my father's legacy, men of discovery had been reaching further into the interior, configuring new boundaries as they sought freedom from the Company's strict rules and its monopolies, and as land and grazing became dearer at the Cape and in the known territories. There was talk, which came to pass, of the establishment of a new district encompassing the Zuurveld, recently inaugurated and named Graaff-Reinet, where, over the years, trekkers from the Cape had settled with their flocks and herds. It was no secret that so far away from any form of Company control, trekkers had assumed heinous liberties: they short-changed the Company's revenue system by neglecting to apply for loan farms and settled wherever they wished, often beyond the Colony's borders. Here they continually skirmished with the Hottentots they encountered, indulged in overgrazing and were, by and large, remiss in paying tax on their livestock. Burghers at the Cape were divided in their regard for and condemnation of the trekkers' behaviour. Some revelled in the cheating of the Company, while others were sticklers for upholding the rules and regulations that governed our society. I myself was conflicted, finding much to commend and to censure.

Inspired by my father's adventuring during his earlier years, I thought of emulating him, of forging my own path and destiny in a less settled area, but I was weighted down with the responsibilities and cares that had been bestowed upon me. Still, I was fortunate, more fortunate than those men delving deeper into the dark territories, for many of them were doing so out of necessity – younger sons, men without my means. Someday I'd travel – into the interior and to Europe too, as men of breeding did – I told myself. Until then, I needed to return to Town. I yearned to ground myself among familiar places, familiar people.

Upon our return, Town seemed deserted and narrower after the expansiveness of the country. Several of the foreign battalions had already left its shores, and due to the high north-westerly winter winds, ships avoided Table Bay altogether, dropping anchor at the safer harbour to be found at False Bay across the peninsula instead. It was not unwarranted that the

Cape of Good Hope had earned first the appellation 'Cape of Storms'. Certain of the more prominent families had removed to the False Bay area to wait out the winter months, but this was the one area in which my father had not been interested, and having had little exposure to it, neither were my sisters and I.

I caught up with the news I'd missed during my interlude in the country. This one had married and his wife was already big with child, despite the short duration of their marriage; a neighbour was having financial difficulties after making foolhardy investments in cotton farming, of all things, and we could anticipate a vendue of his goods soon. Rumours, insistent rumours, that the Company too verged on bankruptcy had grown and continued to reverberate in the drawing rooms and meeting places of Town.

Then the fleets returned to Table Bay, and I busied myself at the docks supplying meat to the Company's and other ships. Those heavily invested in the wine and wheat industries might have experienced fluctuating fortunes over the years, but my father had been correct in his assessment when he'd said that there was nothing safer than meat. He had known his way around the Company's unreasonable demands, and without knowing it then, so had I. The thought solaced me.

Lena, 1854

In this place they do not grow rice, but in the land beneath the skies, it was our main food. The rice we grew was red in colour – white too, of course, but the rice I liked best was red. When boiled, the red grains turned pink, in the same way the shell of the crayfish does when cooked. Here, the rice is white only, or yellow when seasoned with *borrie*. It is not the same. What people eat most here is bread: bread smeared thickly with fat, bread and meat. No wonder the men and women are so stout – Christians and often slaves, too. Only the young are slender, but they do not stay that way for long.

It was from my mother that I learned all I know about rice. With my father gone, she had to take over the sowing and planting. As soon as the Ambiaty bloomed, my mother began preparing the rice seeds. Until then, we'd check the Ambiaty bushes each morning, waiting for the blue flowers to burst forth their buds, as it was then, my mother said, we would know the sowing season had arrived.

First, my mother had me divide the red and white grains into two basins, as the seeds should be planted separately, she explained. We half-filled each basin with water before bringing them inside to germinate in the warmth of our hut, and to protect them from the wild boars and other creatures that on occasion got into the fields at night.

I saw how my mother checked the grains for sprouting several times a day. I checked too, but with more excitement to see the shoots than any sense of trepidation. When I was older I could understand why my mother had been so nervous. It was the first crop for which she alone had been responsible. If the rice failed, all else would fail too.

Before too long, the grains began to sprout tiny yellow-white worms, or at least, that is how it looked to me. My mother drained the water away and planted the sprouts in the patch prepared for them, close to our hut. I had not been allowed to handle the sprouts; they were too delicate and my clumsy fingers might damage them. Once they were in the ground, I helped my mother spread wood ash over the black soil. Curiously, she did not water the sprouts then. Instead, the patch was left dry until the earth cracked. This meant that soon the blades would breach the surface. It was only then that she watered. On the day she drenched the patch my mother told me to watch over Raketaka. She was beginning to crawl then and would have found her way into the muddy ground. Perhaps my mother sensed that so would I.

The morning the first green blades pushed through the soil my mother beamed. It was the first time I had seen her smile since my father had been killed. Even Rakota was pleased, grinning and shaking his head from side to side as he tenderly examined the shoots from the edges of the patch.

Within days the blades became a thick, green carpet. We scrutinised the patch daily, checking for the small, red and brown insects that bored into the stalks and the tiny black and brown spots that grew larger and larger in size until the entire plant was eaten up by mould. But that year the seedlings flourished. Despite all our troubles, it could still in some ways be a good year. We had scares, yes: the thunder that announced itself by bellowing across the valley, the tongues of lightning that flicked out of the sky at night like flames from a monster's mouth. Nothing harmed the seedlings, and our hut and our buildings stood safe. By the time the seedlings were a few hands in height, the first rains had come and it was time for them to be replanted.

This time it was my mother who drove the ox through the fields to loosen the soil. This time she was the one smeared black with mud, her body stiff and sore from struggling with that stubborn animal. I too was smeared black from helping her pinch apart the matted roots of the seedlings. This year it was I who placed the plants into the holes my mother had poked into the ground with a long, sharp stick. It was I who then stamped the soil around them with my feet, carefully, lest I cause any damage to the delicate plants. I can still feel the soft pull of the mud oozing beneath my toes. I remember how I was so afraid of stepping on a snake – snakes were attracted to the dampness of the rice fields, I knew that – but I did what was expected of me because I was a big girl and my mother needed my help.

I learned what was weed and what was plant as I helped my mother tend the vegetable fields where she planted yams and manioc and corn. I discovered the best places in the forest to take honeycomb from the bees, and I learned how not to get stung – a painful lesson. I was busy from morning to sunset. It was hard work, but a girl's work. My brother had a man's work to do: driving the cattle to a nearby stream to drink, leading them to the pasturage to graze and milking the cows each morning. When his work with the cattle was done, he cut cane to burn as nourishment for our crops, chopped wood or collected dried grass for our fires.

Rakota's shoulders broadened, his skin darkened from too many hours in the sun. He grew quieter. Sometimes I'd act playfully with him, tap him on his back or pull his ears, but he did not find it amusing. Now he had no time for a child's games. When we were younger, he had taught me how to train beetles to fight; it was a great sport, but he was not interested in sport. Sometimes I kicked him, softly first, then harder. The kicking game had always been his favourite. He did not kick me back. Nor was he interested in telling me the story of the bullfight to which my father had once taken him, claiming to have forgotten the details; or the story of Ibonia, the handsome hero who'd had to vanquish his enemies to win the hand of his beloved.

'You think you're a hero, that's why you're always talking of Ibonia,' I used to tease Rakota in the days when he liked nothing better than to recite the story.

But that was before.

Without any regard for our mother, Rakota removed himself from our hut, building his own of wood and palm a few strides away from the one we'd all shared.

'Why does brother want to sleep alone? Why does he not want to live with us?' I remember pestering my mother.

My mother sighed, lifted her hands to the sky as if the answer lay there, but she did not answer me. Then Raketaka started up crying; my mother put her teat in her mouth and my question was forgotten. Rakota was a young boy yet – too young to be married and set up his own household. The purpose of his hut was to escape us females, I believe.

Alone in our hut save for Raketaka, who was too little to be of any companionship, my mother and I drew even closer. We were together all the time. People used to say we were like rice and water. Rice grows in water and it is cooked in water, it is eaten with water. That is the thing about rice. You cannot have rice without water.

When my parents had first moved there, my father had dug sloping rills in the ground to channel water from the stream. Raketaka secured to her back with a length of fabric, my mother and I flooded the fields by scooping water from the adjacent rills. In addition to unseen snakes, all sorts of creatures were drawn to the sodden fields. Frogs and fish and eels swam among the roots and stems of the rice plants. On occasion, Rakota would catch an eel and we'd roast it for our evening meal. I was as afraid of eels as I was of their cousins the snakes, but oh, how my mouth watered at the thought of eel meat.

The rice grew greener, taller. From far away, you could hear it whistle in the wind, along with the burps and croaks of the frogs and the twitching chatter of the birds. We examined the rice for signs of rust, for brown spots, for the red worms that feasted on them; we watched the sky for locusts, for hail. As the grain ripened, the green plants turned yellow and red; the heavy heads bent under the weight. We fretted about the strong winds that threatened to upheave and spill the grain before harvest time.

As the rains reached an end, it was time to pick the rice. Growing and tending the rice was a woman's work, but when the ears of grain were heavy and ripe – ready to be picked – Rakota helped with the harvesting. The water came up to his thighs; flecks of mud and ash coated his arms as he brought the long blade down to shear the stalks. Over and over again the blade shone in the sun; the rice shone too, gold and shiny like silk. As he completed each row, my mother followed behind him, tying stalks into small bundles. With Raketaka on my hip, I watched from the side of the field.

'Next season it will be your job to help with the tying of the sheaves,' my mother told me.

After a day, or maybe two, when the bundles were dry, my mother and Rakota carried the bundles to a flattened area some distance from the fields. Here they thrashed them against a rock, loosening the grains from their stalks. Once the bundles had been beaten, my mother placed the sundered beards in a large basin and tossed these in the air to separate the grain from the chaff.

I remember it like it was yesterday, the *shick-shick-shick* sound the grains made as they fell into the container; I remember my brother's face, tense and unmoving, as he watched my mother. I remember Raketaka crawling in the dirt; she was faster than I'd expected and I had to rush to keep her away from the clean rice and from the sharp bits of straw that fluttered in the wind with the winnowing, as they could get in her eyes. And I remember my mother's eyes, how they narrowed, and the way she bit upon her lips as if to swallow them as she concentrated.

I helped to place the winnowed grains in a big, strong basket. Rakota fed the chaff to the cattle. As soon as a basket was filled, my mother lifted it on her head and carried it to our rice store. Each was so heavy that her neck bent and the basket tilted to the side. Looking up at my mother for a moment then, I was reminded of a stalk of rice, ready to be picked, the basket the weighty ear that drooped close to the ground.

The rice was stored in an underground pit next to our hut. The pit was made of clay and had an opening in its roof through which my mother poured and extracted the rice. The opening was just wide enough for me to sidle through. When stores dwindled, my mother lowered me inside to scoop rice from the bottom into a dish. As soon as I'd relinquished the receptacle, she or Rakota would grab me by my arms and pull me up. The rice pit was dark and had a stale, shut-in smell, since for most of the time, a large stone covered the opening to protect our stores against theft or rats or disease or bad weather.

Once all the rice was emptied into the pit, we could stop fretting about what we would do for food with my father gone. The rice was safe there, and a full rice pit meant that we would have enough to eat, without borrowing or going hungry, until the next sowing season. Along with the rice, we had ample manioc, yams and corn to last us during the months when all growing things were cleaned off. Most importantly, we had gathered enough rice to pay the tribute – the portion of rice that each household contributed to the king, regardless of our yields. We knew of families who'd gone into debt so they could pay. With the money my mother had borrowed to retrieve my father's bones, and the expenses incurred in burying them, our family could ill-afford further bondage.

When my father was alive, we had four cattle: an ox, two cows and a bull calf. As I said, it was Rakota's job to look after them. My brother loved those creatures; he even had names for them. When let out of their hut, they followed him around like dogs. Although given to silence, Rakota was a kind person, a gentle person; I think the animals sensed this. He fed the cattle lumps of salt or licks of honey that they nuzzled out of his hand. Often I would catch him stroking their humps when he did not know I was looking.

The calf was slaughtered on the day we buried my father's bones; we could not spare the ox or one of the cows. He had been lazy, with legs too long for his oversized belly. I could not understand why the calf had to be killed for the bones to be buried, but this was my people's way. When someone died, an ox – it was usually an ox – was killed and the meat divided among the guests. We received our portion last, as was custom- ary. My mother insisted Rakota and I eat. Guests ate before the body was buried, not afterwards like here – meat and rice: plain rice, no *borrie*, no raisins.

The men collected money to assist us with the cost of the

food, but it had not amounted to a substantial sum since most of my father's friends and relatives were as needy as we were. I was so young that I never thought in terms of rich or poor. There were rich men in our village, and the chief was rich in cattle and grain, but we'd always had enough to eat so I never suspected we could be in want of anything. We had our animals: the three cattle that remained, a few sheep, chickens too. Our soil was healthy and there was always rice.

One morning I was woken by a commotion that I dimly realised was Rakota calling for help. My first thought was that the bandits were coming. In that moment I believed only an attack could be the reason for my brother to shout like that. It was dark inside our hut – no windows. I shifted on the sleeping mat I shared with my mother and Raketaka. Only Raketaka was there, lightly exhaling her baby's breath. My mother was an early riser, while I was always tired, always trying to keep my eyes shut a bit longer. Ever since my father had died, my mother struggled to sleep, turning this way and that on the narrow mat, trying to find a position that would allow her to rest. There were times when I woke up in the middle of the night to find her wide awake, sitting against the wall on the other side of the room. I turned to look for her. A scraping sound alerted me to her whereabouts. She was standing at the door, her back to me. Hearing the rustle I made as I rose from the rush mat, she spun around.

'Stay there,' she whispered, raising a finger to her lips. 'I will go. Stay with your sister.'

Pulling her *lamba* around her, she darted out. I snuggled closer against Raketaka, almost shrouding her tiny body with mine. The dogs began to bark immediately my mother stepped outside; the rooster stirred to life, trumpeting with displeasure at being woken so early, while the hens clucked and hissed in agreement. My brother was always up before the rooster's crow. He was a light sleeper too, I remember.

I listened, trying to make out individual sounds. To my mind, the lowing of the cattle sounded like wailing. The other animals were waking too; the birds that lived in the forest took to the skies with a loud flap as if with one pair of wings and signalled loudly as they looped our fields; I heard the grunts and clicks of the group of *maki* that lived in the tall trees near our homestead. Rising above the din, the wailing of the cows grew louder. Growing more and more uneasy as the morning light slanted in through the door – in her haste my mother had neglected to close it properly – I waited for her, for Rakota, or for some explanation, but none came. Raketaka woke and began to cry. I put my finger in her mouth, but although she quieted for a bit, she began to cry once again in earnest when she realised that my finger held no sustenance.

Picking her up, I went outside. The courtyard was deserted save for the hens and rooster pecking in the dirt. A thin haze of smoke wisped through the open door of the hut where the cattle were kept. This was most unusual. I went closer.

My mother and Rakota were inside; there was no room for me to enter, so I hovered at the door, Raketaka perched precariously on my hip. Neither my mother nor Rakota paid us any heed, despite my sister's sobbing. I coughed; neither of them reacted. My mother was adding shards of cane to the skimp fire that burned in the centre of the room, hence the smoke. As a rule, we did not make fires there: it was dangerous and disconcerted the animals and the dried *rofia* thatching could easily catch fire if one of the animals excited a spark.

Rakota was kneeling on the ground next to one of the cows. It was a tan colour, almost red. The other cow was black, and her temperament was as dark as her fur. Sweeter natured, the tan cow had birthed the calf they'd slaughtered, and she had pined for days afterwards. Undeterred by the heat and smoke of the fire, the black cow and the bull hovered over Rakota and the other cow as if anxious to see what he was doing. One would emit a woeful groan and the other would answer. But for her laboured breaths, the cow on the ground was silent.

'What's wrong?' I asked, still at the doorway.

Rakota and my mother turned to look at me. An ugly frown transfigured Rakota's face.

My mother too was angry. 'What are you doing here?' she demanded. 'I told you to stay in the hut. And how could you bring your sister out in the cold? Go back inside!'

I did not try to argue with my mother.

When she came back, the sun was high in the sky; the air inside our hut was hot and dry, even though the fire had all but died. Raketaka had cried herself out and had gone back to sleep. I was angry at my mother, and afraid. I was hungry too, but I did not say so. I did not say anything.

'Why so sad, little one?' my mother asked, as if I had no reason to be upset. Without waiting for me to answer, she continued. 'The cow was bitten by *vancoho*. Rakota found her like that this morning. We tried to get the poison out, but it was too late. She is no longer.'

From a young age, I had been taught to be careful of those large black spiders with shells so glossy they looked wet. They were horrid things, with overstuffed round bellies marked with red, and thick legs and pincers, a little like those of a crab. My father had told us the story of how, when he was a young boy, he had fallen into a deep and terrifying sleep that lasted for days after being bitten by a *vancoho*. Scorpions, they call them here.

'The poison had led to fever dreams of the worst kind,' my father had said. 'Your grandparents were not sure that I would wake or if the spirits would take me while I slept. Luckily, I awoke, thanks to the herb tea my father, your grandfather, had administered. Most do not survive the *vancoho*'s bite.'

As soon as my mother related her news about the cow, I darted outside. I was at the age when everything interested me. Even, or especially, death; I was not girlish in that way. I wanted to see for myself how something as small as a spider could kill a creature as large as a cow.

'Let your brother be,' my mother called after me as if sensing my intention to pester him with questions. But Rakota was not there when I entered the cattle hut. Neither were the bull and the other cow. He had likely taken them to drink. The dead cow looked like it was asleep. It used to like nothing more than to lie about in the sun like that, with its legs tucked beneath its body … cows love the sun. It was only when I looked closer that I could see for myself that it *was* dead. Fat, blue-green flies had already begun to bother it, settling on its hide and buzzing around its mouth. I tried to flick them away, but they refused to budge. They were already feasting, laying their eggs in its fur.

Later that day, I watched Rakota cut the cow up for meat. My mother salted most of it and was about to roast some – hair and all – over the fire for our evening meal when she changed her mind, saying that the poison from the spider might have spread. Rakota buried all the meat in a deep hole and we ate roasted manioc instead.

Though only one cow and the bull remained, there was no need to be alarmed, my mother said. The cow would give us milk and the bull was only really needed by the next planting season. We would be fine.

We were fine. It was a time of abundance in our village then, a time of peace. Bellies were full. Our enemies stayed away. Then the dry season was upon us. Trees lost their leaves, our fields, save for the underground vegetables that still grew, were shorn and fallow. The rills dried up and the streams began to run shallow. The weather grew colder, particularly in the morning. Without the rice to keep her busy, my mother found the time to spin and weave, and once more I became an attentive learner.

As with growing rice, the arts of spinning and weaving were necessary for a girl to master. I learned how to split the leaves of the *rofia* palm or banana bark in the correct manner in order to make thread. I learned to twist the thread and draw it out, as much as my hands could stretch, before winding it around the *ampela* and to not stop twisting and drawing and winding until the spindle was full. I was too young to learn more than the rudiments of weaving, but I did learn how to choose dried grass, or use the inner bark of the hibiscus tree which we frayed and twisted into rope. Patiently, my mother showed me how to fashion rushes and grasses into sturdy baskets, complete with lids, for storage.

As the dry season progressed, Rakota spent even less time with us. The grass upon which our cattle grazed frizzled into hay so he sought fresh pasturage further afield. He spent hours away at a stretch, at times with the cattle, at times exploring the peaks and forests surrounding our home. My mother busied herself with various tasks, sometimes teaching me, sometimes working in silence. I too explored when I had the chance, but was careful not to stray too far from home. Raketaka grew, took her first steps and began babbling in her baby tongue.

We told ourselves we were fine. We were not. Perhaps if we had heeded the warnings, our lives might have been different. I thought about that afterwards, if we had changed just one thing, been more vigilant about the signs ... That is the problem with signs. They only make sense once it is too late. Signs such as the time Rakota reported seeing an ill-omened wildcat in the hills above the stream when he took the cattle to drink. Our mother disbelieved him. 'Take back your stories,' she had insisted. 'This boy and his stories!'

'Take back your stories,' I'd parroted proudly.

We all knew that no one had seen a wildcat in our area in many seasons. I've forgotten the exact reasoning about why it was so, except that it was said that a wildcat meant that there would be bad luck for those who encountered it.

Then, for two mornings in a row, I spotted the bird of death, screeching loudly as it tracked my movements as I carried water from the stream to our hut. I had not known then that this bird portended trouble. I did not yet know its name. All I knew was that it sounded like murder. Both occasions, by the time I returned home, I had forgotten all about it. Only once I was older and someone, I forget who, told me the significance of this bird, did I remember seeing it those mornings. Now I'm not sure that I did. There are times when I'm not sure what really happened and what was a dream. Life is like that.

One morning, not long after he claimed to have seen the wildcat, Rakota went to rouse the cattle and discovered the remaining cow lying motionless in its hut. This time he knew what to look for, but there was no sign that it had been bitten. Rakota suggested that we call the diviner in to see what had caused the cow's death; perhaps someone had wished us ill. But before any decision could be made, my uncle, my father's oldest and only surviving brother, surprised us with a visit. My mother begged him to examine the cow, since he was more knowledgeable about those things.

After examining the cow, my uncle said it looked like she was a victim of the cattle sickness, but it was hard to tell. Had Rakota noticed any unusual behaviour in the last few days? Had the cow walked stiffly, or been unable to rise? Rakota could not be certain, but he thought she had walked clumsily the previous morning, and now that he thought about it, she had held her head at a high angle. This is what had made him take note of the cow's gait in the first place. My uncle said that it most definitely sounded like the cattle sickness. He suggested we destroy the carcass and the meat, to be safe. I had not been fond of that mean, black cow, but her death was a big loss as she had been our only source of milk.

My uncle did not stay long that day, as if fearing that our

misfortune was catching. Yet he too was a bearer of unhappy news. A crocodile, as long as the tallest man in our village was tall, had been seen on the banks of the river that hemmed our village on one side. Already a man and two children had gone missing. It could not be a coincidence. We'd heard about the fearsome, yellow-bellied beasts; we'd heard about their hard shells, hardened further with pointed scales; and we'd heard about their teeth like rows of spears. But we had not heard of crocodiles frequenting these parts, for our water was considered to be too cold.

Not so, my uncle insisted. He narrated the story of a young boy who had been guiding his cattle across the river to get to pasturage on the other side. 'Probably in the boy's age group,' he said, pointing at Rakota. 'As they crossed, this boy and eight, maybe nine, heads of cattle, the crocodile launched out of the water and grabbed one of the cows, pulling it beneath the surface. And it wasn't a small cow either!

'That cow bawled and screeched so loudly that several people, including myself, rushed to the riverbank. I thought someone was getting killed,' my uncle explained. 'The boy just stood there shaking … the other cattle had stampeded to the opposite bank … but the boy, he didn't even think to get out of the water … and not a squeak from his mouth, nothing to fight the crocodile.'

'Must have been the shock,' my mother suggested, but my uncle ignored her.

'We grabbed our sticks and tried to beat the crocodile, anything to get it to release its grip. But that monster's jaw was locked into place. It was so strong,' he added, 'that it tossed that cow like it weighed nothing, pounding it against the surface of the water and plunging it underneath until it drowned. They vanished within minutes, cow and crocodile both,' my uncle said, with some satisfaction. 'All that remained was an ever-widening red-brown pool on the surface of the water. I was there; I saw it.'

'What happened to the boy?' asked Rakota, who'd been silent throughout. 'Who is he? Do we know him?'

Disregarding the last two questions, my uncle answered, 'The boy and the rounded-up cattle had to take the long way back home, as he was too afraid to re-enter the water once he stirred himself to get out. Cattle may be stupid creatures, but I don't think they would have followed him even if he had,' my uncle said.

Again, Rakota asked, 'What happened to the boy?'

Again, my uncle ignored him. 'Now the chief is warning people to avoid crossing the river,' he said. 'That is why I came, to see if you had heard.'

'No.' My mother shook her head before turning her attention to Rakota and me. 'See, children, you should not linger far from home. We have our own water that is good. Promise that you will stick to the stream by our lands.'

Rakota and I agreed readily. We knew that we could not afford to take chances with our remaining bull.

But there was no way to avoid the river once the dry season progressed. Streams dried up completely and were baked and cracked by the sun. Rakota accompanied me to the river to fetch water, or I accompanied him to take the bull to drink. The men of our village devised ways of frightening the crocodile away. Fires and loud noises worked for a while, but he always returned, his warty-looking snout and wide nostrils floating above the surface of the water.

Yes, I saw him too.

Going to the river during the time of the crocodile was full of danger, but thrilling. The banks were crowded with men and children; some beat drums, others ensured that the bonfire built there remained fed. The noise and the smoke made for an almost festive atmosphere, but there was nothing merry about it. A few boys played the kicking game, as if to show their bravery; others dared to dip a foot in the water and made as if to jump in, under the glare of their elders. Yet at all times we were careful lest we anger the gods and thus open ourselves to becoming the creature's next victim.

The crocodile grew gigantic on the unwary or reckless villagers who wandered to the river late at night or early in the morning. Others whispered that they were sacrifices, or had sacrificed themselves to sate its greed. Then it became official: the chief decreed that each household was to contribute a bull to appease the crocodile and its gods. We had only one bull, but there was no question of disobeying this command or of requesting dispensation from the dictate.

When the day for the handover arrived, my family made for a sombre party. Rakota led the bull, with my mother, Raketaka on her back, and I following behind. Although unhindered by animal or child, I walked slowly for someone who was always rushed, reluctant to witness the bloodshed. The slaughtering was to take place at the river's edge – a mass slaying – not a matter of throwing in a bull every day or so for the crocodile to feed upon. When we arrived, mayhem greeted us. Families had assembled with their beasts, forming an untidy caravan. The chief and all the nobles were there, ready to oversee the carrying out of the orders.

One by one, families were called up to hand over their bulls. The chief's butcher slit their throats. The noises those wretched creatures made are still hard to describe. In my experience, only pigs, I think, make a worse noise when they are killed. Young children squealed and screamed in sympathy – mothers slapped those who made the most noise – and throughout the carnage drummers beat out a mournful tattoo. Dust rose from countless feet, the air was thick with it. Blood from the oxen fed the river, flowing in thin, red rivulets that lay on the surface like entrails before spreading and turning the muddy water red.

'Wouldn't it be better sense to sacrifice one bull at a time?' I remember my mother asking that morning, before we set off.

She wouldn't have dared ask it outside of our hut.

Whole animals were tossed into the river, clogging the water with their bloating carcasses. Of the crocodile there was no sight. Not of claw, nor scale nor even his large, lizard-eyes bobbing above the ruined river. Not even the blood had drawn him out. People took this as a sign that the sacrifice had worked. A shout rose up from the crowd and some women began singing songs of celebration. The dust rose ever higher as the more spirited villagers stamped their feet and danced in relief. The revelry did not last long. When we turned to go, vultures descended like a dense, dark rain-cloud swollen with malice. As we walked home we heard them: shrieking and sniggering at our folly.

Now we had no cattle left, and no means of procuring replacements. Still, even then, as long as our pits contained rice, as long as there was still some water to be found, we believed we would be fine. The rains would come soon; life would begin again.

Time passed. Buds appeared on the limbs and branches of the Ambiaty. Once more we waited anxiously for the flowers to unfurl from their casings. Our rice stores were running low, but we had enough to plant and enough to eat until the next harvest. The weather that time of year was clement, save for the lightning that sparked across the sky of an evening and presaged that the time to sow was near. Otherwise, it remained dry, with no further hint of the coming rain. Yet when it arrived some days later, the water soaked the earth, creating a rich, glorious mud that helped replenish the arid streams. There is no more welcome smell in my opinion than the musty smell of the earth after the first rainfall. I remember laughing uncontrollably beneath the sky, my arms stretched out as far as they could go as I spun round and round and round.

The rain didn't last long. Days went by. I saw a glimpse of blue petal showing through a tightly closed bud of the Ambiaty, a blue flower showed its face, but it was not yet time. Until one morning we woke to see that a multitude of buds had opened at once, altering the appearance of the trees with their fluffy blossoms.

This time I knew what was expected of me, even though the process was changed. I helped my mother separate the red grains from the white. This time we planted them directly into the ground. The fields had been prepared days earlier with

Rakota's help. He'd gone to fetch one of my uncle's bulls and he was the one who had driven it through the fields. Early the following morning, without waiting for us to stir, Rakota returned the bull, as my uncle could not afford to spare even one from his herd for long.

'In the old days, a man would drive cattle to those in need. Families in particular, helped each other out. Things have changed since then,' my mother mused. 'Or perhaps it is just here. In the village where I was born, men captured wild bulls and cows in the hills when we had none. They hunted wild boars. No one ever went hungry.'

In our mountains there were no wild buffalo to be found, and the boars that roamed there were forbidden to us by the chief.

Abandoning her story of her life long ago, before she'd met my father and moved to his village, my mother made a series of holes in the turned-over soil with her hoe. I followed behind, placing a few grains in each before stamping over the soil with my feet. We planted the white grains in the lower fields and the red grains on the slopes cleared for this purpose. Once all the rice was in the ground, we soaked the lot with buckets and buckets of water, turning the fields into a splendidly sopping state, but older now, I was indifferent to the delights of the mud.

Within days, a smattering of pale-green shoots pushed through the earth; by the next week, the fields were covered. The seedlings strengthened and over time grew thick and high, rustling in the wind and soaking in the rain. The rains had returned in earnest by then, falling regularly from the afternoon until late into the evening, and on occasion lasting all night.

The rills filled quickly and, on days when the water levels in the fields were low, my mother and I sloshed water from the rills onto the thirsty plants.

'Rice must have water,' my mother reminded me.

We scattered wood ash over the plants, turning the dark soil grey; when they formed, we pulled weeds and then threw them back atop the beds to rot and in turn nourish the growing plants. We were wary of snakes, eels and the other creatures that abounded in the waterlogged fields that time of year. Rakota caught eels; we roasted them. Life during the rice season had the comforting quality of sameness, of familiarity. There was a rhythm to our days: sun in the morning, rain in the afternoon. The rainy season was like that. We knew what to expect, so we watched the sky, looked out for pests, checked the lush green leaves for portents of trouble. There were none. The plants grew taller. In no time at all, ears would begin to form on the stalks.

Rakota picked up the story of Ibonia again:

> *Beautiful-Rich was the wife of the Prince of the Middle. The two were happy and blessed: their rice stores brimmed, cattle grazed as far as the eye could see, their treasury glittered with silver coin, expensive jewels and sumptuous silks, but the cradle that the prince had crafted with his own hands shortly after they'd married, remained empty …*

All was well when Rakota shared his favourite tale. I'd thought so. I was wrong.

The ears had not yet formed on the rice when we received word that an official message from the king would be broadcast at the Friday market. All households were required to send a representative to take heed of the king's words. Friday's market was larger than the everyday market. A greater variety of goods was on offer, and many people, not only from our village, but nearby villages too, attended. When my father was alive, he took with him the exquisite cloth woven by my mother to sell for extra money. On those days, Rakota and I could not wait for him to return; as soon we caught sight of the dust thrown up by his feet, we'd race to meet him. We knew he'd be laden with purchases: sugar, fruits, soap, beads, those kinds of things – trifles, but still a treat.

Best of all was when he allowed us to accompany him to one of the other day markets some distance from where we lived. A group from our village would go together to buy special items like cattle, sheep or finely made implements for cooking or for tending the soil. Once business was over, there would be singing and dancing and feasting and games. We'd stay in tents and fall asleep amid the noise and laughter, with the sweet smell of meat and manioc roasting on the huge fires that burned all night, teasing our noses even as we slept.

No one knew what the king's message might contain. As I said, this was a time of rare peace. Villagers walked about unmolested by day, and by night, watchmen patrolled, keeping us safe. Since the last raid, the one that had claimed my father and others besides him, a high, stick fence had been erected all around the village, with the exception of the side by the river, which formed the fourth boundary. Thanks to the peace, our fields thrived. The only blight was the loss of our cattle, but we'd planted more rice than before – enough to sell. If all went well, we would earn enough to buy a cow in another year or two.

For days we puzzled over the king's message. We'd heard no rumours. Since the death of my father, our family had little notion of what was taking place beyond the limits of our village. We relied on our neighbours or my uncle, who visited only sporadically, for news. There was little time to waste on visiting. In our village, everyone was kept busy during the growing season. Visits and amusements had to wait until the harvests were brought in. Knowing this was what made the king's announcement so unsettling, my mother said.

We set off on Friday morning, just after dawn: my mother, Raketaka and I. We had nothing to sell, but I knew that my mother had bundled a few coins into a corner of her *lamba*. The market was held on a flat plain between our village and a neighbouring one – not far, but with Raketaka on my mother's back and my dawdling, the walk there was a long one. The sun rose soon enough and beat down mercilessly. I was thirsty and my legs ached, but I knew better than to complain.

By the time we arrived, traders had begun to set up their wares on a patchwork of mats. Vendors selling similar items clustered together. There were the tailors and clothiers, the sugar and honey sellers, tobacco merchants, purveyors of spades and spears and the formidable *Ody* men with their charms for sale. A throng of flies drew attention to the butchers who, like the livestock dealers, were located on the outer edges of the market.

My mouth watered at the stalls selling cooked meat. It had been a long time since we'd eaten meat. Noticing my longing sighs, my mother promised that if I behaved well, she would buy a portion of roasted meat for us to share with Rakota, who'd stayed home. In the growing season, it would have been unheard of to leave the fields totally unattended.

After inspecting the items on offer, my mother found a spot shaded by a tiny stand of skinny palm trees, but for which the market would have been entirely barren and devoid of vegetation. A group of women were there, legs stretched out before them in relaxation. Several of the women greeted my mother and she joined them on the ground, propping herself against one of the trunks with a measure of satisfaction once Raketaka had been set free. I was allowed to play with the other children so long as I watched my sister while my mother and the women caught up on news.

The morning passed. Raketaka grew tired and went to sleep on my mother's lap. Later, we ate the roasted corn and boiled manioc we'd brought from home; it was cold and unwelcome compared to the pleasing aroma of the grilled meat so provokingly near.

Eventually, the drums sounded, signalling that the king's messenger was ready to speak. A lethargic hush settled over the gathered crowds: some, including my mother and her companions, moved closer to hear him better, but most remained where they had first stood to attention. Children, kept in check by their parents or older siblings, stopped their games. One afforded the king's representative the respect due to the sovereign himself.

Evoking the presence of the king, the messenger began by saying that scores of people in our kingdom had gone missing in recent months. Since we were on friendly terms with our traditional foes then, these disappearances had been attributed to attacks by fierce animals; predators like the crocodile and the wild boars that lived in the bowels of the forest. He reminded the crowd of the crocodile that had terrorised our village, how it had not been seen since the sacrifice of the bulls and that the river was now safe to cross. Our village had been spared so far, but a large number of people had gone missing in one of the more distant villages of the realm. A handful had disappeared singly, others in small parties – hunters, traders, those travelling to visit friends or family in farther villages. All had left; none had returned. Too much time had passed and too many had vanished for there to be any innocent explanation.

The chief of one of the villages affected had sent out trackers to search for those who'd gone missing. Trackers examined the ground for spoor, traces of blood or hair or teeth … any sign that they had fallen prey to animal attackers. They scanned the sky for carrion. If there were bodies, they would find them. The bones of the dead had to be buried in a manner fitting. They delved deeper and deeper into the forest, but of the missing men, women and children there was not a trace. No bodies; no bones to return to the earth.

Wild animals were not responsible for the villager's disappearance. Broken leaves and branches and tracks left behind told a different story. The hoofprints in the dried mud were clearly those of cattle as they were rounded and fat, like two beans squashed together, and they were deeper than the footprints that accompanied them. Most of these were smudged, but the trackers found a few heel prints and deeper imprints where toes had sought purchase. Finally, they found a single villager – an old woman.

Here the messenger called to the figure who'd been standing to the side. Her blue *lamba* hung loosely from her shoulders, as if it belonged to someone else or she had shrunk, and a dusty *kitamby* peeped through its folds and swept the ground. Her hair was short and ashen and there was a white line where age had leached the colour from her skin at the hairline. Her eyes were cloudy and thickened, almost sightless. It was clear that she had seen many years. She squinted before the crowd.

'This woman is from my village,' the messenger intoned, standing behind the woman who barely reached the height of his chest. 'It is this woman who confirmed the trackers' suspicions.' He told the story of how she and her family, numbering a dozen members, had been travelling to other parts to attend a funeral. 'On their way, they were accosted by a band of pirates, and although the men had assegais for protection, they proved useless against the pirate's muskets.' The messenger explained how the group's wrists and feet had been bound together with rope, just long enough to allow them to walk, and how they had been 'forced to march like chickens towards the coast'.

For hours the old woman had marched. For hours she had tried to keep pace. She learned quickly that if she stumbled she would cause the entire chain to falter. Eventually, they stopped. One of the pirates who could speak her language loosened her ties and told her to stay there.

We gasped as the messenger told of how the old woman had

begged to be allowed to continue, of how she promised to keep up. 'She wanted to share her family's fate, whatever it might be,' the messenger said, nodding at the woman in approval, 'but he threatened to kill her then and there if she didn't obey. And so this lady, she followed behind for hours more – until it became dark and she could not see the way before her. So she slept, since the group too would have to stop for rest, she reasoned.'

The messenger continued: 'Next morning she began following again. She walked until her legs gave in and she could not go on. Instead of trying to make her way back to the village and raising the alarm, this poor woman convinced herself that it was a terrible misunderstanding and that her family would return. She was still waiting when our village scouts found her, half dead from hunger and thirst.'

'She didn't know any better,' a lady in the crowd said. 'She had never encountered a pirate before.'

'Although she had heard of them, no doubt about that,' her companion replied, 'like we all have.'

Yes, we *had* all heard the stories of the pirates – ghosts – who had infiltrated the villages nearer the coast. Their pale skin made them as transparent as the spirits that roamed the darker parts of the forest; they were pirates because they snatched people. Though no one in our village could claim to have seen one with their own eyes, we all knew that they spoke in foreign tongues and ate children. Yes, we knew to run or hide if we encountered men we did not recognise, but strangers were few so far inland. We were high and hidden by the mountains, hills and forests, and so we had thought ourselves safe. Indeed, all the villages in our kingdom were a long way from the coast, inaccessible unless you were familiar with the area and knew its secret pathways and passages.

The messenger paused to allow the listeners time to take in the woman's story. She stood there helplessly, swaying slightly as if blown by a breeze only she could feel. I was convinced that if it were not for the messenger's hands, still firmly placed on her shoulders, she would have swooned in the heat.

Then the messenger cleared his throat slowly and deliberately. It was clear even to me, young as I was then, that he relished having an audience. 'Our king has conferred with the other kings of our land,' he said, 'and it's true, pirates have been taking our people.'

According to him, pirates were not new to the island, only to our realm. Those who dwelt on the coast knew them particularly well, or had some memory of the foreigners arriving for trade, or even attempting to set up their own homes on the island. 'Most had fallen victim to the sweating sickness. Others who had met our people with aggression had been driven back to the sea,' the messenger boasted.

We believed in hospitality, my people, but we also believed that if a calf played with a crocodile, it should expect to be bitten. A crocodile might roll on its back, smile and show his teeth, but only a foolish man would forget that it was a crocodile. Nor were the pirates alone the worst of it, we learned. 'False-hearted people in the distant kingdoms have been selling their slaves, servants, members of their households and, in certain shameful instances, even their kin to the pirates.' The messenger paused as a hum rose from the audience.

All fell silent once he resumed his speech. Now was the time for the king's official word. Evoking the name of the king once more, the messenger announced the decree: 'Any villager among you who is suspected of selling another to the foreigners will submit to trial by the poisoned water.'

Mention of the poisoned water attracted the attention of even the most uninterested among us. All of those still lingering in the shadows of the trees and the roast-meat sellers tending their fires, even the children, drew closer, eager for details.

We children knew a bit about what happened during the trial, not enough to form a full picture, but enough to embellish with our own ideas. I'd heard – perhaps from Rakota, perhaps by overhearing grown-up discussions – that people suspected of treachery or of being bewitched were given to eat first a generous portion of boiled rice taken with three pieces of the flesh from a fowl. Then they were given a drink made from the noxious red nut of the Tangena tree – the poisoned water – along with copious amounts of rice water. In order to be proved innocent, the accused had to regurgitate all three pieces. If unable to do so, or if only one or two pieces were retrieved – or if all three were not retrieved intact – then their guilt was clear and they were beaten to death. Likewise, if the poison ended with their death, this too was considered just punishment.

The messenger concluded his speech and took stock of the crowd as if to divine any guilty ones among us. Stifled chatter was let loose, like a breath that had been kept in too long. Noise rose like the buzzing of bees. Now I think of it, I remember feeling like we were in a hive too; packed so closely together, the heat was thick and oozing, almost syrupy. Questions fluttered in the air. Were people in our kingdom really selling their own? Were people in our village capable of doing such things? No one had gone missing, had they? Neighbours and relatives were accounted for, hastily. What about the foreigners? Were they really such a threat?

The adults were still discussing the king's message when the first drops of rain fell – welcome rain, given the stickiness and heat and the hot-tempered conversations that had risen in pitch after the king's messenger had departed. The buzzing had given way to a waspish drone. I watched as my mother shook the raindrops from her *lamba*. I was tired, moody, and anxious for my mother to buy the promised treat before the rain strengthened. Early afternoon, the rain was on time.

Moments before, save for wisps of clouds like freshly spun white silk, the sky had been clear and blue. For the most part, the rain during the rainy season was constant, gentle and soft, falling each day for a few hours only. This is not to say that we did not experience storms, but they tended to announce themselves beforehand. Animals sensed it first, alerting us to an imminent storm with their rattled chatter as they evacuated their burrows and holes in search of higher ground. You needed only to witness the birds flying away in sleek formation to know that rains more violent than usual were coming. Before a storm, the air smelled different too, pungent – almost oniony, or like the smell of the turned-over sods of a prepared field. And it felt dead, weighted and thick, until the rain fell and carried it all away, the smell and that heavy feeling.

On days when we expected stronger rains, we bolstered the sides of the rills with sand. Rice might need water to grow, but too much water could rot the stalks. Nor were burst banks the only threat. When storms threatened, we remained close to our fields to deal with the high winds or hail that oftentimes accompanied the rain. It was well that Rakota had stayed behind, but by himself, my brother would not be able to cope.

I smelled the lightning before it struck – a crinkly smell, like reeds burning or the stench of rotten eggs. I looked at the sky expectantly, without realising I was doing so. I saw the lightning flame towards the staggered line of palms like a brilliant snake of orange-blue and devour one of the trees with its flicked tongue. I realised that I was not shaken by this; it was as if I'd been expecting something dreadful to happen. All morning I'd had that feeling in my stomach, a gnawing sensation that I'd thought could only be sated by the meat. Now the craving was gone and my mouth tasted bitter, like metal, and like blood.

For long seconds the trees faltered, vibrated almost. Then the tallest tree creaked mightily before crashing to the ground with a thud that unsettled the earth around it. The crowd hushed, but only for a moment. Voices took up again, from chanting softly, as to be almost inaudible, to rapidly rising roars. 'It's a sign! It's a sign! It's a sign!' the voices agreed. Then the thunder began, loud and unstopping, as if beating out a monstrous melody upon the earth. Rain spouted from above and angled at us from the sides. In no time we were drenched. The dry, hard soil upon which we stood turned into a morass.

People scattered to escape the downpour, but there was no shelter to be gained. The area of the trees, with the felled palm still smouldering in the rain, was to be avoided at all cost. Mothers gathered their children, fathers herded their families. A woman helped my mother secure Raketaka to her back.

Together, we raced to get back home, to get out of the rain, but most importantly, to return to our crops. There was a portentous vigour and fury to the deluge, telling us that it would only get worse. I ran, trying hard to keep pace with my mother, struggling to remain on my feet with the ground so slippery now. The rain trickled from my hair to my face, making it hard for me to see in front of me, and all the while the thunder reverberated jeeringly. I remembered then that we had another name for the rainy season: the time of the thunder.

The hail began when we weren't even halfway from home. The small beads stung my skin and made seeing even more difficult. I felt that I could not continue, did not want to continue: the muscles in my legs were burning and there was a fire in my chest when I breathed in. Yards ahead of me, my mother was a limping speck of blue; Raketaka's dark head of hair showed above the bump beneath our mother's *lamba*. Never once did my mother turn back to see that I was following, that I had not stopped. Perhaps she knew that I would follow; maybe she knew that one of the others would ensure that I was not left behind. Whenever I slacked for too long, one of the grown-ups or older children would grab my arm and drag me forward. We were a smaller party by then as some had turned off towards their own homesteads. I ran and slowed, ran and slowed, until eventually I reached our homestead.

My mother and Rakota were already in the fields, throwing sacks over the fledgling rice plants as a protection of sorts. Hail was heavy; the worst thing that could have happened. We hoped that the sacks would trap the hail and spare the plants. There was not much more that could be done.

The rigorous task completed, Rakota returned with my

mother to our hut to hear about the king's message. Both were dirty and dishevelled and shivering in their sodden state, but neither made an attempt to clean up or get dry. Rakota listened patiently as our mother recounted the story at the table. Mid-sentence, my mother stood up abruptly, scraping the bottom of her chair. She strode towards the shelves where our food stores were kept. Her eyes had darkened, narrowed, but tiny points of light glinted within their depths. I worried that I'd angered her with my nagging about food before she'd had a chance to tell her story or change out of her wet clothing.

We followed her with our eyes, Rakota and I, curious about what she'd do next. My mother had a quick temperament at times and, if it hadn't been for the day's excitement, I'd have known better than to plague her about food. She snatched the basket of rice off the shelf, removed its lid and stared. It was as if she'd lost her just-gathered momentum. She just stood there, staring at the rice and shaking her head.

'No, no, no,' she whispered.

'What is it?' Rakota demanded.

Slowly, my mother walked back to the table, the basket of rice outstretched before her as if it was something vile.

It was.

When it came to hail, our people had certain practices by which we lived. Charms against the hail we called them. Dur-ing the rainy season we were prohibited from burning straw from rice as a protection against hail. Certain games, such as stone-throwing, were taboo, but the most important rule was that no white rice should remain on the shelves of our homes during the rainy season.

It was an honest mistake. Though there was not much rice left in the basket, it was white. Not that we'd eaten of it since the rainy season had begun, but it was enough that it was there. It should have been removed from the shelves long ago.

Except for Raketaka, that night, we all went to bed hungry, for none of us could bring ourselves to eat. The hail was our fault.

The next morning, we went out to assess the damage. Our transgression was clear: all our rice plants had been destroyed. The sacks had sagged under the weight of the hail, crushing the fragile plantlets. Later on, Rakota discovered that the damage had been worst in our end of the village, which served as further confirmation of our blame.

'Promise you will not talk of this,' our mother insisted. 'Never speak of the rice upon the shelf. Do you hear me?'

Rakota and I shook our heads furiously in assent.

Then my mother burned the basket that had contained the rice, even though it was a perfectly good one that she herself had woven. There would be a hard price to pay if any trace of our guilt was divined. Our neighbours had suffered tremendous losses too.

My mother sent Rakota to borrow rice from my uncle. He didn't have much to spare, he said, but gave us enough to seed nearly the entire patch. This time we seeded the rice the traditional way and watched it even more zealously than before. As soon as they were strong enough, we planted the seedlings in the cleared fields – cleared without the benefit of a loan ox this time, as my mother said we could not impose upon my uncle further. He had his own mouths to feed; he'd made this clear. Nor did we wish to be humps on his back.

There were no further calamities – the rice grew, their heads formed, the plants changed from green to gold. We watered the fields, or relied on the rain to do so. In time the grains were ready to be harvested. Rakota cut the stalks; my mother and I followed behind him, tying the stalks into sheaves. Days later, we carried the sheaves to be winnowed. We separated the grain from the chaff. We filled our baskets.

Even so, there was not enough rice to put away during the cleaned off months and to pay the king's tribute in full. My mother agonised about this, sharing her problems with Rakota and I. We were her only company, her only counsel. Rakota suggested we put away what we needed and borrow the balance required for the tribute from my uncle. My mother was hesitant at first, but eventually she journeyed to my uncle's homestead to put forward the request. As usual, Raketaka and I accompanied her. My aunts made us wait outside until my uncle could see us. They were polite, but chilled. 'They treat us as if we are bitter herbs,' my mother noted. We were not offered the usual libations given to guests – I remember this because I was hot and I was thirsty, but my mother refused to ask for a drink, nor would she allow me to do so.

When my uncle came out, he patted my head and tickled Raketaka underneath her arms, but he shook his head at my mother's request. 'My yields are adequate only to feed my family and pay my own tribute,' he said. He suggested that our mother borrow rice from the chief, or money from one of the lenders who frequented the markets, cutting off pieces of silver as they saw fit. Though it was clear he would not help us, this would not be the last time that we'd seek his assistance.

Since my mother was afraid of owing the money lenders, she approached the chief for the loan, reasoning that my father had lost his life defending the chief's cattle. We were a closely knit village, small enough that everyone knew everyone else. My mother had been born an outsider, but the chief was a just man, she said, a man of honour. He was. He offered more rice than she'd asked for and we were able to pay our tribute to the king in full.

Time passed. Leaves were cleaned off trees; roots were dug up from the ground; the dry season was upon us and we endured. Blossoms appeared on the Ambiaty; we planted our rice, once again doing without the convenience of an ox to help us till the field. We watched the rice grow, taking care not to break any of the taboos this time. All was well. We began to talk about earning enough to buy a cow in a few years' time once the debt to the chief was repaid.

Nor had there been much talk about the pirates of late. Now and then, rumours would abound of folk in far-off villages going missing, but ours remained safe. The king's threat of the trial by the poisoned water had not borne fruit – not where we lived at least – since no one in our village had had any contact with the pirates, let alone become involved in the evil trade. Word reached us of trials in other villages, but they affected people we did not know.

As long as the rice and other crops grew, we would not worry about what was happening in faraway places. Ours was an elemental existence, governed by the seasons and confined to the goings-on in our homesteads, our village. That was what was important. After the incident of the white rice on the shelf, we'd been careful to observe all the rituals – charms against hail, against drought, against the locust – but this time in vain.

The growing season that had begun so promisingly turned catastrophic when the rains stayed away. Days ticked by without rain. No new plants could be coaxed out of the soil. Growing plants withered on the stalk. Honey became scarce as villagers in their numbers resorted to the forest for food. Streams dried up, exposing puffed-up fish and thin reeds. In our village, only the moneylenders had high, rounded bellies, extracting extortionate payments in return for their sliced off bits of silver, *reals* of eight.

Food – the lack of it, the need for it – became our most pressing concern. We had the chickens still and they laid eggs. It is said that as long as you have chickens you'll never go hungry, and this is true. We traded eggs for handfuls of rice, corn, what have you … except most people in the village were hungry too, their rice pits emptied by the long, lean months. Not even the chief was unscathed – another rumour doing the rounds. And so the day arrived that the chief called in his loan. There was no rice to pay the tribute. How would we find the money to repay the chief? My mother spun cloth to sell in the markets, but that year everyone had cloth to sell.

In my family we believed in paying our debts. It was a question of honour. As my father used to say, a man's word was his wealth. In desperation, we once more sought my uncle's help, but he offered no succour. His belly was high too – I remember that, high and round.

I was not unfamiliar with the practice of children being

pawned for their family's debt, and not only children – adults, old people, husbands and wives, too. There was no shame associated with being a pawn as it was only ever a temporary situation until one's family could redeem one's liberty. If one was born free, one would remain so. It was, after all, meant to be temporary.

When it came to choosing, it was easy to decide who should go to live with the chief. My mother needed Rakota more. He was stronger, a boy. He could tend the animals and, when the rain came, as it had to come, he could look after the fields. Raketaka was growing and would soon be of help to my mother. I would be one less mouth, one less belly.

There's no shame, there's no shame, there's no shame …

On the morning I was to leave, I woke without any prodding. I glanced at my mother, lying on her mat next to mine, and thought it strange that on this morning she was able to sleep. She, who found it so difficult to sleep for a time longer than it takes to cook rice at a stretch. Heedless of the disturbance, I unfastened the door and hobbled outside; my legs had not yet woken properly.

Air steamed off the hills. The leaves on the trees in the forest were still green, still lush, offering no hint of the catastrophe that had befallen us. None of our animals stirred, but as I waited for the sun to climb over the hill, a troop of maki, their dark-ringed eyes glowing yellow in the still-grey morning, ambled into my line of sight, first one mother with a baby on her back, then more mothers thus encumbered or with babies clinging to their undersides, older infants and the males of the group. Some walked on two legs; others ran about on all fours, whooping to each other with wide-open mouths exposing all their teeth, their long tails, ringed in black and white, wagging like dogs'. They came to rest on a bare patch that the climbing sun had started to reach. The mothers suckled their young, while the males and the older infants sat, some clutching their knees with their arms, others lounging untidily, all seeking the scant warmth of the sun's new rays.

I thought then of running away, of going far into the hills, or hiding in the caves and caverns in the area, but it was too dangerous. Nor would I conceal myself in the rice pit; there was peril in that too: I might suffocate. No, my mother was count-ing on me. 'The chief's a good man,' she'd said, over and over again, once the agreement had been made. It was only once I was older that I asked myself the question, who had she been trying to convince?

'The chief's a good man; the chief's a good man; the chief's a good man … will take care of you … treat you like one of his own …'

And I remember later that day, when the sun, high then and searing with a white-hot heat, went behind the clouds … clouds so low I felt I could reach out to them. Clouds that greyed, taunting us with the promise of rain, but failed to darken and swell. I remember the sudden coldness that settled when the sun disappeared and I remember the squawking of the birds and the jabbering of that family of *maki* that lived in the tall trees of the forest near our homestead. I remember each hut, each field, each patch of ground, and the dirt where the chickens scratched disconsolately. I remember the rooster crowing once, twice, three times, and I remember my sister hiding behind my mother's legs. I remember my mother hoisting her to her hip, even though she was getting too big to be carried. And I remember that my brother was not there to see me leave, and wondering, where was he?

Yes.

I remember, I remember, I remember that day.

Geert, 1786

Her pains came on just as night settled in, pitching the town into darkness. Here and there, a lamp winked through curtains or the broken chinks in shutters, breaking up the black. Not all burghers were resolute in adhering to the rules regarding the keeping of a burning lantern outside their houses to light the way. Late at night, the streets themselves were a danger, rutted with potholes to trip the unwary; in the inky hours before morning they belonged to wild pigs, stray dogs and the other desperados that roamed then. Except in the most pressing of circumstances, respectable people opted not to venture out then, preferring to wait for sunrise and the safety of the morning.

Despite the traffic outside, the trundle of wagon wheels, the rapid clip of hooves, or watchman calling out the hour, most nights I slept easily.

'Shush!'

Yet no matter how soundly I slept, Barbetje's voice, recognisable by its pitch, ever ruptured my sleep. I'd learned not to pay her much heed. Barbetje was a restless sleeper and, in recent years, had taken to walking about the house at night while we all slumbered. Every so often she would admonish herself when she made an inadvertent noise: scraping a chair, bumping into a table or carelessly trampling on Juko's tail, causing him to yelp and snap at her errant feet. Each time she woke me, I resolved to speak to her about it in the morning, since other than Juko's growls of discontentment it was often her clamorous self-censure, and not whatever had occasioned it, that disturbed my sleep.

'Shush, shush!' Barbetje again.

Mumbling followed, a one-sided conversation from the sounds of it. I tensed. Had Barbetje let a stranger into the house? I dismissed the thought immediately. She had been with us so long that such treachery was unthinkable. Juko would not stand for any intrusion and would have alerted me long before.

I listened.

Soon enough, I gauged the reasons for Barbetje's consternation – the stifled groans of pain, the frantic breathing, audible in the spacious house due to an architectural foible that caused the slightest noise to reverberate within its walls. Though her room was on the far side of the passage, I was not unfamiliar with those sounds. Her time was at hand.

'Bite on this.'

The moans were muffled but perceptible to a keen ear. A

lamp was lit; logs added to the fire in the kitchen; water poured from the pail into the heavy brass kettle that hung over the fire. I lay there listening, identifying each motion by its sound. I could neither sleep, nor could I offer my assistance. It was women's business. They would call me if I was needed.

Part of me felt panicked and frustrated. Three times now I had watched her body swell: the softening that overcame her at first, then the gradual firming as her belly rose, becoming as round and ripe as a pomegranate before it splits open and spills its seeds. That is how I saw her during those times, like an apple, red and sweet; a juicy, tart tomato; some fecund fruit. Except in both of the previous instances, neither child had drawn breath for longer than a day. The first, a girl, had been stillborn and taken away before I could lay eyes on her. I do not know whether she'd seen the child, or what she'd felt about its demise. The less said the better. What use was there in dwelling on what could never be? She was young; there would be more babies.

The boy, born a year later, had been a live birth. I'd been home at the time and saw the boy once he was cleaned, but I must confess that I was not impressed. He was a puny thing, with a pink-grey pallor that looked almost ghostly. A thin layer of a creamy, curd-like substance had coated his skin unevenly, his fluffy dark hair damp and his hands blue. He lay next to her on the bed, not yet swaddled so I could inspect him, I deduced. The women had left the room when I entered. She was awake but barely. She looked debilitated, pathetic, as if the delivery had drained all the blood from her body. I touched her cheek; her skin was clammy, her hair sweaty and tangled. Her lips were bitten red from the struggle – it had been a long birth, lasting all of the previous night and most of the morning. I left her to sleep.

I went about my business that day; I had several matters to attend to in Town. The child had not occupied my mind much, although I was concerned about her welfare. She'd appeared so weakened when I'd looked in on her. I completed my appointments and hastened home lest she need me to send for one of the surgeons that called at the house in those days. Perhaps I should send for him regardless, I thought. He could prescribe a strengthening tonic and look in on the boy.

The very surgeon I'd been thinking about was at the house by the time I returned. My sister Dorothea had called for him when she'd seen the condition of the boy, but it was too late.

'There was something wrong with his breathing … his lungs,' the surgeon said. 'There was nothing I could do.'

I shrugged and shook his hand; tipped him well for his kindness and propriety.

When I went in to see her, the little boy was still there. She clutched his tiny body to her breast and took no notice of Barbetje's entreaties to release him. She took no notice of me either, as I stood there dumbly with my hat in my hand. I left them like that while I went to make the arrangements for the child's burial. In the end, Barbetje had had to prise the morbid, chilled body from her grasp.

She had not spoken for days thereafter. I endured her silence, but it was an oppressive silence that cast a pall over the entire household. Eventually, I suggested that she hearten herself, that there was no need to dwell on such morose matters.

She was young, her body was fruitful; there would be further infants in her future.

I think back to that time with remorse. Had my apathy for the boy had anything to do with his demise, my reckless characterisation of him as a ghost? Or was it as the Good Book warned? The sins of the father were brought to bear upon the child.

As soon as it was light, I arose from my bed and went to her room. I coughed outside the door to announce myself; then I let myself in and leaned against the jamb. She was panting softly through a rag clenched between her teeth. The room smelled faintly of cloves. A decoction of the leaves and flowers of the common pink Pelargonium lay untouched on the small table next to the bed, turning brown in the white porcelain mug. All at once, I was reminded of the hot and odiferous decoctions of bitter *Als* that grew wild in so many places around the Cape – Barbetje's remedy for whatever had ailed us as children. Barbetje herself lay dozing in a chair. She woke when she became aware of me standing there.

'Master, it will be a long time still,' she said, without rising.

I nodded. 'Barbetje, can you excuse us please?'

Without a glance to the bed, she dragged her body from its seat and walked out of the room, her spine rigid.

The rooster had not yet crowed.

I knelt at the bedside. 'My dear, are you comfortable? Is there anything I can do for you?' I whispered, close to her face.

Her breath was erratic and laboured, but when she got the words out, she spoke coherently. 'Get that bad-luck woman away from me! I don't want her here. Send for the Hottentot woman I told you about – Tan' Sanna! Please, Geert.'

In her agitation, she'd referred to me by my Christian name.

I'd forgotten about my promise to send for the midwife when her time came. I felt ashamed that I'd left her to lie there, while knowing full well that she was in labour – and I had known – with only Barbetje to tend her, a woman, for reasons I could not comprehend, but put down to womanish tendencies, she did not trust. Barbetje had all but raised my sisters and I; she had assisted at my sisters' births. How was I to tell her that her assistance was not desired? Perhaps in my cowardice I'd remained in my room, hoping that I would not have to.

'I'll send for her at once,' I said, stroking her brow.

The air was cold for September. No one was astir, save for the dogs that growled as I came outside and settled once they saw that it was I. One bounded towards me, already energetic that early in the morning. The commotion alerted one of the boys, who strolled out of the long house.

'Kammies, make quick. Go fetch the Hottentot woman who delivers the babies,' I said.

He was a useful fellow, Kammies. He hadn't been with us long, but in the year or so he'd been, he'd proven himself.

'*Ja, baas*,' he replied.

'Kammies!' I called, as he scarpered away. 'Her name is Tant Sanna, the woman you must fetch. Tell her to come at once.'

I left the boy to his mission and walked to the front of the house. It was cold on the stoep. A light beading of moisture covered the tiled, stone stools built at right angles to the walls where I'd sometimes sit of an evening and watch the town.

Nevertheless, I sat in my usual place, both wishing and dreading that Barbetje would find me there and bring me a mug of the strong black coffee that I so enjoyed. (The secret was to add a measure of salt to the pot, to bring out the flavour of the beans.)

Though I am by nature an early riser, ingrained by my father's lectures regarding sloth and idleness, I seldom have moments to spare to enjoy the world begin anew. The morning is the best part of the day, to my mind. There is something different about the quality of light then – softer. Later, once the sun attains its heights, the light is almost white, harsh, stripping. The walls of houses appear even whiter too, sharper; the sea burns with a bright glare. At this early hour, the sea appeared perfectly flat and, from this distance, an inviting blue. Up close, it is a different matter entirely; one immediately notices the putrid vapours from the slops the slaves empty into the sea. Even after all these years, delinquent butchers still dispose of their animal waste there, despite renewed regulations against this repugnant practice.

As my eyes adjusted to the distance, I could better make out the shapes and movements I'd discerned at first glance. Fishermen in small boats were casting off from the strand. Further from the shore, others already had their nets out and were sieving the water in search of their bounty. These were the slave fisherman or free blacks who fished for their own account. I wondered what it was in these people that drove them to the sea. Hungry seagulls circled overhead, diving into and agitating the water. They were so loud I could hear their taunts and shrieks from where I sat.

Since it was not the shipping season, there were few visiting ships in the bay. Out of habit, I counted the ships at anchor. The *fluyt*, the Company's distinctive three-masted ship, no longer dominated our waters. Indeed, ever since the war between the English and the Dutch ended these past two years, Danish and French ships abounded, as well as those flying the English flag and those of other seafaring nations.

For me, the war had been beneficial, as it had been for most *pachters*. Business had boomed as never before. With the war, the might the Company had enjoyed in previous years had begun to wane. Rightfully so, most burghers agreed. If the time of war had boded ill for the Company, its aftermath promised to be even more detrimental. The peace granted the English one of their greatest goals: the right to trade freely with every Dutch-owned territory in the East.

Even before the war, the English had been making inroads in crucial markets. The English circumvented the Company's stranglehold on the pepper market by colluding with middlemen and pirates who accepted payment in ammunition and opium for this most precious of spices. When the English merchants took up with the Chinese distributors of opium, the Company's dominance over this trade was likewise destroyed. Long assumed to be preoccupied with tea, the English had begun to encroach upon the coffee market, particularly in the East, where beans were grown on the Company's own plantations on Java. Nor were the English the only threat to the Company's continued success. In the past decade or roundabouts, the French had successfully cultivated cloves on their islands in the Indian Ocean, thus ending the Company's monopoly of that crucial market.

Meanwhile, in the United Provinces, revolution permeated the air, inspired by the American colonists' successful revolt against English rule. William v, Prince of Orange, *stadtholder* and chief director of the Company, had never enjoyed much popularity and was considered an ineffectual and, some say, corruptible ruler. Those in opposition to his rule called themselves Patriots. Disobedience in the United Provinces took different forms. By and large, this was restricted to derisive newspaper articles and other tracts, oratory attacks and other benign forms of agitation.

News might travel slowly to the Cape, but we were no backwater, unapprised as to what was happening in the world. The developments in the United Provinces prompted our own burgeoning Patriot movement, which had grown out of that small group of protestors with whom my father had been involved in the aftermath of Mijneer Buytendacht's arrest and removal to Batavia.

Months after the fact, my father had cause to reconsider his connections with these men. Though I cannot rightly recall his reasoning, I remember precisely what he had said: 'The problem with Mijneer Buytendacht was that they sent caffers to arrest him. That's what started all the trouble. A drunken sot and a wife-beater, but he took exception to the stature of those who enacted his capture and not the circumstances of the arrest. I shouldn't have signed that paper, boy. It is not wise to attract attention to oneself when one depends upon the Company and its fickle officers for a living.'

Years later, when the Company answered the memorandum, finding largely in favour of its own officials, I'd smiled wryly at the notion that my father would have felt vindicated, but that was, as I said, later – towards the end of 1783. When several burghers sent further entreaties to the *Heren* XVII and the States-General, I took no part in it.

In the period immediately following my father's death, however, I'd been less resolute and had felt adrift and over-whelmed as I took up the mantle of my responsibilities. In principle, my father's estate should have remained under the auspices of the Orphan Chamber, since I had not yet reached the majority age of twenty-five years. To my consternation, I found that such precepts were blunted when one inherited holdings the size that I had. Adjusting to my changed position had been instantaneous perforce.

Strangely, the person of the most assistance to me during this time was Titus, my father's body or personal slave. As my father's male heir and eldest son, I'd inherited Titus upon my father's death. This fact had surprised me. My father had been so fond of Titus that I would have wagered good money that Titus would have been freed upon his demise. Still, my father had been a prudent businessman, and slaves, particularly those amenable and well trained, were assets. Or so was my reasoning.

I cannot remember a time when Titus had not been there, but the new status quo unbalanced me. I was unused to Titus's constant presence; the way he pre-empted my desires and needs through the various tasks he unwaveringly determined I re-quired and which, being inexperienced, I had no confidence to deny. I drew the line at allowing him to bathe my feet; it seemed a grossly familiar act, one that made me uncomfortable when I remembered how he had knelt over Father's feet with the basin of warm water, the fat from the soap leaching out and rising to the top in a greasy film, along with grey-white flecks of lye. Sometimes I contemplated asking him what he had felt about performing such intimacies for my father, but I knew to do so would be improper.

Yet as Titus adjusted to our new relationship, he became more loquacious with me. One of his favourite topics of conversation was my father, 'the late Master', as he referred to him. As I gained his trust, Titus would share stories of things he'd seen my father do, heroic feats, meting out ordinary justices, as well as making foolhardy decisions, although these last were only hinted at. Titus even scrupled to tell me whom my father had trusted and whom he had not. This last point proved invaluable to me in business, as more often than not Titus's intelligence was without par.

Shortly after our father's death, my sisters and I had repaired to the Rondebosch farm to escape the heat and vapours that emanated from the Dock in summer. This, the smallest and homeliest of my father's properties, held fond memories for my sisters and me. Here we'd managed without the enormous retinue of servants that our immense Cape house or one of the working farms demanded. My father had spent much of his last years there, either cantering his horse, or walking daily to the Liesbeek River, where perhaps he'd stopped to think of a different river where hundreds of windmills whirred in the wind. It had been cathartic for all three of his children to be there together then, though I'd felt a small tinge of regret that his horse-breeding activities had amounted to so little. Nor ever would they, alas, given that the horse upon which he'd built his dreams had died on the day of his accident.

Since matters were more informal on the Rondebosch farm, my sisters had succeeded in cajoling me to reintroduce the small pleasures enjoyed by young ladies and gentlemen: games of cards, small dinners for our closer acquaintances, evenings of music and dance. For someone who'd longed for such entertainments during my sojourn in Swellendam mere months before, I had found myself disinclined to company. Even then, the companionship I'd missed had been the company of other males, since I had always been rather awkward around females. Indeed, when it came to women and the pursuit of relations – proper or illicit – I had never been very libidinous. This was not due to any high-mindedness on my part; the fact is, I had always been preoccupied with other matters during my calving years. I was well aware that certain of my associates indulged in relations with the women of their households, servants and slaves. Others visited the Slave Lodge where, for a small sum or some favour, they could procure satisfaction of their needs. The predilections of my friends were of no concern to me, though I myself attracted no end of criticism and teasing from these very characters for my abstemious existence.

Thus, it was to no greater astonishment than my own that I had found myself increasingly bewitched by a young woman of my acquaintance. And having noticed her, I'd found it impossible to resist the intense attraction she elicited in me, tempting me away from my ambitions and cares …

These thoughts of her broke my reverie. I had been concentrating so hard on avoiding what was happening inside the house, but the truth was that I was afraid. Afraid for her, for myself, for the baby. Where was that boy?

I paced the flagstone steps on the stoep, one, two, three, four, five, six, seven strides, turn and back again. One, two, three, four … Gradually, the day brightened, the condensation began to dry and fade. The sun climbed steadily over the bay, momentarily painting the sea golden. Strands of virgin-white clouds drifted across the sky and I could see that the long winter had finally come to an end. In the light, the town and the sea before me had even greater clarity. I frowned as the gibbet and wheel loomed to my left, an unwelcome sight, and an untimely reminder of the uncertainty of life. One, two, three … I stopped midway, my ponderings disturbed by the arrival of the boy with the Hottentot woman. How much time had passed since I'd dispatched him I couldn't rightly say – minutes, half an hour, perhaps longer?

The woman looked at me hesitantly but proudly, as if defying me to condescend towards her. I meant to be agreeable only.

'Thank you for coming,' I said, holding out my hand.

Her grip surprised me, but given her profession it shouldn't have.

I tried the front door. It was locked. I hadn't taken the key and I was in no humour to knock upon my own front door. 'We'll go around the back,' I said, motioning for the midwife to follow me.

She walked briskly, keeping pace with me. Wearing a black dress of thick fabric, she was not what I'd expected. Her feet were shod in shined black boots – European clothing. Her hair was pulled back from her face in a bun, no *doek*, and she smelled of lavender water. She carried a bag with her, an ordinary medical supplies bag as belonging to any doctor or surgeon. Odd. I wondered about the curiosities contained within the bag. Would they be normal medicines, or potions and tonics made according to her people's way?

I yielded to the midwife at the doorway, allowing her to enter the house before me. Barbetje was in the kitchen, stirring a pot. Bread rose in pans on the hearth and I could smell coffee brewing over the fire. I realised that I was hungry, but it was not the time to eat. Not yet. I escorted the midwife to the room. Our patient's forehead was bathed in sweat, her breath rapid and erratic. Her eyes glinted at the sight of my companion.

'There, there, my child,' the midwife said, as she leaned over to wipe the sweat off her brow. Inwardly, I cursed Barbetje for not having done anything to ameliorate her condition while we'd waited for the midwife, but I knew that she could be stubborn. Once she decided upon a course of action, nothing could dislodge the idea. So it was with Barbetje. The two women were like thorns stuck in each other's feet.

She raised her eyes to the midwife, expelling a protracted sigh, as if all this time she had been keeping her breath at bay. I found myself sighing too, then inhaling deeply to take as much air into my lungs as possible. Had I too been waiting to breathe?

'*Kom nou, Mijneer,*' the midwife said to me, motioning me to leave. Then softer, she placated, 'Mijneer would only be in the way.'

I nodded, relieved. I had not intended to stay.

It was only once I'd left the room that I realised her eyes had not met mine when I'd brought the midwife in. They'd had some connection, she and the older woman. Never before had I felt as superfluous or unwanted.

A notion caught at the edge of my consciousness. She'd been so desperate for the midwife to come. She must want this child. In my weakest moments, I'd wondered about that. Despite her obvious grief when the last two had died, a part of me still questioned her maternal instincts. If truth be told, perhaps I was merely questioning my own thoughts on the matter. What *were* my thoughts on the matter? I couldn't say. I'd asked myself this question time and time again. It is so difficult, this question of blood, but it calls to one, I think. *Bone of my bone, and flesh of my flesh* ... The words drew down to my marrow, lingered and were gone.

I resumed my pacing, too fraught to eat, although I did accept a cup of coffee from Barbetje. I was glad that Johanna was not there but visiting with her mother's family. Dorothea had been married for several years, but had accompanied our sister out of Town. The good burghers might have their opinions about private matters in our household, but my sisters were loyal, stalwart in their devotion to me. Not once had either of them censured me. No, there had been that one time – Dorothea, after the boy died. I immediately quashed this line of thought and continued pacing.

Throughout the house, shutters were opened to allow in the bright sun that streamed in lines of illuminated motes through the gaping windows. The smell of the fresh bread wafted in agreeably from the kitchen and my stomach clenched due to my unappeased hunger. I heard the clip of passing hooves on the cobbles outside, the shrill trundle of carriages going by as the town went about its business, and the shuffling gait of the servants as they carried out their chores.

'Slaves, not servants,' she'd said.

'I don't like that word,' I'd told her.

'Why?'

'I just don't.

'Why?' she'd persisted. 'It's true.'

I had not known how to answer her then.

Flesh of my flesh.

In that moment, pacing up and down the wide corridor while evading the sunbeams, I missed my father's morning prayers, his words of Scripture. I hadn't realised it before, but they had been comforting in their way. Idly I wondered whether I was too young to reintroduce them, for I was no patriarch and my knowledge of the Scriptures was deficient, restricted to elusive words that rose like ether in my memory, for all my solitary reading of the Good Book.

A tortured cry rang out, disturbing my thoughts. Then the keening and wailing began, accompanied by animalistic panting that could only be emanating from her. I froze mid-stride, as if *my* body was preparing to shut down. I held my breath, counting down the seconds between cries. I told myself that I was man enough to deal with whatever was taking place in that room. Nineteen, twenty, twenty-one … After each wrenching sound, I started again. Forty-one, forty-two, forty-three, forty—

I broke off before I could complete the next number. A softer wail, like a puppy yelping, or the sound a calf makes when it first finds its legs. The baby!

On unsteady legs of my own, I made my way to the door of her room. I stood there for an interminable amount of time, so unsure, so afraid. I listened cautiously, trying to make out what they were saying, but they spoke so low or in some primal language I could not comprehend. Eventually, I knocked.

'Come in, Mijneer.'

Tentatively, I opened the door. The room smelled sweet and ripe and sour and bloody, replacing the vegetal smell of Barbetje's earlier herbal remedies. I surveyed the room swiftly, suddenly nervous and shy to see her, to see the child. On the table next to the bed stood a decoction of crushed pipe-heads steeped in brandy – the sweet smell. Next to it was a small pail of milk that had already formed a skin. The cream had obviously been removed beforehand – sour.

All the bloodied material had been tidied away, out of sight, I noted thankfully, but the metallic smell of blood lingered. I turned my attention to the bed. Her face was flushed and her hair slick. She raised her eyes to me, full of pride. She had never appeared more beautiful. The thought surprised me. I smiled at her warmly and walked towards the bed, stopping about a foot away. The baby lay nestled in her arms, silent, immobile. I stepped closer, inclining my head. 'It's a girl,' she whispered, a slight frown marring her face momentarily.

I extended my arms.

'May I?' I asked. Tenderly, I held the baby in my arms. She was small, so much smaller than I'd expected; I'm not sure why I'd imagined she'd be bigger. I sniffed her skin, her hair. She smelled sweet, like the coconut oil with which her mother anointed her own hair and skin. She remained sleeping while I examined her, her face so pure and untouched, like a story waiting to be written.

I was relieved that she in no way resembled her brother who

had not lived long. There was nothing ghostly about her. Her skin was plump, puckered and pink; soft, downy blonde hairs covered her head and crowned her forehead. The creamy curds had been cleaned off her skin, but had not been completely removed. Her closed eyes were puffy – I wondered what colour they would be.

Looking at her, I felt a vehement swell of emotion deep within me, leaving me breathless once more.

'We'll name her Elisabeth,' I said once my breath returned, 'in memory of my mother.'

'Elisabeth,' she agreed. 'It's a fine name for a girl.'

Lena, 1854

The day my mother walked me to the chief's homestead, delivering me as if I was a cow she had borrowed, she was silent for most of the walk. I was silent too. All we'd needed to say to each other had been said. Young as I was, I refused to hear one more time about what a good man the chief was. Raketaka's happy babbling was the only sound that accompanied us that morning.

Yes, Rakota had been nowhere to be found when the time came for me to leave.

'Where's your brother?' my mother had fussed. 'You two should greet each other properly before you go; it is only right.'

But Rakota had refused to be found and since the hour was growing late, my mother strapped Raketaka to her back and, giving me a quick looking over with her beady eyes, she pronounced us ready to leave. We could have been going anywhere. There was something so ordinary about leaving home. We had not journeyed often, but whether to the market, a celebration, or visiting with family or friends, until then all had concluded in the same way. We had returned.

No, that was wrong. My father had not returned. Was that the first step on this journey? The first step of these steps I was taking? I thought then how odd it was that my father had died in service to the chief, how he had died to protect cattle to which he had held no claim and in which he had had no interest. I thought about the injustice of our cattle dying, another step; the hail yet another, the drought. Shrugging these notions from my mind, I concentrated on landmarks along the way: a pile of rocks, a row of abandoned huts – ragged fronds from their palm roofs fluttering weakly in the wind the only sign of life. I refused to carry my earlier musings further. I was too young, my thinking too muddled. What was the use of such thoughts? They would get me nowhere.

'It's not for long,' my mother reminded me. 'As soon as the debt is paid, you can come home.'

I nodded. The lump in my throat was hard and constricting, like a boulder blocking a path. In the sight of an unforgiving sun, I followed my mother to the chief's home.

What had my mother felt that day? When I became a mother, I wondered this.

The chief's house was built on a soaring but flat hilltop in the centre of our village. Like that of a king's, his homestead was built higher than those of his subjects. That was the way of the island. I kept my eyes out for the commanding structures surrounded by its high palisades I'd seen only from a distance until then. All too soon the hill and the palisades towered into view. I gasped, unable to stem my panic.

Sensing my fear, my mother sought to reassure me. 'The chief's a good man,' she reminded me, as if I did not know that, as if she had not been telling me this every day. I did not answer.

'Obey the chief and his wives in all things and they'll treat you well,' my mother instructed. 'The chief's a good man. You are of his village. He won't let any bad come to you,' she added.

I looked at her in alarm.

'Remember this. You are freeborn. You are your father's daughter. Don't forget that.'

I nodded.

As we scaled the hill, the individual components of the compound shifted into view. The chief's hut was the largest; three smaller dwelling huts radiated around it, and there were the usual rice pits and enclosures for cattle. It looked in many ways similar to our home, but grander, sturdier. Even the chickens pecking in the dirt seemed fatter and shinier, the spurs on the roosters sharper.

A huddle of men stood before the entrance, guarding it with their sharpened sticks. They indicated that we could pass once my mother told them the purpose of our visit. We were expected.

My mother opened the gate. She hesitated at the threshold before placing her hand on my neck and guiding me in front of her. I was no longer a cow, I was a lamb. Alerted to the intrusion, the dogs of the compound came charging towards us in an unruly pack, barking and baring their teeth. I felt my bowels turn to water.

My mother tightened her grip on my neck.

'Stand still,' she whispered.

I held my breath and complied.

We waited like that, not daring to move until the barking dogs announced our arrival to the unseen occupants of the compound. Odd that the sun was so high up, yet no one was about, other than those men guarding the gate. Then a woman around my mother's age came out of one of the huts. Her hair, piled elaborately atop her head, was dressed with beads; her indigo-hued *lamba* was decorated with beads too. She was clad almost too lavishly, I thought, for one at home. Unlike my mother, she looked kempt, pampered; as if she had all the time to ensure she looked her best. She, like the fowls, was plumper, shinier.

Walking towards us, the woman greeted us with a smile that exposed deep dimples in her cheeks and I realised her beauty went beyond ornamentation. After exchanging the usual pleasantries, she asked about the purpose of our visit. Her lips thinned into a line and the hollows in her cheeks vanished when my mother told her why we were there.

'Stay here a moment,' she said. 'I'll call my husband.'

My mother muttered something under her breath, but I could not make out what she said.

Eventually, the chief came out to meet us. He was short in stature and rather more corpulent than the men I was used to – definitely fleshier than my father had been, my uncle too. His complexion was what the Christians here call 'olive', his nose sharp and his long, black hair, oiled to a sheen, flowed down his back in languid curls. I'd seen the chief before, at public meetings and festivals, but never up close. Face to face with him, I noticed his many adornments, which previously I'd only glimpsed from afar: the bracelets and chains that hung from his wrists and neck, the gleaming gold in his ears. These adornments, marking his status and his wealth, made him even more intimidating. I was at once horrified and fascinated.

'Welcome, children,' he greeted us. 'What business brings you here?'

The stone that had been pressing on my heart all morning lifted. Perhaps we were not expected after all.

Dragging me to join her in genuflecting before him in the dust, my mother cleared her throat and paused for breath. 'I give my child to thee, Chief. To do with her as you see fit. Only you know what is best for your subjects, Chief. All I ask is that you treat her kindly. She is a good child, an obedient daughter.' Her voice had started out strong but tapered to nothing. Rising to her feet, she pulled me from my kneeling position and thrust me forward with a force that spun me back to face her. I righted myself at once.

The chief looked at us in confusion, and then gradually a look of recognition altered his expression. 'This child's father died in order to protect the honour of this village,' the chief pronounced. 'We shall treat her as one of our own,' he promised, placing his thick palm against the nape of my neck where my mother's grasp still burned.

My mother lowered her eyes from the chief's to mine. Her eyes spoke of reassurance, and something else – vindication, perhaps. I don't know.

'Thank you, Chief,' she whispered.

'May you live to an old age,' the chief dismissed my mother, who gently touched a finger to my cheek. Then addressing me, he said, 'Go with my wife.'

His wife, who had been standing just within earshot of our conversation, stepped towards us and led me away by my elbow. She introduced herself as Lilisa. At just that moment, the chickens that until then had been pecking placidly, scattered in agitation and a rooster with red and black and brown feathers that glinted dully in the sun began to crow, startling us all. The dogs began to bark once more and were only quieted when the chief made to lash them with an invisible rope. I followed Lilisa to her hut. I heard the gate open and the rustle of their robes as the men guarding the entrance let my mother pass.

I promised myself I would not turn back, that I would not look around to see them go, but at the last possible moment, I did so. I could just make out my mother's figure, the hump on her back that was Raketaka, as she descended the hill. I stared at them intently, as if trying to set the image in my memory. Still, I know that a person's memory is not something that can be relied upon. Why else can't I remember Raketaka's face? Sometimes I think that what I do remember are not memories at all – only lies I tell myself.

Yet I do remember the bile that rushed to my throat as I watched them walk away. That was real. If I swallow, I can taste it. Sometimes I think bile is the true taste of love. Maybe that is how you know you have loved. Maybe that is how you know what you have lost.

—

I remember thinking, treacherously, how it was all so unjust. Why me? Why was I the one? Raketaka was so small; it would not have been hard for her to forget us, forget she had a family. But that was the problem. Raketaka was too small, too young to be parted from my mother, too young to be of any use to anyone else. I knew that, even then, but I was not willing to concede any quarter. And Rakota? Why had he been born a boy? Why was his presence at home more vital than mine? Why was it my fate to have been born a girl-child?

I adjusted as best I could to the rhythm of the chief's homestead. I lived in a hut with others like me, females, and on the whole was treated well – not quite like a family member, but not poorly either. There were rules that governed the way pawns were treated. I had not known them when I arrived, but the rules were made clear by the others who shared my status: 'A pawn has to be treated as family; a pawn cannot be sold beyond the village ...'

Certain of the pawns had been captured in times of war, but even they were treated no differently than if they had been born in the chief's own village. On our island, there was a difference between a pawn who had been born free and one who had been born into slavery, but our chief tolerated no such prejudices and treated us all in a like manner.

I adjusted as best I could to my humbled status by convincing myself of the truth of my mother's words: *it was not for long; it was not forever.* Time and its passage became increasingly important to me. I marked the changing of the seasons fervently: the time when everything was cleaned off, and the time after, when I was watching keenly for those first green knobs to appear on the Ambiaty, telling us that soon we would have to begin all over again.

The chief, his wives and children were distinguished by the richness and newness of their fabrics, their jewels of gold and silver and the elaborate hairstyles of the married women. When they outgrew them, I was given some of the older daughters' clothing: soft, brightly coloured dresses and skirts, much more beautiful than any I'd owned before.

At the time of my arrival, the chief had had three wives: a senior wife by the name of Lahotsy, another called Rabesina, and Lilisa, the one who had met me that morning. His children numbered about twenty and ranged in age from babes in arms to near-grown. Of the pawns, I was one of the youngest, and, as such, was treated rather kindly. Delicately almost, as if I were a child of the household and not one of its servants. My chores were no more taxing than those at home; if anything, probably less so, as there were so many hands to do the work.

From the very first, Lilisa set me apart by her treatment of me, and I was grateful. Lilisa had children of her own, four sons, but no daughters. I followed her as diligently as I had my mother. She was gentler though, kinder too to me, the girl whose mother had left her. She allowed me to comb her long, curly hair and bestowed various benevolences upon me for no reason other than her innate goodness. Perhaps having witnessed the facility with which my mother had handed me over, she'd sought to make amends for this, as if she had colluded in the matter. Then again, maybe she sensed, rightly, how hungry I was for any kind of attention, any kind of interest. There were days when basking in the nearness of her, I imagined that she *was* my real mother. She was not impatient with me as my mother often had been; she never pinched me. Now that I am older, I allow that Lilisa did not have my mother's cares.

Despite my mutinous thoughts and despite the favour shown me by the chief and his family and those who shared my lot, I longed for home. The weather changed and finally came the rains that filled in the cracks in the earth. This year, not in a flood, but as gentle rains that slowly changed the landscape from bare browns and unforgiving greys to a hopeful green. The Ambiaty flowers escaped their buds and then it was time to plant.

Working in the rice fields without my mother was to feel her loss all over again. As I went through the steps, I could only think of her. Separating the grains into red and white, watering the fields then watching for the earth to crack and the shoots to inch out of the ground, yellow at first and then darkening to green. Who would help her pinch apart the muddy roots when it was time to replant? I helped to watch the chief's rice fields, but it was my mother's that concerned me more. Had her seed-lings grown unscathed? When I teased the tiny red worms off the chief's rice plants, it was my mother's plants I fretted over. Her crop could not fail; more than that, it needed to thrive. The output needed to exceed our expectations, for it was the only way she could earn enough to redeem my freedom.

The chief's fields flourished, his animals multiplied and the cursed weather of the previous year was just that, belonging to another time. I was happy for the weather: the steady falling of the rain, the absence of hail and other further disasters – no locusts, no red worms and definitely no searing, dry heat to incinerate the land. If things were so right at the chief's homestead, everything had to be well at ours. I longed for news from home, for a visit from my mother or my brother, but none came. There was no one I could talk to about my fears and longings; no one to ask the question: 'Has my family forgotten about me?'

Lilisa distracted me with her care, turning my various chores into opportunities to learn. 'One day you'll marry one of my sons,' she said. 'You'll need to learn all the things a woman needs to know.' I was never sure if she was serious or whether she was joking at my expense, but as I said, she was not an unkind person. Perhaps she spoke about such things to soften the fact that I was no more than a pawn in their home, for the rules strictly forbade such marriages.

I gladly learned from her, so eager for knowledge, to be useful, to earn her approval. From Lilisa, I learned to make indigo dye from the parts of the Banghets tree. Together we collected its violet blossoms and soaked them in water. When the water was the colour of the petals, we added the leaves and stems to darken it. Then we picked out all the plant material and mixed the water with an equal part of oil. We then strained this mixture, allowing it to draw into a large bucket underneath – in this way dividing the dregs from the liquid over the course of a few days. We drew off any remaining liquid, using more rags, until only the sediment remained, and this was what we mixed with fresh water to stain the silk and other fabrics worn by the chief and his family. My weaving too improved under Lilisa's tutelage.

She was also the one who taught me to cook; how to flavour

my dishes with the plentiful herbs and spices that grew in the fertile soil of the island: peppers, ginger and such, things that don't grow here. Someone once told me that it was spices that started all this business at the Cape and that if it weren't for spices, the Dutch wouldn't be here, none of this … And if the Dutch weren't here, maybe I wouldn't be here. Who knows? If it wasn't spices, it might have been something else.

Anyway, those first few months, the rice grew; the vegetables grew. I saw that soon it would be harvest time and still there was no word from my mother or my brother. The chief was the kind of man who enjoyed the society of others, and men from the village often called upon him to seek his counsel or merely to pass the day. On such days, I would loiter outside his hut, eager to see a familiar face, desperate to gain some scrap of news from home. My uncle was a regular visitor and appeared to be on friendly terms with the chief – not quite an equal, of course not, but not abased either. My uncle was never of much use; he never sought me out, and if I did make myself known to him, he'd greet me with a weak smile and a reminder to obey the chief and not bring shame upon my family nor myself.

Secretly, I'd watch the men playing games in the courtyard until they tired or the sun beat too brightly. When they retired to the chief's hut to recount his heroics and those of his ancestors, I'd make sure to stay close enough to hear them. These visits would be accompanied by much drinking, feasting and merriment. A lamb or sheep would be slaughtered and there'd be meat enough for everyone. At dusk, the dancing would begin, dancing that lasted all night. Those nights I'd fall asleep to the hum and throb of the music, the endless singing and drumming, saddened amid this cheer by unwelcome memories of a different time.

So many seasons passed, it's hard to say when things changed. For someone who watched the changing seasons so carefully, the shifts were too gradual to identify with any accuracy. Who knows when a whisper begins? Whispers and whispering – that's what I remember about that time – secret conversations between men that stilled when women and children came near. The island was a noisy place and the chief's compound the most so. We lived, like now, too closely together for secrets.

Then, as if a spark had caught, lighting a dry palm roof, everyone knew what the whispering was about. There'd been a falling out among the kings and the peace that had lasted since the last cattle raid was under threat. Some of us in the chief's household were surprised. Most were not, not with the talk of pirates so eager to stoke smouldering flames. And the kings? Everyone knew a king is never satisfied. We had all heard stories of greedy, unscrupulous kings, chieftains too – never happy until they had more power, more gold and Spanish silver ... ever jostling for more. This was not new. Skirmishes and wars, with alternating lulls as hostilities came and went and lines were drawn and redrawn, had long been part of life on the island. The coming of the pirates changed everything. For once the pirates reached the highlands, human captives became the object and not the coincidental outcome of wars.

None of us could have ever imagined that the king's long-ago warnings about *our* people selling one another would become true. Other islanders, yes, those without blood ties to our soil, people who would ransom the bones of those who fell on their lands. None of us would have thought that our own people would succumb to the wickedness that spread throughout the isle like fire, consuming it.

The story of our island began with five princes – brothers – who'd crossed the big sea in search of adventure. After many long days of sailing, their ships touched the island's shore. It is said that in those days, the only living things to be found there were tall trees shrouding the land in darkness and countless wild animals, small and large: chameleons, *maki*, wild boar, humped cattle as well as the various creatures that abounded in the seas, rivers and lakes and those that soared and dipped beneath the skies. Seeing all that the island offered, the princes declared themselves kings and swore to share the land equitably. In this way the kingdoms of the south, the north, the east, the west and the middle came about, each ruled by brothers who vowed to live in peace and ensure that their fraternal ties remained strong.

Within each of the five kingdoms there existed smaller territories governed by princes and chiefs, each swearing fealty to their king, since a king could not be in many places at once. It would make ruling over a large space easier, as people would have more respect for the rulers they knew personally. Or so the kings believed. This was how it had been in my village. Everyone knew and revered the chief, no matter the nature of their relationship, whether freeman or pawn or even slave.

For many years, the system worked. At least, as long as

fraternal ties persisted, it worked. Then wives began to inherit and nephews and in-laws – rulers without blood ties or a connection to the land. Then the peace that had lasted for so long, as long as the oldest person could remember, broke. This should not have been so: our land was large enough to share. The rice the brothers had brought along with them adapted well to the rich, black soil. Rains were abundant and the foreign seeds tipped into the land took root and flourished. When they first arrived – those who came with or followed the five kings – there had been ample animals for hunting and taming, but with the new rulers, enough was never enough. Villagers started worrying about their neighbours' rice stores, their fields, whose land was more fertile or received more sun, more rain, was better favoured.

Then came the attacks, as the men on our island remembered the ways of war.

That is how it started: neighbour against neighbour. They began by attacking those closest to themselves, those under the banner of the same king. It was never supposed to be like that: kinsman against kinsman. The old people spoke of the times when the rivers ran red with blood and how the black soil became even blacker. This is where the red rice came from, they said: from the time that blood saturated the soil and a bloody rain watered the fields. This was the sign that the ancestors had been angered by brothers fighting brothers. Slowly, the men in the villages began banding together again, relearning the value of kinship ties, of keeping their enemies close, of finding new enemies …

They began raiding neighbouring villages: taking cattle and

human bounty, taking a hand of territory here, a foot there. It became common for villages to fight each other, for one chief to raise men against another. Before long, fewer of the smaller territories remained, replaced by larger chiefdoms with borders that changed like water upon which the wind blew. By the time I was born, my people had a saying that the chiefs on the island were like turtles tossed in a basket, each one trying to clamber over the next to get out, not caring whose back they crushed or whose neck they snapped, as long as they succeeded.

Then the kings came under attack. Like before, the trouble arose within as chieftains began to attack their kings. None of the kings escaped these threats, the unpredictable, but not utterly unthinkable, attack of a pet goat goring its owner. Certain kingdoms survived intact. Our king entrusted the responsibilities of his domain to a succession of ministers, avaricious men, unworthy of the honour, who to a man sought only to attain riches for themselves and their families. The old people reminded us that while the system of the five kings had not been without fault, it had kept everyone safe. With no one above them to maintain order or keep them in check, the new chieftains became greedier and greedier. By the time I was at the chief's homestead, land and cattle were no longer the highest stakes for which they fought. The pirates changed all that.

It was one thing to imagine that we knew all about the pirates from the stories we'd heard before, second- and third-hand accounts from those who'd survived it when their paths had crossed those of the wicked men. But none of the stories conveyed the true horror. The pirates were the worst thing to happen to our village, and it did not matter that we had had warnings about what they stole, or that we were in some ways prepared for them, should they pierce our village. No, what we were not ready for was the evil they brought about in people who had only ever considered themselves good.

There are dangerous men in the world ...

Sometimes the most dangerous people are the ones you already know. Rakota hadn't told me that when he'd told me the story. Some things you learn yourself.

Our village had always been one of the most serene on the island. Certainly, when we had been raided and had cattle taken, our chief had always sent men to retrieve the beasts, no matter the cost. I knew this all too well. We were not a people to hide from danger, like an animal that bolts into its hole on the forest floor. We believed in defending ourselves, but we did not provoke fights. On occasion, men from our village would make incursions, but these were half-hearted attempts, motivated not by greed but by the necessity of proving our strength lest other villages think us weak.

Perhaps we were deluded, naïve, or merely guilty of pride, but all the while the wars between villages and kingdoms had raged, we had always thought our village and kingdom different. Was not our king good and wise, a strong leader willing to make difficult decisions for the good of the realm? He had indeed been strong and good and wise, but that was before. For reasons no one understood, the king became weary of ruling and handed over his power to a succession of ministers, avaricious men who sought only to attain riches for themselves. Some said the king had been bewitched, others believed his health to be ailing. In the end, the reasons did not matter.

Tributes were raised and new taxes introduced. Spanish silver reached the highlands: *reals*, *piasters*, pieces of eight. So silver became the island's new god. Coins were melted down for adornment and worn by the rich. Money-changers walked around with guardsmen to protect the boxes containing their coins and measures, and the metal clippers they used to cut the Spanish dollars into smaller pieces. These fragments were assessed against iron weights, right down to the tiniest grain of rice. All this meant, of course, was that I would not be returning home soon; my mother's chances of paying off her debt went from a slice to a sliver.

Then we heard anew the stories of the pirates edging ever closer. We heard strange stories of pirates being welcomed in nearby villages, villages too near for comfort. We heard even stranger stories of the pirates fighting alongside island men. We heard of their weapons, valued even more than silver, weapons that struck people from so far and so quickly and left men twitching on the ground in puddles of crimson black. We heard about the prisoners of war, and its bounty: women and children, shared among the pirates and victorious villages. But who, who was stoking the wars?

Despite our king's weaknesses, our chief remained loyal to him. This was a mistake. When the king's enemies began rising up against him, they became the enemies of our people too. The chief needed weapons and he wanted silver, and I was a pawn, only a pawn – no longer protected by my familial ties to the village. My father was dead, my mother the one who'd placed me here. Surely she must have known that she would never be able to pay her debt? Had my mother lied to me when she'd said that she'd return for me? To this day, I still wonder.

I'd like to think that the chief grappled with his decision to trade me to the pirates. I'd like to think that Lilisa tried to convince him to allow me to stay and that losing me would be like losing one of her own children. I'd like to think that my mother and my uncle did everything they could to redeem me, to ensure that I would remain on the island ... I'd like to think that someone said 'no', that someone said 'let's think about this', or 'she's so young'. I'd like to think that I mattered to someone. Maybe these are but more lies that I tell myself.

Mine was such a swift dispatch. Again I thought about the day my mother delivered me to the chief. Was that the day she took her leave of me for good? It was the last day I saw her – not one visit in all that time, not one final goodbye.

While I can recall the day I left my family's home with much clarity, I have few details of the day I left the chief's homestead. It could have been hot, it could have been cold; it could have rained, or been dry, maybe there were clouds block-ing the sky or maybe it had been clear. I don't remember saying goodbye – not to Lilisa, not to any of the pawns who remained behind, nor to any of the chief's children, my one-time play-mates. Maybe there were no such things as goodbyes for those like me, for what I'd become. I learned that.

But some things I do remember.

I remember how we were marched, linked arm to arm, along paths where once men drove cattle to the coast. They drove cattle still, the thick-humped zebu, milk cows and the bulls with their twisted horns. Mules carried sacks of rice. We trod the dark and trampled paths, treacherously placed with hidden roots of overhanging trees that bore a grim testimony to our movements.

I remember the way the sun streamed and broke up through the dense leaves, lighting the dark, only to vanish behind a cloud and was gone. I remember days that the sun sprinkled and dripped onto our shoulders like rain.

I remember the villages we passed along the way: islanders, men and women too, eagerly proffering fruit, corn, some roots – manioc, a ewe for a few pieces of silver, Spanish *piasters*, *reals* of eight.

And I remember they did not notice us, the villagers, or if they did, they pretended not to, looking instead at the tracks made by our feet from tramping barefooted through the forest, or at the sky of blinding blue.

I remember how the air changed as we neared the sea, the fabled coast so far away; cold and tangy and salt like tears, while all around me, people panicked like mules, upsetting the chain.

I remember then the soft, brown sand of the strand, too soft for highland-hardened heels, which sank into the dried-damp, a lurch to the left, a run for the shore and the shots that put paid to escape.

I remember being made to bare my teeth, my thighs, my breasts. And the examination of my eyes, my feet, my hands, and then careless hands that strayed into forbidden places.

I remember pieces of silver glinting dully in the gloom: Spanish *piasters* and *reals* of eight, but I never knew my worth.

I remember a boat tethered to the shore: so close, we imagined throwing ourselves overboard like refuse slopped from deck; men spoke of grabbing pistols, a knife.

I remember time came when we stopped smelling the sea, but were instead overcome by the intimate smells of each other: our breath, our waste, the acrid reek of our fear in the confines of our shared space.

I remember the day the ropes were cut and the heaving waves that elbowed the boat, the steam billowing through the hold, and I remember it was a day of hysteria, but also one of resignation, even calm, once we were adrift.

I remember floating in that dark coffin, and I remember how it was always night, and that the men entered only to drag women to their quarters or to cart away the sick, the dying and the dead.

I remember when next we saw land: the blinding glare from the white buildings and the burnished grey-black sea. I remember, too, the snorting of shiny, fat seals amid the noise, noise everywhere, crashing around me like waves.

I remember the feel of the harsh cobbles beneath my bare feet and I remember the surprise of the light, and how the sun, high up, but oh so close, touched our backs and shoulders, not like rain, but like stinging sand scattered by the wind.

I remember.

I remember the tree beneath which they made me stand: for twenty-five rix-dollars, they knocked me down – I was young, I was strong and look at my teeth …

I was raised to believe in fate. If something happened, good or bad, we said it was due to their destiny. Yet, I look at my life now and can't help but think this is not mine. This is not the life set out for me. I was not greedy; my hopes had been little hopes. All that happened, how could it be destiny? My father dying, losing all our cattle, the hail … Was that fate?

My people had a saying: 'If I go away, my father is dead; if I come back, my mother is dead,' and this is true, I think. Misfortune follows us wherever we place our feet.

Geert, 1792

A Cape wedding is never a simple matter. It is less so when the groom is counted as one of the most prosperous men in the Colony, young or old, and the bride is a daughter of a wealthy and connected man; a woman who could have had any man given the scarcity of estimable women of marriageable age, and yet she chose me. I had known Magdalena since her birth practically. Her father and mine had been well acquainted. Moreover, she had always been a dear friend of Johanna, being but a few years younger than my youngest sister. Had our families not been intimates, our town, though the first and largest in the Colony, was yet so small that, in the normal course of events, we'd have been acquainted soon enough, meeting either at the weekly church service, promenading in the Company's Garden, or while attending dinner at the home of one or other of the Cape's eminent citizens.

In all ways, Magdalena was the kind of lady that I had been fated to marry. Our mutual eligibility had made our union almost inevitable – unless Magdalena sought a groom with a smaller fortune, or I a bride with a lesser pedigree. Neither of these options was viable; Magdalena was a dutiful daughter and I would never have been able to escape my obligations to my family, nor all the responsibilities and rewards my father had bestowed upon me. Had I wanted another, or preferred a different course, there was the fact that I was no longer as eligible as might once have been supposed. Few knew of my situation, but suffice to say that, by the age of two and thirty years, I had learned about the caprices of fate. Magda was in no way disagreeable and her substantial dowry would right all my missteps of the previous years. Marriage between the two of us was a necessary affair. Even my sisters, always so possessive over their older brother, had agreed upon my choice. There was no use in concerning myself overly much in how they would have reacted were I to have taken another ... less suitable ... bride. No, no use at all.

I told myself that it was for my sisters' sake that I had made my matrimonial decisions. My father had entrusted them into my care; it was a great honour and spoke of his belief in me. He knew that whatever happened I would make the right choices for my family.

Dorothea and Johanna had been such high-spirited young ladies that it surprised me how they'd both turned into such proper matrons. Perhaps marriage and responsibilities collaborated to ensure that fancy-free maidens became respectable mothers. I was certain that, all their charms and other considerations aside, their marriage prospects would have been demonstrably diminished had I allowed my heart to dictate whom I married. Yes, it was easier when I convinced myself – for no matter how short a span – that it was for them that I had postponed marriage until the time proved opportune.

At the time of my betrothal, Dorothea had been married eight years and was the mother of three sturdy children: a son and two daughters. I had hoped that she would entertain various suitors before settling on one, but Dorothea had always been of a romantic nature. She had married at the age of nineteen – fortunately to one of my childhood friends. Dorothea was prized by her husband for the way she managed their household, and for the dowry she'd brought with her.

Johanna had been married these past four years and was the mother of a toddling son and infant daughter. She too had married well, perhaps even better than Dorothea had. I'd long suspected this would be the case. For in addition to being a romantic, Dorothea's feelings were gentler, nobler, while my younger sister was ambitious and, I am loath to admit, avaricious. Her husband's family was wealthier than our own. This favourable match was to be expected, for when the time came for her to choose a groom, she was arguably regarded as the best-favoured among the pool of potential brides at the Cape and possessed a beauty that was almost astonishing in our plainer-featured family. Furthermore, she'd possessed a generous dowry of her own.

As a young married woman, Johanna set the fashion at the Cape – fashions copied from Europe, if copied at all. She despised the gauche and pretentious wives, returning from the

East with their silks and other Eastern fabrics, attempting to condescend upon our local women, she said. Many within the Company at large still regarded the Cape as some kind of untamed outpost, deeming all its denizens savages. Johanna bristled against such prejudice and took great pleasure in inviting appropriate visitors from the ships to dine at her table and attend her dances.

'It's strange that Magdalena didn't marry sooner,' I had mentioned to Johanna, trying to puzzle out my betrothed's secrets.

Magdalena was three and twenty years then; it was not rare for girls as young as fifteen, or sixteen years of age to enter into marriage.

I realised that a part of me would have preferred that Magdalena entered into our marriage fraught too, whether by heartbreak or an unsuitable beau. It would diminish the discomfort I felt on all fronts as I hurtled towards becoming a man I never thought I would. The whispers about my father's ventures into matrimony, and the genesis of his fortune, came back to me at such inconvenient times.

'You can be so very obtuse, my dear brother,' Johanna replied. 'You must know she was waiting for you to ask?'

I frowned.

'Perhaps she was waiting for you to get over your proclivities,' she murmured archly, lest I misunderstand her insinuations.

My frown deepened. My 'proclivities', as she called them, were the concern of no one but myself. Yet I was unable to remain vexed with her long. My thoughts brightened at the idea of my bride-to-be admiring me from afar. A man should rule in his home, my father had always said, and a besotted wife was one who would prove easier to govern. With luck, her feelings would prevent her from examining my affairs too closely. In any event, I saw no reason for my so-called proclivities to end. Yet, I was not some injudicious cad, rutting with any number of women in order to satisfy my base nature. Rather, there had always been only one woman for me, a woman I'd loved without reservation these past ten and more years. Had circumstances been different, had society been different, I would have proven this to be the case.

As soon as we were granted an appointment, Magdalena and I appeared before the Matrimonial Court, a prerequisite to ensure that no impediments existed to our union. None were found and we were granted permission for the banns to be announced. After our appearance, my future in-laws hosted a celebratory dinner attended by our relations and more than one hundred friends and acquaintances. The dinner alone consisted of five courses: all kinds of meats roasted on a spit, chickens, guinea fowl, vegetables, sauces, soups, breads and puddings. It was a Bacchanalian feast with the health of the betrothed pair toasted by only the finest wines, in keeping with the fact that the bride's father was one of the main wine *pachters* at the Cape. The dancing lasted all night until languid ladies and enervated men sought out their beds in the early hours of the morning. It was the sole occasion that the groom-to-be relaxed his usual temperance, which necessitated his being escorted home before the end of the festivities by friends to sleep off the evening's excesses.

I was ignorant of Magdalena's thoughts on my unseemly exit from our engagement party, but by Sunday all was forgiven, as the first of the banns was called out during the service at the Great Church. The next few weeks followed in a tumult of activity. In keeping with tradition, our marriage was officiated during the Sunday morning service after the banns had been called for the third time. When we'd first begun negotiating the betrothal, my wife's father had suggested that the formalities be concluded before the time came to celebrate the New Year. There being no cause for delay and several compelling reasons for haste, I'd agreed. December was always an agreeable time of year for a wedding at the Cape.

By dawn, the day was already bright and warm, a perfect summer's day, a perfect day for a marriage to take place. I felt hopeful, almost eager, as I watched the lucent morning moon fade into the clear blue of the sky. I dressed quickly and meandered around Town to marshal my thoughts and ruminate over all that had taken place to bring me to this, my wedding day.

All things considered, the years following my father's death had been good and profitable. I discovered that, contrary to my initial thinking, but a small proportion of my father's sheep and cattle holdings was destined for slaughter – far less than a tenth. My forays to buy up sheep and cattle from smaller stock farmers during my initiation into the business in Swellendam had led me to believe that most of my father's wealth had been due to meat and that he'd bought up additional livestock to supply an endless appetite for beef and mutton. I later realised that he bought stock from smaller, more indigent farmers because he could – whether from altruism or because it made business sense to do so.

My father's real wealth had resided in the sheer numbers of sheep and cattle he owned, and these were not sold only for meat. For example, thanks to the sweet pasture he'd allowed his cattle to graze upon, and not simply letting them scrabble for whatever greenery they could find, the butter produced by his cows was as highly sought after as his meat. Yet even with these additional markets, his animal holdings were valuable only when converted into specie, and this was no longer a simple matter.

Paper currency had been introduced during the war, as silver supplies were disrupted. Cartoon money, we called it. These bills, ranging from six *stuivers* to sixty rix-dollars were to be redeemed by the Company once the war was over or more silver became available, whichever occurred first. Burghers were banned from sending precious metals from the Colony, a dictate which most deigned to ignore. My father, with his vast holdings of coin, had often served as a moneylender and I was astonished to discover the extent of his debtors. Given the fluctuations in currency after the Company abandoned the silver standard, I was even less interested in usury, despite the interest he'd earned on his loans. For during these uncertain times, I felt it would have been better had my father held on to more of his funds, and I resolved to make this right.

Money – paper and otherwise – flowed into our coffers during the war. Indeed, the war years had been a propitious time to be a meat man such as I, with contracts to supply the Company and the larger numbers of foreign ships that docked at the Cape. The meat tenders awarded for five-year periods meant stability – important for any man of business. However, the duration of the contracts meant that we were forced to accept the prices offered, prices that lagged during years of high demand, or were even inadequate, as had been the case scant years ago when our sales of livestock to the Company were conducted at a loss. The only exception in recent years had been in 1786, when a grain shortage caused the Company to buy increased quantities of meat at prices above that of the *pacht* level. This had been but a temporary respite; once the shortage was resolved by the importation of grain from America, the situation reverted.

Sales to foreign ships had long compensated for the periodic losses we suffered as a result of our contracts with the Company. For most of the past decade, this had served us well, for we had the Company's sanction to set our own prices. Between 1781 and 1782 alone, my fellow meat *pachters* and I sold several million pounds of meat to the French and the Dutch navies. Those were exceptional times; as prices rose, foreign captains began to complain about the high prices. Several bypassed the Cape, which affected not only those in the meat business, but also landlords and inn-keepers and who knows who else. Other visiting ships' captains tried to bargain down the prices or bought smaller and smaller quantities, while yet others procured their meat illegally from private butchers, who had been barred from making such sales. These unscrupulous characters flouted the regulation openly and seemingly without fear. Admittedly, the Company attempted to end such transgressions, but their teeth had been blunted. Sales continued to diminish; between September 1789 and September 1790, we *pachters* sold little more than two hundred thousand pounds of meat to the foreign ships. To compensate, I began selling tallow to the chandlers in Town and looked for markets for our hides.

With the war ended, most of the foreign troops decamped, leaving our shores. We believed that peace reigned across Europe. All the auguries were there, but it proved nothing more than a respite, the deceptive lull before a devastating storm.

It began in France, a nation experiencing droughts, grain shortages and rising bread prices. At the Cape, midway between Europe and the East, stories were told of how the citizens of France were becoming increasingly disenchanted with their profligate king and their men's involvement in costly wars waged faraway. French soldiers, so recently stationed here, had spoken of how a select few enjoyed unparalleled perquisites amid an impoverished populace. It was no wonder that revolutionary inclinations had been fomenting. Facing bankruptcy, the French king had essayed to persuade his fellow nobles into making economic reforms, but to no avail.

We heard no further news for months until a visiting ship's captain from Marseille recounted the remarkable story of an attack on the Bastille for guns and ammunition. 'Following the assault on the fortress in Paris, the troubles spread as far as the countryside … homes of landlords and tax collectors made prime targets for looting and torching,' he said with a wink, making it clear where his sympathies lay. 'Vast numbers of aristos fled the country and are fleeing still. Even the king tried to escape the land over which he's said to reign,' the captain said.

'What of the king now?' I asked. 'And the queen? Is she not the sister of the Holy Roman Emperor?'

'Don't talk to me of *the queen*,' the captain declaimed. 'That Austrian bitch! All across the land she is detested for her arrogance and her squandering ways.'

'I've heard that said,' I agreed.

'And that brother of hers, the high and mighty emperor threatening war if the king's rights are threatened. Bah, the king! He's king in name only, that's what the problem is, when some foreign emperor has to threaten war against his own people,' the captain spat.

Troubled by other concerns, his tale remained far from my mind until months later, when another ship's captain, a Dane this time, arrived with word that France had declared war against Austria and Prussia and that an invasion of France by the foreign forces had been in the wind when he'd left the *entrepôt* of Brussels, from whence he'd sailed.

Despite our distance from the centres of these conflicts, we at the Cape felt the ravages of the war. This time, the impact was dissimilar to that of the Anglo-Dutch war, which had been profitable for so many. Instead of an increase in foreign ships, the numbers began to dwindle.

Closer to home, the Graaff-Reinet settlement was becoming a niggling factor in the lives of all of us involved in the meat business. Five years ago, when the town was first established, many stock farmers and those seeking to make a living from it moved there, joining those who'd trekked into the interior earlier, attracted by the area's expansiveness and climate. Though not without an adventurous spirit myself, after undertaking an exploratory journey to our Colony's newest district a year after my father's death, I decided against acquiring a farm of my own there. This proved a mistake. Within a matter of years, Graaff-Reinet had become the main area for sheep-rearing and, to a lesser extent, cattle. Indeed, it was reckoned that the district supplied the entire Colony with meat for nine months out of twelve.

With the fighting in Europe, a decrease in shipping and the resultant attenuation of sales to foreign ships, the domestic market, particularly Cape Town, was becoming increasingly important to all of us involved in the meat trade. However, it had become easy for individuals with very little skills to set up shop as butchers. As evinced by their under-handed dealings with the foreign captains, these private butchers were a constant nuisance to those of us in possession of honest contracts with the Company. Though they could not compete against us on quality, they did not scruple to compete on the basis of price. Their practices hurt our business, but I negated them, believing their model to be unsustainable in the long term. Underestimating the threat posed by these private butchers was another mistake.

It was an infelicitous time to be making mistakes in the meat business. The fact that our own herds and flocks had shrunk had not helped matters. I'd seen no reason to increase our herds aggressively, since our agents could as easily acquire cattle and sheep from farmers inland, which we drove to and resold in the Cape in fulfilment of our contract. During my father's time, the bulk of the meat and live animals supplied had been our own, bred and reared on my family's farm in Swellendam. The meat that bore my family's name was renowned for its quality, but I'd reasoned that, in a short while, and with good grazing, the animals my agents bought could as easily be fed and brought to our high standard. My agents went out several times a year, keeping me apprised of developments further from Town.

In recent years, one of the things they'd reported was that stock farmers were refusing to accept the prices we were willing and able to pay for slaughter animals due to the high prices that butter was commanding at the time. Our own butter sales were but a negligible contributor to our overall profits, but had I foreseen this development, I would have set aside more cows for its making. It was a small miscalculation, but it nettled.

Another factor that worked against us was the burgeoning market for draught cattle. It seemed as if anyone with a few guilders to spare did not consider himself risen in the world unless he had a wagon and a span of ten to twelve oxen. Since these beasts of burden typically endured their existence for two or three years, or thereabouts, a cattle farmer was not always disposed to selling his bullocks for slaughter. As a meat man, I felt myself becoming squeezed in every direction, as even the prices demanded for sheep were rising. Still, I had no cause for alarm. My other ventures were faring satisfactorily and, with luck, would hold, until I found myself on surer footing.

All the while I had one very real consideration I was loath to voice: I was unsure for how long I could rely on my contracts with the Company as the primary source of my income. For the very first time, we *pachters* were unsure whether the Company was willing to renew our contracts. More importantly, there were loud whispers that *were* the Company willing, that it would be in a position to do so was tenuous.

As the century drew to a close, the Company's hold upon our growing settlement, and indeed on its factories in other parts of the world, weakened further. Relations between its officials and citizens continued to decline here and elsewhere. In the past three years alone, the Company's directors had recalled a spendthrift governor and withdrawn a large component of the Cape garrison. Recently, two commissioners had arrived to investigate the dire state of its coffers, and there was already talk that tax collection would be tightened, new taxes levied and official spending reined in. The only positive outcome of the Company's precarious position, and particularly its probing into matters at the Cape, was that the list of grievances sent to the *Heren* xvii more than a decade ago were finally being addressed.

Given these circumstances, I looked at ways of curtailing expenses. The Rondebosch farm, vacant for most of the year, was a luxury I could no longer afford. The proceeds from the sale of the farm that had meant so much to my father helped for a while, but not in any meaningful way. Fortunately, the innovations I'd since introduced at the Stellenbosch farm made it profitable, but the revenues remained ever small. I was certain, however, that my luck with meat would turn. My instincts could not desert me forever. I convinced myself, even as I watched the losses accumulate in my books, that my seven years of lean would not last forever. And if they were indeed to last that long, by such reckoning, I had but one more year to endure.

There was the grain farm in the Drakenstein, of course. Other than what was retained for our own consumption, most of the grain grown there was sold in Town, since we had neither a contract to sell to the Company nor to passing ships. Nor did we grow enough to export to Batavia or Europe, although I believed this to have been my father's initial plan. As to why this had not been realised, I was unsure, but surmised that it had more to do with yields than the lack of a market.

At one stage I'd had high hopes of effecting my father's plans, but grain harvests had been deficient during the first five years of my taking over, including that disastrous year when American grain had been bought to satisfy the palates of a Cape citizenry accustomed to bread. Although harvests had begun to improve, I'd decided a few months ago to sell the Drakenstein farm to make up for my losses elsewhere. I deemed it wiser to focus all my energies on one area of business only. Since my miscalculations with meat, I'd felt torn, as if my attentions were scattered, and that this was the reason for my mistakes. It had to be. I was at ease in every other aspect of my life. Still, the decision to sell was not an easy one, given my father's connection to the property through his late wife, and my own upbringing, which had for so long equated land and property with prosperity. Before I sought a buyer, I decided to visit the farm one last time.

And I will pour out mine indignation upon thee; I will blow against thee in the fire of my wrath.

Curiously, it was not the smell that woke me, but the sound, the hiss and spatter as the stalks burned. I jolted upright in the narrow cot in which I slept whenever I visited the farm, pressed my knuckles to my face and rubbed my eyes. In the seconds it took me to wake properly, I saw how strangely illuminated the room was. Through the open shutters I noted the colours first: the seething oranges and vivid blues of the blazing fields. Transfixed, I marvelled at how quickly the light-grey plumes of smoke rising from the flames turned thicker, darker, almost black, until I registered that these were my fields that were being devoured and that something needed to be done to stop flaming tongues from reaching the house.

In the time it took me to dress, the plumes had dissipated and formed a thick scrim that befouled the air and obscured my vision at first. Once my wits adjusted I saw that my men were already battling the greedy flames, rushing about with feeble buckets of water while others beat at them with blankets and sticks.

The wheat fields were situated closer to the house than was wise. From the back stoep, I could make out individual stalks being consumed by the inferno. The fully ripened crop crackled and sparked as it burned. Though I could not see the animals at first, I heard them: a keening roar, panicked and murderous as they stumbled over one another in an attempt to escape. As I took in the hellish panorama before me, I felt once more the disjuncture I'd experienced earlier, as if these were another's lands, another's fields, another's animals being burned alive. Then, coming to my senses, I too grabbed a blanket and began to beat at the flames.

By morning, the fields lay smouldering before me. Some of the animals had been rescued and tethered to a fence, since the barns had been razed. Most were lost. I wanted to avert my eyes from the burnt carcasses of sheep and cattle in the soot-smeared soil. Nor had the house survived unscathed: the fire had reached the reed roof and burned from the top down, consuming all that was possible. The walls remained standing, but the woodwork was charred and damaged irreparably, the ceilings gutted. I looked to the gable with the date etched upon it and remembered my father's pride at the renovations and refurbishment. They had lasted twelve years only. This that had once been a place of beauty, reduced to a scene of desolation. I knew I would not rebuild it. I had neither the heart, nor the purse for such a resurrection.

Standing on the ruined land, I thought how ironic it was that I had timed my trip to coincide with the bringing in of the harvest; how I so enjoyed the festivities that concluded each day, the exuberant levity and carousing a natural panacea for strained muscles burnished by the sun. Yet I could appreciate the symmetry of wheat being the final catastrophe to hit in my series of calamitous years. As a meat man, my father had had a favourite parable to relate: Pharaoh's dream, in which seven scrawny cows devoured seven plump, healthy ones. This dream had been followed by another, in which seven full and robust heads of grain had been swallowed by seven meagre ones.

'Those dreams had been a warning,' my father had always reminded my sisters and I – we were subjected to additional sermonising over and above the daily meetings to which his entire household were obligated. 'If one does not protect against it, disaster can follow abundance. Take heed of my words, children,' he'd say, 'just as Pharaoh heeded Joseph's interpretation of his dreams and prepared for darker days.'

'Yes, Father,' I'd reply, but I had not heeded his words. I'd believed myself set apart – cushioned by wealth and privilege, I'd believed myself inured from disaster.

Now, as I surveyed my losses, the stench of smoke in my hair and tasting its acridity on my tongue, I knew that I had no option but to find a suitable woman to marry. Best to do so before word of this latest disaster reached Town. Thankfully, I knew it would take a while for the extent of my losses to be broadcast widely, and even then, few men would be able to accurately gauge the change in my fortunes, since I was known to have a skillet in many fires.

Thankfully too, I remembered the ardent manner in which one of my sister's friends had admired me over the years. The time had come for me to renew our acquaintance. I'd enlist Johanna's help, but tactfully. Before our meeting ended, my sister would be persuaded that I was the one who had needed convincing and that she had succeeded in playing matchmaker. Yes, her friend would be an ideal choice. It always paid to remain appraised of the marriageable women at the Cape, even if one were not in the market for a wife.

For my part, ours would be a marriage of necessity, occasioned by my waning fortunes. And for this I was willing to assume full responsibility. I had never been one to suffer under the weight of self-delusion.

Magdalena made a truly beautiful bride. Looking at her face in the church, her sweet, hopeful face, before the *dominee* launched into the rites of matrimony, I promised that I would do my best to be a good husband to her. The *dominee* asked if there was any reason why the two of us should not be married, and again, no one came forth to repudiate our union. I had always been a discreet man, and one would be wise to heed the words of gospel that only the blameless among us might cast aspersions against others.

When Magdalena and I walked out of the church together as man and wife, her tiny hand in its white glove tucked beneath my elbow, I saw that it had begun to pour while we'd been inside. The sun continued to shine through the gaps between, gilding the grey clouds that patterned the sky like torn lace on an old nightdress. Though it had rained lightly earlier that week, such a deluge was unseasonal, muddying the streets and adding a layer of gloom to what had started out as such a flawless day. We hastened towards our waiting carriage, so gaily bedecked with flowers upon which diamonds and pearls of moisture glinted as if by design. I saw Magdalena grimace, taking great pains to protect the long, dragging skirts of her pale-blue dress. For a moment I wondered whether I should chivalrously offer to bear her to our awaiting conveyance lest she soil her bridal finery, but I am not one for ostentatious displays and decided against doing so for decorum's sake. Luckily, the walk was short and our carriage enclosed.

Our first destination was the home of my newly acquired parents-in-law for a discreet luncheon with family and close friends. Their home, located close to mine, had been decked out superbly, but in not too flamboyant a manner. The great room was filled with silver bowls containing roses and greenery, while gilt and silver tinselling adorned the walls. On our arrival, Magdalena and I were seated beneath an ornate mirror wreathed with myrtle and other blooms. Wearing our fussy wedding garb and wilting along with the flowers in the heat, we two sat with broad smiles plastered on our faces as our guests were introduced one by one – the ladies ushered in by my nephew, Jacobus, Dorothea's son, and the men by one of Magdalena's nieces, a pretty child with long, russet-brown hair and pink cheeks.

Then it was time for our luncheon, a feast even more extravagant than that which had marked our betrothal. I'd supplied the meat, my father-in-law the wine and brandy. No beer was served on this occasion, as only the finest of everything was served at my in-laws' table and the beer produced at the Cape was known for its mediocrity. Magdalena was a cherished eldest daughter for whom only the best would do and I had been assured by more than one person that her parents held me in the highest estimation.

A long, wide yellowwood table ran the length of the great room, the centrepiece of which, right in front of where Magdalena and I sat, was a large suckling pig, its dead eyes open and staring, an orange wedged in its gaping mouth. Looking at this grim tribute perturbed me, a peculiar reaction indeed for someone able to slaughter and skin an animal in short minutes. Perhaps a lamb would have been more fitting, or a calf, I mused, but then admonished myself to cast such thoughts from my mind, cast away all thoughts of the various mishaps and missteps that had cost me so dearly and led me here to this very table, on this very day. I concentrated instead on the cornucopia before me: the broiled fish, the baked chicken and pheasants and squab, roasted venison, so many different kinds of flesh if one eschewed that on which my family's fortune had been founded, but to be sure, of beef and mutton there was plenty too.

Clearly, the kitchens had been kept busy for days. Vegetables of all varieties – stewed, boiled, roasted; sauces savoury and sweet; and breads served with butter that pooled in shallow dishes due to the heat. Coffee, accompanied by a variety of cakes and fruit, was served once the dishes from the main course had been cleared. As appetites were sated and over-sated and just before that sense of lassitude descended upon the guests, one of the servants entered the room holding a heavy crystal loving cup aloft. This was traditionally brought out at the end of the wedding meal and contained wine enough to be passed around the table to ensure that each guest could indulge in a sip and so drink to the health of the newlyweds.

Engraved upon the cup was my wife's family's motto: *In vino veritas*, an appropriate verse given their business. I nearly choked on my drink as I contemplated what they would think of the truth behind my wanting to marry their daughter. Again putting such morbid thoughts from my mind, I raised my glass to my wife and smiled at the latent eagerness I glimpsed in her eyes before she lowered them shyly. The skin on her face flamed. She *was* an innocent, I mused, in relief. And yes, it appeared she *did* love me. Johanna's intimations had been correct.

I smiled at her and raised my glass.

'To your beauty,' I whispered.

I smiled again as she blushed even deeper.

My father-in-law chose that moment to wish us many sons and I felt my wife squirm in embarrassment. I wondered whether she was looking forward to our wedding night. In my albeit limited experience, Cape women, well-bred Cape women, were either wanton or naïve, and in that moment I had no doubt as to which of these characteristics was embodied in my wife.

After the meal, a group of singers entertained the guests, some of whom began making overtures to dance once the space was cleared; others regrouped at little tables set up for the playing of cards. I knew I was expected to dance with my wife and I have never been one of those men who feign the inability to dance. I am a good dancer and enjoy the pastime, but I was tired and impatient and perhaps just a bit worried about the reception that awaited us when we returned home, my bride and I, for the first time. I hoped my people would give her a good welcoming. She was after all so young, so innocent and so very, very eager to please.

To be honest, there was only one person's reaction I feared. Had I been a stronger man, I'd have sent her away long ago. Indeed, there were so many things I would have done differently had I been a stronger man.

When we left the reception the night was dark, but just. Magdalena's parents were the last to wish her well as we took our leave. Their farewell was sad, sweet, but swift. I was grateful for this. It appeared my wife was not one for histrionics. I thanked Magdalena's parents for all they had done. All in all, it had been a good wedding. Despite my misgivings, I hoped that our marriage would prove so too.

Alone at last, except for my driver, I scanned the street. A line of carriages waited for their owners still enjoying the festivities inside. The summer air felt clean and mild, no doubt freshened by the rain that had fallen earlier. The best part about this time of night at this time of year is the way the skies seem crowded with stars, the stalwart Southern Cross and the evening star pulsing so brightly. Looking at the heavens had always made me feel that I was alone in the world, so alone, but strangely at peace. I squeezed my wife's hand. 'You are Venus,' I told her.

I would have preferred to walk home, the houses were proximate enough and the ground had dried, but tradition dictated otherwise. I wanted to tell the driver to take us for a circuit around the quieted town. I pictured my new wife and I sprawled out on the seat while I showed her the constellations; I imagined us driving for hours until the town went to sleep and we could sneak into my house unannounced, with no need for a great ado.

I did no such thing.

'Home, driver,' I directed.

My wife's face lit up to rival the moon.

In that moment I vowed that I would try to be a faithful husband, repaying the trust she placed in me. I would honour my vows. I wanted to believe those words, the words that said we were no longer two, but one. I promised I would not sunder nor sully a union that God had joined. I would not, could not, allow unsanctified vows to take precedence over my anointed marriage.

When we arrived, my entire household was waiting to greet my wife. In the short time it had taken for us to reach our destination, my vow to be faithful had strengthened into resolve. I was more than convinced of my wife's fidelity and feeling. Still, I have to confess to a frisson of dread as I prepared to carry her over the threshold, disheartened once more by the reception she might receive from one person in particular.

In preparation for this night, my staff, supervised by Dorothea and Johanna, had cleaned and scoured the house, going into every corner and crevice. Given the crowd around us, I chose not to carry my bride over the threshold as was customary. After partaking of a dish of coffee in the small parlour to help her acclimate to her changed surroundings, I lifted her over my shoulder and carried her to the bedroom, relieved that our wedding night would be taking place under my own roof, away from her family and the usual retinue of married couples to escort us to bed as if we could not find the way by ourselves.

The room had been transformed into a bridal chamber worthy of a princess. Prim pink rosebuds just come into bloom perched prettily in bowls of beaten silver. Beneath the roses' perfume hovered the scent of lemon, subtly attesting to the cleaning that had gone into readying the room. Silver tinsel garlanded the walls and bits of the same material lay strewn upon a newly purchased rug knotted into some leafy pattern of browns and greens. The dark wood furniture shone and glowed in the candlelight – good white candles procured from the Chinese chandlers in Town and not the everyday tallow candles I was more apt to use. A fire had been lit in the fireplace, which meant that the room was heated, but overly so. It felt so sweltering that I longed to throw open the shutters and windows to allow the night air in, but did not. Instead, I intended to tamp down the fire as soon as I had the chance.

More tinsel had been suspended around the draperies of the canopied bed. With one hand, I drew the drapes aside then gingerly settled my wife in the centre of what would become our marital bed. The bed was dressed in fresh linens of the purest white in homage to my wife's virtue. I glanced down at her. Still wearing her bridal best, she looked scattered and strange. I reproached myself immediately. What ill-considered words to describe one's wife! Her blue eyes, so light they looked watered down, were not the deep brown pools I craved. Eyes that I had been unable to meet as I'd ushered my wife into her new home. Her creamy, pink limbs, already showing the signs of the softness that would one day overwhelm her flesh, as it had overtaken her mother and all Christian women here, were not the slender, dusky limbs I was used to seeing on this bed. Nor were her yellow curls the long, black hair I'd once brushed in the candle-glow of this room. That night, as I made my bride my wife in every sense of the word, I could not help but wonder which one of us was the imposter: she or I?

I lay awake for hours the next morning while my new wife lay sleeping next to me. Despite the seductive smell of the brewing coffee that permeated the house, I had no wish to rise and pour myself a cup. I'd have given anything for a cup, but I had no desire to see her face, to stand aloof as she searched mine.

'I've made my decision,' I'd told her the day I had finally summoned the courage to inform her of my plans. 'This doesn't change anything.'

Of course I dissembled. It changed everything.

I tried to explain the parlous state of my finances; tried to persuade her that there was no choice. Had there been another option, I would have taken it, I told her. I shall never forget the look of venom in her eyes that day, dangerous and dark like those of a snake. That made it easier, I warrant. I don't know what I'd have done if I had seen hurt. Yet it angered me too. I wanted to see something, anything to prove that she felt for me the way I did her.

Not once had she returned the words of love I'd press into her hair, her skin, the spot above her heart.

Lena, 1854

'Lena,' he said, nervously twisting that old hat he used to wear all the time in those days. 'Lena, I need to tell you something.'

Right away I knew it was trouble. A man never has to tell a woman anything, least of all a man like him and especially not to a woman like me.

'I did not want you to hear from one of the others. The matter is, I need to take a wife.'

Since I had not asked him the matter and did not want to hear his reasons, I found myself paying attention to the hat in his hands. It was sun-baked and battered, and with his busy fingers he wrung its rough leather straps, but whether in agitation or despair, I could not tell.

'Will you say something, Lena?'

He stepped towards me, so close I could feel the rasp of the strap, and I knew that if I touched it, I would feel the places where hands had worn it smooth. Whoever had made the hat had not skinned the animal carefully; here and there tufts of hair sprouted from the straps. I thought about how I knew that hat so well. He wore it always – when the sun was at its worst and burnt pale skin so red that not even the juice of the aloe could take away the sting, and in winter, when it rained. Only at night would he take that hat off, and then no matter what the weather was like outside, his hair would be flattened and damp with an almost sour smell, like milk left in the sun too long.

'Say something, Lena, say something.'

I will want no other woman …

Once, long, long ago, I had told him the story of the baby who had fallen in love while yet in his mother's womb. What had I been thinking when I told him that story, the story that Rakota had told me in the days when I was someone else?

'Talk to me, Lena.'

I could not find the words to say what I felt; he would not have understood, that man. How could I tell him that my first thought was what kind of woman would he choose? He would think I was being covetous, womanish. Would she treat us kindly, or would she be schooled in cruelty, the sort of woman who did not spare the whip? I wanted to say, 'Make sure to choose well.' I wanted to ask the questions: 'Do you have some-one in mind? Is it all arranged?'

To no other woman will I give my name …

'Lena!'

I lifted my head and stared into his eyes, golden and green, and I almost pitied him.

'Yes,' I said. 'I heard you.'

I am proud to say that I kept myself in check and did not add the word I knew would hurt him, no matter how much I wanted to hurt him then – *Baas*.

He looked into my face, as if trying to read the questions that I would not ask; I kept my face blank, like river water before a stone is thrown across its surface, or maybe after the stone has been thrown and the water is settled again. On my face he would see no ripples, no disturbance of any kind.

He sighed; a heavy sigh like a man relieved, a man who discovers peace when he'd expected hostilities. What did he think I was capable of doing? He reached for my hand, perhaps to draw me close or perhaps to keep me there, but before I could be sure of his intent, we heard the slap of approaching feet and he quickly dropped my hand and walked to the opened door. He bashed his hat on his head before going outside to face the sun's glare. Summer was early.

A man who goes in search of a wife can be killed …

I thought that maybe, yes, I hated him, hated him enough to kill him, but with us it was never about love or hate. How could it be?

Barbetje entered the room. Older now, her face was like that of a Chinaman's, with so many wrinkles and folds, and small, narrow eyes that shone brilliantly and missed nothing.

'*Wat is dit?*' I asked insolently, addressing her in her language.

She looked at me carefully, almost kindly. I lifted my chin

and met her eyes. She could look at me and see what she wanted; I had always been good at keeping my feelings under control. Staring her straight in her eyes – those eyes that upon my first glance I'd thought shone so brightly with glee, but glistened with moisture instead – I realised that if there was one person in the house who knew what I was feeling, it was she. How many times had she found herself set aside for another? I had no idea and had no wish to know. I resented our sudden familiarity, although that was an overstatement. Perhaps we would forever be like two hens in a henhouse, but that's the thing. Unlike cocks, two hens will not fight each other to the death, yet we had that familiar way of pecking at each other, sometimes drawing blood, but nothing fatal.

I thought about when I'd first arrived and how Barbetje had treated me – not with outright malice, but with a grim impatience that expected the worst from a young girl who barely understood a word of her language. I had sensed her authority and had despised her for it, seeing it as meaningless. Deep down, I knew that the animosity that had existed between us was as much my fault as hers. Ever since Lilisa, I had never allowed myself to trust another woman. I'd long ago stopped looking for replacement mothers. Even if Barbetje had softened towards me, or been tender towards me from the first, I would have remained suspicious, disdainful, afraid. I had hardened my heart from a young age, but that is not to say that I did not have hopes – if not for myself, then for the child.

Barbetje had had hopes once too. Once I'd been in the house a few years and could speak better, understand better, I heard the stories of the children Barbetje had carried – the old man's children. No one would tell me what had happened to them, or indeed whether any had survived beyond infancy. Or had even drawn breath, for that matter. I didn't know the old man well; he died soon after I arrived here, so I couldn't tell if he was the kind of man who could sell his own children. I liked to think that Barbetje's children were living somewhere in Town, cared for by a kind freewoman; that they were free too and one day would buy their mother's freedom. I don't know why I cared enough to make up stories for children I hadn't met. For all I knew, they were all dead, if they'd ever been born in the first place.

I wondered whether Raketaka ever made up stories of what had become of me. Or if mine was a name she remembered at all.

Barbetje cleared her throat loudly. This habit of hers always annoyed me; she always made such a to-do about the simplest of actions. Sometimes at night I'd hear her clear her throat just as loudly, not caring whom she woke. Perhaps it was just her way of saying without saying that she saw what was happening. That woman saw everything. There were no secrets from her. There were no secrets from anybody. We all lived so closely, those of us in the house and even those who stayed in the quarters outside.

I tried to keep my daughter away from the outside people, but she was young, always smiling, that child. She thought everyone was her friend and, yes, it was true. People took to her, even Barbetje always had a bit of something nice or a kind word for the girl. I would almost go as far to say that though she treated me the same as always, she treated my child like she used to those misses all those years ago, when they were young and used to live in the house.

Barbetje cleared her throat again.

'Just say what you want to say,' I told her, addressing her in English this time. My English was better than hers by then.

Barbetje ignored me and instead bustled about the kitchen while I watched her with defiant expectation. She took out two cups and saucers: not the good stuff the family used, but not the worst. She placed the sugar and a jug of milk next to them and then poured the tea that had been warming on the stove all morning into the cups. She stirred them briskly, then passed me one.

'Hot, sweet tea always makes me feel better,' she explained. I could believe it; she drank several cups a day.

'Why don't we sit?' she suggested, pulling out a chair at the table. We seldom sat there; the table had always been reserved for the family, even once the misses left. When we worked we stood, but Barbetje was having none of that. 'My legs are sore.'

I sat down, since I knew that no one would actually tell me that I could not. Anyway, it was usually Barbetje who watched me, to make sure that I didn't overstep my bounds, and if she told me to sit then I would sit. We sipped our tea in silence. I decided that I would not goad her to talk. Maybe I was afraid of what she'd say.

'His father was exactly the same,' Barbetje said, once I had nearly finished my tea.

I stirred the bottom of my cup, thinking that the words alone must have tasted like sugar on her tongue, but she had surprised me with the tea. Such a sweet irony, I thought, that Barbetje should be the one to show me how I too had been deluded enough to believe that a man like that would keep his word: 'I will marry you one day; I will give our children my name'. That's what he used to say on the nights he wanted to talk.

I was glad that Barbetje hadn't required me to confirm the news of his marriage; she probably already knew, perhaps she was privy to the details. I didn't know and I didn't ask. I let her speak.

'Always promising one thing but doing another,' Barbetje said.

I wanted to ask her about the children she'd borne; I wanted to know what had happened to them, whether she'd thought they'd make a difference. I wanted to know whether the old man had been able to sell his own flesh and blood. If his son was exactly like his father, I needed to know that.

Barbetje had helped me with the first two births – the unsuccessful births. Motherhood had never been my desire. Not to be hurtful, but it had never been my plan. The hopeful among us saw children as negotiating instruments, a tool when we had so little with which to bargain. Others bore children to punish, a constant reminder of the sins of the fathers. All those fathers sinning so unconscionably, ardently, what was another child when compared to able hands, strong arms, feet? A baby for some was gold, and if not gold, then silver.

A baby is not a bird …

I remembered the words from Rakota's tale; had always wondered what it meant. Those words were the first thing that came to mind when I saw the child, the first one, a girl. Birdlike bones and damp feathers of hair like a newly hatched chick.

A baby is not a bird …

Barbetje's words disturbed my thoughts. '*'n Stywe lat het geen konsensie nie,*' she said, placing a hand on my shoulder.

It was true what she said. A stiff rod has no conscience. I'd never had any illusions about that, except sometimes I'd forgotten. Or maybe, after everything that had happened to me, a small part of me, a hidden part, was still hopeful that someone would see more value in me than whatever my worth had been decided on at the open market under the tree.

Gathering the cups, Barbetje stood up, abruptly ending our conversation. I was grateful for this. One conversation would not make us friends. Both of our positions in this house had been too precarious for that. In a way, I supposed, I'd usurped her. I'd wanted to, but there had been no way to shake her. She'd been with the family too long; she'd known him as a boy.

'Why don't you go for a walk, Lena?' Barbetje suggested. 'Get some fresh air. If anyone asks, I'll tell them you went to the market.'

I don't know who was more surprised when I turned around and thanked her. I smiled, I remember, a thin, weak smile, but a smile nonetheless, even if it did not reach my eyes.

In the past years, I'd begun experiencing greater freedoms. People would say it was because of my relationship with him, and perhaps this was true, but it was more than that. My languages had improved and I became accustomed to the cobbled streets, the gabled houses, the large, open squares that were so different to the land of my birth. I decided to walk in the Company's Garden to clear my head. I wanted to be as far away from his house as possible, that big house that he'd inherited and made bigger. 'A man's vanity is his folly,' someone once said.

The old house had been more than adequate, stately even. 'But men like to build monuments to themselves and monuments cost money,' someone else had said. His money problems were no secret to those of us of his household. If I thought about it, I could not blame him for wanting a bride who came with a heavy purse. I wasn't sure if I wanted him for myself, or if I had ever wanted him for myself, but he was the one who mentioned it. He was the one who made the promise.

I walked the length of the Company's Garden, which had always been a place of calm for me, even though it was always so busy. Something about the colourful and exotic trees and the animals in the menagerie reminded me of home. Though I was in no mood to be lulled, after a while, my furious-paced walk helped to calm my mind so that I was able to think about my situation dispassionately. So he was to be married and there was nothing I could say, nothing I could do to stop him. I would not say, 'Marry me,' or, 'You promised!' I vowed that I would not remind him of his words uttered not so long ago. Had it been that long ago? My life had taught me patience. I saw now how this was my downfall. As to weaknesses, I had always known he was a weak man. He thought he was not, but he was. I knew better to wish that he could have been otherwise. This man believed himself to be honourable; I knew that, I knew all his vanities and conceits. He was not honourable, but nor was he overly bad. I knew that there were worse men, whether freemen or slaves. He was merely a man, a man in need of a wife, and I was not the kind of woman he could consider marrying. I had never forgotten this, not even when he kissed my neck or squeezed my shoulder like a man who loves a woman would; not even when he whispered the words I would never allow myself to echo. I never believed him. But yes, I hoped, I hoped; I hoped not for myself, but for my child. It was my fault she was here; my fault she was born into this. I was born free, but there were too many days I wished I had not been born at all.

Being born free had not stopped me from being sold. Freedom had not stopped my mother from bartering me. I knew what it was like to be a child with no freedom or security. I had stopped wishing for my own freedom long ago, but I mourned for that of the child I'd brought into the world. I would rather have had no children if I could spare them the pain of this life. I was relieved when the first two died. It's a terrible thing to say, but it was better, for as a mother I was powerless. I had only begun to hope that things would be different shortly before my daughter was born. That was when the promises had first started. He claimed her, or so it seemed; cared for her, I convinced myself. Perhaps I was no better than Barbetje; like her, I had believed a man's lies when I should have known better. I was grateful to her that she had not thrown that in my face.

Thinking of Barbetje and her unexpected kindness, my mind went back to earlier in the day, when he'd first broken the news. Just before leaving, he'd lowered his voice, leaned closer. 'Please, Lena, I love you. This doesn't change anything.'

He was not telling the truth, but I think that I realised enough to know that he believed his lies. If he'd honestly loved me, he would have married me long ago, long before it came to this. No, I was not free, but this could have changed, should have changed.

Even here at the Cape, there were men who'd freed and married their slaves. It was his decision, always his decision. I was so tired of this life where every big decision about me was made by someone else. What I wanted for my child, wished for her, even though it was probably too late, was that one day she would have a life in which she could decide for herself.

Before much time had passed, the household was preparing for a wedding. I had to wonder how far in advance the plans had been when he'd first told me the news, but I refused to dwell. With a week to go, his sisters visited every day, supervising the cleaning of the house from top to bottom and muttering about the lack of standards in a home where there was no woman to order things.

'But that's all about to change,' the younger one, Johanna was her name, said. She looked at me and smiled, but it was a false smile.

I was once more reminded how I had never liked those girls, who were now no longer misses, but mothers with a clutch of fair-haired children between them, children who ran amok in the house and made our tasks harder.

I cleaned diligently, careful not to draw any attention to myself, though of course they knew who I was. My daughter, fair-haired too, played with their children and it was nice to see how all the children played together like that, but then she was such a sweet child, my daughter, so pretty. She drew people to her, even if they could not abide her mother. The older sister brought her clothes her daughters had outgrown. I tried to ignore the burning feeling that rose from my belly to my chest, wishing that my daughter had new clothes to wear. She was always so excited about the dresses, even if they were sometimes a little tight. But it didn't really matter that much because she was small and slender like me.

If I'd entertained any hopes of escaping a role in this palaver, I was mistaken. The morning of the wedding, his sisters insisted upon decorating the room for the night. He had risen early, dressed in his wedding clothes: a pale-blue jacket with embroidery, tight trousers of a darker blue, shined shoes. His leaving allowed the women the space to do their best. Armed with tiny pink roses, they came full of excitement and good intentions, but simmering beneath it all was spite, I think. Spite aimed at me.

There were others who could have assisted with the preparation of the room, but the sisters must have considered it an exquisite torture for one such as myself. I never could understand this compulsion that drove some people to be unnecessarily cruel. I never knew what it was about me they felt wronged them so. Well-raised young misses that they'd been when they still lived there, they'd pretended not to notice where their brother spent his nights, or I mine. During the day, they'd make sure to remind me of my place, sniping at me like cats. Only one time had either of his sisters shown me any kindness and that was the day my son was born. She, the older one, had insisted on calling the surgeon, but only once the child was born. By the time he came, it was too late. I still don't know if I was grieved or relieved that he had not lived, for how can a mother take comfort in such a thing? I refused to think about such things and instead focused on the task at hand.

All the furniture had been moved out of the room, even the

old woollen mat from the East that had always been there. Someone handed me a broom and then rags to wash the floor once the sweeping was done. Even though the room had been swept days before, there was so much dust where the mat had always sat. It was my own fault; I should never have let the dust get so thick. Once the floor was dried, two men brought in a new carpet and unrolled it under the sisters' instructions. 'This carpet will trap the dust; I'll need to use a hard broom to keep it clean,' I remember thinking, until I realised that cleaning the room would be at the discretion of the new lady of the house. I'd have to earn her trust and any other privileges. Maybe she'd bring her own people with her and all of that wouldn't matter. Not that it mattered to me; I'd always preferred working in the kitchen anyway.

The heavy bed I knew so well was the first item of furniture brought back inside. I rubbed a soft cloth dipped in beeswax over its carved lines before buffing it to a shine. One of the sisters brought in fresh bedclothes and instructed me to dress the bed. As I smoothed the white sheets, the younger one stepped closer to inspect.

'We should have made him buy a new bed,' she said.

The other sister coughed, but other than that did not acknowledge her sister's comment. I concentrated on placing the lavender-scented slips over the pillows; lavender for sweet dreams.

Once the rest of the furniture was put back in, then arranged and rearranged in various combinations, the real decoration of the room began: the stupid tinsel, the leaves and flowers that turned it into a bridal bower. The smell of the roses was overpowering. I would have left a window open but for the rain. Strange things always happened when it rained while the sun was shining.

The sisters left, the groom returned, hesitated at the front door and then he too left, this time for his wedding that was to be held in the big church down the road. I washed my hands; my nails had been bleached white by the lemons I'd used to clean. I scrubbed and scrubbed my hands, but I could not get rid of the lemon smell. Nor could I escape the sweet, rotting smell of the roses that had taken over the house, spilling out of silver bowls and glass vases.

I thought of offering Barbetje help in the kitchen – we'd been getting along better these past few days – but thought she'd understand that I needed to be left alone. In the rain, my feet led me to the church, but I did not linger, not even to visit with the other slaves who gossiped under the trees there in good weather or bad. 'What if you just walk?' I wondered aloud. 'What if you just carry on walking and see what happens?' I was not afraid of the consequences; I was not afraid of getting caught, but I knew I would not leave. I needed to return to my daughter. She'd be worried about where I was.

For weeks, he'd been training her. 'Call me "master".'

He pretended it was a new game they played, their secret, but she would only call him 'mijneer' or 'mister'. 'My mijneer, my mister,' she'd said, possessively, confident. He bent down to her level to let her know from his face that he was serious.

'Master!'

She tugged at his thick beard, yellow like the hair on his head, but reddish too, like rust.

'Ouch!' he laughed, before leaning forward to tickle her.

She, the instigator, laughed loudest: the deep, unaffected laughter of a child.

I had to stop myself from laughing too, as once I might have, before.

There was a carnival atmosphere at the house when I returned. All the work had been finished and the groom would only return much later with his bride. Men and women lolled about under the shelter of trees; others sang and danced, oblivious to the rain. Above the sounds of merriment, I heard the bells ringing from the church and imagined them making their way to their wedding feast. Nodding at the revellers outside, I watched my daughter as she played with the other children.

'For her I can survive anything,' I promised myself.

She will cast bad looks on her husband as she enters …

I remembered my promise when the time came to welcome the bridal pair home. They were late, much later than we'd expected; a boy had come with a message hours before. I was glad that my child was asleep by the time they arrived. Mistakes would have been unbearable, chastisement worse. Changed into our best outfits, our hair neatened and faces clean, we lined up to welcome the bride to her new home. He ushered her down the line, a hand placed firmly on the small of her back. I could see she was a skittish thing, young and nervous. Her eyes swept over ours, and she made pleasant comments, but she shook no hands and her lips were firm, showing me then that she was tougher than she seemed to be. With her husband, she was all small smiles and nervous laughter. 'She'll be smarter than she appears,' I warned myself.

So they drifted into the house, Barbetje following, eager to make herself indispensable. Maybe I was just being mean. After all, Barbetje was indispensable if I had to think about it. Most of us began to take our leave. Bedtime would be hours away; there'd still be lots of celebrations to get through until the last wine was drunk and the last song sung. I did not want to join in the party. I'd never been one for drinking or carousing, and in any case, I was an inside girl. I hadn't mixed much with the outside people. But that night I knew I would forsake my comfortable bed inside the house. My daughter was already asleep on our bed and for a moment I considered leaving her there. Barbetje could look after her for once, but after seeing her lying there so innocently, so vulnerable, I decided to carry her outside with me. Someone would give us a mat. I was certain of it.

They remained in the bedroom until late the next morning; the coffee had already turned bitter, and I knew how that man used to complain if the coffee stewed for too long. Knowing his peculiarities, Barbetje had begun to fret about whether or not she was expected to take in breakfast on a tray. 'But no one said anything about it last night,' she reasoned.

'If he wanted a tray, he'd have told you,' I said.

That morning, for the first time in days, his sisters stayed away. At least there was a mercy in that. I did not think I could handle their gleeful, shiny faces that morning. Especially when I knew that I would at some time or later have to face the new lady of the house again.

Eventually, they exited the bedroom. I waited in the kitchen. A part of me thought that perhaps he had hoped to avoid me by staying in bed so late, but no, that man was too arrogant to consider how I would feel. I wasn't even sure what I felt. Not jealousy, though I confess I felt displaced. Overnight, mine and my child's position in his household had become precarious, uncertain. My nerves are for my child; that is what I told myself.

I was washing the breakfast dishes when they came in. She was clasping his hand as if for courage. I made sure to assume the appropriate demeanour: friendly, but not too friendly, servile but not overly so. Still, I gave my curiosity free rein. I studied her features: her small eyes the colour of glass, her straw-coloured hair, pink cheeks, pink lips; the button of her nose. She was as tiny and delicate as a doll; I conceded she was pretty, if ordinary. I took note of her lowered lashes, the blush on her cheeks and the softness in her eyes. She looked happy, secure. She greeted Barbetje with familiarity.

Then she smiled and addressed me: 'And what's your name, girl?'

'Lena, Mewrouw,' I answered clearly; I would not be cowed.

'And how long have you been here, Lena?'

I shrugged.

'Lena's been with us for more than ten years, now,' he answered for me. 'She was here during my father's time.'

'And how do you like it here?'

'It's good, Mewrouw, it's a very good house.'

'This man is not a good man,' I wanted to warn her instead. 'His word is not to be trusted. He thinks if he can say he inherited all of us from his father, that's an excuse. But there were others. Those he bought and those he sold. One day, maybe, he'll sell my daughter and me too. Because he can. Because you're here now ...' I did not say any of these things. Not with him standing there, watching me in that careful way of his. She would not have believed me anyway. I saw that.

Seeming satisfied with my answers, she returned her attentions to Barbetje, who'd begun to set out the breakfast dishes before them.

She will soon know what kind of man she has married, I thought. I waited until they began eating before I excused myself from the room.

In the days that followed, I watched her; I watched him. She began to settle in, began to become a bit more comfortable than when she'd first arrived and had reminded me of nothing more than a white mouse with her fair hair, her tiny teeth and eyes so pale they were rimmed with red. Her family visited often and her friends, especially his younger sister, who was there constantly, taking over the house with her opinions, her comments and complaints. I saw how she was instructing the bride on how to run the house in which she had been raised. I wondered whether she'd told her about the old man's spirit that walked the house at night. Was that why Barbetje roamed too? Were they trying to find each other in the wide, dark halls of the house at night? Sometimes I thought that she was haunting the old man as much as he was haunting the house. Maybe the old man's ghost rested easily and it was just another story that people in the house told. No, the sister would not have mentioned it to her friend.

This is what I noticed about Mewrouw in those first days: she had many dresses and seldom wore the same outfit more than once in one week; her shoes, of which she had several pairs, were made of the softest leather, but she preferred wearing slippers inside the house. She favoured tea over coffee and would sometimes have a *sopie* of wine after breakfast; she asked many questions, but had a habit of wincing before you could reply as if she was afraid of the answer; she stared at my daughter a lot, also as if asking a question that she did not want answered. 'She's a beautiful child,' she'd say instead, 'and so well-spoken.' This was true. I'd nod and thank her.

After that first night, I returned to my and my daughter's little bedroom in the house. The outside quarters, though not crowded, were too confining with the intimacies people looking for a little solace shared. It made me want to seek solace of my own, but I knew there was danger in that.

'I will not share you, Lena,' he'd once said, and even though I was not looking to be shared at the time, let alone thinking such thoughts, the one warning had been enough.

He did not come to my room at night. I was glad. Barbetje continued to roam. Sometimes I thought I heard the old man's heavy tread marching down the passage. The summer nights were too hot and the mosquitoes kept us all awake.

Weeks passed, we celebrated the passing of the old year and the coming of the new. For one whole day, we enjoyed what felt almost like freedom, but even with our new clothes, the feeling didn't last. In February, they left for his wine farm in Stellenbosch. It was believed that her family owned several large properties there and were big wine contractors, just as he was with meat. With them gone, I experienced a greater taste of freedom. Before, my daughter, several members of the Cape household and I used to accompany him on his journeys. I welcomed staying behind this time. Things were different far from Town. Masters and their wives had very strict ideas about how those such as I should be treated. I was certain they spoke about us too, me and him and my light-skinned daughter.

Though it was the hottest month of the year, as it always is, February was a good month. February was also the shortest month, over too soon.

It started, as it had begun, with little touches: a heavy hand on the back of my neck, a squeeze of my shoulder, a finger lightly brushing my cheek. Before March had ended, those hands had made their way down again. They strayed, a reminder of the power he had over me, but they did not delve. There were days when I was confused as to how I felt about those hands, days when I wasn't sure whether I wanted to welcome them or push them away. I did neither, transporting myself to that place in my head where I had to make no such choices.

Ever since she'd arrived, the large house had felt smaller. There were no shadowy corners in which to hide, no unused cupboards, no empty rooms. And my room was no longer my own, since we were kept busy during the day and locked in at night. 'It is safer this way,' she said with a shy smile. 'We've all heard about the bad things that are happening in Town.'

Outside was the same story; outside was where we all watched each other, saw each other, knew each other's business. Outside where there were no secrets. I can't explain my yearning for secrets, or even what secrets exactly I was looking for. It wasn't another man. Perhaps I wanted something that was all my own.

His house, he knew it well; he knew all its secret spaces and he demanded his secrets be kept. No one had ever had any choice in the matter. In time she would learn that she too would yield to his will, but for now he appeared the devoted husband. His hands teased, taunted. He stalked me in quiet, dark corners, but no more than that. It was merely a reminder, a taste.

Soon, the reason for his devotion became clear. It was clear in the way she rubbed her belly indulgently, wistfully. Barbetje busied herself carrying in trays and tisanes while Mewrouw lay abed.

'These women are not like you or me,' Barbetje grumbled under her breath.

I nodded, distracted.

I knew he was biding his time.

I cannot stay away from you, Lena.

I knew that.

While Mewrouw was keeping her strength up in bed, there was one less pair of eyes to keep watch. There were always eyes watching. She had visitors constantly. Intimate visitors she allowed into her bedroom; the rest she indulged in her small parlour, decorated to her taste in pinks and blues and with silly pictures on the walls – shepherdesses, pink, round-faced children, flowers. On calling days, Barbetje and I were kept busy, bearing tea and cakes between the kitchen and the rooms. Eyes looked to find fault. Eyes peered for traces of defiance. I held my head up high, but not too high. I had no cause to attract attention to myself, but I should have been more circumspect.

'Be careful,' Barbetje warned me one day. 'People are telling her you wish her harm. There's been bleeding. They're worried about the child.'

I would never wish ill on an innocent person, and who was there more innocent than a child? I knew of the men and women in Town one could go to for spells and charms, but that sort of thing had never interested me. Long ago, Lilisa had taught me: 'Whatever harm you wish on another will come back to you.' And, 'To call evil upon another is to call evil upon yourself.'

After that, I saw how she watched me, how her eyes followed my every move. She had not yet schooled her face to hide her feelings. I saw her fear and it made me afraid. I saw how her fear would work against me, and against my child. I wondered who had told her that I was someone for whom she should watch out.

I was not that dangerous.

'I do not want this man,' I wanted to explain, 'I never chose him for myself. I had no choice.' Yet I said nothing; it was easier for her to see me as her enemy. It may have been that to her I was that dangerous, even if I had no power of my own. I wanted to tell her that she had all the power I desired and that she should use it wisely. She was not a bad woman. It would have been easy not to hate her if she was not herself and I was not me.

Marriage is an imperative … Do not loosen the ties of marriage …

'Family is foremost to me, Lena.' He'd always said this in the days when the words meant something else.

I knew he wanted a son, an heir, someone to carry his name

and continue his works, just as he had done for his father. Those things were important to him, but his eyes and his hands told me that he wanted me too.

Geert, 1796

From the beginning, ours was a docile union. My wife endeavoured to please me, and I aimed to be a dutiful husband. The only spot of blight during that first summer was the other woman whom, for so many years, I'd regarded as my wife in everything but name. I had tried to make her see my reasons for marrying someone of Magda's stature. I know this. I can't rightly recall whether I'd made her, Lena, any promises in the past, but who can award currency to words spoken in the frenzy of lust or the satiated murmurs of a mortal man? While I'd made no mention of discontinuing our liaison once I married, in those days and weeks after entering into the bonds of matrimony, by my behaviour, I allowed Lena to understand that I was of a mind to honour the vows I'd made to myself on the night of my wedding.

Lena might have captured my heart at one time, but my wife was an easier woman to abide with comfortably. Magda was more biddable, with a sweeter temperament than she. We had much in common, Magda and I, coming from similar backgrounds and having both been born and raised at the Cape. Our world was the known world.

As I'd anticipated, Magda brought to our marriage a sizeable dowry. This dowry saved my home, as well as the remaining properties, my businesses, and righted the reversal of my fortune. Our marriage enhanced my standing at the Cape. No longer was I regarded in some quarters as a feckless man with a felicitous inheritance. As a married man, a husband, I was seen as a man in my own right, a man building a legacy of his own. Certain of my indiscretions which had denied me access into the strictest echelons of Cape society were no longer deemed relevant and were instead bantered about, if alluded to at all.

My wife's family was large, loyal and held fast to the adage that charity begins at home. Indeed, with their connections, I was able to restructure my meat business into more profitable avenues, such as exporting salted beef to the Mascarene Islands, and began experimenting with breeding merino sheep for their wool.

A few months after the wedding, Magda and I departed the Cape for Stellenbosch, and my father-in-law, who had his own extensive wine farm nearby, visited often, 'to check up on the happy pair', as he expressed it, and to advise me on wisdoms and innovations with regard to viticulture and oenology. Similar to my late father, despite his numerous farms, my father-in-law's true wealth stemmed not from husbandry but from successful bidding for the Cape wine and brandy *pachten*, auctioned by the Company each year, not every five as with the meat *pacht*. Magda's father spoke about helping me acquire a share in one of the lucrative alcohol *pachten* when they were put on the block later in the year. I felt accepted and optimistic about my marriage, even if I at times found myself longing for another: her comforting familiarity, her silent acquiescence in the dark.

After this brief sojourn, Magda and I returned to the Cape. We were not back long when an American ship sailing via Amsterdam brought the grave news that the French king had been tried and found guilty of crimes against the people of the newly established Republic of France.

'Sentenced to death by guillotine.'

'And they gave him less than one day to make peace with his fate.'

'Give the king his due, he showed great courage as he approached the scaffold.'

'Courage not expected from Louis 'til then.'

'No, he was arrogant to the last,' another of the sailors interjected.

'You saw this with your own eyes?' I asked.

'Not exactly, no,' he replied.

'But we have it on good authority,' insisted the sailor who'd spoken first.

By means of probing, I learned that none of the sailors had been in Paris at the time of Louis XVI's execution and had all heard these accounts from other parties. Gleefully, they concurred on the detail that the king's severed head had been held up for everyone to see.

Some said that a silence had reigned over that cold, Parisian square named for one of Louis's ancestors; others said that the crowd had rejoiced upon the sight of that decapitated head: 'Hats were hoisted into the air to the riotous refrain of *Vive la Republique!*'

Over the years, though I'd become increasingly republican in my way of thinking, I admit to being nauseated by the purported violence of the king's death.

Within days of his execution, France declared war against England and its ally, the United Provinces. 'This, despite the lily-livered Dutch government's great care not to antagonise the revolutionaries in France,' the sailors embellished.

At the Cape we'd already heard of the French revolutionists' promise to assist with the liberation of any oppressed peoples. We'd known too that the new regime had enjoyed several military gains, including stalling an invasion at Valmy and successfully annexing the Austrian Netherlands. The Dutch rulers had therefore stinted on offering any great support to aristocrats fleeing France and had gone as far as seeking friendly relations with Republican France. These measures were in vain. According to the American captain himself, the French had based their decision on the fact that the *stadtholder* was subservient to the British and Prussian courts.

Far from this theatre of action, Cape burghers knew that after the Patriots' triumph in Holland, the *stadtholder*'s return to power could solely be attributed to English diplomacy and Prussian might. Consequently, the Dutch Republic was a republic in name only, reliant on foreign powers for internal and external stability and governed by an unpopular and weak heredity ruler.

Many of us had for some time wondered how long the *stadtholder*'s restored rule would last. We appreciated that the stability of the Dutch Republic affected all of us, from the gluttonous share-holders in Holland and other provinces to the citizens of the humblest factory under the Company's control. The *stadtholder* was the head of the Company, after all. Thus, we devoured news when we received it, and the passing ships derived great profit and pleasure from our desire for knowledge.

A mere two months into our marriage, a red-faced but jubilant Magda told me that we were in 'expectation of an interesting event', as she termed it. My pride was boundless. 'Expectation' was a fitting word to describe how I felt those days, as if I were poised on the cusp of promising prospects.

In the first months of my marriage, I felt ever optimistic. The commissioners-general sent to investigate matters at the Cape had announced a number of concessions to sweeten the pain of their straitening measures. Most importantly, we burgh-ers were given the right to trade freely with foreign ships and could now purchase surplus produce once the Company's ini-tial orders had been fulfilled – at fixed prices of course, but it was an improvement nevertheless. Additionally, those so in-clined were granted the right to outfit ships in order to ply the lucrative routes between the Colony and the East, a crucial concession. With the events in Europe, fewer and fewer ships passed this way, and we were facing shortages of goods we had once taken for granted.

With the assistance of my father-in-law, I expanded the wine farm at Stellenbosch and began exporting the surplus vintage to Batavia, where it gained no small amount of favour. I was unsuccessful in acquiring the wine and brandy *pachten* on which I'd bid, but there would be further opportunities to do so in future years. I joined my brothers-in-law in investing in a small importing business that entailed bringing in manufactured goods from Europe and selling them for a small profit at home. Despite entrenched competition from the existing import firms established by Company men before the changes had been introduced, our venture surprised me with healthy returns almost immediately. My purse fattened and I looked forward to my seven years of fat after suffering through my lean years.

Magda grew fat too, her body swollen with my child. I engaged builders to resume the alterations to my Cape home initiated years earlier, and which had been stalled when my money troubles had first begun. We would require more room in the house once the children came. I continued to maintain a distance between my old life and the new. Granted, I was being unfair, but there is a difference between a child who carries your name and one who does not. I wished it were not so; I wished I'd felt differently. Feelings of guilt never sat well with me, so I tamped them down. On the days when they persisted, I reminded myself that, throughout this period, I had remained faithful to my marriage vows, and to the decision I'd made on the night of my wedding.

'You're a good man, Geert,' Magda assured me. 'You'll make a good father.'

I told myself I was pleased, that my life had never been better.

This I told myself until the day Magda lost our baby. It's odd that, despite what had happened with Lena's first two pregnancies, I had thought her birthing troubles an aberration. Rationally, I knew all too well the dangers and difficulties attendant with bringing a child into the world, but in my ignorance or pride I'd assumed that my legitimate offspring would come naturally and without fuss. A perverse part of me believed that this was because with any children created between my wife and myself there would be no mixing of the blood, no taint on a child born out of the bonds of marriage. The church – and science – has much to answer for, I know.

Unlike Lena's, Magda's loss was without drama or fuss. It occurred early in the pregnancy, a lump of tissue, bleeding when there should have been none. I was spared the image of a fully formed but lifeless infant, or of one who didn't draw breath for long. There was a mercy in that, for Magda too, especially for her. Days afterward, I recall her stoicism, her pitiful smile as I murmured the words by rote: 'There'll be other children.' Hollow words, but ones I had no reason to doubt. There would be more children; there'd been before.

Other children, yes, another child, there'd been another child, and I'd felt everything a father should that day. Her birth had been a relief, a vindication of sorts when I'd not known I'd been seeking absolution. *The sins of the father* ... When had I become so fatalistic? Doubts persisted in the tenebrous hours of night, and I could find no way to clear them or escape their snare other than to wait for the dawn. On more than one occasion, I'd wondered whether the child's failure to thrive was payment exacted for my own sin. Now I did not have to wonder: I had denied my own child, *flesh of my flesh, before the cock crowed thrice* … I am no better than Judas.

While I had set Lena aside safe in the assumption that to do so was the correct course, the narrow and winding way, I could not say the same about her child. The girl had long been the joy of my household, holding everyone in her thrall with her kindness and beaming smile, her insouciance that I encouraged, I confess. I cared for her in my fashion, but I did not feel for her as a father should. Had she carried my name, perhaps I would have thought of her more as a daughter than a winsome child who happened to live in my home.

I lie. There were days that she was the dearest thing to me, and I denied her. I cast her aside as the mistake of my youth, except I had been a grown man when she'd been bred and birthed. I could not action the excuse of immaturity.

I could have insisted she be baptised. I could have offered her the protection of my name. I could have claimed her, claimed her even if I were unwilling to claim her mother. At this no one would have looked askance; though not common, it was not unheard of for a Christian man at the Cape to sponsor the baptism of fair-skinned infants born to favoured slaves. Several men of my distant acquaintance had gone as far as legitimising their natural children and marrying their mothers even if it meant being ostracised by the more genteel members of Cape society.

At one time I believed I might have considered such a course, but prudence, and then circumstance, had prevented those flights of fancy from growing wings. It was only afterwards, in the months it had taken a child to root in Magda's belly, and after that, when it became dislodged, that I entertained the question: would I have cleared a way had Lissie been born a boy-child? In the mornings, I excused my nocturnal musings as the natural anxieties of a man worried about the continuation of his line. And there was no need to worry, I reminded myself.

At this stage, I believed that Magda was still unknowing of Lena's child. Though she'd been aware of my so-called 'proclivities', my wife had neither name nor face to put to my liaison, nor could she possibly know the finer details.

I was mistaken. Women talk.

I, however, found myself distracted by the drought of 1793 – raging in the eastern parts of the Colony, it made grazing even dearer. Having learned my lesson regarding the district's value, I now sourced most of my mutton and beef from Graaff-Reinet, and as such, paid close attention to the politics there. In addition, I installed a new overseer and built up my herds in Swellendam. I had considered consolidating my livestock on one large farm in Graaff-Reinet, but the area was volatile and unsettled, a place where heathen and Christian still jostled for land and cattle. I had just begun to rebuild my fortune after my marriage and did not want to risk further losses in an area where stock theft was commonplace. Visitors to the Cape told alarming tales of heathen marauders roaming in bands of ten or twelve looking for mischief and ignoring genial advice to respect the boundaries and property of others.

Then rumours began to swirl that certain burghers in the district were embarking on their own incursions for cattle, though no names were given. Nor was the aggression one-sided. Arming themselves with guns and ammunition procured from absconding Hottentots, several of the heathen tribesmen became increasingly belligerent, demanding tributes from Christian farmers, raiding farms and threatening violence against those who dared deny them succour. The longer the drought lasted, the more convinced I became that the smallest spark could cause the tensions between heathen and Christian to ignite there.

When the unpopular district secretary, Honoratus Maynier, was provisionally appointed as *landdrost*, matters deteriorated even further. Barend Lindeque, a Zuurveld burgher, preferred to join forces with a heathen chief, one Ndlambe, rather than rely on the Company and its officials to drive marauding clans from the region. Though this coalition was but of short duration, Lindeque and Ndlambe's men attacked a heathen kraal, dividing the spoils of eight hundred head of cattle between them.

Within days, reprisals of great savagery ensued: bolstered by comrades from further afield, the heathens exacted their revenge on the hapless inhabitants of the Zuurveld. Scores of homesteads were torched and men, both Christian and Hottentot, were executed. Only the women and children were spared, though as always in war, there were exceptions that proved the rule. An estimated sixty thousand cattle, ten thousand sheep and two hundred horses were taken as booty, dwarfing the eight hundred horses captured by Lindeque and his cronies by many multiples.

I did not know what to make of the matter. My allegiance

to the Company had always been tenuous, though symbiotic. I deplored Lindeque and his ilk for resorting to their own justice, but it was a frontier kind of justice, and one that we had come to expect from burghers living in such combustive conditions, far away from the civilising influence of Town. A different set of rules prevailed there, with or without the Company and its courts.

While I, along with most Christian men at the Cape, lamented the bloodshed and the concomitant loss of farms and cattle, certain townsmen, particularly those of us in the meat trade, could not desist from speculating how very wondrous it was that the frontier farmers had contrived to lose more cattle than they'd claimed to own at the time of the census.

My father-in-law had become increasingly belligerent against the Company and its laws, and as such, sided with the burgers of Graaff-Reinet. Yet, while I regarded myself as a progressively minded thinker, I was not wholly unsympathetic to the Company's problems with the Graaff-Reinet burghers. I too had my own problems with these good burghers.

Due to the instability of the farther regions and various other practicalities, my agents sent to buy cattle from farmers in the stock-farming areas outside of the Cape did not pay for purchases in coin but in promissory notes redeemable in Town. All the other *pachter*s and butchers followed this practice. There'd been no problems in the past, but now farmers were refusing to sell meat to my men for paper money, claiming that the notes were too easily forged and myriad other excuses. I was not the only *pachter* to be affected, though I wondered whether my straitened circumstances of the previous years had influenced this decision. And despite my fortunes improving due to my marriage and family connections, I could no longer afford to be complacent as far as business was concerned.

During the previous year, the Company had declared itself unable to pay its outstanding debts, an action long-anticipated. To maintain appearances, in recent years the Company's directors had continued to vote for the payment of plump dividends to their shareholders – financed out of the Company's capital. Riddled with debt due to such excesses, the Company was forced to look to the state for assistance. Huge loans were made, with the Dutch government offering guarantees for a portion of the debt, but given the ruinous war with the English and the many concessions to which the Company had been forced to agree, informed men believed the Company would be unable to reverse its decline. My father had always quoted his own father as having said that, 'It pays to be aware of the winds and the tides.' This time, I promised myself, I would not be caught unprepared.

Partway into 1795, news reached us that the French army had entered the United Provinces and captured town after town, with little resistance, until eventually reaching Amsterdam in the January. The *stadtholder* fled once more – to England this time. American sailors who brought the news said that, as in America and France, Dutch citizens were attracted to the idea of the sovereignty of the people and the abolition of heredity rights and privileges. They told of how ordinary burghers had welcomed the dissolution of the old regime, greeting the French troops as liberators, planting boldly painted trees of liberty in public squares and donning caps of liberty as they sought their own sense of *liberté*, *fraternité* and *egalité*.

Whether one had called it the Dutch Republic, the United Provinces or the United Netherlands, the country was no more. Renamed the Batavian Republic, the new nation was autonomous, but in name only – coerced by France into agreeing to a number of military and economic conditions. We only discovered the full details regarding these later.

The primary consequence of this treaty was renewed enmity with the English navy, which blockaded the coast and halted all commercial shipping around the waters of the former United Provinces. Prior to the arrival of the first ships of the year, we had but an inkling of what was taking place there. A Swedish ship that arrived in November of the previous year had brought rumours regarding the fall of Nijmegen, but this remained unconfirmed until the April arrival of the Dutch frigate *Medenblik*.

Captain Dekker, the frigate's commander, informed the council that the French had been holding Breda to siege by the time he'd set sail and that the French had looked likely to cross further into the Republic. No further news was heard until early June, when word reached the Castle that a fleet flying without flags was steaming into False Bay.

These we soon learned were British warships, under the command of a vice-admiral and accompanied by a detachment of troops. According to the English commanders, they possessed a letter penned by the Prince of Orange, the *stadtholder* himself, instructing Commissioner Sluysken to allow the ships entry into the ports and the troops billet at the forts. This, they said, was to prevent a French invasion. We were to regard them as allies. I appreciated the irony that the situation was much like ten years ago, when the French had come to our aid to protect the Cape from the English. Alliances were reconfiguring in Europe, but we had only the Englishmen's word for it, since they made every effort to withhold newspapers and mail from the Company's officials and ordinary citizens alike.

In letters delivered to Commissioner Sluysken, the English commanders reported that, though Dutch forces had capitulated to the French and the *stadtholder* had been forced to flee, Great Britain and her allies would again muster in the Republic's defence and oust the interlopers. What they neglected to mention was how Dutch patriots had welcomed the French; nor was there the slightest intimation that the office of the *stadtholder* had been abolished in favour of a more Republican government. This, too, we discovered later.

The English hoped that we would construe them as protectors, upholders of the Company and the old ways. But as the events in Graaff-Reinet had shown, many citizens were ready to shirk off the Company's reins as we sought our own independence in our affairs. A few months before the arrival of the British warships, Graaff-Reinet rebels had refused to swear fealty to the Company, promising allegiance to the States-General instead. In June, burghers in Swellendam had followed this example, divesting their *landdrost* and other court officials of their positions. And at the Cape, the Patriot movement was growing, drawing new recruits from the rank and file of the Company's servants – not only menials but those holding high office too.

For two weeks, a diplomatic stalemate existed between the English and Sluysken and his council. Then, a ship flying the American standard, but originating in Amsterdam, arrived in Simon's Bay. The purpose of its journey, we learned, was to convey official messages to the Cape and Batavia. Suspecting such motives, the English commandeered the ship's mail and newspapers. But one newspaper found its way into the hands of a Cape burgher and there, published for all to see, was a notice signed by the States-General abnegating allegiance to the Prince of Orange and stating the amity that existed between the citizens of the French and Batavian Republics.

With this new intelligence in hand, Commissioner Sluysken and the council resolved that under no circumstances would the Colony be relinquished to the English usurpers. Via a series of intrigues, word was sent to Batavia to inform the authorities of the developments in Europe – the council hoped to wait out the English until such time that Dutch or French reinforcements arrived to defend the Colony. As soon as information of the English commanders' perfidy infiltrated the Colony, burghers who had at times been antagonistic towards the Company and its officials began to muster to protect our land. I too declared myself willing to take up arms in the nation's defence and was encouraged in this by Magda and her family.

Along with Magda's two brothers, Justus and Septimus, I joined the camp at Muizenberg, where we waited for a salvo to be fired that would break the tedious deadlock between ourselves and the English. Finally, during the first week of August, English ships began bombarding our camp. At the same time, troops under General Craig marched from Simon's

Town, forcing our limping legion to abandon post, since the two twenty-four-pounders mounted there were inadequate to answer the English long nines and carronades.

Pandemonium reigned as our various companies sought their escape. As soon as we were safely out of range, our burgher cavalry and sundry members of the infantry attempted to make a stand, but we were no opposition for the English troops advancing by land. The infantry brigade under Colonel De Lille was the first to flee. The defence of the Colony was left largely in the hands of burghers and the Hottentot Pandour corps. Together we checked the advance of the English columns near Muizenberg and once more settled into stalemate.

Tempers frayed within the confines of our camp. Justus, Septimus and I were likewise divided. Septimus, who lived in Stellenbosch, was strongly influenced by the stories percolating in Town of heathens, slaves and Hottentots – as close by as Stellenbosch and the Drakenstein – making mischief while the men were away.

'It's my family, what can I do?' Septimus asked Justus and me. Since we both called Town home, we had no rebuttal when he joined the growing number of men who packed up and returned to their farms due to these rumours.

Even Justus, who'd argued loudly against his brother's decision at first, was forced to concede. 'Men are naturally more inclined to protect their own homes and families than they are to protect a detested government.'

The Company attempted to bolster its Hottentot corps, but met with limited success. The existing Pandour troops were no more loyal, threatening mutiny due to poor pay, the declining welfare of their families back home and inadequate liquor rations. Even Commissioner Sluysken's offer to raise their pay and increase their wine and spirit rations had little effect.

By the time the vaunted English reinforcements arrived from India, there remained fewer than two thousand men to defend the Colony. The five thousand or so Englishmen marching two abreast from Muizenberg to the Cape fully overwhelmed us. For the most part, however, burghers are men of honour, and on the final day of battle our numbers were swelled by many members of the burgher cavalries who'd regrouped upon hearing of the renewed crisis, Septimus among them.

Perhaps our valour would have triumphed over the greater numbers. I like to think so. Yet valour cannot compensate for poor military strategy and direction. Overriding the concerns of a few battle-hardened officers, Major van Baalen, the officer in charge of the camp, martialled his forces in a haphazard fashion and insisted that the cannon be placed in a less than optimal position. His most reprehensible act, however, was to abscond with the largest part of the national battalion once the English came into range. Together with its more stalwart members, we burghers cobbled together a defence until we were forced to retreat, lest we be taken as prisoners of war.

In the hours that followed, Commissioner Sluysken agreed to the terms of our surrender. All the Company's holdings in our land passed to the British Crown and not to the Prince of Orange, as we'd been led to believe would happen. As for burghers, our property rights and religion were to be respected and no new taxes levied in terms of the truce. I, always so eager to see history in the making, was loath to witness the changing of the guard. For one hundred and forty-three years the Company had governed the Cape, and despite my latent hostility to the organisation and the way it had treated its burghers, I noted its usurpation with no small degree of sadness and regret.

'Send them away, Geert.'

Magda did not have to name them; I knew to whom she was referring. It was becoming an old argument between the two of us.

'I have never been one of those owners who threaten to sell my people, Magda. You know that. Some of them are like family.'

'Like family?' she spat.

'Barbetje, Titus – they were with my family before I was born.' I tried to deflect Magda's rage. She appeared fond of Barbetje in her way.

'But it's not Barbetje or Titus we're talking about, is it Geert? As long as that child lives in my home, you will never have a son to continue your name.'

'Is that a threat, Magda?'

'No, Geert, it's a promise. A promise on blood. My blood. And yours. I will not be humiliated any longer. I will not be cursed, as I am every day, by her presence.'

'What do you mean?' I asked, although I knew there was no reasoning with her when she was in this state of mind. Magda believed that hers was the side of righteousness. 'Are you telling me you will no longer lie with me? You are my wife, Magda, joined to me by the Lord. What can you do, return to your father's home?'

Magda snorted. 'Yes, bring the Lord into this matter, Geert.

How like you to do so! You may lie with me all you want, Geert, but your seed will not take root. I will do my duty, I will never give you cause to doubt my fidelity to this marriage; I will never give you reason to repudiate me, if that is your intent. I am merely telling you that as long as that girl remains in our home, there will be neither son nor daughter to carry your name.'

'Dare you curse me? Do you realise you curse yourself? Be careful of the words you speak with your tongue, Magda,' I warned her. 'You are talking of evil things.'

'Evil? Do not talk to me of evil! Not when that *meid* is a curse on me. She is what is evil, that abomination of a *meid*.'

Lissie had never before been called *meid*. Her name had been a mark of favour. By naming her after my mother, I had set her apart, and that, along with her light complexion and green eyes, made her an easy target for Magda's jealousy and vitriol. I know I should have sent them both away years ago, Lissie and her mother, but I was weak. My daughter was not her first target, but as a weapon, she was the most effective stratagem for a woman bemoaning her childlessness.

Interpreting my silence as capitulation, Magda continued, repeating her theme. 'That child is a curse on me, a curse to me; a constant reminder of your faithlessness.'

'It was long ago, Magda. Before we married.' I tried to defend myself. 'I have never dishonoured my vows.'

'Vows, what vows?' Magda demanded. 'I was nothing more than an expedience, our marriage an arrangement.'

'You can't say that,' I argued. 'I learned to love you. You cannot fault me on that.'

'Love, bah! You did not even carry me over the threshold

when I first came here,' Magda accused. 'You were more interested in soothing that … that harlot's feelings.'

'No, Magda, you're wrong—'

'No, *you're* wrong,' Magda said. 'And love? You dare talk about love? Does she love you, Geert? No, don't answer, I already know.' Magda laughed, a hoarse cackle that brought to mind the witches in the stories that Barbetje had told my sisters and me when we were little. 'All this for a woman who flinches at the sight of you … Don't worry, Geert. I see every sly pinch, I feel it. Each time she recoils at your touch, I recoil too. Perhaps we have much in common, she and I.'

I had tried to stay away from Lena, but I could not. I tried to be a good husband, yet I was not.

'This is not about her.' I tried to calm Magda. 'She means nothing to me. Less than nothing; you know that.'

'I don't know which is worse, the mother or the child …' Magda admitted. She looked at me piteously, the lost look reminding me of the young woman I'd courted so ruthlessly. 'It is her fault, husband. That girl is to blame. I will neither eat nor drink from her hand. She wishes me harm; she curses my womb so it will not bear fruit.'

'She's a child! She would never do such a thing, wouldn't even know of such things. And you know there's no truth in the stories the old people tell of potions and charms.'

'I know!' Magda screamed, not caring who heard her. 'Not the child, the mother. *That* girl! But if she will try to stop me from carrying a child to term, I must separate her from her child. What does that book you're always reading say? *An eye for an eye …*'

'You can't seriously think to part them? That would be cruel, unconscionably cruel.'

'She loves that girl. That much I do see.' Magda's eyes glistened. 'Perhaps if her child were taken away, she will think twice about bespelling me.'

'You don't know that, Magda. She's not like that.'

It was the wrong thing to say.

'I know that she is a woman without morals. I know that you made her that way. I know that you lie with her still, and as your wife, I am powerless against your inclinations. I am forced to smile and act the mistress of this house, while your bastard and your whore sleep under my roof. I am tired of playing the role of your fool, Geert. Is this the kind of home into which my father sold me, Geert? Is this what his money paid for?'

'You wanted me, Magda,' I reminded her. 'You knew everything about me.'

'Not everything, Geert. I was deluded, I told myself that you were a man of honour. I told myself that marriage would be the making of you and that you would change your lascivious ways.'

I had no response to her accusation. It was what I feared in my weakest moments; that as a man, I lacked honour. Yet there would be no honour in what Magda was demanding of me if I consented.

'Send her away.'

'And if I refuse?' I asked, wishing to bring an end to our discourse.

Magda smiled brilliantly. 'Tell me, Geert, how goes your business?'

I felt myself chill.

—

After the French Republic declared war on Austria, England and their allies in 1792, shipping traffic began to decline, and markedly so. By 1794, only eighty-six vessels put into Cape ports, with the result that those of us reliant on foreign commerce suffered grave losses. Visiting ships had been a prime source of metal currency, and their diminished numbers further contributed to the dire shortage of gold and silver coin.

The British government, as the Company had done before, set the prices of goods entering Town. Our new masters had made no changes to the *pacht* system, but they had only been in power for a few months. Who knew what their plans were? Most likely, British officials would prefer to transact with British contractors. Already we had seen English traders gain ascendancy over burghers with longstanding ties to this land.

The merino breeding scheme, of which I'd been so optimistic, particularly since the offspring of the imported Spanish rams we'd bred with common ewes had been well favoured, was less viable than I'd hoped. While the wool produced was of a superior quality, when sent to Amsterdam, the prices we received were inadequate to cover our costs.

The one bright spot of my financial outlook was the importing firm in which I'd invested along with Justus and Septimus. With the slowdown in shipping, several goods such as timber, coal and fabric were scarce at the Cape. However, our ships were able to navigate the troubled waters of the world to satisfy this demand in some small way. For how much longer they could travel unharmed was uncertain, though the rewards outweighed the risks.

—

Sensing victory in sight, Magda became even more animated, more sanctimonious.

'It is my dowry that has made you rich, and it is my dowry and my family contacts that will keep you rich, no matter how many misjudgements you make. Marriage to me has given you the status you so craved; don't think I don't know this about you. Don't think I don't know how you strut, how you compare yourself to your father. "A man should always excel his father." Isn't that what you say? Is that why it is so important you have a son? Yet here stands the high-and-mighty Geert with no son to inherit his name.

'Tell me, are you waiting for me to die? That was the way of your father, they say, and indeed a son should always exceed his father. How many wives do you plan to bury, Geert? How many wives do you plan to bring into this house? The house in which your heathen whore sleeps, under the very same roof as I. And your heathen daughter? She *is* a heathen, is she not? That child, I know she is, even with that name, your mother's name. You don't believe in baptising your chattel, do you Geert? Don't tell me you believe that nonsense that Christian slaves cannot be sold,' Magda laughed.

Lena, 1854

There was the story of the boy I told you about. Who, as a baby, had insisted on becoming betrothed in his mother's womb. The story my brother, Rakota, used to tell me. About Ibonia and how he refused to consider any other bride than his beloved Joy-Giving Girl. Even when she was taken from him. And he not yet born.

If the girl should die, I will not bury her in the earth.

If the girl should live, I will not give her to another.

'What does it mean, he will not bury her in the earth?' I remember asking Rakota.

'Nothing, it's just a story, R—'

Those were the days when I was called something else. They took everything, even my name. I used to think that that was the worst thing they could take from a person, for a name represented everything you were or thought you were.

When my daughter was a baby, I used to whisper her secret name in her left ear. Left for all the good things; in her right ear I whispered all the bad. So, in her left ear, I told her of where we came from, an island that we called the land beneath the sun. When I was older, someone explained that the land was an island because it was surrounded by water. But when I was a young child, the land had seemed so endless beyond the green and brown hills and mountains that repeated for as far as the eye could see. It was easy to believe that this land was all there was to the world. It took a walk to the coast and a ride in a pitching ship before I grasped that there was much more to this world than I'd known.

I whispered in my daughter's left ear the names of her grandfather and her grandmother; I whispered my name, my true name, so she would not forget it, and the names of my brother and my sister. I told her of animals called *maki* with dark rings around their eyes and the colour-changing creature I used to let walk along my arms when I was a girl. I told her the story of the crocodile that terrorised our village and the story of the cattle bandits and how her grandfather had been a brave man. I recited how to spin cloth, and about Lilisa, who had taught me to weave in place of my mother.

I told my daughter about rice. In the morning when we woke and at night when we went to sleep, I whispered into her left ear: 'We are like rice and water. Rice needs water to grow, it is cooked in water and it is eaten with water.'

Just as my mother and I were not like rice and water – not when it counted – so too were my daughter and I.

I learned to grow without my mother, but it is a hard thing

for a mother to learn to live without her child. Sometimes I feel better about my mother when I acknowledge this. Then I remember that my mother had had three children at the time and I was the one she chose to send away. And I remember that she and I had been freeborn and how we'd called no one *Baas* or *Mewrouw*.

I remember when my daughter was born. That man Geert told me the name he had chosen. Later on, I learned that it had been the name of his mother, and by naming her thus he was conferring upon her a mark of honour, a sign of his favour for the child and for me. He said he would have her baptised in that big church and give her his name. He said: 'One day I will make an honest woman of you, Lena. Would you like that?'

Would his false words have turned true if I'd smiled and said something gentle and womanish like: 'Would you really, Geert? Would you free me and make me your wife?'

His name was a stone in my craw; I could not use it even when he begged. Did he detest the power I'd had over him, power to make him beg?

'You're a Jezebel, Lena. Your name should be Jezebel.'

I did not know who Jezebel was, but I knew that this was no sign of favour.

All the time he had all the power over me and I don't know what was worse, that I refused to remember or that I refused to forget it was so?

On an evening when he'd come to my bed or taken me to his, and after he'd done what he'd wanted to do, he might become expansive. Such and such a person freed his slave and married her, he'd say. 'Have you heard? One day that will be you.' The joke is that there were days I think he really believed his words. Then he married and I knew there would be no more lies. At least no more lies of that nature. 'His father buried four women, but still he never married me,' Barbetje had once said within my hearing. Deliberately, I thought, though she had not addressed me. I recalled other conversations: of how the old man would free her in his final testament, or of a Mewrouw she believed to be her dearest friend, but who had not kept her promise either. So I forgave her, Barbetje. Maybe I was tired of fighting on all fronts.

Yes. He sent her away.

I begged him then, the day he told me it would be so, fell to my knees, clutching at his trousers. I promised that I would do anything if I could go too. 'This is not what I want, Lena, believe me,' he said. I never knew if he meant that she should go or that I should stay.

It makes my head sore just to think of that day. My heart can't take it. I'm an old woman now. My heart can't take it.

But I remember. No matter how much my head aches and my heart pains, I remember.

I remember every detail of the day she left. I remember feeling her little-body bones, her eyes so like his, and the expression in her eyes was one I'd only seen in a dog when it's been kicked or punished for no very good reason at all. Seeing her cowering like a dog that's been beaten, feeling the thundering in her chest when I held her close, I remember how her heart had quickened in the time before she was born and before I knew to expect her. I remember how I'd never wanted that man's child, but by the time she made herself known by the quickening and burn of my own heart, it was too late to do anything about it. Too late to take any herbs, or visit any skilled midwife willing to risk the law.

I remember those darkest parts of night. Once my bed was cold and everyone else was asleep, I remember how I would place my palm upon the hard skin of my belly and whisper to the child growing there – stories of a locust that became a baby and who took many years to be born. I remember warning the child in my belly not to be like that baby, the one who'd cut open his mother's womb with a razor blade ... Ibonia, who'd warned that curses only made one stronger. Because even then I remembered, when my baby was nothing more than a quickening pulse, that a child can be a blessing and a curse. For a child teaches love to those who will not – or believe that they cannot – love.

And I wished that I had always remembered this, because the day came when I was reminded that, yes, to love is both a blessing and a curse, because if one does not love, then one cannot hurt. But my daughter was one against whom it was difficult to harden one's heart. And so I'd allowed myself to believe that she had captured the heart of the man who believed he was a good man; a man who believed he knew all there was to know about love.

Lena, I love you. Lena, I love you. I love you.
I love our child.

I remember how the usual fears I had for her were compounded from the very night that woman came and how I wished to hide my child somewhere far away and how I regretted that I had not taught her the lessons I should have: how to be servile; how to be unseen.

Fears, yes. A mother always has fears for her child, a daughter, especially. Always I'd feared that my daughter would be taken from me. Sometimes I remembered wrongly and imagined that I had been taken from my mother. This was easier than to remember how she had handed me over to the chief. But no matter what my life had become, until the day my daughter was taken, I never believed that she would leave.

I lie. There were days when all I thought about was how she would leave. But always, the two of us together, my daughter and me.

I remember, oh, how I remember the words 'bastard' and 'curse' and 'this *meid* is a curse to me', and sometimes I think we were both cursed, that woman and I, and how always love was a curse that a wiser woman would not wish for.

Wise! That woman was cunning. I often thought it would have been better if Mewrouw had beaten me, marked my body, inflicted the wounds upon me suffered by so many of my kind. But the punishment meted out by that woman was no less painful than had she taken a switch to my bare back and then dressed the lacerations with salt.

The day my daughter left, yes. I remember how the sun was hidden by the clouds and how it was winter-cold, and yet I still felt I would swoon as if it were the hottest day. And I remember thinking that I would never be warm again and that the sun would forever remain hiding.

That morning I remember studying my child with the eye of an assessor, as once I had been made to bear teeth and show eyes and limbs. My intention was not to ascribe a value to the girl, but to catalogue her every virtue and attribute. And despite his promises regarding the nature of the transaction, I remember thinking – how could I not? – will they evaluate her, this child, this untouched girl? And what of the promise that she could not be sold?

I remember he promised this; that she would not be sold, but I remember that once this too had been said of me. That morning I remembered too many of his promises to believe his lies. That morning, when he was nowhere to be seen, I knew why Rakota had hidden himself away the morning I left, and I remember wondering why a man is like that when bad things happen.

I remember: *the chief's a good man, the chief's a good man*, but I could not find the words to comfort my daughter, or myself. I remember how my legs faltered and seemed unable to hold me, and the weight upon my heart that felt so unbearable, but I stood firm. I remember and I remember the words I whispered as I embraced my daughter one last time: words of love and of hate, words of retribution and revenge.

I remember my daughter's dark-yellow plaits and the red ribbons she wore in her hair, and I remember those red ribbons waving in the wind and the rains that drenched us as the clouds burst, weeping for me when I could not. I remember, I remember, yes, until all I can remember and all I can see is the rain upon my face.

—

The worst thing about it all is that she lied, Mewrouw. Everything she said was a lie. I never cursed her. Not before, at least. I had no feelings about whether his line died out or carried on. It was not my business. I was not one to place potions in food or collect the hair from another's brush for charms. The *Ody* men of my childhood had always frightened me. My mother had believed in offerings to pacify troubled spirits, but Lilisa had told me this was wrong, and that when beings died they became part of the soil, that was all.

My feelings changed after my daughter was spirited away. Mewrouw quickened with her first daughter, who was born shortly after the celebration of the new year. As soon as Mewrouw rose from her childbed I watched her take to motherhood like a cat with kittens. I watched him too, that proud rooster strut as he strode across the stoep. I remember her words, Mewrouw's words, as she fought her war to have my daughter removed from her home: 'As long as that girl lives in our home, you will have neither son nor daughter to carry your name.'

I had tarried too long to do anything about daughters, but as long as I lived under their roof, no sons came.

I do not speak against my friends,
I ignore those who leave me be,
But I insult those who spread lies about me,
And curse those who besmirch my name …

I was always glad that my brother had told me stories of a wily boy and not a weakling fool.

Geert, 1806

We have a saying here at the Cape: '*die bloed trek*'. The blood pulls. Another interpretation, and the one with which I am more apt to agree, is that blood will draw blood. This is not in the sense of 'an eye for an eye and a tooth for a tooth', as the Good Book will have it, but rather, the strange yearnings in one's marrow that have no explicable cause other than that they are inherent, innate, or as the English adage has it: 'What is bred in the bone will come out of the flesh.'

I'd been reminded of these sentiments when I first began making preparations for my trip, when recalling my father's wanderlust and desire to see the world. His plans had been changed by happenstance: a plague, an offer of a better position within the Company, a fortuitous marriage. While it had been my father himself who'd thwarted my intentions to see Europe, to be a man of learning, perhaps I too have to accept some culpability in the matter. I might have been a braver man, disdained my father's wealth and holdings, eschewed his designs for me, as he'd abandoned his own father and his designs.

Perhaps, with time, I would have been able to look him in the eye and tell him that I had my own desires for my future, but I had neither the chance nor the opportunity to pursue alternate avenues upon his death. After his passing, I could not deny my sisters succour any less than I could renege on caring for the many souls he'd entrusted into my hands. Once I accepted the reins of responsibility so prematurely thrust upon me, I became too busy striving to be obedient to the memory of that stern man who was my father, too busy trying to maintain the endowments he'd left me, to follow the dictates of my heart.

During this time, I found my small comforts certainly, tender mercies that made the weight of my responsibilities easier to bear, but it had been instilled into me from a young age that tenderness was for women. Men had loftier concerns and expectations. What loftier ambitions than travel, discovering new people and places, was something I'd always wondered.

'For dilettantes and idlers.' My father's voice rang in my head. 'For those without cares.'

Even now, I am not sure whether those are fragments of a remembered conversation or whether, with his death, my father's voice had become that of my conscience.

I'd ever known of my father's yearnings for travel, and even in short trousers, I could volubly relate the story of how he had left his father's home in Zaanstreek. Yet by the time I was of an age to voice similar ideas, my father's yen for travel had been imbued with a practicality and nobility he judged my own to be lacking. And so it was that my father managed to convince me that I was unwilling to forego the trappings of my status as his son and of the legacy for which he'd worked so hard, which would one day be mine. In my very acquiescing to his will, I discovered that I was not the man my father was. This was not about half measures or measures of any kind; we were merely different from each other, my father and I.

I might have imagined otherwise, but with this discovery, I became aware of myself and the man I would ever be; that I was a conventional man raised for a conventional life. I would not cause ructions in the thin fabric of society; I would not change the world. Nor could I contemplate leaving my family and all I loved completely behind as my father had done. Comfort too had been a factor of consideration, comfort and complacency.

Perhaps I have always known this about myself: that, given the option, I shall always accede to the easiest route. This is an exceedingly onerous thing for a man to admit. Still, I flattered myself that my stymied aspirations to travel by sea to foreign lands was in its own way proof that I was indeed my father's son in more than name and that the same notions that had stirred his blood stirred mine.

On the morrow, finally, after years of thwarted ambitions, I am to depart for Amsterdam – aboard the *Bellona*. While I intend to pass most of my time in Amsterdam, that centre of culture and commerce, I am determined to travel to Zaanstreek, where I hope to find trace of my grandfather's shipyard, perhaps search out those who'd known either my father or my grandsire and see for myself the church named for a bull. I want to witness the myriad windmills my father described along the river Zaan, their blades twirling lazily in the wind. And at each windmill I encounter I shall doff my hat in honour of a Spanish nobleman my father told me about – an imbecile who'd believed himself a knight, the windmills his many adversaries. This was one of the few purely enjoyable stories my father told, a welcome deviation from his usual sermonising.

'The fatherland' is how my father would refer to the land of his birth. I'd often wondered about his insistence on referring to it thus, for other than intellectual curiosity I'd always felt that I'd owed no allegiance to the United Provinces or 'The Kingdom of Holland', as it is latterly known ever since that Corsican general who now calls himself Emperor of France in-stalled his brother Louis Bonaparte as king in June.

It is not my fatherland. My home is here in Africa, the land where I was born, where my father and his wives are buried in the soil, where one day too my body will find rest. Perhaps, once I visit those places in Europe about which I've only heard, I will feel a familial pull. Perhaps all I wanted, all these years when I spoke about travelling, was to see for myself the sites of which my father had spoken so warmly, particularly in his last years. Perhaps I longed to escape, to escape the women in my household and the sameness of my existence, despite the many changes of the past years.

A discordant noise, like the scrape of steel-soled boots on tile, distracts me from my thoughts. I look around, but no one is there. No one wears steel-soled boots these days, especially not indoors. The sound must have been conjured by my mind in consequence of all that musing on knights in armour. I know that I should retire for the night and attempt to capture at least an hour or two of sleep, one last time in my own bed, under my own roof. Instead, I sit with a glass of brandy warmed by my hands and my favourite pipe in my mouth (though the bowl requires filling), thinking of my past and the things I am unable to change. A folio of vellum sheets, a metal pen, imported from France, and a pot of ink are set on the table before me. Next to the ink, the only candle that remains aglow in this room in which I sit, surrounded by my salvaged prosperity and newer acquisitions, has burned down low and is guttering and spattering as it endeavours to stay aflame. I should seek out replenishments, I know, or light a lamp should I plan to write further.

It has been a while since I last committed my thoughts to paper. From my youth, I have been of the habit to maintain a record of both my daily life and momentous events, but the more vindictive my wife became, the more reason I had to guard my innermost thoughts. Before marriage, I'd had no reason to keep my papers private as no one in my household could read – with the exception of my sisters when they'd lived here. Even then, I'd trusted them implicitly, we being a family that valued privacy. Magda, however, has no such scruples, except when they pertain to her own private yearnings. It came to me, during the course of an argument one day, that she was privy to secrets she had no way of knowing, other than if she'd read the bound journals I'd deemed safe in my father's old sea chest.

I'd been tempted to set fire to the books then, but a man owes it to those who come after him to keep a record, as it were, of his life and achievements. Despite this duty to future generations, I could no longer bring myself to set out my musings, my questions, my histories of this Colony and its people when I knew that whatever I wrote would be but fodder for my wife's increasingly addled mind. It is hard to look at her in the unflinching light of day and not wonder about the docile and sweet-tempered woman I married. Had marriage to me turned my wife into a termagant? It must have, unless this tendency had been latent within her all the time. Who can say? Of women, it seems, I know very little.

The replacement candle I'd lit went out long ago, as did the fire in the grate. Soft, lemon rays squeeze into the room through the gaps in the wooden shutters, uniform and ordered. In this wan morning light, all is well in the world again. With my back to the door, I hear the salver first, smell the aroma of coffee, before I see who it is who enters the room. Most mornings I take my coffee in the kitchen. I turn in my chair.

'Geert,' Magda says softly, fussing with the tray as she places it on the table beside me. 'Let us part as friends. You will be away for months, let us end this ill-will between us.'

'What ill-will?' I ask, not expecting an answer.

Shrewish though she may be, Magda is mostly decorous, having been raised that way, and so we present a civil pairing to the rest of the world. Oftentimes, this pretend-civility translates into days and weeks of peace until some or other infraction on my part sets her off.

'You are my wife,' I iterate as I always do. 'I admire you, can you conceive?'

My admission surprises us both.

'I agree, Magda, with what you said. There should be no bad

242

blood between the two of us. Six months is a long time, and who knows what the shipping will be like when it is time for me to return.'

Magda smiles but does not tarry. 'Yes, let us not forget that the war is still on,' she says as she leaves the room.

I wonder whether she'd been referring to the war in Europe – the peace between France and Great Britain and those two nations' allies had lasted one year only – or the war between the two of us. In the spirit of that abandoned peace, I choose to take her words at their most generous. The coffee must have cost my wife dearly in terms of pride. Accepting her largesse, I wait for the strong, sweet liquid to cool.

It was in this very room, all those years ago, when a maid, or I should rightly say, a maiden, served coffee to me. Yes, that was the first time, the first time I'd noticed her, just after she'd lit the lamps. Perhaps she had served me before then; I'd been too overwrought in the preceding days to tell. Here, where it all began, what was it, nearly twenty-five years ago? Oh, how much easier my life would have been had there been no lamps, no coffee, no maiden that night when I'd been feeling particularly susceptible, I think briefly, treacherously. But I shall countenance no regrets. I am a man, and as a man, I must stand by my actions.

I had been a boy then. A man in years, true, but a boy nevertheless; a boy trying to live up to the man his father was and had been. Perhaps now, nearly midway through my fourth decade, I can stop balancing my life against my father's. He was not perfect, my father, but nor was he the benevolent tyrant I had deemed him when in my youth. Now that I have made my own decisions and my own mistakes, I understand him better, I believe. For despite the heinous stories of my father having made his fortune by marriage and the subsequent deaths of his wives, in truth, he was a man who'd buried four wives and must have grieved them. He had buried at least one child that I know of, too.

We had not discussed such matters as mourning, my father and I. He had never been one to tolerate sensitivity in his son or himself, believing sentiment a weakness that a truly great man could not afford.

I could never contemplate burying a wife. Even at the height of the hostilities between the three of us, I'd not allowed myself to consider that the death of one or the other would be expedient. This is the most difficult consideration when a man has two wives, for I could not but regard both women as such. They both have my heart, if not my name.

I have not drunk all my coffee when Magda returns. She has a preternatural ability to divine my thoughts at times, even without the benefit of my journals.

'Did you ever think to marry her, Geert?' Magda asks, as if she'd known to whom my thoughts had wondered.

I am so taken aback by the question that I answer honestly.

'At times, yes; there were times when I thought I should marry her.' I want to explain that it was because of the child, but that would not be wholly true.

'There've been times during our marriage when I've wished you had married another.' Magda's voice drops and I strain to hear her. 'There were times that I'd thought you'd have been better off with her; better off with any other than me.'

I want to tell her that our marriage is not all bad. I want to tell her that we might have lived peacefully together, Magda and I, had she not made me choose. All three, four of us, the other girls too, we could have abided well together. I want to ask her what makes her speak now, after so many years. So many years after she'd won.

'But you would never have married her, would you, Geert?'

Magda is the kind of person to poke at an open wound. I wish she were more gracious in victory, for that is the true test of grace, how one treats those they defeat.

'My father always said,' Magda continues, 'back when he first heard I was considering you as a husband, that you were the type of man who respected hierarchy; one's status within society. And let us be honest, among each other if no one else. Burghers of our class do not marry baseborn slaves, do we? Not these days, at least.'

I wish I could tell Magda that, try as I may, I cannot compel myself to see our union as a hardship or a curse. I've accrued far too many benefits from it, but oh, yes, there is bitterness in my heart towards her, bitterness for so long. For what she demanded of me and for what I acceded to doing. She should not have expected that of me.

'What choice do you have, Geert?' I'd asked myself time over time.

Certainly, it was easier for me to believe that I'd had none.

Magdalena, the name of the women I love. Magda and Lena, the first a family name, chosen by her father to honour one of his forebears; the other a name chosen by my father, a name given without thought or wit. Simply a name. I always made sure to adhere to the two names. In this I learned I am not unique – not about the names, but in regard to loving two women at the same time. At the Cape I am just one of many: with my Christian wife and my wife who is not. Though I married only one in a church, in my heart I am married to both. I am not sure whether this makes me an adulterer or a bigamist, but I am in truth just a man, an ordinary man.

Thus, as a man, let any remonstrations be between me and my maker, to whom I shall give account when the time for so doing is at hand. *For as you judge, so shall you be judged; and as you punish, by that same measure shall you be punished.*

Oh, that I'd remembered this.

My daughter was in her tenth year when I sent her away. I had never called her daughter, never acknowledged her as such to anyone of import, or even to herself, but most of my intimates and my kin knew the relationship, or knew that she was special to me. I'd loved her mother, yes, but with my daughter there was a tenderness of feeling, an innocence or sense of blood calling blood. She had my eyes, golden like the eyes of a cat in a certain light; her skin was the colour of weak coffee, her hair the colour of straw.

Before this, had anyone asked, I would have said: 'Family is foremost to me; the greatest consideration of them all.'

I had lived my life thus.

She was family, and she was not family. She was of my blood, yet I denied her. I was at her birth, I had held her in my arms as I'd named her, and still I denied her. There came a day when Magda wore me down with her arguments. There came a time when it was easier to grant my wife her will. I had denied her and denied her and denied her. I did not need a rooster's crow to remind me of this. Sometimes my scriptural learnings came to me most inconveniently. Sometimes I thought my life would have been easier had I not been born my father's son. No, my father had nothing to do with it. It was me, all me, and I shall have to live with that to the end of my days. The Good Book tells children to honour their parents, but what does it say of a parent's duty to a child?

Like many men, I have always turned to the Scriptures in moments of turmoil. So it was that I found comfort once more in the story of Abraham, or Abram as he'd been known before. The Lord's promise to Abram: that his offspring would be as innumerable as the sand of the earth, or the stars in the heavens, had been particularly reassuring while Magda struggled to carry a child to term. I saw similarities between my own situation and that of Abram, though unlike him and his wife, Magda had youth on her side and was of childbearing age. When Abram was in his eighty-fifth or eighty-sixth year, and his wife some ten years younger, Sarai, as she was known then, suggested that her husband take her Egyptian slave Hagar as a wife. Abram duly did so and she gave him a son, Ishmael. But it came to pass that when Abraham reached one hundred years of age, a son was born to him and his first wife, who had been renamed Sarah, as he himself had been renamed Abraham as a reflection of God's promise that he would father a host of nations.

With a son of her own, Sarah began to worry that Ishmael too would inherit. She demanded that Abraham cast out Hagar and Ishmael, a demand that caused no little consternation to Abraham on account of the boy. He took the matter to the Lord, who told him to attend to Sarah's wishes, as it would be through Isaac, Sarah's son, that his name would be carried. Thus Abraham sent Hagar and Ishmael away.

I was not as presumptuous, or indeed as blasphemous, as to compare myself and my sacrifice to that of Abraham, but I found solace in the parallels. The Lord had differentiated between Abraham's child with his wife and that of the slave. Abraham had had to sacrifice one son to ensure the continuation of his line to perpetuity. I knew then that I had to find the courage to make a similar sacrifice if I wanted my name to live on. It was not as if I had planned to cast my daughter into the wilderness as Abraham had Ishmael.

I arranged to send Lissie to stay with my sister Dorothea, who, together with her family, lived a mere two streets away. The girls often played together when Dorothea visited, and it was sweet, and alarming too, to watch them play, running down the long passages of my home and chasing each other like ordinary cousins in so many ways.

On her free day, Lena could visit with her child. Whether it pleased my wife or not, I intended to make certain of that.

'You should let them go, Master Geert. It's the right thing to do, to free the mother and child, like your father said he was going to free me the time before he died.' Barbetje had come to me the night before the child was to leave.

Barbetje's and my relationship was thus: though she was my chattel, she remained my elder and I respected her. She had reared my sisters and I like chicks in a nest and we loved her in our way. On a certain level, I must have been aware of the role she had served in my father's life, and I had never been disgusted by that fact, realising even in my youth that one takes consolation where it can be found. That had ever been the nature of Barbetje's role in our household: to offer solace where there was none.

After my father's funeral, I became aware of the rumours that my father had promised to free Barbetje and Titus. In different ways, and with varying degrees of subtlety, both Barbetje and Titus had apprised me of the insinuation as if it were fact and not conjecture or a case of 'counting leaves', as Lena used to say.

In truth, I had toyed with freeing Barbetje, if not Titus – I relied on him too much in the immediate aftermath of my father's death. Yet it would have been unfair to manumit one and not the other when both intimated that this had been my father's will. And what of the other slaves, I had asked myself. In the end, I'd taken my father's will as gospel, the last word on the matter. If he had wanted to free them, he would have stipulated so in his testament. It had been easier for me to be guided by an out-of-date document written shortly after the birth of my younger sister than to make such a momentous decision for myself.

'I cannot free them, my wife—' I tried to explain the situation, though Barbetje knew very well what my wife was like. There was no privacy in my home.

'If Master cannot free them, Master must not separate a mother and a child, it is not right. Do not send the girl away.'

I was not in the habit of justifying myself to servants, but this was Barbetje, the woman who'd raised me more than any other. She knew me. Part of me believed then that if I could make her accept the decision, I could make peace with it too.

'You know my wife will not allow the girl to stay,' I said, unable to look up from the ledgers that I'd been arranging and rearranging on my desk, physically unable to make the requisite notation in my book of holdings. 'Transferred to Dorothea Baardwijk, Lissie van de Caab, aged ten years on this date ...'

'Master must make his wife understand. After all, is a man not the head of his household?' Barbetje persisted in a way she had not done for her own freedom when I had been younger and greener.

'It is not a matter of head of the household, Barbetje,' I protested.

Barbetje stared at me, forcing me to look up. Her face was shaped in readiness for remonstrance, fierce and with furrowed brow, then her features smoothed.

'Master Geert, you will tell your wife to let the girl stay?' she said softly.

I shook my head, picked up the ledgers again. I waited for her to leave.

As softly as she'd beseeched, Barbetje castigated me.

'Your father would have been proud of you on this day, I think.' Looking directly at me, so I was forced to meet her eyes once more, she continued: 'You are your father's son in so many ways. I never thought so before, not exactly like him, but you are ... in a way your brother – my son – never was and never could be. He sent him away too, did you know that? This was a few months before you'd been born; perhaps you weren't told, but I had a child, and he sent him away "to be raised a Christian" he said. He gave him to a couple with no children of their own – the Van Graans. You know them, I believe, though your father made sure that they lived far away in Swellendam. Too far away for me to see the boy was his thinking, I'm sure. "It was for the best," he said. For who was it best? Not for me! Not for the boy. Now, when my son comes to Town, I find ways to see him, each and every time. He is a man now, with children of his own. Think, I am a grandmother! But if he notices me looking, this boy, this flesh of my flesh, what does he see? Nothing but a *meid*. No, I am nobody and nothing to him!' Though Barbetje's voice had risen during the course of her tantrum, she'd ended on a sob.

'I had not known, truly,' I said, aghast at the thought that I had a brother I had not known was my kin, though I roughly recalled the man of whom she spoke.

'Yes, your mother and I had been increasing at the same time, and she, my dearest companion, but that was the kind of man your father was.'

The import of Barbetje's earlier words had not yet struck me, now I knew.

When deliberating my options, I had thought about what my father would have done had he had to make the same decision as I. This was how I routinely assessed myself, by considering how my father would have acted in the same situation. At my age, I should have stopped filtering all my thoughts and opinions through the fabric of his; I should have ceased comparing myself to him long ago. There were times, such as with Barbetje's revelation, that I saw that I had not known him much at all.

'I used to think that what your father did was the worst thing a man could do to his natural child, and to the mother of that child. But do you know, Master Geert? Finally, I think, you have surpassed him. Indeed, you have, for your father at least did not send his child to be raised a slave in another man's house.'

Before waiting for a response, Barbetje gathered the phlegm in her throat loudly, but did not expectorate – that would have been an unforgivable offence, as it would be for me to then heap physical punishment upon an elderly female slave. She must have left the room then, for when I next looked up I saw that I was alone. As I sat there, absorbing her words, I realised, as I had not done before: Lena had not tried to negotiate with me after the first time, not for her daughter's freedom, not for her own, and not that they stay together or leave together. I wondered whether this meant that she knew me well or whether her pride was, as always, too strong. I do not know what I would have done *had* she asked again. Or if my daughter had asked me not to send her away. But her mother had taught Lissie her lessons well.

Lissie left the next day without any fuss. Though I entrusted her into Dorothea's care and asked her to treat the child kindly, this did not lessen my feelings of shame. I had not needed Barbetje's admonition to feel that way. A better man would have manumitted mother and daughter and sent them far, far away. An honourable man would not have separated mother and daughter, but I'd told myself I could lose only one, not both. Magda's reprisals, I knew, would not be complete if Lena and

Lissie were to remain together. She would rather be tormented by Lena's presence if she, in turn, could be a torment too. And by allowing myself to be swayed, I placed myself in position to be tormented by them both.

There were compensations. Perhaps this makes me most guilty. Conversely, perhaps these developments exonerate me. My daughter was born nine months after Lissie left us. Magda named her Hester, for her mother, since she would not think of naming her after mine. Thereafter, it seemed that the babies came one each year for the next several years. We had five children in all, Magda and I, all girls. The boys would come later, or so people said. 'There is still time,' everyone told us. After all, the girls were healthy, each one of them, pink-cheeked children with hair the colour of straw and with either my green or Magda's blue eyes. I shall miss them while I'm away, but the trip has been too long in the making for regrets of any kind. And where would I start with regrets? No, there's no use in dwelling on regrets. No use at all.

Lena, 1854

In the kitchen was where I always remembered. After all the time that had passed, my mind still travelled over the sea, through the cattle paths and up the hills, scaling the higher mountains and then low into a valley to a village that had once been my world. But I did not linger there long. I closed my eyes and was led away once more through the forest as the clammy smell of rotting leaves filled my nostrils. I stepped closer to the table and for a moment I felt cold mud beneath my soles, not the unyielding surface of the *mis* floor.

I closed my eyes again, rubbing at the lids as if to scrape away the memories of the forest and that walk in chains. Over the years, memories had come out of nowhere, like forgotten pathways, the smell of damp places, the taste of roasted manioc on my tongue. Manioc, yes; think of that. Think of your brother over the sea. Rakota must be a grown man now, with children of his own. Does he tell them stories, these children of his? Perhaps grandchildren too?

There was another beyond the sea. Nearly three moons he'd been gone, but I would not think of him. I'd promised myself. There was no need to think about him, but perhaps it was my dream, yes, that had made me think about him. The dream meant nothing and had been nothing out of the ordinary. Just a man on a horse, not moving, almost frozen. And in my dream I'd wondered why they'd just stood there and how could a horse stand so still? The streets in my dream were blue-grey cobbles like here, but the sun was weak, dimming the day with a dull glow that made the gabled buildings unfamiliar. I shut my eyes again.

I will prefer no other land, no other person …

Again, Rakota's story of the baby who'd insisted on becoming betrothed in his mother's womb and had undertaken all sorts of quests to prove his devotion. In my mind's eye, I saw Rakota: tall, yes – then again, maybe he's not so tall now that I am taller too – and lean, but solid from all the hard work. I remembered his silences after our father died and how I'd beg him to tell me stories – stories he'd always claim he'd forgotten – and finally, the reedy timbre of his voice when he resumed his tale.

He is unchallenged in his village, a master of many servants …

Odd how I always thought of Rakota as silent when he must have been talkative once; odd how when I remembered his story it was in a language he did not speak. Who had told him the story? My father probably; my mother had no time for stories, but my father, like most men of the island, had been a frequent storyteller. I saw my father too, before he went away, but I could not recall any of his features other than his great height and the dull timber colour of his skin.

The onions were braising and I added the chopped mutton to the pot. The raw meat shrank immediately upon contact with the pot's heated base, quickly going from red to pink, to grey before browning. I sniffed; the aroma was not displeasing though I had not yet added any spices.

He may be a calamity, but I am a catastrophe ...

Then it was neither my brother nor my father whom I saw before me, but another. A man with green eyes flecked with gold, eyes that in an instant could darken dangerously; yellow hair that stuck up like straw and the red-gold hairs that dusted his cheeks and jaw; a long, narrow body, a neck that stooped lightly as if under the weight of his hat, and the hat, yes, a line of moisture along the brim when he took it off and the dampness that softened the straw. It was the dream that had made me think of him, yes, nothing more than the dream.

To stop these thoughts, I concentrated on peeling the potatoes I'd taken out earlier. I was making pumpkin *bredie* with chillies. The pumpkin was already peeled and lay on the table in front of me, orange with green stippling where the skin had been, waiting to be cut into smaller pieces and rinsed with the potatoes.

'Lena.' A voice behind me disturbed my thoughts. I turned around though I knew who it was. Titus was an old man now, with arms and legs like sticks and skin like leather that had been left out too long in the sun and the rain. His face was wrinkled and scrunched up; his muscles and skin creped from his bones, but his features were sharper, bonier. All these years and still the malice in his eyes burned as brightly as ever.

'Did you hear?' Titus wheezed as he limped into the kitchen. 'The *baas*, they just got a letter to say that he died over there in that place.'

The knife slackened in my hand. I gripped it tightly before it could fall, but my grasp was so tight that it raised a ribbon of blood along the exposed surface of my palm. I pressed my thumb into the shallow wound to stop the bleeding.

'No, Titus, I have not heard,' I wanted to say, but did not. Who would have told me? Mewrouw? Ha! I had not heard a sound out of the ordinary – no sobs, no wails, no shrieks from Mewrouw or her children – nothing to alert me to the tidings of his death. If she could be calm, I would be calm too. If she could be silent, I would be silent too.

I stared at Titus insolently, looking right into the cold blackness of his eyes, and held his gaze. If he was waiting for a reaction, let him wait. I would give nothing away. I had nothing to say to him, Titus. Though we had lived in the same house for so many, many years, we had never been friends. He was a jealous man; anyone else's success was his failure. Accordingly, he had always revelled when the tides had turned against me. 'That's the nature of tides,' I'd wanted to warn him, time and time again. They ebb and they flow, changing one way and then back again. So it had always been with me and the man.

I remained silent, holding his gaze until, eventually, he looked away and tried to catch the eye of Agnes, the new girl, who was helping me with the cooking. She'd been with the house more than two years now. Agnes was from the Cape; her mother still lived at the Lodge, and she was usually a nice, respectable kind of girl, if a little full of herself for being born at the Cape and all. My daughter's the same, was what I liked to imagine.

I glared at Agnes and then allowed myself to nod at Titus, finally acknowledging the news. Turning back to the pot, I saw I needed to add water before the meat and onions began to stick and burn. Agnes was chunking more of the mutton for *denningsvleis*. They ate so lavishly here: a soup or something light to start with, two, often three choices of main course and then pudding. Mewrouw and her children kept us busy.

After I'd added the pumpkin – potatoes cooked quicker and should be added later – I realised that Titus was still standing there. Usually he avoided the kitchen. It was my space. I watched the looks passing between him and the girl, but I did not want to know what they were thinking.

I focused my gaze on Agnes as she came to stand next to me in order to add dripping to the pot she had placed there to heat before Titus had come in. I stepped aside as she added the meat, along with chopped onions, garlic, allspice, cloves, a grating of nutmeg and two bay leaves, to the smoking fat.

'Careful, Agnes,' I warned. 'Make sure the pot isn't too hot.'

Aside from tamarind, which gives it its sour taste and is added later, the secret of *denningsvleis* is to cook the mutton over a low heat and to add enough water so the meat doesn't dry out or burn. I'd taught her that. She should have known better.

As she dashed to fetch a cup of water from the jug on the table, I sighed, all at once remembering the time when I was the new girl in this house and worried about burning the food. Had it really been so long ago? And even though it was long ago, I remembered clearly all those conversations that Barbetje and Titus had had in the kitchen and in the quiet, hidden places of the house, in the days we were waiting for the old man to die; the whispered hope on their breath.

Barbetje, aai, Barbetje.

I remember how we'd all looked at her, waiting to see her reaction the morning after the old man died. She'd appeared upset then, focused on his daughters, fussing with them to eat, to rest. Everyone could tell she was upset. Even Titus, I thought, had been truly doleful. The night of the man's funeral, Titus had got so drunk, but that was because once the old man's will was read, everyone knew that he had not kept his word to free Titus as promised, or as Titus always said he had promised. It's not nice for me to admit this, but part of me was satisfied that the old man had not kept his word. I don't know why this was. It must have been about more than my desire to be right in my instincts, but I cannot say.

I thought of the years Barbetje and I had wasted on antagonising each other when we could have been friends. Yet when Mewrouw came, and after she sent my daughter away, and then when Lissie moved with that man's sister's family to Graaff-Reinet, so far away and with all the trouble and all, it had been Barbetje who'd comforted me. And although I had been suspicious at first, I was grateful. Barbetje knew what it was like to be me. She'd told me about her son and how she could stake no claim to him, could not approach him or greet him, but at least she could see him, she'd said. Our relationship changed after that, growing so strong that we became good friends. Not quite like a mother and daughter, but we were allied. I respected that. It would have been easy for her to creep into Mewrouw's good books and work against me, but as I said, Barbetje surprised me.

I nursed her during her final illness and was there with her at the very last. I washed her body and dressed it before they buried her. In a small way, I was doing it for Barbetje and for what might have been if I had not been so stubborn. And perhaps, in another way, I was doing it for my mother, thinking: who would dress her when she died? I would not allow myself to consider that maybe she had already departed this world.

Thinking about what was and what could have been made me long for Barbetje even more. She would have known what to do. She would have already begun checking to see what was needed, already begun cooking for the funeral. Would there even be a funeral if the man had died over there? Surely his body would have been buried by now. The ships travelled so slowly and the news we received from them was old. Would there be a tea, men coming to the house for their brandy and meat, the bread and cakes that took us days to make and then, finally, the coffee, as the last visitors stayed to remember the deceased?

I remember that the first time I took notice of him, real notice, was when I took in the coffee on the day of his father's funeral and the last guests were still there. I remember that though I had no reason to, I had felt sorry for him. He'd looked like a boy dressed in a man's clothes, overwhelmed by the weight of his responsibilities. Now I can see that it was a good thing I felt sorry for him; it meant that I wasn't bitter all the way through, not totally consumed by my hatred. I had only tamped my feelings down. Sometimes it is better to hold on to the hate if you want to survive this life. I saw this with Barbetje, and I saw this with Titus, the crush of disappointment when hope was extinguished. It would almost have been better to die upon the wheel. I'd stopped hoping a long time ago and, like Titus, I had allowed my malice to fester but never to show.

I began wiping down the table, putting the spices away, anything to keep busy. I waited for Mewrouw to come in. The matter of the funeral was her decision, let her make it. Agnes added another log to the fire that sent up sparks at once, the wood was so dry. She looked at me questioningly before walking outside to talk to Titus. From the window, I watched them as they cast sly glances in my direction. I could not hear them and had no wish to know what they were saying. I would stay in the kitchen watching over the food.

When it thunders, when the rain falls and the skies weep, lament for him ...

He was dead, but the sky outside was clear; this was not the time to weep. If I started, I would not stop. I would lament them all, including myself, as well as the teller of the tale. I would lament the tellers of all tales.

Man shall turn again unto dust.

The biblical verse came back to me unbidden; it was from the Book of Job; I knew that much. Job, a man subjected to many trials. I must have paid more attention to his preaching after all, every morning in the later years, just like his father. Who knew that I would remember so much? I've never had much use for religion.

The Lord giveth and the Lord taketh away.

Job again.

A blameless man.

To clear my head, I went back to the cupboard. I traced my hand over the tin of raisins. Funeral rice: raisins and *borrie*. Would I need to make funeral rice once again? I would wait for her to tell me. Talking of rice, I needed to make fresh rice to go with the *bredie*, and maybe some of that cucumber and onion salad with vinegar. They always liked that. It was getting late, nearly time to eat. Where had the day gone?

As I washed the rice, I thought about her and of the decisions that would have to be made – Mewrouw, his wife. She too had been left behind when he went across the seas. I'd wondered about that at the time. Had she not wanted to go too? Had she not expected to go with him? Never mind, it was none of my concern. Perhaps it was enough for her that I had remained behind too. As if there'd been any real chance of my going. That man knew better than to promise me things he could not deliver. What use would it be for me to cross the seas? I could never go back home again.

'If you go with, you will be free,' Titus had said on one of the days we'd been talking. 'In the old country there's no such thing as free and not free.'

Aai, Titus, still so determined to die a free man, I'd thought to myself at the time, feeling uncharacteristically sad for him. Instead, I'd asked him why there were rules for people in the old country and rules for people here, the same people, but he had not known the answer, said he would ask Mewrouw. Maybe she would tell him.

Aai, Mewrouw. Perhaps now it would all be over, now that he was gone, the hatred she and I felt for each other. I thought back again to the first day she'd come here, so young, so determined to be a good mistress, determined to treat us all well. New clothes, school for the children, it had not lasted long. There were worse mistresses, I admit, but maybe she'd admit that there were worse ones such as me.

I thought then how both of us would try to sleep that night, me in my little bed, and her in that big bed with the curtains she had shared with him. She could draw the curtains and shut the door and … and maybe she would weep for him. Or maybe she would be glad he was gone. I knew that she would not sleep and neither would I. On our opposite sides of the house, both of us would lie awake and think of him, that man, and wonder what it was that we had both lost, if we had lost anything. But I would remind myself that you cannot lose something you never really had. I'd remember also that whatever we had was something I had not asked for. And in the darkest hour before the morning's first light, before I got up to stir the fire in the kitchen to life again, before I got the things ready to make the coffee, they would come to me, his words. How his eyes had begged me to say them, but my mouth could not form the words, could not tell him what he wanted to hear. I had that, at least.

Lena, I love you. Lena, I love you. I love you.

I never believed him; never returned the words. What did love mean to me? It could neither warm you nor feed you. It could not make me free. If there was love, it was not an equal love; we were never equals, so how could it be? *Alles is oor.* Everything is over. No, love was not for me and my kind, not then.

Still, I remember his tenderness when our child was born, your mother, you know? Oh, he loved her! Of that there was no doubt. Sometimes I even thought that he loved her more than I did because I was afraid, so afraid I could lose her anytime, but that man loved that child and sometimes it's enough for a mother that a man loves her child. But he did not love her adequately, not when it counted. He sent her away and for that I could never forgive him and never forgive her, Mewrouw. Whenever I felt myself softening, I remembered that.

The night my daughter left, he came to my room and told me that he would see that she was freed when she reached the age of one and twenty years. He said he would settle money upon her, and it was for the best that she left. But he died before Lissie reached that age, so who knows whether he meant to keep his promise. Who knows anything about anything? I'm sure he never expected to die on that trip. I never expected it either, but that's how his story ended.

As long as I live, you will live …

Both that man's wife and I lived long after he died. Together, under the same roof, until the day they came to say we were free. No, I never expected to live so long … to see the day I was freed, not by a man, but by laws, English laws … to hear that my child was free, to see her and my grandchildren alive and well after all that time …

Oh, it's too much. It's too much. It's too much for me.

I'm tired now. I want to go home.

When it thunders and the winds blow, it is a bad day for an old woman …

Author's Note

For most people of my generation, South African history began with the date 6 April 1652. This was when a man by the name of Jan van Riebeeck landed at the Cape. At schools around the country, children learned how Van Riebeeck had 'founded' the nation.

So, dutifully we memorised the important details, knowing we'd be tested on them later. The *Dromedaris*, the name of the ship on which Van Riebeeck sailed; the *Reiger* and the *Goede Hoop* (Good Hope), the names of the two ships that accompanied him. The *Walvis* and the *Oliphant*, the ships in his fleet that arrived later. We knew that he'd sailed from Texel in the Netherlands, a journey that lasted three months, and that along with his wife Maria, Van Riebeeck had landed with eighty-nine others – eighty-two men and seven women.

We learned why he had come: to establish a 'refreshment station' and a hospital to cater for beleaguered but brave sailors plying the lucrative trade route between Europe and the East. Looking at maps, we saw how the Cape was a logical place to stop, positioned almost halfway between these two centres of trade.

Some of our tongues struggled with the words *Vereenigde Oost-Indische Compagnie*, the Dutch East India Company, which had instructed Van Riebeeck to build the settlement at the Cape. We heard about the immense wealth of this organisation that today is regarded as the world's first multinational. We were told how Van Riebeeck had been forced to introduce slavery, as the Khoisan he encountered here (and who themselves had settled from elsewhere in Africa, it was stressed) were deemed too lazy and disobliging to work for an honest wage.

At home, some of us were told different stories – of violence and occupation and how the coming of the European settlers had reduced the Khoisan to beggars, stealing their cattle, and of the deadly consequences of the smallpox they brought with them on an isolated local population. We learned how slavery was an evil, evil thing and how some of us were the descendants of the white men and their slaves.

When I was five or six years old, my maternal grandmother Barbara told me the story of our slave ancestress Lena and how her master had loved her so much that he'd disinherited his children with his white wife in favour of Lena and her children. In her cupboard in her bedroom, my grandmother kept a yellowing and much-handled newspaper story of this man, Geert

Bantjes, which described the mythical fortune he'd left for his descendants to be claimed one hundred years after his death.

We were the true descendants to this fortune, Ma insisted. The *Sunday Times* article 'Bantjes Millions: Now Coloureds Stake Claim' picked up on the story. Dated 2 September 1973, it describes how my great-great-grandmother had destroyed the proof in order to hide her slave blood and to protect three of her children who'd been reclassified as 'white' to escape the full brunt of apartheid laws.

It was only when I was older that I began to wonder at Ma's pride in her slave heritage when all around her people were claiming instead a Scottish grandfather, a German grandmother. I can only ascribe this to her dark skin, which left her no choice but to embrace the heritage so many of her family were eschewing, changing names and moving countries to escape the same. I don't know whether Geert really did love Lena as Ma claimed. I found his details easily enough in the Archives in Cape Town, but of Lena there is no trace.

This, then, is what I imagine their stories would be if they were to have told them.

Cape Town, 2017

Acknowledgements

For the gift of time, I'd like to thank the University of Iowa International Writing Program, and the City of Asylum/Pittsburgh. It was while I was a writer-in-residence at the latter that I first resolved to write this book. Likewise, I owe the Ford Foundation a debt of gratitude for allowing me the freedom to write and research this book for nearly two years in New York City. Thanks to Jackson Taylor and Susan Cheever, mentors at the New School, and to my first readers: Amanda Harris, Brandon Covey, Mani Parchem, Sheryl Heefner and Stephanie Nikolopoulos.

To Beth Lindop and Fourie Botha at Umuzi, it was wonderful working with you both, and a special thanks to my editor, Frances Marks.